S0-CBR-166

The
Human Search

The Human Search

An Introduction to Philosophy

edited by

JOHN LACHS
CHARLES E. SCOTT

New York Oxford
OXFORD UNIVERSITY PRESS
1981

Copyright © 1981 by Oxford University Press, Inc.

Library of Congress Cataloging in Publication Data
Main entry under title:

The Human search.

1. Life—Addresses, essays, lectures.   I. Lachs,
John.   II. Scott, Charles E.
BD431.H73   100   79-19230
ISBN 0-19-502675-6

Since this page cannot accommodate all the copyright notices, the pages that follow constitute an extension of the
copyright page.

Printed in the United States of America

L.I.F.E. College Library
1100 Glendale Blvd.
Los Angeles, Calif. 90026

Acknowledgments

A. Alvarez. From *The Savage God: A Study of Suicide*. Copyright © 1970, 1971, 1972 by A. Alvarez. Reprinted by permission of Random House, Inc. Published in England by George Weidenfeld & Nicolson Ltd. Reprinted by permission.

Aristotle. From "Nicomachean Ethics" trans. W. D. Ross, from *The Oxford Translation of Aristotle* ed. W. D. Ross, Vol. 9, 1925. Reprinted by permission of Oxford University Press.

John Barth. "Night Sea Journey," copyright © 1966 by John Barth, first published in *Esquire* Magazine from the book *Lost in the Funhouse* by John Barth. Reprinted by permission of Doubleday & Company, Inc.

Medard Boss. Excerpted from *A Psychiatrist Discovers India*. Reprinted by permission of Oswald Wolff Publishers, Ltd.

Martin Buber. Reprinted by permission of Charles Scribner's Sons from *I and Thou* (translated by Walter Kaufmann), copyright © 1970 by Charles Scribner's Sons.

Nancy Caroline. "Dying in Academe," *The New Physician*. Copyright © 1972 by the American Medical Student Association. Reprinted by permission from *The New Physician*.

John Compton. "Death and the Philosophical Tradition," *Soundings*, Vol. LXI, No. 2, Summer, 1978. Reprinted by permission of the editor.

E. E. Cummings. "dying is fine)but Death" and excerpt on p. 371. Copyright 1949 by E. E. Cummings. Reprinted from his volume *Complete Poems 1913–1962* by permission of Harcourt Brace Jovanovich, Inc.

John Dewey. "Force, Violence, and Law" was first printed in *The New Republic*, V (1916). It was subsequently reprinted in John Dewey, *Characters and Events*, edited by Joseph Ratner, 1929. This selection is excerpted from Joseph Ratner, ed., *Intelligence in the Modern World: John Dewey's Philosophy*, 1939 and is reprinted by arrangement with the estate of Joseph Ratner.

028559

Mircea Eliade. Reprinted from *The Two and the One*, translated by J. M. Cohen, a Phoenix Edition reprint, by permission of The University of Chicago Press. © 1962 Editions Gallimard, © 1965 in the English translation Harvill Press, London, and Harper and Row, Publishers, Inc., New York. All rights reserved. Published 1965, Phoenix Edition 1979.

Epictetus. From *Epictetus: The Discourses and Manual* trans. P. E. Matheson, 2 vols. 1917. Reprinted by permission of Oxford University Press.

Viktor Frankl. *Man's Search for Meaning*. Copyright © 1959, 1962 by Viktor Frankl. Reprinted by permission of Beacon Press.

Erich Fromm. From pp. 22–27, 50–53, 72–78 in *The Art of Loving*. Volume Nine of the World Perspective Series edited by Ruth Nanda Anshen. Copyright © 1956 by Erich Fromm. Reprinted by permission of Harper & Row, Publishers, Inc.

James Hillman. Excerpted from *Suicide and the Soul*. J.H. Spring Publications Inc., University of Dallas, Irving, Texas 75061. All rights Reserved. Reprinted by permission of the author.

William James. From *The Varieties of Religious Experience,* published by the New American Library in 1958.

Immanuel Kant. Excerpted from *Lectures on Ethics*, trans. Louis Infield, published by Methuen & Co., Ltd. Reprinted by permission of Methuen & Co., Ltd.

Nikos Kazantzakis. From *Saint Francis*. Copyright © 1962 by Simon & Schuster, Inc. Reprinted by permission of Simon & Schuster, a Division of Gulf & Western Corporation.

Søren Kierkegaard. Excerpts from *Fear and Trembling and The Sickness unto Death*, translation with Introduction and Notes by Walter Lowrie (copyright 1941, 1954 by Princeton University Press): pp. 91–92, 121–129. Reprinted by permission of Princeton University Press. Excerpts from *Concluding Unscientific Postscript* trans. David F. Swenson and Walter Lowrie copyright 1941 © 1969 by Princeton University Press; Princeton Paperback, 1968): pp. 169–217. Footnotes omitted. Reprinted by permission of Princeton University Press and the American-Scandinavian Foundation.

John Lachs. "To Have and To Be," *The Personalist*, Vol. 45, No. 1, 1964. Reprinted by permission.

Abraham Maslow. Taken from *Toward A Psychology of Being*, 2nd ed., © 1968 by Litton Educational Publishing, Inc. Reprinted by permission of D. Van Nostrand Company.

Rollo May. From "Contributions of Existential Psychotherapy," *Existence: A New Dimension in Psychiatry and Psychology*, edited by Rollo May, Ernest Angel, and Henri F. Ellenberger, pp. 42–44, © 1958 by Basic Books, Inc., Publishers, New York.

Friedrich Nietzsche. "Joyful Wisdom and the Death of God" from *The Joyful Wisdom*. Copyright 1916. Reprinted by permission from Frederick Ungar Publishing Co., Inc. Excerpts from *Beyond Good and Evil*, by Friedrich Nietzsche, translated, with commentary, by Walter Kaufmann. Copyright © 1966 by Random House, Inc. Reprinted by permission.

C. S. Peirce. Excerpted from *Philosophical Writings of Peirce*. Ed. Justus Buchler. New York: Dover Publications, Inc., 1940. Reprinted by permission.

Plato. From *The Republic of Plato* translated by F. M. Cornford and published by Oxford University Press (1941). Reprinted by permission of the publisher.

His Divine Grace A. C. Bhaktivedanta Swami Prabhupada. Reprinted from *Beyond Birth and Death*, by His Divine Grace A. C. Bhaktivedanta Swami Prabhupada, founder-Acarya of the International Society for Krishna Consciousness, © 1972 by the Bhaktivedanta Book Trust. All rights reserved. Reprinted by permission.

Ted Rosenthal. Excerpts from *How Could I Not Be Among You*. Copyright © 1973. Reprinted by permission of George Braziller, Inc.

Bertrand Russell. Selection is reprinted from *Power*, with the permission of W. W. Norton & Company, Inc. Copyright 1938 by Bertrand Russell. Copyright renewed 1966 by Bertrand Russell.

George Santayana. Reprinted by permission of Charles Scribner's Sons from *The Realm of Truth* copyright 1937, 1938 by George Santayana.

Arthur Schopenhauer. Excerpted from *Schopenhauer Selections*, ed. DeWitt Parker. New York: Charles Scribner's Sons, 1928. Reprinted by permission.

Charles E. Scott. From David Barton, M.D., ed., *Death and Dying*, © 1977, which included Charles E. Scott's "Healing and Dying." Copyright © 1977, The Williams & Wilkins Company. Reproduced by permission.

Wallace Stevens. "Of Mere Being," copyright © 1957 by Elsie Stevens and Holly Stevens. Reprinted from *Opus Posthumous*, by Wallace Stevens, ed. Samuel French Morse, by permission of Alfred A. Knopf, Inc.

Elie Wiesel. A selection from *Night*. Translated from the French by Stella Rodway © Les Editions de Minuit, 1958. English translation © MacGibbon & Kee, 1960. Reprinted with the permission of Hill and Wang (now a division of Farrar, Straus and Giroux, Inc.).

About this Book

An introduction to philosophy must be more than an introduction to an academic specialty. The history of reflective thought as well as its latest developments exhibit the tendency of philosophy to burst its disciplinary bounds. Inside the university, philosophy reaches out to establish contact with literature and psychology, with the social and the natural sciences. It builds bridges to the professional schools and serves as the critic of teaching styles and administrative procedures. Both within and beyond institutions of higher education, philosophical reflection connects with experience directly; it sheds light on passion, engenders passions of its own, and helps direct human activity to life-giving ends. Those who think of philosophy as wisdom for living are not wrong after all. The discipline always returns to its permanent task of tackling the largest questions and to its highest calling: to be a way of life beyond any particular method of thinking.

Many introductory texts proceed on the assumption that there are a certain number of standard philosophical problems; to introduce students to philosophy is, therefore, to lay out for them the structure of these difficulties. There is wide agreement on what the problems are and on their proposed solutions. This is what accounts for the remarkable similarity of philosophy texts: many share the same structure and reprint identical selections.

None can quarrel with the philosophical substance of these strikingly similar books, which present material from such great figures as

Descartes and Hume and St. Thomas. But they suffer from two serious problems, one pedagogic, the other philosophical. First of all, many of the conceptual issues they present do not readily connect with the experience of young people. Subtle points about the mind-body relation appear irrelevant to pressing problems of fulfillment or sexuality; discussions of the self as substance do little to resolve anxieties about happiness or identity.

As a result, many students come to see philosophy as discursive thought in its most abstract and unproductive mode. They observe it exhausting itself in futile precision and endless argument. They are encouraged to think that doing it well is a matter of deft moves and clever premises, that—in short—philosophy is conceptual gamesmanship and not serious reflection. To teach philosophy in this way is the surest prescription for losing the respect and interest of most students, while capturing those few pure minds whose love is chess or conundrums.

The philosophical problem of these introductory texts is that they present our discipline as one-dimensional and isolated. They tend to restrict philosophical subject-matter to conceptual puzzles, method to analysis and inference, results to statable conclusions. And they draw sharp lines between philosophy and other activities, encouraging the impression that ours is a purely conceptual—or even linguistic—study to which facts are irrelevant and for which experience is either unnecessary or positively harmful.

By contrast with this narrow view, philosophy is intrinsically pluralistic and interdisciplinary. Its subject-matter includes but is not limited to conceptual difficulties and paradoxes. Facets of experience in all their baffling complexity, the unexplained interconnections of human feeling and belief, the preconceptual structures of consciousness are all proper subjects for philosophical reflection. Analysis and reasoning are appropriate philosophical methods. But so are description and insight, the interpretation of texts and imaginative construction, conjecture and synthetic vision.

And, finally, philosophy is not a science. Some of its results may be confirmed hypotheses, but it also creates commands and injunctions, structured lives and reorganized societies, control over feelings or new-found spontaneity, and the growth of inexpressible convictions. To present an adequate picture of our discipline, an introductory text must do justice not only to the diversity of conclusions in the field, but also to the experiential basis of our questions, the broad spectrum of philosophical activities, and the wide variety of uses to which philosophy is put.

The departmentalization of knowledge involves both loss and gain.

The freedom to pursue advanced, narrow lines of specialization is offset by increasing isolation, atomicity, impoverishment. The cost to philosophy has been particularly high. For the conceptual skills of philosophers are well employed in the clarification of problems in other disciplines. Other fields, in turn, provide the material so essential for the synthesizing function of philosophical thought. In fact, without fertilization by the arts and sciences, philosophy can fulfill neither its traditional function as the critic and interpreter of values and of culture, nor its calling to envision and present new possibilities for human growth. And without this relevance to life, it is condemned to sterility and frustration.

In this book we present philosophy as a diverse set of activities not easily confined within disciplinary bounds. Selections from the analytic tradition, from phenomenological and existentialist sources, and from American philosophy provide for the student a significant cross-section of divergent ways of thinking. Substantial material from major historical figures gives added depth to our treatment of several topics. We have purposely kept our introductions short; the selections are clear enough to speak for themselves and to require little interpretation.

As further enrichment, we include literary selections and writings from psychology and religion. One of our reasons for doing so is that professional philosophers are by no means the only ones who make important contributions to problems of special interest to philosophy. Another and related reason is that the lines between philosophy and other disciplines are relative and fluid: it is more accurate to think of a work as more or less philosophical than to think of it as purely philosophical or not at all so. We think that several of the selections that are not technically philosophical are particularly effective in stimulating reflection. And to stimulate reflection is to launch the student on a career of philosophical activity.

Our book is designed specifically to initiate in students the activities of disciplined questioning and structured reflection. We believe that it is better to start students in philosophy with selections that arouse their interest and naturally engage them in the work of thought than simply to acquaint them with the results of the reflection of others. This fundamental premise has served to structure the entire volume: we have sought both by the choice of topics and by the treatments selected to pique curiosity, to arouse the imagination, to stimulate judgment, as well as to increase understanding. Philosophy is learned best—perhaps only—by doing; if we provide students with material that is of immediate interest to them, they can engage in philosophical reflection from the start.

Focusing on areas of intense human concern, on some of the pervasive desires and aversions in our experience, is singularly well suited to accomplish this end. The seeds of thought are already there in the soil of experience; a little sunshine and water, a little conscious cultivation should yield flowers before long. Simply to bring the great search in which we are all engaged to the foreground of consciousness is to stimulate self-knowledge. To go beyond this by providing the ideas and the language in terms of which the search can be examined and understood is to establish philosophy not only as relevant to life but also as indispensable to intelligent action.

We have been especially careful to avoid two temptations. Many philosophers and most of the rest of us believe that for every problem there is a definite solution and suppose that such solutions can be known with certainty. On the contrary, we think that philosophy is much more like life at large than like a restricted science: the solution of its problems is improbable and, in any case, of less importance than the search for resolution and understanding. Moreover, certainty about matters of great significance is an ideal elusive because illusory; since it cannot be achieved, it ought not to be sought. Consequently, we have laid little stress on single or ultimate solutions to any problems. Both the broad spectrum of our selections and the structure of our chapters discourage the natural hope that there are incontestable answers and saving certainties.

Those who engage in the philosophical enterprise have to learn to live with uncertainty, to accept finitude, to embrace our ambiguous estate. And even in the face of daily failure, they must ever reinstitute the search for understanding, as we do in life for everything we want and hope to gain. It is to this philosophical search, in which teachers and students are partners, that our book serves as an introduction and an invitation.

Contents

The
Human Search

Introduction

Human life is a stream of activities. We strive to attain a variety of objectives, obtain a diversity of goods, retain what we have once achieved. We, like streams, are the flow of these activities. Purposes enfold us and make demands on us from every side. If we are not conscious of them, they shape our existence and define our responses, regardless of our own identity, as though they were final or were definitive of our being. Yet we may learn to hear and reflect the depth of our goals and interests. If we do not, we forget the most human of our abilities: to know and to think with depth of insight and growth of consciousness. In other words, we fail to become philosophers.

The stream of activity is not only at the center of human life. It is also the heart of philosophy. For, first of all, human aims and meanings, which are a part of the stream, constitute primary objectives of philosophy. We must study them first because we always find the world bathed in the light they shed on it. And, secondly, philosophy itself is an activity, which lights up the stream of which it is a part. It is one of the great ventures of which life consists, an effort to grasp the connections of our searches, and the way in which the world and our search for meaning and understanding in the world are related.

If we think of philosophy *as an activity*, we will not be misled into supposing that it is only a method of inquiry or a set of conclusions we maintain. For as disciplined and discriminative reflection on facts and experiences, it is first and foremost our struggle to understand the

3

complexity, significance, and value of existence. As any activity, it has its rules and requires skill. It also yields results, although none that are certain or uncontested. It is unavoidably diverse in its premises, procedures, and conclusions. Even its uses are varied. For sometimes we want only to understand, although more frequently philosophy plays a role in our attempts to change the world or to accept it.

In this volume, we present philosophy in its attempt to address important problems of life. Our intention is to exhibit our discipline as indispensable for dealing with the recurrent questions and crises of individuals and societies. The process of gaining this insight will naturally involve students in self-exploration and self-discovery. Growing grasp of the nature and relevance of philosophy will, therefore, be proportional to their improved self-understanding, to an enhanced consciousness of their values and intentions. This is why the choice of topics is so important: students should be able to see themselves as seeking power, knowledge, and happiness and as struggling with the problems that accompany this search. And they should find no difficulty in encountering in themselves the great problems of identity, meaning in life, and fulfillment.

As is appropriate to philosophy, we foster a critical, questioning attitude. The readings have been selected partly for their promise of initiating and guiding reflection. They are intellectually varied; we have aimed throughout at opening alternatives and stimulating the imagination. As a result, nothing here presents *the* truth or offers certainty. On the contrary, learning to live without solutions is one of the important skills philosophy teaches and its results justify.

A significant part of Western philosophy has revolved around the quest for certainty. Philosophers have looked for reasons grounded in necessity, for timeless structures, for indubitable ideas. This search has led to dogmatism, intolerance and, above all, disappointment. The time may be near when we can place proper limits on this search or at least see it in a larger context. This is all the more important because acceptance of uncertainty and acceptance of self seem to be deeply related. Accordingly, this book focuses on fundamental human concerns with the assumption that the acceptance of uncertainty must be preserved among the rightful goals of philosophy.

We made our selections with the conviction that the richest and most provocative material for philosophical discussion is not always the product of philosophers. In fact, the more narrowly we draw the limits of philosophy, the more we find it impoverished and imprisoned in irrelevance. Discursive thought and intuitive insight are not the sole property of any discipline. The educational task of the philosopher is continuous with that of the sociologist, the psychologist, the poet: we all work to render the thin stream of reflection and appreciation richer and more free.

In this spirit of human cooperation, among disciplines, philosophers, students and teachers, we offer this book to taste the joys and start the work of thought.

JOHN BARTH

Night–Sea Journey

"One way or another, no matter which theory of our journey is correct, it's myself I address; to whom I rehearse as to a stranger our history and condition, and will disclose my secret hope though I sink for
it.

"Is the journey my invention? Do the night, the sea, exist at all, I
ask myself, apart from my experience of them? Do I myself exist, or is
this a dream? Sometimes I wonder. And if I am, who am I? The Heritage I supposedly transport? But how can I be both vessel and contents? Such are the questions that beset my intervals of rest.

"My trouble is, I lack conviction. Many accounts of our situation
seem plausible to me—where and what we are, why we swim and
whither. But implausible ones as well, perhaps especially those, I
must admit as possibly correct. Even likely. If at times, in certain
humors—striking in unison, say, with my neighbors and chanting
with them 'Onward! Upward!'—I have supposed that we have after all
a common Maker, Whose nature and motives we may not know, but
Who engendered us in some mysterious wise and launched us forth
toward some end known but to Him—if (for a moodslength only) I
have been able to entertain such notions, very popular in certain quar-
ters, it is because our night-sea journey partakes of their absurdity.
One might even say: I can believe them *because* they are absurd.

"Has that been said before?

"Another paradox: it appears to be these recesses from swimming that sustain me in the swim. Two measures onward and upward, flailing with the rest, then I float exhausted and dispirited, brood upon the night, the sea, the journey, while the flood bears me a measure back and down: slow progress, but I live, I live, and make my way, aye, past many a drownèd comrade in the end, stronger, worthier than I, victims of their unremitting *joie de nager*. I have seen the best swimmers of my generation go under. Numberless the number of the dead! Thousands drown as I think this thought, millions as I rest before returning to the swim. And scores, hundreds of millions have expired since we surged forth, brave in our innocence, upon our dreadful way. 'Love! Love!' we sang then, a quarter-billion strong, and churned the warm sea white with joy of swimming! Now all are gone down—the buoyant, the sodden, leaders and followers, all gone under, while wretched I swim on. Yet these same reflective intervals that keep me afloat have led me into wonder, doubt, despair—strange emotions for a swimmer!—have led me, even, to suspect . . . that our night-sea journey is without meaning.

"Indeed, if I have yet to join the hosts of the suicides, it is because (fatigue apart) I find it no meaningfuller to drown myself than to go on swimming.

"I know that there are those who seem actually to enjoy the night-sea; who claim to love swimming for its own sake, or sincerely believe that 'reaching the Shore,' 'transmitting the Heritage' (*Whose* Heritage, I'd like to know? And to whom?) is worth the staggering cost. I do not. Swimming itself I find at best not actively unpleasant, more often tiresome, not infrequently a torment. Arguments from function and design don't impress me: granted that we can and do swim, that in a manner of speaking our long tails and streamlined heads are 'meant for' swimming; it by no means follows—for me, at least—that we *should* swim, or otherwise endeavor to 'fulfill our destiny.' Which is to say, Someone Else's destiny, since ours, so far as I can see, is merely to perish, one way or another, soon or late. The heartless zeal of our (departed) leaders, like the blind ambition and good cheer of my own youth, appalls me now; for the death of my comrades I am inconsolable. If the night-sea journey has justification, it is not for us swimmers ever to discover it.

"Oh, to be sure, 'Love!' one heard on every side: 'Love it is that drives and sustains us!' I translate: we don't know *what* drives and sustains us, only that we are most miserably driven and, imperfectly, sustained. *Love* is how we call our ignorance of what whips us. 'To reach the Shore,' then: but what if the Shore exists in the fancies of us swimmers merely, who dream it to account for the dreadful fact that we swim, have always and only swum, and continue swimming without respite (myself excepted) until we die? Supposing even that there *were* a Shore—that, as a cynical companion of mine once imagined, we rise from the drowned to discover all those vulgar superstitions and exalted metaphors to be literal truth: the giant Maker of us all, the Shores of Light beyond our night-sea journey!—whatever would a swimmer do there? The fact is, when we imagine the Shore, what comes to mind is just the opposite of our condition: no more night, no more sea, no more journeying. In short, the blissful estate of the drowned.

" 'Ours not to stop and think; ours but to swim and sink. . . .' Because a moment's thought reveals the pointlessness of swimming. 'No matter,' I've heard some say, even as they gulped their last: 'The night-sea journey may be absurd, but here we swim, will-we nill-we, against the flood, onward and upward, toward a Shore that may not exist and couldn't be reached if it did.' The thoughtful swimmer's choices, then, they say, are two: give over thrashing and go under for good, or embrace the absurdity; affirm in and for itself the night-sea journey; swim on with neither motive nor destination, for the sake of swimming, and compassionate moreover with your fellow swimmer, we being all at sea and equally in the dark. I find neither course acceptable. If not even the hypothetical Shore can justify a sea-full of drownèd comrades, to speak of the swim-in-itself as somehow doing so strikes me as obscene. I continue to swim—but only because blind habit, blind instinct, blind fear of drowning are still more strong than the horror of our journey. And if on occasion I have assisted a fellow-thrasher, joined in the cheers and songs, even passed along to others strokes of genius from the drownèd great, it's that I shrink by temperament from making myself conspicuous. To paddle off in one's own direction, assert one's independent right-of-way, overrun one's fellows without compunction, or dedicate oneself entirely to pleasures and diversions without regard for conscience—I can't finally condemn those who journey in this wise; in half my moods I envy them and despise the weak vitality that keeps me from following their example. But in reasonabler moments I remind myself that it's their very freedom and self-responsibility I reject, as more dramatically absurd, in our senseless circumstances, than tailing along in conventional fashion. Suicides, rebels, affirmers of the paradox—nay-sayers and yea-sayers alike to our fatal journey—I finally shake my head at them. And splash sighing past their corpses, one by one, as past a hundred sorts of others: friends, enemies, brothers; fools, sages, brutes—and no-bodies, million upon million. I envy them all.

"A poor irony: that I, who find abhorrent and tautological the doctrine of survival of the fittest (*fitness* meaning, in my experience, nothing more than survival-ability, a talent whose only demonstration is the fact of survival, but whose chief ingredients seem to be strength, guile, callousness), may be the sole remaining swimmer! But the doctrine is false as well as repellent: Chance drowns the worthy with the unworthy, bears up the unfit with the fit by whatever definition, and makes the night-sea journey essentially *haphazard* as well as murderous and unjustified.

" 'You only swim once,' Why bother, then?

" 'Except ye drown, ye shall not reach the Shore of Light.' Poppycock.

"One of my late companions—that same cynic with the curious fancy, among the first to drown—entertained us with odd conjectures while we waited to begin our journey. A favorite theory of his was that the Father does exist, and did indeed make us and the sea we swim—but not a-purpose or even consciously; He made us, as it were, despite Himself, as we make waves with every tail-thrash, and may be unaware of our existence. Another was that He knows we're here but doesn't care what happens to us, inasmuch as He creates (voluntarily or not) other seas and swimmers at more or less regular intervals. In bitterer moments, such as just before he drowned, my friend even supposed that our Maker wished us unmade; there was indeed a Shore, he'd argue, which could save at least some of us from drowning and toward which it was our function to struggle—but for reasons unknowable to us He wanted desperately to prevent our reaching that happy place and fulfilling our destiny. Our 'Father,' in short, was our adversary and would-be killer! No less outrageous, and offensive to traditional opinion, were the fellow's speculations on the nature of our Maker: that He might well be no swimmer Himself at all, but some sort of monstrosity, perhaps even tailless; that He might be stupid, malicious, insensible, perverse, or asleep and dreaming; that the end for which He created and launched us forth, and which we flagellate ourselves to fathom, was perhaps immoral, even obscene. Et cetera, et cetera: there was no end to the chap's conjectures, or the impoliteness of his fancy; I have reason to suspect that his early demise, whether planned by 'our Maker' or not, was expedited by certain fellow-swimmers indignant at his blasphemies.

"In other moods, however (he was as given to moods as I), his theorizing would become half-serious, so it seemed to me, especially upon the subjects of Fate and Immortality, to which our youthful conversations often turned. Then his harangues, if no less fantastical, grew solemn and obscure, and if he was still baiting us, his passion undid the joke. His objection to popular opinions of the hereafter, he would declare, was their claim to general validity. Why need believers hold that *all* the drownèd rise to be judged at journey's end, and nonbelievers that drowning is final without exception? In *his* opinion (so he'd vow at least), nearly everyone's fate was permanent death; indeed he took a sour pleasure in supposing that every 'Maker' made thousands of separate seas in His creative lifetime, each populated like ours with millions of swimmers, and that in almost every instance both sea and swimmers were utterly annihilated, whether accidentally or by malevolent design. (Nothing if not pluralistical, he imagined there might be millions and billions of 'Fathers,' perhaps in some 'night-sea' of their own!) However—and here he turned infidels against him with the faithful—he professed to believe that in possibly a single night-sea per thousand, say, one of its quarter-billion swimmers (that is, one swimmer in two hundred fifty billions) achieved a qualified immortality. In some cases the rate might be slightly higher; in others it was vastly lower, for just as there are swimmers of every degree of proficiency, including some who drown before the journey starts, unable to swim at all, and others created drowned, as it were, so he imagined what can only be termed impotent Creators, Makers unable to Make, as well as uncommonly fertile ones and all grades between. And it pleased him to deny any necessary relation between a Maker's productivity and His other virtues—including, even, the quality of His creatures.

"I could go on (*he* surely did) with his elaboration of these mad notions—such as that swimmers in other night-seas needn't be of our kind; that Makers themselves might belong to different *species*, so to speak; that our particular Maker mightn't Himself be immortal, or that we might be not only His emissaries but His 'immortality,' continuing

His life and our own, transmogrified, beyond our individual deaths. Even this modified immortality (meaningless to me) he conceived as relative and contingent, subject to accident or deliberate termination: his pet hypothesis was that Makers and swimmers *each generate the other*—against all odds, their number being so great—and that any given 'immortality-chain' could terminate after any number of cycles, so that what was 'immortal' (still speaking relatively) was only the cyclic process of incarnation, which itself might have a beginning and an end. Alternatively he liked to imagine cycles within cycles, either finite or infinite: for example, the 'night-sea,' as it were, in which Makers 'swam' and created night-seas and swimmers like ourselves, might be the creation of a larger Maker, Himself one of many, Who in turn et cetera. Time itself he regarded as relative to our experience, like magnitude: who knew but what, with each thrash of our tails, minuscule seas and swimmers, whole eternities, came to pass—as ours, perhaps, and our Maker's Maker's, was elapsing between the strokes of some supertail, in a slower order of time?

Naturally I hooted with the others at this nonsense. We were young then, and had only the dimmest notion of what lay ahead; in our ignorance we imagined night-sea journeying to be a positively heroic enterprise. Its meaning and value we never questioned; to be sure, some must go down by the way, a pity no doubt, but to win a race requires that others lose, and like all my fellows I took for granted that I would be the winner. We milled and swarmed, impatient to be off, never mind where or why, only to try our youth against the realities of night and sea; if we indulged the skeptic at all, it was as a droll, half-contemptible mascot. When he died in the initial slaughter, no one cared.

"And even now I don't subscribe to all his views—but I no longer scoff. The horror of our history has purged me of opinions, as of vanity, confidence, spirit, charity, hope, vitality, everything—except dull dread and a kind of melancholy, stunned persistence. What leads me to recall his fancies is my growing suspicion that I, of all swimmers, may be the sole survivor of this fell journey, tale-bearer of a generation. This suspicion, together with the recent sea-change, suggests to me now that nothing is impossible, not even my late companion's wildest visions, and brings me to a certain desperate resolve, the point of my chronicling.

"Very likely I have lost my senses. The carnage at our setting out; our decimation by whirlpool, poisoned cataract, sea-convulsion; the panic stampedes, mutinies, slaughters, mass suicides; the mounting evidence that none will survive the journey—add to these anguish and fatigue; it were a miracle if sanity stayed afloat. Thus I admit, with the other possibilities, that the present sweetening and calming of the sea, and what seems to be a kind of vasty presence, song, or summons from the near upstream, may be hallucinations of disordered sensibility. . . .

"Perhaps, even, I am drowned already. Surely I was never meant for the rough-and-tumble of the swim; not impossibly I perished at the outset and have only imaged the night-sea journey from some final deep. In any case, I'm no longer young, and it is we spent old swimmers, disabused of every illusion, who are most vulnerable to dreams.

"Sometimes I think I am my drownèd friend.

"Out with it: I've begun to believe, not only that *She* exists, but that She lies not far ahead, and stills the sea, and draws me Herward! Aghast, I recollect his maddest notion: that our destination (which existed, mind, in but one night-sea out of hundreds and thousands) was no Shore, as commonly conceived, but a mysterious being, indescribable except by paradox and vaguest figure: wholly different from us swimmers, yet our complement; the death of us, yet our salvation and resurrection; simultaneously our journey's end, mid-point, and commencement; not membered and thrashing like us, but a motionless or hugely gliding sphere of unimaginable dimension; self-contained, yet dependent absolutely, in some wise, upon the chance (always monstrously improbable) that one of us will survive the night-sea journey and reach . . . Her! *Her,* he called it, or *She,* which is to say, Other-than-a-he. I shake my head; the thing is too preposterous; it is myself I talk to, to keep my reason in this awful darkness. There is no She! There is no You! I rave to myself; it's Death alone that hears and summons. To the drowned, all seas are calm. . . .

"Listen: my friend maintained that in every order of creation there are two sorts of creators, contrary yet complementary, one of which gives rise to seas and swimmers, the other to the Night-which-contains-the-sea and to What-waits-at-the-journey's-end: the former, in short, to destiny, the latter to destination (and both profligately, involuntarily, perhaps indifferently or unwittingly). The 'purpose' of the night-sea journey—but not necessarily of the journeyer or of either Maker!—my friend could describe only in abstractions: *consummation, transfiguration, union of contraries, transcension of categories.* When we laughed, he would shrug and admit that he understood the business no better than we, and thought it ridiculous, dreary, possibly obscene. 'But one of you,' he'd add with his wry smile, 'may be the Hero destined to complete the night-sea journey and be one with Her. Chances are, of course, you won't make it.' He himself, he declared, was not even going to try; the whole idea repelled him; if we chose to dismiss it as an ugly fiction, so much the better for us; thrash, splash, and be merry, we were soon enough drowned. But there it was, he could not say how he knew or why he bothered to tell us, any more than he could say what would happen after She and Hero, Shore and Swimmer, 'merged identities' to become something both and neither. He quite agreed with me that if the issue of that magical union had no memory of the night-sea journey, for example, it enjoyed a poor sort of immortality; even poorer if, as he rather imagined, a swimmer-hero plus a She equaled or became merely another Maker of future night-seas and the rest, at such incredible expense of life. This being the case—he was persuaded it was—the merciful thing to do was refuse to participate; the genuine heroes, in his opinion, were the suicides, and the hero of heroes would be the swimmer who, in the presence of the Other, refused Her proffered 'immortality' and thus put an end to at least one cycle of catastrophes.

"How we mocked him! Our moment came, we hurtled forth, pretending to glory in the adventure, thrashing, singing, cursing, strangling, rationalizing, rescuing, killing, inventing rules and stories and relationships, giving up, struggling on, but dying all, and still in darkness, until only a battered remnant was left to croak 'Onward, upward,' like a bitter echo. Then they too fell silent—victims, I can only presume, of the last frightful wave—and the moment came when I also, utterly desolate and spent, thrashed my last and gave myself over to the current, to sink or float as might be, but swim no more. Whereupon, marvelous to tell, in an instant the sea grew still! Then warmly, gently, the great tide turned, began to bear me, as it does now, onward and upward will-I nill-I, like a flood of joy—and I recalled with dismay my dead friend's teaching.

"I am not deceived. This new emotion is Her doing; the desire that possesses me is Her bewitchment. Lucidity passes from me; in a moment I'll cry 'Love!' bury myself in Her side, and be 'transfigured.' Which is to say, I die already; this fellow transported by passion is not I; *I am he who abjures and rejects the night-sea journey!* I. . . .

"I am all love. 'Come!' She whispers, and I have no will.

"You who I may be about to become, whatever You are: with the last twitch of my real self I beg You to listen. It is *not* love that sustains me! No; though Her magic makes me burn to sing the contrary, and though I drown even now for the blasphemy, I will say truth. What has fetched me across this dreadful sea is a single hope, gift of my poor dead comrade: that You may be stronger-willed than I, and that by sheer force of concentration I may transmit to You, along with Your official Heritage, a private legacy of awful recollection and negative resolve. Mad as it may be, my dream is that some unimaginable embodiment of myself (or myself plus Her if that's how it must be) will come to find itself expressing, in however garbled or radical a translation, some reflection of these reflections. If against all odds this comes to pass, may You to whom, through whom I speak, do what I cannot: terminate this aimless, brutal business! Stop Your hearing against Her song! Hate love!

"Still alive, afloat, afire. Farewell then my penultimate hope: that one may be sunk for direst blasphemy on the very shore of the Shore. Can it be (my old friend would smile) that only utterest nay-sayers survive the night? But even that were Sense, and there is no sense, only senseless love, senseless death. Whoever echoes these reflections: be more courageous than their author! An end to night-sea journeys! Make no more! And forswear me when I shall forswear myself, deny myself, plunge into Her who summons, singing . . .

" 'Love! Love! Love!' "

1

The Uses of Power

Our interest in power is pervasive and understandable. The need and the desire for it are present even in the infant. The ability to control the movements of one's body is a great and primary power; children achieve it with difficulty, old people surrender it in sorrow. Without it, life is impotent or impossible. Each limitation of power is framed in pain and experienced as a burden.

We learn to operate our bodies with delight. Before long, our interests expand and we wish to control portions of the surrounding world the way we can control our hands and feet. Power, in the broadest sense, is the ability to do what we want; its source is desire with its imperatives, its focus is as multiple as our needs.

The first bitter lesson about power is that it is costly to achieve. The physical world and other humans resist our efforts, and the struggle exhausts as often as it exhilarates. The second lesson teaches that all power is limited. Nature and society wield far more force than any individual, yet even their power wanes. And individuals with their small spheres of power suffer assaults until all fight, and all life, are pounded out of them.

The limits of physical force move us to think that at least the power of mind is infinite. Intellectual dominion through understanding then becomes our goal. And if we cannot control the world around us, we strive to master at least our hopes and fears. True power is then thought to reside in control over self, in overcoming our desires, in accepting our fate.

The shift from physical, social, or political power to self-mastery opens new possibilities and kindles a new search. The power of wisdom, virtue, and imagination move to center stage. Worldly weakness itself may become a virtue, particularly when it is tied to intellectual or spiritual power, or to the moral force of innocence.

Paradoxically, it may well be that we never achieve moral and spiritual powers while we seek them. Indeed perhaps only our culture, devoted as it is to manipulation and to making things happen, thinks of them as achievements based on skill and effort. When we have them at last, they feel effortless and seem past all desire. To the spiritual person his/her power is a way of being, a gift received. His/her weakness will seem despicable to the burly fighters of the world. Yet, to him/her, their muscles, their thunder will always be signs of their weakness.

THOMAS HOBBES

First Distinctions

Of Power, Worth, Dignity, Honour, and Worthinesse

The Power *of a Man,* (to take it Universally,) is his present means, to obtain some future apparent Good. And is either *Originall,* or *Instrumentall.*

Naturall Power, is the eminence of the Faculties of Body, or Mind: as extraordinary Strength, Forme, Prudence, Arts, Eloquence, Liberality, Nobility. *Instrumentall* are those Powers, which acquired by these, or by fortune, are means and Instruments to acquire more: as Riches, Reputation, Friends, and the secret working of God, which men call Good Luck. For the nature of Power, is in this point, like to Fame, increasing as it proceeds; or like the motion of heavy bodies, which the further they go, make still the more hast.

The Greatest of humane Powers, is that which is compounded of the Powers of most men, united by consent, in one person, Naturall, or Civill, that has the use of all their Powers depending on his will; such as is the Power of a Common-wealth: Or depending on the wills of each particular; such as is the Power of a Faction, or of divers factions leagued. Therefore to have servants, is Power; To have friends, is Power: for they are strengths united.

Also Riches joyned with liberality, is Power; because it procureth friends, and servants: Without liberality, not so; because in this case they defend not; but expose men to Envy, as a Prey.

Reputation of power, is Power; because it draweth with it the adherence of those that need protection.

So is Reputation of love of a mans Country, (called Popularity,) for the same Reason.

Also, what quality soever maketh a man beloved, or feared of many; or the reputation of such quality, is Power; because it is a means to have the assistance, and service of many.

Good successe is Power; because it maketh reputation of Wisdome, or good fortune; which makes men either feare him, or rely on him.

Affability of men already in power, is encrease of Power; because it gaineth love.

Reputation of Prudence in the conduct of Peace or War, is Power; because to prudent men, we commit the government of our selves, more willingly than to others.

Nobility is Power, not in all places, but onely in those Commonwealths, where it has Priviledges: for in such priviledges consisteth their Power.

Eloquence is power; because it is seeming Prudence.

Forme is Power; because being a promise of Good, it recommendeth men to the favour of women and strangers.

The Sciences, are small Power; because not eminent; and therefore, not acknowledged in any man; nor are at all, but in a few; and in them, but of a few things. For Science is of that nature, as none can understand it to be, but such as in a good measure have attayned it.

Arts of publique use, as Fortification, making of Engines, and other Instruments of War; because they conferre to Defence, and Victory, are Power: And though the true Mother of them, be Science, namely the Mathematiques; yet, because they are brought into the Light, by the hand of the Artificer, they be esteemed (the Midwife passing with the vulgar for the Mother,) as his issue.

The *Value*, or WORTH of a man, is as of all other things, his Price; that is to say, so much as would be given for the use of his Power: and therefore is not absolute; but a thing dependant on the need and judgement of another. An able conductor of Souldiers, is of great Price in time of War present, or imminent; but in Peace not so. A learned and uncorrupt Judge, is much Worth in time of Peace; but not so much in War. And as in other things, so in men, not the seller, but the buyer determines the Price. For let a man (as most men do,) rate themselves at the highest Value they can; yet their true Value is no more than it is esteemed by others.

BERTRAND RUSSELL

The Nature of Power

The Impulse To Power

Between man and other animals there are various differences, some intellectual, some emotional. One of the chief emotional differences is that some human desires, unlike those of animals, are essentially boundless and incapable of complete satisfaction. The boa constrictor, when he has had his meal, sleeps until appetite revives; if other animals do not do likewise, it is because their meals are less adequate or because they fear enemies. The activities of animals, with few exceptions, are inspired by the primary needs of survival and reproduction, and do not exceed what these needs make imperative.

With men, the matter is different. A large proportion of the human race, it is true, is obliged to work so hard in obtaining necessaries that little energy is left over for other purposes; but those whose livelihood is assured do not, on that account, cease to be active. Xerxes had no lack of food or raiment or wives at the time when he embarked upon the Athenian expedition. Newton was certain of material comfort from the moment when he became a Fellow of Trinity, but it was after this that he wrote the *Principia*. St. Francis and Ignatius Loyola had no need to found Orders to escape from want. These were eminent men, but the same characteristic, in varying degrees, is to be found in all but a small exceptionally sluggish minority. Mrs. A, who is quite sure of her husband's success in business, and has no fear of the work-house, likes to be better dressed than Mrs. B, although she could es-

cape the danger of pneumonia at much less expense. Both she and Mr.
A are pleased if he is knighted or elected to Parliament. In daydreams
there is no limit to imagined triumphs, and if they are regarded as
possible, efforts will be made to achieve them.

Imagination is the goad that forces human beings into restless exertion after their primary needs have been satisfied. Most of us have
known very few moments when we could have said:

> If it were now to die,
> 'Twere now to be most happy, for I fear
> My soul hath her content so absolute
> That not another comfort like to this
> Succeeds in unknown fate.

And in our rare moments of perfect happiness it is natural, like Othello, to wish for death, since we know that contentment cannot last.
What we need for lasting happiness is impossible for human beings:
only God can have complete bliss, for His is "the kingdom and the
power and the glory." Earthly kingdoms are limited by other kingdoms; earthly power is cut short by death; earthly glory, though we
build pyramids or be "married to immortal verse," fades with the
passing of centuries. To those who have but little of power and glory,
it may seem that a little more would satisfy them, but in this they are
mistaken: these desires are insatiable and infinite, and only in the infinitude of God could they find repose.

While animals are content with existence and reproduction, men
desire also to expand, and their desires in this respect are limited only
by what imagination suggests as possible. Every man would like to be
God, if it were possible; some few find it difficult to admit the impossibility. These are the men framed after the model of Milton's Satan,
combining, like him, nobility with impiety. By "impiety" I mean
something not dependent upon theological beliefs: I mean refusal to
admit the limitations of individual human power. This Titanic combination of nobility with impiety is most notable in the great conquerors, but some element of it is to be found in all men. It is this that
makes social co-operation difficult, for each of us would like to conceive of it after the pattern of the co-operation between God and His
worshipers, with ourself in the place of God. Hence competition, the
need of compromise and government, the impulse to rebellion, with
instability and periodic violence. And hence the need of morality to
restrain anarchic self-assertion.

Of the infinite desires of man, the chief are the desires for power and glory. These are not identical, though closely allied: the Prime Minister has more power than glory, the King has more glory than power. As a rule, however, the easiest way to obtain glory is to obtain power; this is especially the case as regards the men who are active in relation to public events. The desire for glory, therefore, prompts, in the main, the same actions as are prompted by the desire for power, and the two motives may, for most practical purposes, be regarded as one.

The orthodox economists, as well as Marx, who in this respect agreed with them, were mistaken in supposing that economic self-interest could be taken as the fundamental motive in the social sciences. The desire for commodities, when separated from power and glory, is finite, and can be fully satisfied by a moderate competence. The really expensive desires are not dictated by a love of material comfort. Such commodities as a legislature rendered subservient by corruption, or a private picture gallery of Old Masters selected by experts, are sought for the sake of power or glory, not as affording comfortable places in which to sit. When a moderate degree of comfort is assured, both individuals and communities will pursue power rather than wealth: they may seek wealth as a means to power, or they may forgo an increase of wealth in order to secure an increase of power, but in the former case as in the latter their fundamental motive is not economic.

This error in orthodox and Marxist economics is not merely theoretical, but is of the greatest practical importance, and has caused some of the principal events of recent times to be misunderstood. It is only by realizing that love of power is the cause of the activities that are important in social affairs that history, whether ancient or modern, can be rightly interpreted. . . .

There are many ways in which different societies differ in relation to power. They differ, to begin with, in the degree of power possessed by individuals or organizations; it is obvious, for example, that, owing to increase of organization, the State has more power now than in former times. They differ, again, as regards the kind of organization that is most influential: a military despotism, a theocracy, a plutocracy, are very dissimilar types. They differ, thirdly, through diversity in the ways of acquiring power: hereditary kingship produces one kind of eminent man, the qualities required of a great ecclesiastic produce another kind, democracy produces a third kind, and war a fourth.

Where no social institution, such as aristocracy or hereditary monarchy, exists to limit the number of men to whom power is possible, those who most desire power are, broadly speaking, those most likely to acquire it. It follows that, in a social system in which power is open to all, the posts which confer power will, as a rule, be occupied by men who differ from the average in being exceptionally power-loving. Love of power, though one of the strongest of human motives, is very unevenly distributed, and is limited by various other motives, such as love of ease, love of pleasure, and sometimes love of approval. It is disguised, among the more timid, as an impulse of submission to leadership, which increases the scope of the power-impulses of bold men. Those whose love of power is not strong are unlikely to have much influence on the course of events. The men who cause social changes are, as a rule, men who strongly desire to do so. Love of power, therefore, is a characteristic of the men who are causally important. We should, of course, be mistaken if we regarded it as the sole human motive, but this mistake would not lead us so much astray as might be expected in the search for causal laws in social science, since love of power is the chief motive producing the changes which social science has to study.

The laws of social dynamics are—so I shall contend—only capable of being stated in terms of power in its various forms. In order to discover these laws, it is necessary first to classify the forms of power, and then to review various important historical examples of the ways in which organizations and individuals have acquired control over men's lives. . . .

Leaders and Followers

The power impulse has two forms: explicit, in leaders; implicit, in their followers. When men willingly follow a leader, they do so with a view to the acquisition of power by the group which he commands, and they feel that his triumphs are theirs. Most men do not feel in themselves the competence required for leading their group to victory, and therefore seek out a captain who appears to possess the courage and sagacity necessary for the achievement of supremacy. Even in religion this impulse appears. Nietzsche accused Christianity of inculcating a slave-morality, but ultimate triumph was always the goal. "Blessed are the meek, *for they shall inherit the earth.*" Or as a well-known hymn more explicitly states it:

The Son of God goes forth to war,
A kingly crown to gain.
His blood-red banner streams afar.
Who follows in His train?
Who best can drink his cup of woe,
Triumphant over pain,
Who patient bears his cross below,
He follows in His train.

If this is a slave-morality, then every soldier of fortune who endures
the rigors of a campaign, and every rank-and-file politician who works
hard at electioneering, is to be accounted a slave. But in fact, in every
genuinely co-operative enterprise, the follower is psychologically no
more a slave than the leader.

It is this that makes endurable the inequalities of power which organization makes inevitable, and which tend to increase rather than
diminish as society grows more organic.

Inequality in the distribution of power has always existed in human
communities, as far back as our knowledge extends. This is due partly
to external necessity, partly to causes which are to be found in human
nature. Most collective enterprises are only possible if they are
directed by some governing body. If a house is to be built, someone
must decide on the plans; if trains are to run on a railway, the timeta-
ble cannot be left to the caprices of engine drivers; if a new road is to
be constructed, someone must decide where it is to go. Even a demo-
cratically elected government is still a government, and therefore, on
grounds that have nothing to do with psychology, there must, if collective enterprises are to succeed, be some men who give orders and
others who obey them. But the fact that this is possible, and still more
the fact that the actual inequalities of power exceed what is made necessary by technical causes, can only be explained in terms of individual psychology and physiology. Some men's characters lead them
always to command, others' always to obey; between these extremes
lie the mass of average human beings, who like to command in some
situations, but in others prefer to be subject to a leader.

Adler, in his book on *Understanding Human Nature,*[1] distinguishes a
submissive type and an imperious type. "The servile individual," he
says, "lives by the rules and laws of others, and this type seeks out a
servile position almost compulsively." On the other hand, he con-

1. New York: Greenberg.

tinues, the imperious type, which asks: "How can I be superior to everyone?" is found wherever a director is needed, and rises to the top in revolutions. Adler regards both types as undesirable, at any rate in their extreme forms, and he considers both as products of education. "The greatest disadvantage of an authoritative education," he says, "lies in the fact that it gives the child an ideal of power, and shows him the pleasures which are connected with the possession of power." Authoritative education, we may add, produces the slave type as well as the despotic type, since it leads to the feeling that the only possible relation between two human beings who co-operate is that in which one issues orders and the other obeys them.

Love of power, in various limited forms, is almost universal, but in its absolute form it is rare. A woman who enjoys power in the management of her house is likely to shrink from the sort of political power enjoyed by a prime minister; Abraham Lincoln, on the contrary, while not afraid to govern the United States, could not face civil war in the home. Perhaps Napoleon, if the "Bellerophon" had suffered shipwreck, would have tamely obeyed the orders of British officers as to escaping in boats. Men like power so long as they believe in their own competence to handle the business in question, but when they know themselves incompetent they prefer to follow a leader.

The impulse of submission, which is just as real and just as common as the impulse to command, has its roots in fear. The most unruly gang of children ever imagined will become completely amenable to the orders of a competent adult in an alarming situation, such as a fire; when the War came, the Pankhursts made their peace with Lloyd George. Whenever there is acute danger, the impulse of most people is to seek out authority and submit to it; at such moments, few would dream of revolution. When war breaks out, people have similar feelings towards the government. . . .

The Forms of Power

Power may be defined as the production of intended effects. It is thus a quantitative concept: given two men with similar desires, if one achieves all the desires that the other achieves, and also others, he has more power than the other. But there is no exact means of comparing the power of two men of whom one can achieve one group of desires, and another another; e.g., given two artists of whom each wishes to paint good pictures and become rich, and of whom one succeeds in painting good pictures and the other in becoming rich, there is no way of estimating which has the more power. Nevertheless, it is easy to say, roughly, that A has more power than B, if A achieves many intended effects and B only a few.

There are various ways of classifying the forms of power, each of which has its utility. In the first place, there is power over human beings and power over dead matter or nonhuman forms of life. I shall be concerned mainly with power over human beings, but it will be necessary to remember that the chief cause of change in the modern world is the increased power over matter that we owe to science.

Powers over human beings may be classified by the manner of influencing individuals, or by the type of organization involved.

An individual may be influenced: **A.** By direct physical power over his body, e.g., when he is imprisoned or killed; **B.** By rewards and punishments as inducements, e.g., in giving or withholding employment; **C.** By influence on opinion, i.e., propaganda in its broadest sense. Under this last head I should include the opportunity for creating desired habits in others, e.g., by military drill, the only difference being that in such cases action follows without any such mental intermediary as could be called opinion.

These forms of power are most nakedly and simply displayed in our dealings with animals, where disguises and pretenses are not thought necessary. When a pig with a rope round its middle is hoisted squealing into a ship, it is subject to direct physical power over its body. On the other hand, when the proverbial donkey follows the proverbial carrot, we induce him to act as we wish by persuading him that it is to his interest to do so. Intermediate between these two cases is that of performing animals, in whom habits have been formed by rewards and punishments; also, in a different way, that of sheep being induced to embark on a ship, when the leader has to be dragged across the gangway by force, and the rest then follow willingly.

All these forms of power are exemplified among human beings.

The case of the pig illustrates military and police power.

The donkey with the carrot typifies the power of propoganda.

Performing animals show the power of "education."

The sheep following their unwilling leader are illustrative of party politics, whenever, as is usual, a revered leader is in bondage to a clique or to party bosses.

Let us apply these Aesopian analogies to the rise of Hitler. The carrot was the Nazi program (involving, e.g., the abolition of interest); the donkey was the lower middle class. The sheep and their leader were the Social Democrats and Hindenburg. The pigs (only so far as their misfortunes are concerned) were the victims in concentration camps, and the performing animals are the millions who make the Nazi salute.

The most important organizations are approximately distinguishable by the kind of power that they exert. The army and the police exercise coercive power over the body; economic organizations, in the main, use rewards and punishments as incentives and deterrents; schools, churches, and political parties aim at influencing opinion. But these distinctions are not very clear-cut, since every organization uses other forms of power in addition to the one which is most characteristic.

The power of the Law will illustrate these complexities. The ultimate power of the Law is the coercive power of the State. It is the characteristic of civilized communities that direct physical coercion (with some limitations) is the prerogative of the State, and the Law is a set of rules according to which the State exercises this prerogative in dealing with its own citizens. But the Law uses punishment, not only for the purpose of making undesired actions physically impossible, but also as an inducement; a fine, for example, does not make an action impossible, but only unattractive. Moreover—and this is a much more important matter—the Law is almost powerless when it is not supported by public sentiment, as might be seen in the United States during Prohibition, or in Ireland in the eighties, when moonlighters had the sympathy of a majority of the population. Law, therefore, as an effective force, depends upon opinion and sentiment even more than upon the powers of the police. The degree of feeling in favor of Law is one of the most important characteristics of a community.

This brings us to a very necessary distinction, between traditional power and newly acquired power. Traditional power has on its side the force of habit; it does not have to justify itself at every moment, nor to prove continually that no opposition is strong enough to overthrow it. Moreover, it is almost invariably associated with religious or quasi-religious beliefs purporting to show that resistance is wicked. It can, accordingly, rely upon public opinion to a much greater degree than is possible for revolutionary or usurped power. This has two more or less opposite consequences: on the one hand, traditional power, since it feels secure, is not on the lookout for traitors, and is likely to avoid much active political tyranny; on the other hand, where ancient institutions persist, the injustices to which holders of power are always prone have the sanction of immemorial custom, and can therefore be more glaring than would be possible under a new form of government which hoped to win popular support. The reign of terror in France illustrates the revolutionary kind of tyranny, the *corvée* the traditional kind.

Power not based upon tradition or assent I call "naked" power. Its characteristics differ greatly from those of traditional power. And where traditional power persists, the character of the regime depends, to an almost unlimited extent, upon its feeling of security or insecurity.

Naked power is usually military, and may take the form either of internal tyranny or of foreign conquest. Its importance, especially in the latter form, is very great indeed—greater, I think, than many modern "scientific" historians are willing to admit. Alexander the Great and Julius Caesar altered the whole course of history by their battles. But for the former, the Gospels would not have been written in Greek, and Christianity could not have been preached throughout the Roman Empire. But for the latter, the French would not speak a language derived from Latin, and the Catholic Church could scarcely have existed. The military superiority of the white man to the American Indian is an even more undeniable example of the power of the sword. Conquest by force of arms has had more to do with the spread of civilization than any other single agency. Nevertheless, military power is, in most cases, based upon some other form of power, such as wealth, or technical knowledge, or fanaticism. I do not suggest that this is always the case; for example, in the War of the Spanish Succession Marlborough's genius was essential to the result. But this is to be regarded as an exception to the general rule.

When a traditional form of power comes to an end, it may be succeeded, not by naked power, but by a revolutionary authority commanding the willing assent of the majority or a large minority of the population. So it was, for example, in America in the War of Independence. Washington's authority had none of the characteristics of naked power. Similarly, in the Reformation, new churches were established to take the place of the Catholic Church, and their success was due much more to assent than to force. A revolutionary authority, if it is to succeed in establishing itself without much use of naked power, requires much more vigorous and active popular support than is needed by a traditional authority. When the Chinese Republic was proclaimed in 1911, the men of foreign education decreed a parliamentary Constitution, but the public was apathetic, and the regime quickly became one of naked power under warring Tuchuns (military governors). Such unity as was afterwards achieved by the Kuomintang depended on nationalism, not parliamentarianism. The same sort of thing has happened frequently in Latin America. In all these cases, the authority of Parliament, if it had had sufficient popular support to succeed, would have been revolutionary; but the purely military power which was in fact victorious was naked.

The distinction between traditional, revolutionary, and naked power is psychological. I do not call power traditional merely because it has ancient forms: it must also command respect which is partly due to custom. As this respect decays, traditional power gradually passes over into naked power. The process was to be seen in Russia in the gradual growth of the revolutionary movement up to the moment of its victory in 1917.

I call power revolutionary when it depends upon a large group united by a new creed, program, or sentiment, such as Protestantism, Communism, or desire for national independence. I call power naked when it results merely from the power-loving impulses of individuals or groups, and wins from its subjects only submission through fear, not active co-operation. It will be seen that the nakedness of power is a matter of degree. In a democratic country, the power of the government is not naked in relation to opposing political parties, but is naked in relation to a convinced anarchist. Similarly, where persecution exists, the power of the Church is naked in relation to heretics, but not in relation to orthodox sinners.

Another division of our subject is between the power of organizations and the power of individuals. The way in which an organization acquires power is one thing, and the way in which an individual acquires power within an organization is quite another. The two are, of course, interrelated: if you wish to be Prime Minister, you must acquire power in your Party, and your Party must acquire power in the nation. But if you had lived before the decay of the hereditary principle, you would have had to be the heir of a king in order to acquire political control of a nation; this would, however, not have enabled you to conquer other nations, for which you would have needed qualities that kings' sons often lack. In the present age, a similar situation still exists in the economic sphere, where the plutocracy is largely hereditary. Consider the two hundred plutocratic families in France against whom French Socialists agitate. But dynasties among the plutocracy have not the same degree of permanence as they formerly had on thrones, because they have failed to cause the widespread acceptance of the doctrine of Divine Right. No one thinks it impious for a rising financial magnate to impoverish one who is the son of his father, provided it is done according to the rules and without introducing subversive innovations.

Different types of organization bring different types of individuals to the top, and so do different states of society. An age appears in history through its prominent individuals, and derives its apparent character from the character of these men. As the qualities required for achieving prominence change, so the prominent men change. It is to be presumed that there were men like Lenin in the twelfth century, and that there are men like Richard Coeur de Lion at the present time; but history does not know of them. Let us consider for a moment the kinds of individuals produced by different types of power.

Hereditary power has given rise to our notion of a "gentleman." This is a somewhat degenerate form of a conception which has a long history, from magic properties of chiefs, through the divinity of kings, to knightly chivalry and the blue-blooded aristocrat. The qualities which are admired, where power is hereditary, are such as result from leisure and unquestioned superiority. Where power is aristocratic rather than monarchical, the best manners include courteous behavior towards equals as an addition to bland self-assertion in dealing with inferiors. But whatever the prevalent conception of manners may be, it is only where power is (or lately was) hereditary that men will be judged by their manners. The *bourgeois gentilhomme* is only laughable when he intrudes into a society of men and women who have never had anything better to do than study social niceties. What survives in the way of admiration of the "gentleman" depends upon inherited wealth, and must rapidly disappear if economic as well as political power ceases to pass from father to son.

A very different type of character comes to the fore where power is achieved through learning or wisdom, real or supposed. The two most important examples of this form of power are traditional China and the Catholic Church. There is less of it in the modern world than there has been at most times in the past; apart from the Church, in England, very little of this type of power remains. Oddly enough, the power of what passes for learning is greatest in the most savage communities, and steadily decreases as civilization advances. When I say "learning" I include, of course, reputed learning, such as that of magicians and medicine men. Twenty years of study are required in order to obtain a Doctor's Degree at the University of Lhasa, which is necessary for all the higher posts except that of Dalai Lama. The position is much what it was in Europe in the year 1000, when Pope Sylvester II was reputed a magician because he read books, and was consequently able to increase the power of the Church by inspiring metaphysical terrors.

The intellectual, as we know him, is a spiritual descendant of the priest; but the spread of education has robbed him of power. The power of the intellectual depends upon superstition: reverence for a traditional incantation or a sacred book. Of these, something survives in English-speaking countries, as is seen in the English attitude to the Coronation Service and the American reverence for the Constitution; accordingly, the Archbishop of Canterbury and the Supreme Court Judges still have some of the traditional power of learned men. But this is only a pale ghost of the power of Egyptian priests or Chinese Confucian scholars.

While the typical virtue of the gentleman is honor, that of the man who achieves power through learning is wisdom. To gain a reputation for wisdom a man must seem to have a store of recondite knowledge, a mastery over his passions, and a long experience of the ways of men. Age alone is thought to give something of these qualities; hence "presbyter," "seigneur," "alderman," and "elder" are terms of respect. A Chinese beggar addresses passers-by as "great old sire." But where the power of wise men is organized, there is a corporation of priests or literati, among whom all wisdom is held to be concentrated. The sage is a very different type of character from the knightly warrior, and produces, where he rules, a very different society. China and Japan illustrate the contrast.

We have already noted the curious fact that, although knowledge plays a larger part in civilization now than at any former time, there has not been any corresponding growth of power among those who possess the new knowledge. Although the electrician and the telephone man do strange things that minister to our comfort (or discomfort), we do not regard them as medicine men, or imagine that they can cause thunderstorms if we annoy them. The reason for this is that scientific knowledge, though difficult, is not mysterious, but open to all who care to take the necessary trouble. The modern intellectual, therefore, inspires no awe, but remains a mere employee; except in a few cases, such as the Archbishop of Canterbury, he has failed to inherit the glamour which gave power to his predecessors.

The truth is that the respect accorded to men of learning was never bestowed for genuine knowledge, but for the supposed possession of magical powers. Science, in giving some real acquaintance with natural processes, has destroyed the belief in magic, and therefore the respect for the intellectual. Thus it has come about that, while men of science are the fundamental cause of the features which distinguish our time from former ages, and have, through their discoveries and inventions, an immeasurable influence upon the course of events, they have not, as individuals, as great a reputation for wisdom as may be enjoyed in India by a naked fakir or in Melanesia by a medicine man. The intellectuals, finding their prestige slipping from them as a result of their own activities, become dissatisfied with the modern world. Those in whom the dissatisfaction is least take to Communism; those in whom it goes deeper shut themselves up in their ivory tower.

The growth of large economic organizations has produced a new type of powerful individual: the "executive," as he is called in America. The typical "executive" impresses others as a man of rapid decisions, quick insight into character, and iron will; he must have a firm jaw, tightly closed lips, and a habit of brief and incisive speech. He must be able to inspire respect in equals, and confidence in subordinates who are by no means nonentities. He must combine the qualities of a great general and a great diplomatist: ruthlessness in battle, but a capacity for skillful concession in negotiation. It is by such qualities that men acquire control of important economic organizations.

Political power, in a democracy, tends to belong to men of a type which differs considerably from the three that we have considered hitherto. A politician, if he is to succeed, must be able to win the confidence of his machine, and then to arouse some degree of enthusiasm in a majority of the electorate. The qualities required for these two stages on the road to power are by no means identical, and many men possess the one without the other. Candidates for the Presidency in the United States are not infrequently men who cannot stir the imagination of the general public, though they possess the art of ingratiating themselves with party managers. Such men are, as a rule, defeated, but the party managers do not foresee their defeat. Sometimes, however, the machine is able to secure the victory of a man without "magnetism"; in such cases, it dominates him after his election, and he never achieves real power. Sometimes, on the contrary, a man is able to create his own machine; Napoleon III, Mussolini, and Hitler are examples of this. More commonly, a really successful politician, though he uses an already existing machine, is able ultimately to dominate it and make it subservient to his will.

The qualities which make a successful politician in a democracy vary according to the character of the times; they are not the same in quiet times as they are during war or revolution. In quiet times, a man may succeed by giving an impression of solidity and sound judgment, but in times of excitement something more is needed. At such times, it is necessary to be an impressive speaker—not necessarily eloquent in the conventional sense, for Robespierre and Lenin were not eloquent, but determined, passionate, and bold. The passion may be cold and controlled, but must exist and be felt. In excited times, a politician needs no power of reasoning, no apprehension of impersonal facts, and no shred of wisdom. What he must have is the capacity of persuading the multitude that what they passionately desire is attainable, and that he, through his ruthless determination, is the man to attain it.

The most successful democratic politicians are those who succeed in abolishing democracy and becoming dictators. This, of course, is only possible in certain circumstances; no one could have achieved it in nineteenth-century England. But when it is possible, it requires only a high degree of the same qualities as are required by democratic politicians in general, at any rate in excited times. Lenin, Mussolini, and Hitler owed their rise to democracy.

When once a dictatorship has been established, the qualities by which a man succeeds a dead dictator are totally different from those by which the dictatorship was originally created. Wire-pulling, intrigue, and court favor are the most important methods when heredity is discarded. For this reason, a dictatorship is sure to change its character very considerably after the death of its founder. And since the qualities by which a man succeeds to a dictatorship are less generally impressive than those by which the regime was created, there is a likelihood of instability, palace revolutions, and ultimate reversion to some different system. It is hoped, however, that modern methods of propaganda may successfully counteract this tendency, by creating popularity for the Head of the State without the need for any display of popular qualities on his part. How far such methods can succeed it is as yet impossible to say.

There is one form of the power of individuals which we have not yet considered, namely, power behind the scenes: the power of courtiers, intriguers, spies, and wire-pullers. In every large organization, where the men in control have considerable power, there are other less prominent men (or women) who acquire influence over the leaders by personal methods. Wire-pullers and party bosses belong to the same type, though their technique is different. They put their friends, quietly, into key positions, and so, in time, control the organization. In a dictatorship which is not hereditary, such men may hope to succeed to the dictator when he dies: but in general they prefer not to take the front of the stage. They are men who love power more than glory; often they are socially timid. Sometimes, like eunuchs in oriental monarchies, or kings' mistresses elsewhere, they are, for one reason or another, debarred from titular leadership. Thier influence is greatest where nominal power is hereditary, and least where it is the reward of personal skill and energy. Such men, however, even in the modern forms of government, inevitably have considerable power in those departments which average men consider mysterious. Of these the most important, in our time, are currency and foreign policy. In the time of the Kaiser William II, Baron Holstein, permanent Head of the German Foreign Office, had immense power, although he made no public appearances. How great is the power of the permanent officials in the British Foreign Office at the present day, it is impossible for us to know; the necessary documents may become known to our children. The qualities required for power behind the scenes are very different from those required for all other kinds, and as a rule, though not always, they are undesirable qualities. A system which accords much power to the courtier or the wire-puller is, therefore, in general not a system likely to promote the general welfare.

JOHN DEWEY

Force, Violence and Law

The empirical perplexities which attend the question of the relationship of force and law are many and genuine. The war brings home to us the question not only of the relation of force to international law, but the place of force in the economy of human life and progress. To what extent is organization of force in the multitude of ways required for the successful conduct of modern war a fair test of the work of a social organization? From another angle, the reform of our criminal law and our penal methods compels us to consider the significance of force. Are the Tolstoians right in holding that the state itself sets the great example of violence and furnishes the proof of the evils which result from violence? Or, from the other side, is not the essence of all law coercion? In the industrial domain, direct actionists lead us to inquire whether manifestation of force, threatened and veiled if not overt, is not, after all, the only efficacious method of bringing about any social change which is of serious import. Do not the usual phenomena attending strikes show us that the ordinary legal forms are just a kind of curtain drawn politely over the conflicts of force which alone are decisive? Are our effective legislative enactments anything more than registrations of results of battles previously fought out on the field of human endurance? In many social fields, reformers are now struggling for an extension of governmental activity by way of supervision and regulation. Does not such action always amount to an effort to extend the exercise of force on the part of some section of society, with a corresponding restriction of the forces employed by others? In spite of the fact that the political thinking of the seventeenth and eighteenth centuries is out of date, were not the thinkers of that period clearer headed than we are in acknowledging that all political questions are simply questions of the extension and restriction of exercise of power on the part of specific groups in the community? Has the recent introduction of an idealistic terminology about moral and common will, about juridical and moral personalities, done anything but muddle our minds about the hard fact that all our social questions at bottom concern the possession and use of force; and the equally hard fact that our political and legal arrangements are but dispositions of force to make more secure the other forms of its daily use?

In taking up the writings of the theorists it is not easy to persuade oneself that they are marked by much consistency. With a few notable exceptions, the doctrine that the state rests upon or is common will seems to turn out but a piece of phraseology to justify the uses actually made of force. Practices of coercion and constraint which would be intolerable if frankly labeled "Force" seem to become laudable when baptized with the name of "Will," although they otherwise remain the same. Or, if this statement is extreme, there seems to be little doubt that the actual capacity of the state to bring force to bear is what has most impressed theorists, and that what they are after is some theoretical principle which will justify the exercise of force; so that in a great many cases such terms as common will, supreme will, supreme moral or juridical personality, are eulogistic phrases resorted to in behalf of such justification. The one thing that clearly stands out is that the use of force is felt to require explanation and sanction. To make force itself the ultimate principle is felt to be all one with proclaiming anarchy and issuing an invitation to men to settle all their difficulties by recourse to fighting it out to see which is the stronger. And yet what every political student is profoundly convinced of, is, I suppose, that at bottom every political struggle is a struggle for control, for power.

Although I have raised large questions, it is not my ambition to answer them. I have but outlined a large stage upon which to move about some quite minor figures. In the first place, something can be done, I think, by clarifying certain of the ideas which enter into the discussion. We may, I think, profitably discriminate the three conceptions of power or energy, coercive force, and violence. Power or energy is either a neutral or an eulogistic term. It denotes effective means of operation; ability or capacity to execute, to realize ends. Granted an end which is worth while, and power or energy becomes a eulogistic term. It means nothing but the sum of conditions available for bringing the desirable end into existence. Any political or legal theory which will have nothing to do with power on the ground that all power is force and all force brutal and non-moral is obviously condemned to a purely sentimental, dreamy morals. It is force by which we excavate subways and build bridges and travel and manufacture; it is force which is utilized in spoken argument or published book. Not to depend upon and utilize force is simply to be without a foothold in the real world.

Energy becomes violence when it defeats or frustrates purpose instead of executing or realizing it. When the dynamite charge blows up human beings instead of rocks, when its outcome is waste instead of production, destruction instead of construction, we call it not energy or power but violence. Coercive force occupies, we may fairly say, a middle place between power as energy and power as violence. To turn to the right as an incident of locomotion is a case of power: of means deployed in behalf of an end. To run amuck in the street is a case of violence. To use energy to make a man observe the rule of the road is a case of coercive force. Immediately, or with respect to his activities, it is a case of violence; indirectly, when it is exercised to assure the means which are needed for the successful realization of ends, it is a case of constructive use of power. Constraint or coercion, in other words, is an incident of a situation under certain conditions—namely, where the means for the realization of an end are not naturally at hand, so that energy has to be spent in order to make some power into a means for the end in hand.

If we formulate the result, we have something of this kind. Law is a statement of the conditions of the organization of energies which, when unorganized, conflict and result in violence—that is, destruction or waste. We cannot substitute reason for force, but force becomes rational when it is an organized factor in an activity instead of operating in an isolated way or on its own hook. For the sake of brevity, I shall refer to the organization of force hereafter as efficiency, but I beg to remind you that the use of the term always implies an actual or potential conflict and resulting waste in the absence of some scheme for distributing the energies involved.

These generalities are, it will be objected, innocuous and meaningless. So they are in the abstract. Let us take the question of the justification of force in a strike. I do not claim, of course, that what has been said tells us whether the use of force is justified or not. But I hold that it suggests the way of finding out in a given case whether it is justifiable or not. It is, in substance, a question of efficiency (including economy) of means in the accomplishing of ends. If the social ends at stake can be more effectively subserved by the existing legal and economic machinery, resort to physical action of a more direct kind has no standing. If, however, they represent an ineffective organization of means for the ends in question, then recourse to extra-legal means may be indicated; provided it really serves the ends in question—a very large qualification be it noted. A recourse to direct force is a supplementation of existent deficient resources in effective energy under some circumstances.

Such a doctrine is doubtless unwelcome. It is easily interpreted so as to give encouragement to resorting to violence and threats of violence in industrial struggles. But there is a very large "if" involved—the "if" of greater relative economy and efficiency. And when so regarded, it at once occurs to mind that experience in the past has shown that it is not usually efficient for parties to be judges in their own cause: that an impartial umpire is an energy saver. It occurs to mind, also, that the existing legal machinery, whatever its defects, represents a contrivance which has been built up at great cost, and that the tendency to ignore its operation upon special provocation would so reduce the efficiency of the machinery in other situations that the local gain would easily be more than offset by widespread losses in energy available for other ends. In the third place, experience shows that there is general presumption on the side of indirect and refined agencies as against coarse and strikingly obvious methods of utilizing power. The fine mechanism which runs a watch is more efficient than the grosser one which heaves a brick. Thus the bias against any doctrine which seems under any circumstances to sanction resort to personal and primitive methods of using force against the more impersonal juridical contrivances of society turns out to be *prima facie* justified on the principle of efficiency in use of means.

Over and above this bare presumption, it must be admitted that our organized contrivances are still so ineffective that it is a delicate matter to tell how far a standing menace to resort to crude methods may be a necessary stimulus to the better working of the more refined methods.

There is a general presumption in politics against doing anything till it is clearly necessary; and indication of potential force operates as a sign of necessity. In other words social reorganization is usually a response to a threatened conflict.

This conclusion that violence means recourse to means which are relatively wasteful may be strengthened by considering penal measures. Upon the whole, the opinion seems to be current that in such matters force is hallowed by the mere fact that it is the State which employs it, or by the fact that it is exercised in the interests of "justice"—retribution in the abstract, or what is politely called "vindicating the law." When the justification of force is sought in some kind of abstract consideration of this sort, no questions are to be raised about the efficiency of the force used, for it is not conceived as a specific means to a specific end. It is the sacrosanct character thus attributed to the state's use of force which gives pungency to the Tolstoian charge that the State is the archcriminal, the person who has recourse to violence on the largest scale. I see no way out except to say that all depends upon the efficient adaptation of means to ends. The serious charge against the State is not that it uses force—nothing was ever accomplished without using force—but that it does not use it wisely or effectively. Our penal measures are still largely upon the level which would convince a man by knocking him down instead of instructing him.

My treatment is of course very summary. But I hope that it suggests my main point. No ends are accomplished without the use of force. It is consequently no presumption against a measure, political, international, jural, economic, that it involves a use of force. Squeamishness about force is the mark not of idealistic but of moonstruck morals. But antecedent and abstract principles cannot be assigned to justify the use of force. The criterion of value lies in the relative efficiency and economy of the expenditure of force as a means to an end. With advance of knowledge, refined, subtle and indirect use of force is always displacing coarse, obvious and direct methods of applying it. This is the explanation to the ordinary feeling against the use of force. What is thought of as brutal, violent, immoral, is a use of physical agencies which are gross, sensational and evident on their own account, in cases where it is possible to employ with greater economy and less waste means which are comparatively imperceptible and refined.

It follows from what has been said that the so-called problem of "moralizing" force is in reality a problem of *intellectualizing* its use: a problem of employing so to say neural instead of gross muscular force as a means to accomplish ends. An immoral use of force is a stupid use. I sometimes hear apologies for war which proceed by pointing out how largely all social life is a disguised contest of hostile powers. Our economic life, so it is said, is but a struggle for bread where the endurance and even the lives of laborers are pitted against the resources of employers. Only lack of imagination fails to see the economic war, the industrial battlefield with its ammunition trains and human carnage. Let the point be admitted. What still remains true is that the decisive question is the level of efficiency and economy upon which the deploying of force goes on. Our present economic methods may be so wasteful, so destructive, as compared with others which are humanly possible, as to be barbarous. Yet competitive commercial methods may represent an advance in the utilization of human and natural resources over methods of war. In so far as they involve greater indirection and complexity of means, the presumption is that they are an advance.

No matter what idealists and optimists say, the energy of the world, the number of forces at disposal, is plural, not unified. There are different centers of force and they go their ways independently. They come into conflict; they clash. Energy which would otherwise be used in effecting something is then used up in friction; it goes to waste. Two men may be equally engaged about their respective businesses, and their businesses may be equally reputable and important, and yet there may be no harmony in their expenditures of energy. They are driving opposite ways on the road and their vehicles collide. The subsequent waste in quarreling is as certain as the immediate waste in a smash-up. The rule that each shall turn to the right is a plan for organizing otherwise independent and potentially conflicting energies into a scheme which avoids waste, a scheme allowing a maximum utilization of energy. Such, if I mistake not, is the true purport of all law.

Either I am mistaken, or those persons who are clamoring for the "substitution of law for force" have their language, at least, badly mixed. And a continuous use of mixed language is likely to produce a harmful mixture in ideas. Force is the only thing in the world which effects anything, and literally to substitute law for force would be as intelligent as to try to run an engine on the mathematical formula which states its most efficient running. Doubtless those who use the phrase have their hearts in the right place; they mean some method of regulating the expenditure of force which will avoid the wastes incident to present methods. But too often the phrase is bound up with intellectual confusion. There is a genuine emotional animosity to the very idea of force. The "philosophy of force" is alluded to scornfully or indignantly—which is somewhat as if an engineer should speak deprecatingly of the science of energy.

At various times of my life I have, with other wearied souls, assisted at discussions between those who were Tolstoians and—well, those who weren't. In reply to the agitated protests of the former against war and the police and penal measures, I have listened to the time-honored queries about what you should do when the criminal attacked your friend or child. I have rarely heard it stated that since one cannot even walk the street without using force, the only question which persons can discuss with one another concerns the most effective use of force in gaining ends in specific situation. If one's end is the saving of one's soul immaculate, or maintaining a certain emotion unimpaired, doubtless force should be used to inhibit natural muscular reactions. If the end is something else, a hearty fisticuff may be the means of realizing it. What is intolerable is that men should condemn or eulogize force at large, irrespective of its use as a means of getting results. To be interested in ends and to have contempt for the means which alone secure them is the last stage of intellectual demoralization. . . .

JOHN LOCKE

Power and Liberty

The mind being every day informed, by the senses, of the alteration of those simple ideas it observes in things without; and taking notice how one comes to an end, and ceases to be, and another begins to exist which was not before; reflecting also on what passes within itself, and observing a constant change of its ideas, sometimes by the impression of outward objects on the senses, and sometimes by the determination of its own choice; and concluding from what it has so constantly observed to have been, that the like changes will for the future be made in the same things, by like agents, and by the like ways,— considers in one thing the possibility of having any of its simple ideas changed, and in another the possibility of making that change; and so comes by that idea which we call *power*. Thus we say, Fire has a power to melt gold, i.e. to destroy the consistency of its insensible parts, and consequently its hardness, and make it fluid; and gold has a power to be melted; that the sun has a power to blanch wax, and wax a power to be blanched by the sun, whereby the yellowness is destroyed, and whiteness made to exist in its room. In which, and the like cases, the power we consider is in reference to the change of perceivable ideas. For we cannot observe any alteration to be made in, or operation upon anything, but by the observable change of its sensible ideas; nor conceive any alteration to be made, but by conceiving a change of some of its ideas.

Power thus considered is two-fold, viz. as able to make, or able to receive any change. The one may be called *active,* and the other *passive* power. . . .

[We are abundantly furnished with the idea of *passive* power by almost all sorts of sensible things. In most of them we cannot avoid observing their sensible qualities, nay, their very substances, to be in continual flux.] And therefore with reason we look on them as liable still to the same change. Nor have we of *active* power (which is the more proper signification of the word power) fewer instances. Since whatever change is observed, the mind must collect a power somewhere able to make that change, as well as a possibility in the thing itself to receive it. But yet, if we will consider it attentively, bodies, by our senses, do not afford us so clear and distinct an idea of active power, as we have from reflection on the operations of our minds. For all power relating to action, and there being but two sorts of action whereof we have an idea, viz. thinking and motion, let us consider whence we have the clearest ideas of the powers which produce these actions. 1. Of thinking, body affords us no idea at all; it is only from reflection that we have that. 2. Neither have we from body any idea of the beginning of motion. A body at rest affords us no idea of any active power to move; and when it is set in motion itself, that motion is rather a passion than an action in it. For, when the ball obeys the motion of a billiard-stick, it is not any action of the ball, but bare passion. Also when by impulse it sets another ball in motion that lay in its way, it only communicates the motion it had received from another, and loses in itself so much as the other received: which gives us but a very obscure idea of an *active* power of moving in body, whilst we observe it only to *transfer,* but not *produce* any motion. For it is but a very obscure idea of power which reaches not the production of the action, but the continuation of the passion. For so is motion in a body impelled by another; the continuation of the alteration made in it from rest to motion being little more an action, than the continuation of the alteration of its figure by the same blow is an action. The idea of the *beginning* of motion we have only from reflection on what passes in ourselves; where we find by experience, that, barely by willing it, barely by a thought of the mind, we can move the parts of our bodies, which were before at rest. So that it seems to me, we have, from the observation of the operation of bodies by our senses, but a very imperfect obscure idea of *active* power; since they afford us not any idea in themselves of the power to begin any action, either motion or thought. . . .

This, at least, I think evident,—That we find in ourselves a power to begin or forbear, continue or end several [actions] of our minds, and motions of our bodies, barely by [a thought] or preference of the mind [ordering, or as it were commanding, the doing or not doing such or such a particular action.] This power which the mind has [thus to order] the consideration of any idea, or the forbearing to consider it; or to prefer the motion of any part of the body to its rest, [and *vice versâ*, in any particular instance,] is that which we call the *Will*. The actual [exercise of that power, by directing any particular action, or its forbearance,] is that which we call *volition* or *willing*. [The forbearance of that action, consequent to such order or command of the mind, is called *voluntary*. And whatsoever action is performed without such a thought of the mind, is called *involuntary*.] The power of perception is that which we call the *Understanding*. Perception, which we make the act of the understanding, is of three sorts:— 1. The perception of ideas in our minds. 2. The perception of the signification of signs. 3. The perception of the [connexion or repugnancy,] agreement or disagreement, [that there is between any of our] ideas. All these are attributed to the understanding, or perceptive power, though it be [the two latter only that use allows us to say we understand.] . . .

Every one, I think, finds in *himself* a power to begin or forbear, continue or put an end to several actions in himself. [From the consideration of the extent of this power of the mind over the actions of the man, which everyone finds in himself, arise the *ideas* of *liberty* and *necessity*.]

All the actions that we have any idea of reducing themselves, as has been said, to these two, viz. thinking and motion; so far as a man has power to think or not to think, to move or not to move, according to the preference or direction of his own mind, so far is a man *free*. Wherever any performance or forbearance are not equally in a man's power; wherever doing or not doing will not equally *follow* upon the preference of his mind directing it, there he is not free, though perhaps the action may be voluntary. So that the idea of *liberty* is, the idea of a power in any agent to do or forbear any particular action, according to the determination or thought of the mind, whereby either of them is preferred to the other: where either of them is not in the power of the agent to be produced by him according to his volition, there he is not at liberty; that agent is under *necessity*. So that liberty cannot be where there is no thought, no volition, no will; but there may be thought, there may be will, there may be volition, where there is no liberty. . . .

Again: suppose a man be carried, whilst fast asleep, into a room where is a person he longs to see and speak with; and be there locked fast in, beyond his power to get out: he awakes, and is glad to find himself in so desirable company, which he stays willingly in, i. e. prefers his stay to going away. I ask, is not this stay voluntary? I think nobody will doubt it: and yet, being locked fast in, it is evident he is not at liberty not to stay, he has not freedom to be gone. So that liberty is not an idea belonging to volition, or preferring; but to the person having the power of doing, or forbearing to do, according as the mind shall choose or direct. Our idea of liberty reaches as far as that power, and no farther. For wherever restraint comes to check that power, or compulsion takes away that indifferency of ability to act, or to forbear acting, there liberty, and our notion of it, presently ceases. . . .

If this be so, (as I imagine it is,) I leave it to be considered, whether it may not help to put an end to that long agitated, and, I think, unreasonable, because unintelligible question, viz. *Whether man's will be free or no?* For if I mistake not, it follows from what I have said, that the question itself is altogether improper; and it is as insignificant to ask whether man's *will* be free, as to ask whether his sleep be swift, or his virtue square: liberty being as little applicable to the will, as swiftness of motion is to sleep, or squareness to virtue. Every one would laugh at the absurdity of such a question as either of these: because it is obvious that the modifications of motion belong not to sleep, nor the difference of figure to virtue; and when any one well considers it, I think he will as plainly perceive that liberty, which is but a power, belongs only to *agents,* and cannot be an attribute or modification of the will, which is also but a power. . . .

Will, then, is nothing but such a power. *Liberty,* on the other side, is the power a *man* has to do or forbear doing any particular action according as its doing or forbearance has the actual preference in the mind; which is the same thing as to say, according as he himself wills it.

It is plain then that the will is nothing but one power or ability, and *freedom* another power or ability so that, to ask, whether the will has freedom, is to ask whether one power has another power, one ability another ability; a question at first sight too grossly absurd to make a dispute, or need an answer. . . .

I grant, that this or that actual thought may be the occasion of volition, or exercising the power a man has to choose; or the actual choice of the mind, the cause of actual thinking on this or that thing: as the actual singing of such a tune may be the cause of dancing such a dance, and the actual dancing of such a dance the occasion of singing such a tune. But in all these it is not one *power* that operates on another: but it is the mind that operates, and exerts these powers; it is the man that does the action; it is the agent that has power, or is able to do. For powers are relations, not agents: and that which has the power or not the power to operate, is that alone which is or is not free, and not the power itself. For freedom, or not freedom, can belong to nothing but what has or has not a power to act.

PLATO

What Is the Best Kind of Power?

The whole imaginary conversation is narrated by Socrates to an unspecified audience. The company who will take part in it assemble at the house of Cephalus, a retired manufacturer living at the Piraeus, the harbour town about five miles from Athens. It includes, besides Plato's elder brothers, Glaucon and Adeimantus, Cephalus' sons, Polemarchus, Lysias, well known as a writer of speeches, and Euthydemus; Thrasymachus of Chalcedon, a noted teacher of rhetoric, who may have formulated the definition of justice as "the interest of the stronger," though hardly any evidence about his opinions exists outside the Republic; *and a number of Socrates' young friends. The occasion is the festival of Bendis, a goddess whose cult had been imported from Thrace. Cephalus embodies the wisdom of a long life honorably spent in business. He is well-to-do, but values money as a means to that peace of mind which comes of honesty and the ability to render to gods and men their due. This is what he understands by "right" conduct or justice.*

SOCRATES. I walked down to the Piraeus yesterday with Glaucon, the son of Ariston, to make my prayers to the goddess. As this was the first celebration of her festival, I wished also to see how the ceremony would be conducted. The Thracians, I thought, made as fine a show in the procession as our own people, though they did well enough. The prayers and the spectacle were over, and we were leaving to go back to the city, when from some way off Polemarchus, the son of Cephalus, caught sight of us starting homewards and sent his slave running to ask us to wait for him. The boy caught my garment from behind and gave me the message.

I turned round and asked where his master was.

There, he answered; coming up behind. Please wait.

Very well, said Glaucon; we will.

A minute later Polemarchus joined us, with Glaucon's brother, Adeimantus, and Niceratus, the son of Nicias, and some others who must have been at the procession.

Socrates, said Polemarchus, I do believe you are starting back to town and leaving us.

You have guessed right, I answered.

Well, he said, you see what a large party we are?

I do.

Unless you are more than a match for us, then, you must stay here.

Isn't there another alternative? said I; we might convince you that you must let us go.

How will you convince us, if we refuse to listen?

We cannot, said Glaucon.

Well, we shall refuse; make up your minds to that.

Here Adeimantus interposed: Don't you even know that in the evening there is going to be a torch-race on horseback in honour of the goddess?

On horseback! I exclaimed; that is something new. How will they do it? Are the riders going to race with torches and hand them on to one another?

Just so, said Polemarchus. Besides, there will be a festival lasting all night, which will be worth seeing. We will go out after dinner and look on. We shall find plenty of young men there and we can have a talk. So please stay, and don't disappoint us.

It looks as if we had better stay, said Glaucon.

Well, said I, if you think so, we will.

Accordingly, we went home with Polemarchus; and there we found his brothers, Lysias and Euthydemus, as well as Thrasymachus of Chalcedon, Charmantides of Paeania, and Cleitophon, the son of Aristonymus. Polemarchus' father, Cephalus, was at home too. I had not seen him for some time, and it struck me that he had aged a good deal. He was sitting in a cushioned chair, wearing a garland, as he had just been conducting a sacrifice in the courtyard. There were some chairs standing round, and we sat down beside him.

As soon as he saw me, Cephalus greeted me. You don't often come down to the Piraeus to visit us, Socrates, he said. But you ought to. If I still had the strength to walk to town easily, you would not have to come here; we would come to you. But, as things are, you really ought to come here oftener. I find, I can assure you, that in proportion as bodily pleasures lose their savour, my appetite for the things of the mind grows keener and I enjoy discussing them more than ever. So you must not disappoint me. Treat us like old friends, and come here often to have a talk with these young men.

To tell the truth, Cephalus, I answered, I enjoy talking with very old people. They have gone before us on a road by which we too may have to travel, and I think we do well to learn from them. . . .

You strike me as not caring overmuch about money; and that is generally so with men who have not made their own fortune. Those who have are twice as fond of their possessions as other people. They have the same affection for the money they have earned that poets have for their poems, or fathers for their children: they not merely find it useful, as we all do, but it means much to them as being of their own creation. That makes them disagreeable company; they have not a good word for anything but riches.

That is quite true.

It is indeed, I said; but one more question: what do you take to be the greatest advantage you have got from being wealthy?

One that perhaps not many people would take my word for. I can tell you, Socrates, that, when the prospect of dying is near at hand, a man begins to feel some alarm about things that never troubled him before. He may have laughed at those stories they tell of another world and of punishments there for wrongdoing in this life; but now the soul is tormented by a doubt whether they may not be true. Maybe from the weakness of old age, or perhaps because, now that he is nearer to what lies beyond, he begins to get some glimpse of it himself—at any rate he is beset with fear and misgiving; he begins thinking over the past: is there anyone he has wronged? . . .

Now in this, as I believe, lies the chief value of wealth, not for everyone, perhaps, but for the right-thinking man. It can do much to save us from going to that other world in fear of having cheated or deceived anyone even unintentionally or of being in debt to some god for sacrifice or to some man for money. Wealth has many other uses, of course; but, taking one with another, I should regard this as the best use that can be made of it by a man of sense.

You put your case admirably, Cephalus, said I. But take this matter of doing right: can we say that it really consists in nothing more nor less than telling the truth and paying back anything we may have received? Are not these very actions sometimes right and sometimes wrong? Suppose, for example, a friend who had lent us a weapon were to go mad and then ask for it back, surely anyone would say we ought not to return it. It would not be "right" to do so; nor yet to tell the truth without reserve to a madman.

No, it would not.

Right conduct, then, cannot be defined as telling the truth and restoring anything we have been trusted with.

Yes, it can, Polemarchus broke in, at least if we are to believe Simonides.

Well, well, said Cephalus, I will bequeath the argument to you. It is time for me to attend to the sacrifice.

Your part, then, said Polemarchus, will fall to me as your heir.

By all means, said Cephalus with a smile; and with what he left us, to see to the sacrifice. . . .

Then, said I, if you are to inherit this discussion, tell me, what is this saying of Simonides about right conduct which you approve?

That it is just to render every man his due. That seems to me a fair statement. . . .

Obviously it does not mean what we were speaking of just now—returning something we have been entrusted with to the owner even when he has gone out of his mind. And yet surely it is his due, if he asks for it back?

Yes.

But it is out of the question to give it back when he has gone mad?

True.

Simonides, then, must have meant something different from that when he said it was just to render a man his due.

Certainly he did; his idea was that, as between friends, what one owes to another is to do him good, not harm.

I see, said I; to repay money entrusted to one is not to render what is due, if the two parties are friends and the repayment proves harmful to the lender. That is what you say Simonides meant?

Yes, certainly.

And what about enemies? Are we to render whatever is their due to them?

Yes certainly, what really is due to them; which means, I suppose, what is appropriate to an enemy—some sort of injury.

It seems, then, that Simonides was using words with a hidden meaning, as poets will. He really meant to define justice as rendering to everyone what is appropriate to him; only he called that his "due."

Well, why not?

But look here, said I. Suppose we could question Simonides about the art of medicine—whether a physician can be described as rendering to some object what is due or appropriate to it; how do you think he would answer?

That the physician administers the appropriate diet or remedies to the body.

And the art of cookery—can that be described in the same way?

Yes; the cook gives the appropriate seasoning to his dishes.

Good. And the practice of justice?

If we are to follow those analogies, Socrates, justice would be rendering services or injuries to friends or enemies.

So Simonides means by justice doing good to friends and harm to enemies?

I think so.

And in matters of health who would be the most competent to treat friends and enemies in that way?

A physician.

And on a voyage, as regards the dangers of the sea?

A ship's captain.

In what sphere of action, then, will the just man be the most competent to do good or harm?

In war, I should imagine; when he is fighting on the side of his friends and against his enemies.

I see. But when we are well and staying on shore, the doctor and the ship's captain are of no use to us.

True.

Is it also true that the just man is useless when we are not at war?

I should not say that.

So justice has its uses in peace-time too?

Yes.

Like farming, which is useful for producing crops, or shoemaking, which is useful for providing us with shoes. Can you tell me for what purposes justice is useful or profitable in time of peace?

For matters of business, Socrates.

In a partnership, you mean?

Yes.

But if we are playing draughts, or laying bricks, or making music, will the just man be as good and helpful a partner as an expert draught-player, or a builder, or a musician?

No.

Then in what kind of partnership will he be more helpful?

Where money is involved, I suppose.

Except, perhaps, Polemarchus, when we are putting our money to some use. If we are buying or selling a horse, a judge of horses would be a better partner; or if we are dealing in ships, a ship-wright or a sea-captain.

I suppose so.

Well, when will the just man be specially useful in handling our money?

When we want to deposit it for safe-keeping.

When the money is to lie idle, in fact?

Yes.

So justice begins to be useful only when our money is out of use?

Perhaps so.

And in the same way, I suppose, if a pruning-knife is to be used, or a shield, or a lyre, then a vine-dresser, or a soldier, or a musician will be of service; but justice is helpful only when these things are to be kept safe. In fact justice is never of any use in using things; it becomes useful when they are useless.

That seems to follow.

If that is so, my friend, justice can hardly be a thing of much value. And here is another point. In boxing or fighting of any sort skill in dealing blows goes with skill in keeping them off; and the same doctor that can keep us from disease would also be clever at producing it by stealth; or again, a general will be good at keeping his army safe, if he can also cheat the enemy and steal his plans and dispositions. So a man who is expert in keeping things will always make an expert thief.

Apparently.

The just man, then, being good at keeping money safe, will also be good at stealing it.

That seems to be the conclusion, at any rate.

So the just man turns out to be a kind of thief. You must have learnt that from Homer, who showed his predilection for Odysseus' grandfather Autolycus by remarking that he surpassed all men in cheating and perjury. Justice, according to you and Homer and Simonides, turns out to be a form of skill in cheating, provided it be to help a friend or harm an enemy. That was what you meant?

Good God, no, he protested; but I have forgotten now what I did mean. All the same, I do still believe that justice consists in helping one's friends and harming one's enemies.

[*The argument now becomes more serious. Polemarchus, though puzzled, clings to the belief that it must be right to help friends and harm enemies. This was a traditional maxim of Greek morality, never doubted till Socrates denied it: no one had ever said that we ought to do good, or even refrain from doing harm, to them that hate us. Socrates' denial rests on his principle, later adopted by the Stoics, that the only thing that is good in itself is the goodness, virtue, well-being of the human soul. The only way really to injure a man is to make him a worse man. This cannot be the function of justice.*]

Which do you mean by a man's friends and enemies—those whom he believes to be good honest people and the reverse, or those who really are, though they may not seem so?

Naturally, his loves and hates depend on what he believes.

But don't people often mistake an honest man for a rogue, or a rogue for an honest man; in which case they regard good people as enemies and bad people as friends?

No doubt.

But all the same, it will then be right for them to help the rogue and to injure the good man?

Apparently.

And yet a good man is one who is not given to doing wrong.

True.

According to your account, then, it is right to ill-treat a man who does no wrong.

No, no, Socrates; that can't be sound doctrine.

It must be the wrongdoers, then, that it is right to injure, and the honest that are to be helped.

That sounds better.

Then, Polemarchus, the conclusion will be that for a bad judge of character it will often be right to injure his friends, when they really are rogues, and to help his enemies, when they really are honest men—the exact opposite of what we took Simonides to mean.

That certainly does follow, he said. We must shift our ground. Perhaps our definition of friend and enemy was wrong.

What definition, Polemarchus?

We said a friend was one whom we believe to be an honest man.

And how are we to define him now?

As one who really is honest as well as seeming so. If he merely seems so, he will be only a seeming friend. And the same will apply to enemies.

On this showing, then, it is the good people that will be our friends, the wicked our enemies.

Yes.

You would have us, in fact, add something to our original definition of justice: it will not mean merely doing good to friends and harm to enemies, but doing good to friends who are good, and harm to enemies who are wicked.

Yes, I think that is all right.

Can it really be a just man's business to harm any human being?

Certainly; it is right for him to harm bad men who are his enemies.

But does not harming a horse or a dog mean making it a worse horse or dog, so that each will be a less perfect creature in its own special way?

Yes.

Isn't that also true of human beings—that to harm them means making them worse men by the standard of human excellence?

Yes.

And is not justice a peculiarly human excellence?

Undoubtedly.

To harm a man, then, must mean making him less just.

I suppose so.

But a musician or a riding-master cannot be exercising his special skill, if he makes his pupils unmusical or bad riders.

No.

Whereas the just man is to exercise his justice by making men unjust? Or, in more general terms, the good are to make men bad by exercising their virtue? Can that be so?

No, it cannot.

It can no more be the function of goodness to do harm than of heat to cool or of drought to produce moisture. So if the just man is good, the business of harming people, whether friends or not, must belong to his opposite, the unjust.

I think that is perfectly true, Socrates.

So it was not a wise saying that justice is giving every man his due, if that means that harm is due from the just man to his enemies, as well as help to his friends. That is not true; because we have found that it is never right to harm anyone.

I agree.

Then you and I will make common cause against anyone who attributes that doctrine to Simonides or to any of the old canonical sages, like Bias or Pittacus.

Yes, he said, I am prepared to support you.

Do you know, I think that account of justice, as helping friends and harming enemies, must be due to some despot, so rich and powerful that he thought he could do as he liked—someone like Periander, or Perdiccas, or Xerxes, or Ismenias of Thebes.

That is extremely probable.

Very good, said I; and now that we have disposed of that definition of justice, can anyone suggest another? . . .

All this time Thrasymachus had been trying more than once to break in upon our conversation; but his neighbors had restrained him, wishing to hear the argument to the end. In the pause after my last words he could keep quiet no longer; but gathering himself up like a wild beast he sprang at us as if he would tear us in pieces. Polemarchus and I were frightened out of our wits, when he burst out to the whole company:

What is the matter with you two, Socrates? Why do you go on in this imbecile way, politely deferring to each other's nonsense? If you really want to know what justice means, stop asking questions and scoring off the answers you get. You know very well it is easier to ask questions than to answer them. Answer yourself, and tell us what you think justice means. I won't have you telling us it is the same as what is obligatory or useful or advantageous or profitable or expedient; I want a clear and precise statement; I won't put up with that sort of verbiage.

I was amazed by this onslaught and looked at him in terror. If I had

not seen this wolf before he saw me, I really believe I should have been struck dumb;[1] but fortunately I had looked at him earlier, when he was beginning to get exasperated with our argument; so I was able to reply, though rather tremulously:

Don't be hard on us, Thrasymachus. If Polemarchus and I have gone astray in our search, you may be quite sure the mistake was not intentional. If we had been looking for a piece of gold, we should never have deliberately allowed politeness to spoil our chance of finding it; and now when we are looking for justice, a thing much more precious than gold, you cannot imagine we should defer to each other in that foolish way and not do our best to bring it to light. You must believe we are in earnest, my friend; but I am afraid the task is beyond our powers, and we might expect a man of your ability to pity us instead of being so severe.

Thrasymachus replied with a burst of sardonic laughter.

Good Lord, he said; Socrates at his old trick of shamming ignorance! I knew it; I told the others you would refuse to commit yourself and do anything sooner than answer a question. . . .

But really, I protested, what can you expect from a man who does not know the answer or profess to know it, and, besides that, has been forbidden by no mean authority to put forward any notions he may have? Surely the definition should naturally come from you, who say you do know the answer and can tell it us. Please do not disappoint us. I should take it as a kindness, and I hope you will not be chary of giving Glaucon and the rest of us the advantage of your instruction.

Glaucon and the others added their entreaties to mine. Thrasymachus was evidently longing to win credit, for he was sure he had an admirable answer ready, though he made a show of insisting that I should be the one to reply. In the end he gave way and exclaimed:

So this is what Socrates' wisdom comes to! He refuses to teach, and goes about learning from others without offering so much as thanks in return.

I do learn from others, Thrasymachus; that is quite true; but you are wrong to call me ungrateful. I give in return all I can—praise; for I have no money. And how ready I am to applaud any idea that seems to me sound, you will see in a moment, when you have stated your own; for I am sure that will be sound.

1. A popular superstition, that if a wolf sees you first, you become dumb.

Listen then, Thrasymachus began. What I say is that "just" or "right" means nothing but what is to the interest of the stronger party. Well, where is your applause? You don't mean to give it me.

I will, as soon as I understand, I said. I don't see yet what you mean by right being the interest of the stronger party. For instance, Polydamas, the athlete, is stronger than we are, and it is to his interest to eat beef for the sake of his muscles; but surely you don't mean that the same diet would be good for weaker men and therefore be right for us?

You are trying to be funny, Socrates. It's a low trick to take my words in the sense you think will be most damaging.

No, no, I protested; but you must explain.

Don't you know, then, that a state may be ruled by a despot, or a democracy, or an aristocracy?

Of course.

And that the ruling element is always the strongest?

Yes.

Well then, in every case the laws are made by the ruling party in its own interest; a democracy makes democratic laws, a despot autocratic ones, and so on. By making these laws they define as "right" for their subjects whatever is for their own interest, and they call anyone who breaks them a "wrongdoer" and punish him accordingly. That is what I mean: in all states alike "right" has the same meaning, namely what is for the interest of the party established in power, and that is the strongest. So the sound conclusion is that what is "right" is the same everywhere: the interest of the stronger party.

Now I see what you mean, said I; whether it is true or not, I must try to make out. When you define right in terms of interest, you are yourself giving one of those answers you forbade to me; though, to be sure, you add "to the stronger party."

An insignificant addition, perhaps!

Its importance is not clear yet; what is clear is that we must find out whether your definition is true. I agree myself that right is in a sense a matter of interest; but when you add "to the stronger party," I don't know about that. I must consider.

Go ahead, then.

I will. Tell me this. No doubt you also think it is right to obey the men in power?

I do.

Are they infallible in every type of state, or can they sometimes make a mistake?

Of course they can make a mistake.

In framing laws, then, they may do their work well or badly?

No doubt.

Well, that is to say, when the laws they make are to their own interest; badly, when they are not?

Yes.

But the subjects are to obey any law they lay down, and they will then be doing right?

Of course.

If so, by your account, it will be right to do what is not to the interest of the stronger party, as well as what is so.

What's that you are saying?

Just what you said, I believe; but let us look again. Haven't you admitted that the rulers, when they enjoin certain acts on their subjects, sometimes mistake their own best interests, and at the same time that it is right for the subjects to obey, whatever they may enjoin?

Yes, I suppose so.

Well, that amounts to admitting that it is right to do what is not to the interest of the rulers or the stronger party. They may unwittingly enjoin what is to their own disadvantage; and you say it is right for the others to do as they are told. In that case, their duty must be the opposite of what you said, because the weaker will have been ordered to do what is against the interest of the stronger. You with your intelligence must see how that follows.

Yes, Socrates, said Polemarchus, that is undeniable.

No doubt, Cleitophon broke in, if you are to be a witness on Socrates' side.

No witness is needed, replied Polemarchus; Thrasymachus himself admits that rulers sometimes ordain acts that are to their own disadvantage, and that it is the subjects' duty to do them.

That is because Thrasymachus said it was right to do what you are told by the men in power.

Yes, but he also said that what is to the interest of the stronger party is right; and, after making both these assertions, he admitted that the stronger sometimes command the weaker subjects to act against their interests. From all which it follows that what is in the stronger's interest is no more right than what is not.

No, said Cleitophon; he meant whatever the stronger *believes* to be in his own interest. That is what the subject must do, and what Thrasymachus meant to define as right.

That was not what he said, rejoined Polemarchus.

No matter, Polemarchus, said I; if Thrasymachus says so now, let us take him in that sense. Now, Thrasymachus, tell me, was that what you intended to say—that right means what the stronger thinks is to his interest, whether it really is so or not?

Most certainly not, he replied. Do you suppose I should speak of a man as "stronger" or "superior" at the very moment when he is making a mistake?

I did think you said as much when you admitted that rulers are not always infallible.

That is because you are a quibbler, Socrates. Would you say a man deserves to be called a physician at the moment when he makes a mistake in treating his patient and just in respect of that mistake; or a mathematician, when he does a sum wrong and just in so far as he gets a wrong result? Of course we do commonly speak of a physician or a mathematician or a scholar having made a mistake; but really none of these, I should say, is ever mistaken, in so far as he is worthy of the name we give him. So strictly speaking—and you are all for being precise—no one who practises a craft makes mistakes. A man is mistaken when his knowledge fails him; and at that moment he is no craftsman. And what is true of craftsmanship or any sort of skill is true of the ruler: he is never mistaken so long as he is acting as a ruler; though anyone might speak of a ruler making a mistake, just as he might of a physician. You must understand that I was talking in that loose way when I answered your question just now; but the precise statement is this. The ruler, in so far as he is acting as a ruler, makes no mistakes and consequently enjoins what is best for himself; and that is what the subject is to do. So, as I said at first, "right" means doing what is to the interest of the stronger.

Very well, Thrasymachus, said I. So you think I am quibbling?

I am sure you are.

You believe my questions were maliciously designed to damage your position?

I know it. But you will gain nothing by that. You cannot outwit me by cunning, and you are not the man to crush me in the open.

Bless your soul, I answered, I should not think of trying. But, to prevent any more misunderstanding, when you speak of that ruler or stronger party whose interest the weaker ought to serve, please make it clear whether you are using the words in the ordinary way or in that strict sense you have just defined.

I mean a ruler in the strictest possible sense. Now quibble away and be as malicious as you can. I want no mercy. But you are no match for me.

Do you think me mad enough to beard a lion or try to outwit a Thrasymachus?

You did try just now, he retorted, but it wasn't a success.

[*Thrasymachus has already shifted his ground. At first "the stronger" meant only the men ruling by superior force; but now their superiority must include the knowledge and ability needed to govern without making mistakes. This knowledge and ability constitute an art of government, comparable to other useful arts or crafts requiring special skill. The ruler in his capacity as ruler, or the craftsman* qua *craftsman, can also be spoken of as the craft personified, since a craft exists only in the man who embodies it, and we are considering the man only as the embodiment of this special capacity, neglecting all personal characteristics and any other capacities he may chance to have. When Socrates talks of the art or craft in this abstract way as having an interest of its own, he means the same thing as if he spoke of the interest of the craftsman* qua *craftsman. Granted that there is, as Thrasymachus suggested, an art of government exercised by a ruler who,* qua *ruler, is infallible and so in the full sense "superior," the question now is, what his interest should be, on the analogy of other crafts.*] . . .

Socrates now turns from the art of government to Thrasymachus' whole view of life: that injustice, unlimited self-seeking, pursued with enough force of character and skill to ensure success, brings welfare and happiness. This is what he ultimately means by the interest of the stronger.

Socrates and Thrasymachus have a common ground for argument in that both accept the notion of an art of living, comparable to the special crafts in which trained intelligence creates some product. The goodness, excellence, or virtue of a workman lies in his efficiency, the Greek areté, *a word which, with the corresponding adjective* agathos, *"good", never lost its wide application to whatever does its work or fulfils its function well, as a good knife is one that cuts efficiently. The workman's efficiency involves trained intelligence or skill, an old sense of the word* sophia, *which also means wisdom. None of these words necessarily bears any moral sense; but they can be applied to the art of living. Here the product to be aimed at is assumed to be a man's own happiness and well-being. The efficiency which*

makes him good at attaining this end is called "virtue"; the implied knowl-
edge of the end and of the means to it is like the craftsman's skill and may
be called "wisdom." But as it sounds in English almost a contradiction to
say that to be unjust is to be virtuous or good and wise, the comparatively
colourless phrase "superior in character and intelligence" will be used in-
stead.

Where Socrates and Thrasymachus differ is in their views of the nature
of happiness or well-being. Thrasymachus thinks it consists in getting more
than your fair share of what are commonly called the good things of life,
pleasure, wealth, power. Thus virtue and wisdom mean to him efficiency
and skill in achieving injustice.

However, I continued, we may return to that question later. Much
more important is the position Thrasymachus is asserting now: that a
life of injustice is to be preferred to a life of justice. Which side do you
take, Glaucon? Where do you think the truth lies?

I should say that the just life is the better worth having.

You heard Thrasymachus' catalogue of all the good things in store
for injustice?

I did, but I am not convinced.

Shall we try to convert him, then, supposing we can find some way
to prove him wrong?

By all means.

We might answer Thrasymachus' case in a set speech of our own,
drawing up a corresponding list of the advantages of justice; he would
then have the right to reply, and we should make our final rejoinder;
but after that we should have to count up and measure the advantages
on each list, and we should need a jury to decide between us.
Whereas, if we go on as before, each securing the agreement of the
other side, we can combine the functions of advocate and judge. We
will take whichever course you prefer.

I prefer the second, said Glaucon.

Come then, Thrasymachus, said I, let us start afresh with our questions. You say that injustice pays better than justice, when both are
carried to the furthest point?

I do, he replied; and I have told you why.

And how would you describe them? I suppose you would call one of
them an excellence and the other a defect?

Of course.

Justice an excellence, and injustice a defect?

Now is that likely, when I am telling you that injustice pays, and justice does not?

Then what do you say?

The opposite.

That justice is a defect?

No; rather the mark of a good-natured simpleton.

Injustice, then, implies being ill-natured?

No; I should call it good policy.

Do you think the unjust are positively superior in character and intelligence, Thrasymachus?

Yes, if they are the sort that can carry injustice to perfection and make themselves masters of whole cities and nations. Perhaps you think I was talking of pickpockets. There is profit even in that trade, if you can escape detection; but it doesn't come to much as compared with the gains I was describing.

I understand you now on that point, I replied. What astonished me was that you should class injustice with superior character and intelligence and justice with the reverse.

Well, I do, he rejoined.

That is a much more stubborn position, my friend; and it is not so easy to see how to assail it. If you would admit that injustice, however well it pays, is nevertheless, as some people think, a defect and a discreditable thing, then we could argue on generally accepted principles. But now that you have gone so far as to rank it with superior character and intelligence, obviously you will say it is an admirable thing as well as a source of strength, and has all the other qualities we have attributed to.justice.

You read my thoughts like a book, he replied.

However, I went on, it is no good shirking; I must go through with the argument, so long as I can be sure you are really speaking your mind. I do believe you are not playing with us now, Thrasymachus, but stating the truth as you conceive it.

Why not refute the doctrine? he said. What does it matter to you whether I believe it or not?

It does not matter, I replied.

[*Socrates attacks separately three points in Thrasymachus' position: 1. that the unjust is superior to the just in character ("virtue") and intelligence; 2. that injustice is a source of strength; 3. that it brings happiness.*

1. *The first argument (349 B–350 C) is omitted here, because only a very*

loose paraphrase could liberate the meaning from the stiff and archaic form of the original. Thrasymachus has upheld the superman who will try to outdo everyone else and go to any lengths in getting the better of his neigh-bours. Socrates attacks this ideal of unlimited self-assertion, relying once more on the admitted analogy between the art of living and other arts. The musician, tuning an instrument, knows that there is for each string a certain pitch which is absolutely right. He shows his excellence and mastery of the art by aiming at that "limit" or "measure" (as the Greeks would call it), and he would be satisfied if he could attain it. In doing so he would be out-doing or "going one better than" less skilful musicians or the unmusical; but he would not be showing superior skill if he tried to outdo a musician who acknowledged the same measure and had actually attained it. Socrates holds that in moral conduct also there is a measure which is absolutely right, whether we recognize it or not. The just man, who does recognize it, shows a wisdom and virtue corresponding to the skill of the good musician. The unjust, who acknowledges no measure or limit, because there is no limit to getting more and more for yourself at others' expense and that is his object, is, by all analogy, exhibiting rather a lack of intelligence and char-acter. As a man, and therefore a moral agent, he is no more "wise and good" than an instrumentalist who should refuse to recognize such a thing as the right pitch. Jowett quotes: "When workmen strive to do better than well, They do confound their skill in covetousness" (K. John iv. 2.). Socrates concludes:

"It is evident, then, that it is the just man that is wise and good (superior in character and intelligence), the unjust that is ignorant and bad."

2. In the following passage Socrates has little difficulty in showing that unlimited self-assertion is not a source of strength in any association formed for a common purpose. "Honour among thieves" is common sense, which Thrasymachus cannot challenge. Socrates infers that injustice will have the same effect within the individual soul, dividing a man against himself and destroying unity of purpose. The various desires and impulses in his nature will be in conflict, if each asserts an unlimited claim to satisfaction. This view of justice as a principle of internal order and unity will become clearer when the soul has been analysed into its principal elements.]

Thrasymachus' assent was dragged out of him with a reluctance of which my account gives no idea. He was sweating at every pore, for the weather was hot; and I saw then what I had never seen before— Thrasymachus blushing. However, now that we had agreed that justice implies superior character and intelligence, injustice a deficiency in both respects, I went on:

Good; let us take that as settled. But we were also saying that injustice was a source of strength. Do you remember, Thrasymachus?

I do remember; only your last argument does not satisfy me, and I could say a good deal about that. But if I did, you would tell me I was haranguing you like a public meeting. So either let me speak my mind at length, or else, if you want to ask questions, ask them, and I will nod or shake my head, and say "Hm?" as we do to encourage an old woman telling us a story.

No, please, said I; don't give your assent against your real opinion.

Anything to please you, he rejoined, since you won't let me have my say. What more do you want?

Nothing, I replied. If that is what you mean to do, I will go on with my questions.

Go on, then.

Well, to continue where we left off. I will repeat my question: What is the nature and quality of justice as compared with injustice? It was suggested, I believe, that injustice is the stronger and more effective of the two; but now we have seen that justice implies superior character and intelligence, it will not be hard to show that it will also be superior in power to injustice, which implies ignorance and stupidity; that must be obvious to anyone. However, I would rather look deeper into this matter than take it as settled off-hand. Would you agree that a state may be unjust and may try to enslave other states or to hold a number of others in subjection unjustly?

Of course it may, he said; above all if it is the best sort of state, which carries injustice to perfection.

I understand, said I; that was your view. But I am wondering whether a state can do without justice when it is asserting its superior power over another in that way.

Not if you are right, that justice implies intelligence; but if I am right, injustice will be needed.

I am delighted with your answer, Thrasymachus; this is much better than just nodding and shaking your head.

It is all to oblige you.

Thank you. Please add to your kindness by telling me whether any set of men—a state or an army or a band of robbers or thieves—who were acting together for some unjust purpose would be likely to suc-

ceed, if they were always trying to injure one another. Wouldn't they
do better, if they did not?

Yes, they would.

Because, of course, such injuries must set them quarrelling and hat-
ing each other. Only fair treatment can make men friendly and of one
mind.

Be it so, he said; I don't want to differ from you.

Thank you once more, I replied. But don't you agree that, if injustice
has this effect of implanting hatred wherever it exists, it must make
any set of people, whether freemen or slaves, split into factions, at
feud with one another and incapable of any joint action?

Yes.

And so with any two individuals: injustice will set them at variance
and make them enemies to each other as well as to everyone who is
just.

It will.

And will it not keep its character and have the same effect, if it
exists in a single person?

Let us suppose so.

The effect being, apparently, wherever it occurs—in a state or a family or an army or anywhere else—to make united action impossible
because of factions and quarrels, and moreover to set whatever it
resides in at enmity with itself as well as with any opponent and with
all who are just.

Yes, certainly.

Then I suppose it will produce the same natural results in an individual. He will have a divided mind and be incapable of action, for
lack of singleness of purpose; and he will be at enmity with all who
are just as well as with himself?

Yes.

And "all who are just" surely includes the gods?

Let us suppose so.

The unjust man, then, will be a god-forsaken creature; the goodwill
of heaven will be for the just.

Enjoy your triumph, said Thrasymachus. You need not fear my con-
tradicting you. I have no wish to give offence to the company.

[3. *The final question is, whether justice (now admitted to be a virtue) or
injustice brings happiness. The argument turns on the doctrine (adopted as*

fundamental in Aristotle's Ethics) *that man, like any other living species, has a peculiar work or function or activity, in the satisfactory exercise of which his well-being or happiness will consist; and also a peculiar excellence or virtue, namely a state of his soul from which that satisfactory activity will result. Aristotle argues* (Eth. Nic. i. 7) *that, a thing's function being the work or activity of which it alone is capable, man's function will be an activity involving the use of reason, which man alone possesses. Man's virtue is "the state of character which makes him a good man and makes him do his work well"* (ibid. ii. 6). *It is the quality which enables him to "live well," for living is the soul's function; and to live well is to be happy. . . .*]

You will make my enjoyment complete, I replied, if you will answer my further questions in the same way. We have made out so far that just men are superior in character and intelligence and more effective in action. Indeed without justice men cannot act together at all; it is not strictly true to speak of such people as ever having effected any strong action in common. Had they been thoroughly unjust, they could not have kept their hands off one another; they must have had some justice in them, enough to keep them from injuring one another at the same time with their victims. This it was that enabled them to achieve what they did achieve: their injustice only partially incapacitated them for their career of wrongdoing; if perfect, it would have disabled them for any action whatsoever. I can see that all this is true, as against your original position. But there is a further question which we postponed: Is the life of justice the better and happier life? What we have said already leaves no doubt in my mind; but we ought to consider more carefully, for this is no light matter: it is the question, what is the right way to live?

Go on, then.

I will, said I. Some things have a function;[2] a horse, for instance, is useful for certain kinds of work. Would you agree to define a thing's function in general as the work for which that thing is the only instrument or the best one?

I don't understand.

Take an example. We can see only with the eyes, hear only with the

---

2. The word translated "function" is the common word for "work." Hence the need for illustrations to confine it to the narrower sense of "function," here defined for the first time.

ears; and seeing and hearing might be called the functions of those organs.

Yes.

Or again, you might cut vine-shoots with a carving-knife or a chisel or many other tools, but with none so well as with a pruning-knife made for the purpose; and we may call that its function.

True.

Now, I expect, you see better what I meant by suggesting that a thing's function is the work that it alone can do, or can do better than anything else.

Yes, I will accept that definition.

Good, said I; and to take the same examples, the eye and the ear, which we said have each its particular function: have they not also a specific excellence or virtue? Is not that always the case with things that have some appointed work to do?

Yes.

Now consider: is the eye likely to do its work well, if you take away its peculiar virtue and substitute the corresponding defect?

Of course not, if you mean substituting blindness for the power of sight.

I mean whatever its virtue may be; I have not come to that yet. I am only asking, whether it is true of things with a function—eyes or ears or anything else—that there is always some specific virtue which enables them to work well; and if they are deprived of that virtue, they work badly.

I think that is true.

Then the next point is this. Has the soul a function that can be performed by nothing else? Take for example such actions as deliberating or taking charge and exercising control: is not the soul the only thing of which you can say that these are its proper and peculiar work?

That is so.

And again, living—is not that above all the function of the soul?

No doubt.

And we also speak of the soul as having a certain specific excellence or virtue?

Yes.

Then, Thrasymachus, if the soul is robbed of its peculiar virtue, it cannot possibly do its work well. It must exercise its power of controlling and taking charge well or ill according as it is itself in a good or a bad state.

That follows.

And did we not agree that the virtue of the soul is justice, and injustice its defect?

We did.

So it follows that a just soul, or in other words a just man, will live well; the unjust will not.

Apparently, according to your argument.

But living well involves well-being and happiness.

Naturally.

Then only the just man is happy; injustice will involve unhappiness.

Be it so.

But you cannot say it pays better to be unhappy.

Of course not.

Injustice then, my dear Thrasymachus, can never pay better than justice.

Well, he replied, this is a feast-day, and you may take all this as your share of the entertainment.

For which I have to thank you, Thrasymachus; you have been so gentle with me since you recovered your temper. It is my own fault if the entertainment has not been satisfactory. I have been behaving like a greedy guest, snatching a taste of every new dish that comes round before he has properly enjoyed the last. We began by looking for a definition of justice; but before we had found one, I dropped that question and hurried on to ask whether or not it involved superior character and intelligence; and then, as soon as another idea cropped up, that injustice pays better, I could not refrain from pursuing that.

So now the whole conversation has left me completely in the dark; for so long as I do not know what justice is, I am hardly likely to know whether or not it is a virtue, or whether it makes a man happy or unhappy.

PLATO

The Power of Insight

Now, I continued, if we are to elude those assailants you have described, we must, I think, define for them whom we mean by these lovers of wisdom who, we have dared to assert, ought to be our rulers. Once we have a clear view of their character, we shall be able to defend our position by pointing to some who are naturally fitted to combine philosophic study with political leadership, while the rest of the world should accept their guidance and let philosophy alone.

Yes, this is the moment for a definition.

Here, then, is a line of thought which may lead to a satisfactory explanation. Need I remind you that a man will deserve to be called a lover of this or that, only if it is clear that he loves that thing as a whole, not merely in parts?

You must remind me, it seems; for I do not see what you mean.

That answer would have come better from someone less susceptible to love than yourself, Glaucon. You ought not to have forgotten that any boy in the bloom of youth will arouse some sting of passion in a man of your amorous temperament and seem worthy of his attentions. Is not this your way with your favourites? You will praise a snub nose as piquant and a hooked one as giving a regal air, while you call a straight nose perfectly proportioned; the swarthy, you say, have a manly look, the fair are children of the gods; and what do you think is that word "honey-pale," if not the euphemism of some lover who had no fault to find with sallowness on the cheek of youth? In a word, you will carry pretence and extravagance to any length sooner than reject a single one that is in the flower of his prime.

If you insist on taking me as an example of how lovers behave, I will agree for the sake of argument.

Again, do you not see the same behaviour in people with a passion for wine? They are glad of any excuse to drink wine of any sort. And there are the men who covet honour, who, if they cannot lead an army, will command a company, and if they cannot win the respect of important people, are glad to be looked up to by nobodies, because they must have someone to esteem them.

Quite true.

Do you agree, then, that when we speak of a man as having a passion for a certain kind of thing, we mean that he has an appetite for everything of that kind without discrimination?

Yes.

So the philosopher, with his passion for wisdom, will be one who desires all wisdom, not only some part of it. If a student is particular about his studies, especially while he is too young to know which are useful and which are not, we shall say he is no lover of learning or of wisdom; just as, if he were dainty about his food, we should say he was not hungry or fond of eating, but had a poor appetite. Only the man who has a taste for every sort of knowledge and throws himself into acquiring it with an insatiable curiosity will deserve to be called a philosopher. Am I not right?

That description, Glaucon replied, would include a large and ill-assorted company. It is curiosity, I suppose, and a delight in fresh experience that gives some people a passion for all that is to be seen and heard at theatrical and musical performances. But they are a queer set to reckon among philosophers, considering that they would never go near anything like a philosophical discussion, though they run round at all the Dionysiac festivals in town or country as if they were under contract to listen to every company of performers without fail. Will curiosity entitle all these enthusiasts, not to mention amateurs of the minor arts, to be called philosophers?

Certainly not; though they have a certain counterfeit resemblance.

And whom do you mean by the genuine philosophers?

Those whose passion it is to see the truth.

That must be so; but will you explain?

It would not be easy to explain to everyone; but you, I believe, will grant my premiss.

Which is——?

That since beauty and ugliness are opposite, they are two things; and consequently each of them is one. The same holds of justice and injustice, good and bad, and all the essential Forms: each in itself is one; but they manifest themselves in a great variety of combinations, with actions, with material things, and with one another, and so each seems to be many.

That is true.

On the strength of this premiss, then, I can distinguish your amateurs of the arts and men of action from the philosophers we are concerned with, who are alone worthy of the name.

What is your distinction?

Your lovers of sights and sounds delight in beautiful tones and colours and shapes and in all the works of art into which these enter; but they have not the power of thought to behold and to take delight in the nature of Beauty itself. That power to approach Beauty and behold it as it is in itself, is rare indeed.

Quite true.

Now if a man believes in the existence of beautiful things, but not of Beauty itself, and cannot follow a guide who would lead him to a knowledge of it, is he not living in a dream? Consider: does not dreaming, whether one is awake or asleep, consist in mistaking a semblance for the reality it resembles?

I should certainly call that dreaming.

Contrast with him the man who holds that there is such a thing as Beauty itself and can discern that essence as well as the things that partake of its character, without ever confusing the one with the other—is he a dreamer or living in a waking state?

He is very much awake.

So may we say that he knows, while the other has only a belief in appearances; and might we call their states of mind knowledge and belief?

Certainly.

But this person who, we say, has only belief without knowledge may be aggrieved and challenge our statement. Is there any means of soothing his resentment and converting him gently, without telling him plainly that he is not in his right mind?

We surely ought to try.

Come then, consider what we are to say to him. Or shall we ask him a question, assuring him that, far from grudging him any knowledge he may have, we shall be only too glad to find that there is something he knows? But, we shall say, tell us this: When a man knows, must there not be something that he knows? Will you answer for him, Glaucon?

My answer will be, that there must.

Something real or unreal?

Something real; how could a thing that is unreal ever be known?

Are we satisfied, then, on this point, from however many points of view we might examine it: that the perfectly real is perfectly knowable, and the utterly unreal is entirely unknowable?

Quite satisfied.

Good. Now if there is something so constituted that it both *is* and *is not*, will it not lie between the purely real and the utterly unreal?

It will.

Well then, as knowledge corresponds to the real, and absence of knowledge necessarily to the unreal, so, to correspond to this intermediate thing, we must look for something between ignorance and knowledge, if such a thing there be.

Certainly.

Is there not a thing we call belief?

Surely.

A different power from knowledge, or the same?

Different.

Knowledge and belief, then, must have different objects, answering to their respective powers.

Yes.

And knowledge has for its natural object the real—to know the truth about reality. However, before going further, I think we need a definition. Shall we distinguish under the general name of "faculties"[1] those powers which enable us—or anything else—to do what we can do? Sight and hearing, for instance, are what I call faculties, if that will help you to see the class of things I have in mind.

Yes, I understand.

Then let me tell you what view I take of them. In a faculty I cannot find any of those qualities, such as colour or shape, which, in the case

1. The Greek here uses only the common word for "power" (*dynamis*), but Plato is defining the special sense we express by "faculty."

of many other things, enable me to distinguish one thing from another. I can only look to its field of objects and the state of mind it produces, and regard these as sufficient to identify it and to distinguish it from faculties which have different fields and produce different states. Is that how you would go to work?

Yes.

Let us go back, then, to knowledge. Would you class that as a faculty?

Yes; and I should call it the most powerful of all.

And is belief also a faculty?

It can be nothing else, since it is what gives us the power of believing.

But a little while ago you agreed that knowledge and belief are not the same thing.

Yes; there could be no sense in identifying the infallible with the fallible.[2]

Good. So we are quite clear that knowledge and belief are different things?

They are.

If so, each of them, having a different power, must have a different field of objects.

Necessarily.

The field of knowledge being the real; and its power, the power of knowing the real as it is.

Yes.

Whereas belief, we say, is the power of believing. Is its object the same as that which knowledge knows? Can the same things be possible objects both of knowledge and of belief?[3]

Not if we hold to the principles we agreed upon. If it is of the nature of a different faculty to have a different field, and if both knowledge and belief are faculties and, as we assert, different ones, it follows that the same things cannot be possible objects of both.

So if the real is the object of knowledge, the object of belief must be something other than the real.

2. This marks one distinction between the two states of mind. Further, even if true, belief, unlike knowledge, is 1. produced by persuasion, not by instruction; 2. cannot "give an account" of itself; and 3. can be shaken by persuasion (*Timaeus* 51 E).

3. If "belief" bore its common meaning, we might answer, yes. But in this context it is essentially belief in *appearances*. It includes perception by the senses, and these can never perceive objects of thought, such as Beauty itself.

Yes.

Can it be the unreal? Or is that an impossible object even for belief? Consider: if a man has a belief, there must be something before his mind; he cannot be believing nothing, can he?

No.

He is believing something, then; whereas the unreal could only be called nothing at all.

Certainly.

Now we said that ignorance must correspond to the unreal, knowledge to the real. So what he is believing cannot be real nor yet unreal.

True.

Belief, then, cannot be either ignorance or knowledge.

It appears not.

Then does it lie outside and beyond these two? Is it either more clear and certain than knowledge or less clear and certain than ignorance?

No, it is neither.

It rather seems to you to be something more obscure than knowledge, but not so dark as ignorance, and so to lie between the two extremes?

Quite so.

Well, we said earlier that if some object could be found such that it both *is* and at the same time *is not*, that object would lie between the perfectly real and the utterly unreal; and that the corresponding faculty would be neither knowledge nor ignorance, but a faculty to be found situated between the two.

Yes.

And now what we have found between the two is the faculty we call belief.

True.

It seems, then, that what remains to be discovered is that object which can be said both to be and not to be and cannot properly be called either purely real or purely unreal. If that can be found, we may justly call it the object of belief, and so give the intermediate faculty the intermediate object, while the two extreme objects will fall to the extreme faculties.

Yes.

On these assumptions, then, I shall call for an answer from our friend who denies the existence of Beauty itself or of anything that can be called an essential Form of Beauty remaining unchangeably in the same state for ever, though he does recognize the existence of beautiful things as a plurality—that lover of things seen who will not listen to anyone who says that Beauty is one, Justice is one, and so on. I shall say to him, Be so good as to tell us: of all these many beautiful things is there one which will not appear ugly? Or of these many just or righteous actions, is there one that will not appear unjust or unrighteous?

No, replied Glaucon, they must inevitably appear to be in some way both beautiful and ugly; and so with all the other terms your question refers to.

And again the many things which are doubles are just as much halves as they are doubles. And the things we call large or heavy have just as much right to be called small or light.

Yes; any such thing will always have a claim to both opposite designations.

Then, whatever any one of these many things may be said to be, can you say that it absolutely *is* that, any more than that it *is not* that?

They remind me of those punning riddles people ask at dinner parties, or the child's puzzle about what the eunuch threw at the bat and what the bat was perched on.[4] These things have the same ambiguous character, and one cannot form any stable conception of them either as being or as not being, or as both being and not being, or as neither.

Can you think of any better way of disposing of them than by placing them between reality and unreality? For I suppose they will not appear more obscure and so less real than unreality, or clearer and so more real than reality.

Quite true.

It seems, then, we have discovered that the many conventional notions of the mass of mankind about what is beautiful or honorable or just and so on are adrift in a sort of twilight between pure reality and pure unreality.

We have.

And we agreed earlier that, if any such object were discovered, it should be called the object of belief and not of knowledge. Fluctuating

---

4. A man who was not a man (eunuch), seeing and not seeing (seeing imperfectly) a bird that was not a bird (bat) perched on a bough that was not a bough (a reed), pelted and did not pelt it (aimed at it and missed) with a stone that was not a stone (pumice-stone).

in that half-way region, it would be seized upon by the intermediate faculty.

Yes.

So when people have an eye for the multitude of beautiful things or of just actions or whatever it may be, but can neither behold Beauty or Justice itself nor follow a guide who would lead them to it, we shall say that all they have is beliefs, without any real knowledge of the objects of their belief.

That follows.

But what of those who contemplate the realities themselves as they are for ever in the same unchanging state? Shall we not say that they have, not mere belief, but knowledge?

That too follows.

And, further, that their affection goes out to the objects of knowledge, whereas the others set their affections on the objects of belief; for it was they, you remember, who had a passion for the spectacle of beautiful colours and sounds, but would not hear of Beauty itself being a real thing.

I remember.

So we may fairly call them lovers of belief rather than of wisdom— not philosophical, in fact, but philodoxical. Will they be seriously annoyed by that description?

Not if they will listen to my advice. No one ought to take offence at the truth.

The name of philosopher, then, will be reserved for those whose affections are set, in every case, on the reality.

By all means. . . .

I will tell you, though only if you wish it, what I picture to myself as the offspring of the Good and the thing most nearly resembling it.

Well, tell us about the offspring, and you shall remain in our debt for an account of the parent.

I only wish it were within my power to offer, and within yours to receive, a settlement of the whole account. But you must be content now with the interest only;[5] and you must see to it that, in describing this offspring of the Good, I do not inadvertently cheat you with false coin.

5. The Greek has a play on two meanings of the word *tokos*—"offspring" and "interest" on a loan, "a breed for barren metal."

We will keep a good eye on you. Go on.

First we must come to an understanding. Let me remind you of the distinction we drew earlier and have often drawn on other occasions, between the multiplicity of things that we call good or beautiful or whatever it may be and, on the other hand, Goodness itself or Beauty itself and so on. Corresponding to each of these sets of many things, we postulate a single Form or real essence, as we call it.

Yes, that is so.

Further, the many things, we say, can be seen, but are not objects of rational thought; whereas the Forms are objects of thought, but invisible.

Yes, certainly.

And we see things with our eyesight, just as we hear sounds with our ears and, to speak generally, perceive any sensible thing with our sense-faculties.

Of course.

Have you noticed, then, that the artificer who designed the senses has been exceptionally lavish of his materials in making the eyes able to see and their objects visible?

That never occurred to me.

Well, look at it in this way. Hearing and sound do not stand in need of any third thing, without which the ear will not hear nor sound be heard; and I think the same is true of most, not to say all, of the other senses. Can you think of one that does require anything of the sort?

No, I cannot.

But there is this need in the case of sight and its objects. You may have the power of vision in your eyes and try to use it, and colour may be there in the objects; but sight will see nothing and the colours will remain invisible in the absence of a third thing peculiarly constituted to serve this very purpose.

By which you mean——?

Naturally I mean what you call light; and if light is a thing of value, the sense of sight and the power of being visible are linked together by a very precious bond, such as unites no other sense with its object.

No one could say that light is not a precious thing.

And of all the divinities in the skies is there one whose light, above all the rest, is responsible for making our eyes see perfectly and making objects perfectly visible?

There can be no two opinions: of course you mean the Sun.

And how is sight related to this deity? Neither sight nor the eye which contains it is the Sun, but of all the sense-organs it is the most sun-like; and further, the power it possesses is dispensed by the Sun, like a stream flooding the eye. And again, the Sun is not vision, but it is the cause of vision and also is seen by the vision it causes.

Yes.

It was the Sun, then, that I meant when I spoke of that offspring which the Good has created in the visible world, to stand there in the same relation to vision and visible things as that which the Good itself bears in the intelligible world to intelligence and to intelligible objects.

How is that? You must explain further.

You know what happens when the colours of things are no longer irradiated by the daylight, but only by the fainter luminaries of the night: when you look at them, the eyes are dim and seem almost blind, as if there were no unclouded vision in them. But when you look at things on which the Sun is shining, the same eyes see distinctly and it becomes evident that they do contain the power of vision.

Certainly.

Apply this comparison, then, to the soul. When its gaze is fixed upon an object irradiated by truth and reality, the soul gains understanding and knowledge and is manifestly in possession of intelligence. But when it looks towards that twilight world of things that come into existence and pass away, its sight is dim and it has only opinions and beliefs which shift to and fro, and now it seems like a thing that has no intelligence.

That is true.

This, then, which gives to the objects of knowledge their truth and to him who knows them his power of knowing, is the Form or essential nature of Goodness. It is the cause of knowledge and truth; and so, while you may think of it as an object of knowledge, you will do well to regard it as something beyond truth and knowledge and, precious as these both are, of still higher worth. And, just as in our analogy light and vision were to be thought of as like the Sun, but not identical with it, so here both knowledge and truth are to be regarded as like the Good, but to identify either with the Good is wrong. The Good must hold a yet higher place of honour.

You are giving it a position of extraordinary splendour, if it is the source of knowledge and truth and itself surpasses them in worth. You surely cannot mean that it is pleasure.

Heaven forbid, I exclaimed. But I want to follow up our analogy still further. You will agree that the Sun not only makes the things we see visible, but also brings them into existence and gives them growth and nourishment; yet he is not the same thing as existence.[6] And so with the objects of knowledge: these derive from the Good not only their power of being known, but their very being and reality; and Goodness is not the same thing as being, but even beyond being, surpassing it in dignity and power.

Glaucon exclaimed with some amusement at my exalting Goodness in such extravagant terms.

It is your fault, I replied; you forced me to say what I think.

Yes, and you must not stop there. At any rate, complete your comparison with the Sun, if there is any more to be said.

There is a great deal more, I answered.

Let us hear it, then; don't leave anything out.

I am afraid much must be left unspoken. However, I will not, if I can help it, leave out anything that can be said on this occasion.

Please do not.

Conceive, then, that there are these two powers I speak of, the Good reigning over the domain of all that is intelligible, the Sun over the visible world—or the heaven as I might call it; only you would think I was showing off my skill in etymology. At any rate you have these two orders of things clearly before your mind: the visible and the intelligible?

I have.

Now take a line divided into two unequal parts, one to represent the visible order, the other the intelligible; and divide each part again in the same proportion, symbolizing degrees of comparative clearness or obscurity. Then (A) one of the two sections in the visible world will stand for images. By images I mean first shadows, and then reflections in water or in close-grained, polished surfaces, and everything of that kind, if you understand.

6. The ambiguity of *genesis* can hardly be reproduced. The Sun "gives things their *genesis*" (generation, birth), but "is not itself *genesis*" (becoming, the existence in time of things which begin and cease to exist, as opposed to the real being of eternal things in the intelligible world).

Yes, I understand.

Let the second section (B) stand for the actual things of which the first are likenesses, the living creatures about us and all the works of nature or of human hands.

So be it.

Will you also take the proportion in which the visible world has been divided as corresponding to degrees of reality and truth, so that the likeness shall stand to the original in the same ratio as the sphere of appearances and belief to the sphere of knowledge?

Certainly.

Now consider how we are to divide the part which stands for the intelligible world. There are two sections. In the first (C) the mind uses as images those actual things which themselves had images in the visible world; and it is compelled to pursue its inquiry by starting from assumptions and travelling, not up to a principle, but down to a conclusion. In the second (D) the mind moves in the other direction, from an assumption up towards a principle which is not hypothetical; and it makes no use of the images employed in the other section, but only of Forms, and conducts its inquiry solely by their means.

I don't quite understand what you mean.

Then we will try again; what I have just said will help you to understand. (C) You know, of course, how students of subjects like geometry and arithmetic begin by postulating odd and even numbers, or the various figures and the three kinds of angle, and other such data in each subject. These data they take as known; and, having adopted them as assumptions, they do not feel called upon to give any account of them to themselves or to anyone else, but treat them as self-evident. Then, starting from these assumptions, they go on until they arrive, by a series of consistent steps, at all the conclusions they set out to investigate.

Yes, I know that.

You also know how they make use of visible figures and discourse about them, though what they really have in mind is the originals of which these figures are images: they are not reasoning, for instance, about this particular square and diagonal which they have drawn, but about *the* Square and *the* Diagonal; and so in all cases. The diagrams they draw and the models they make are actual things, which may have their shadows or images in water; but now they serve in their turn as images, while the student is seeking to behold those realities which only thought can apprehend.

True.

This, then, is the class of things that I spoke of as intelligible, but with two qualifications: first, that the mind, in studying them, is compelled to employ assumptions, and, because it cannot rise above these, does not travel upwards to a first principle; and second, that it uses as images those actual things which have images of their own in the section below them and which, in comparison with those shadows and reflections, are reputed to be more palpable and valued accordingly.

I understand: you mean the subject-matter of geometry and of the kindred arts.

(D) Then by the second section of the intelligible world you may understand me to mean all that unaided reasoning apprehends by the power of dialectic, when it treats its assumptions, not as first principles, but as *hypotheses* in the literal sense, things "laid down" like a flight of steps up which it may mount all the way to something that is not hypothetical, the first principle of all; and having grasped this, may turn back and, holding on to the consequences which depend upon it, descend at last to a conclusion, never making use of any sensible object, but only of Forms, moving through Forms from one to another, and ending with Forms.

I understand, he said, though not perfectly; for the procedure you describe sounds like an enormous undertaking. But I see that you mean to distinguish the field of intelligible reality studied by dialectic as having a greater certainty and truth than the subject-matter of the "arts," as they are called, which treat their assumptions as first principles. The students of these arts are, it is true, compelled to exercise thought in contemplating objects which the senses cannot perceive; but because they start from assumptions without going back to a first principle, you do not regard them as gaining true understanding about those objects, although the objects themselves, when connected with a first principle, are intelligible. And I think you would call the state of mind of the students of geometry and other such arts, not intelligence, but thinking, as being something between intelligence and mere acceptance of appearances.

You have understood me quite well enough, I replied. And now you may take, as corresponding to the four sections, these four states of mind: *intelligence* for the highest, *thinking* for the second, *belief* for the third, and for the last *imagining*.[7] These you may arrange as the terms in a proportion, assigning to each a degree of clearness and certainty corresponding to the measure in which their objects possess truth and reality.

I understand and agree with you. I will arrange them as you say. . . .

The Allegory of the Cave

The progress of the mind from the lowest state of unenlightenment to knowledge of the Good is now illustrated by the famous parable comparing the world of appearance to an underground Cave. In Empedocles' religious poem the powers which conduct the soul to its incarnation say, "We have come under this cavern's roof." The image was probably taken from mysteries held in caves or dark chambers representing the underworld, through which the candidates for initiation were led to the revelation of sacred objects in a blaze of light. The idea that the body is a prison-house, to which the soul is condemned for past misdeeds, is attributed by Plato to the Orphics.

One moral of the allegory is drawn from the distress caused by a too sudden passage from darkness to light. The earlier warning against plunging untrained minds into the discussion of moral problems, as the Sophists and Socrates himself had done, is reinforced by the picture of the dazed prisoner dragged out into the sunlight. Plato's ten years' course of pure mathematics is to habituate the intellect to abstract reasoning before moral ideas are called in question.

Next, said I, here is a parable to illustrate the degrees in which our nature may be enlightened or unenlightened. Imagine the condition of men living in a sort of cavernous chamber underground, with an entrance open to the light and a long passage all down the cave.[8] Here they have been from childhood, chained by the leg and also by the neck, so that they cannot move and can see only what is in front of them, because the chains will not let them turn their heads. At some

7. Plato never uses hard and fast technical terms. The four here proposed are not defined or strictly employed in the sequel.
8. The *length* of the "way in" (*eisodos*) to the chamber where the prisoners sit is an essential feature, explaining why no daylight reaches them.

distance higher up is the light of a fire burning behind them; and between the prisoners and the fire is a track[9] with a parapet built along it, like the screen at a puppet-show, which hides the performers while they show their puppets over the top.

I see, said he.

Now behind this parapet imagine persons carrying along various artificial objects, including figures of men and animals in wood or stone or other materials, which project above the parapet. Naturally, some of these persons will be talking, others silent.[10]

It is a strange picture, he said, and a strange sort of prisoners.

Like ourselves, I replied; for in the first place prisoners so confined would have seen nothing of themselves or of one another, except the shadows thrown by the fire-light on the wall of the Cave facing them, would they?

Not if all their lives they had been prevented from moving their heads.

And they would have seen as little of the objects carried past.

Of course.

Now, if they could talk to one another, would they not suppose that their words referred only to those passing shadows which they saw?[11]

Necessarily.

And suppose their prison had an echo from the wall facing them? When one of the people crossing behind them spoke, they could only suppose that the sound came from the shadow passing before their eyes.

No doubt.

In every way, then, such prisoners would recognize as reality nothing but the shadows of those artificial objects.

Inevitably.

9. The track crosses the passage into the cave at right angles, and is *above* the parapet built along it.

10. A modern Plato would compare his Cave to an underground cinema, where the audience watch the play of shadows thrown by the film passing before a light at their backs. The film itself is only an image of "real" things and events in the world outside the cinema. For the film Plato has to substitute the clumsier apparatus of a procession of artificial objects carried on their heads by persons who are merely part of the machinery, providing for the movement of the objects and the sounds whose echo the prisoners hear. The parapet prevents these persons' shadows from being cast on the wall of the Cave.

11. Adam's text and interpretation. The prisoners, having seen nothing but shadows, cannot think their words refer to the objects carried past behind their backs. For them shadows (images) are the only realities.

Now consider what would happen if their release from the chains and the healing of their unwisdom should come about in this way. Suppose one of them set free and forced suddenly to stand up, turn his head, and walk with eyes lifted to the light; all these movements would be painful, and he would be too dazzled to make out the objects whose shadows he had been used to see. What do you think he would say, if someone told him that what he had formerly seen was meaningless illusion, but now, being somewhat nearer to reality and turned towards more real objects, he was getting a truer view? Suppose further that he were shown the various objects being carried by and were made to say, in reply to questions, what each of them was. Would he not be perplexed and believe the objects now shown him to be not so real as what he formerly saw?

Yes, not nearly so real.

And if he were forced to look at the fire-light itself, would not his eyes ache, so that he would try to escape and turn back to the things which he could see distinctly, convinced that they really were clearer than these other objects now being shown to him?

Yes.

And suppose someone were to drag him away forcibly up the steep and rugged ascent and not let him go until he had hauled him out into the sunlight, would he not suffer pain and vexation at such treatment, and, when he had come out into the light, find his eyes so full of its radiance that he could not see a single one of the things that he was now told were real?

Certainly he would not see them all at once.

He would need, then, to grow accustomed before he could see things in that upper world. At first it would be easiest to make out shadows, and then the images of men and things reflected in water, and later on the things themselves. After that, it would be easier to watch the heavenly bodies and the sky itself by night, looking at the light of the moon and stars rather than the sun and the Sun's light in the day-time.

Yes, surely.

Last of all, he would be able to look at the Sun and contemplate its nature, not as it appears when reflected in water or any alien medium, but as it is in itself in its own domain.

No doubt.

And now he would begin to draw the conclusion that it is the Sun that produces the seasons and the course of the year and controls everything in the visible world, and moreover is in a way the cause of all that he and his companions used to see.

Clearly he would come at last to that conclusion.

Then if he called to mind his fellow prisoners and what passed for wisdom in his former dwelling-place, he would surely think himself happy in the change and be sorry for them. They may have had a practice of honouring and commending one another, with prizes for the man who had the keenest eye for the passing shadows and the best memory for the order in which they followed or accompanied one another, so that he could make a good guess as to which was going to come next.[12] Would our released prisoner be likely to covet those prizes or to envy the men exalted to honour and power in the Cave? Would he not feel like Homer's Achilles, that he would far sooner "be on earth as a hired servant in the house of a landless man"[13] or endure anything rather than go back to his old beliefs and live in the old way?

Yes, he would prefer any fate to such a life.

Now imagine what would happen if he went down again to take his former seat in the Cave. Coming suddenly out of the sunlight, his eyes would be filled with darkness. He might be required once more to deliver his opinion on those shadows, in competition with the prisoners who had never been released, while his eyesight was still dim and unsteady; and it might take some time to become used to the darkness. They would laugh at him and say that he had gone up only to come back with his sight ruined; it was worth no one's while even to attempt the ascent. If they could lay hands on the man who was trying to set them free and lead them up, they would kill him.[14]

Yes, they would.

Every feature in this parable, my dear Glaucon, is meant to fit our earlier analysis. The prison dwelling corresponds to the region revealed to us through the sense of sight, and the fire-light within it to the power of the Sun. The ascent to see the things in the upper world you may take as standing for the upward journey of the soul into the region of the intelligible; then you will be in possession of what I sur-

12. The empirical politician, with no philosophic insight, but only a "knack of remembering what usually happens." He has *eikasia* = conjecture as to what is likely (*eikos*).
13. This verse (already quoted at 386 c, p. 76), being spoken by the ghost of Achilles, suggests that the Cave is comparable with Hades.
14. An allusion to the fate of Socrates.

mise, since that is what you wish to be told. Heaven knows whether it is true; but this, at any rate, is how it appears to me. In the world of knowledge, the last thing to be perceived and only with great difficulty is the essential Form of Goodness. Once it is perceived, the conclusion must follow that, for all things, this is the cause of whatever is right and good; in the visible world it gives birth to light and to the lord of light, while it is itself sovereign in the intelligible world and the parent of intelligence and truth. Without having had a vision of this Form no one can act with wisdom, either in his own life or in matters of state.

So far as I can understand, I share your belief.

Then you may also agree that it is no wonder if those who have reached this height are reluctant to manage the affairs of men. Their souls long to spend all their time in that upper world—naturally enough, if here once more our parable holds true. Nor, again, is it at all strange that one who comes from the contemplation of divine things to the miseries of human life should appear awkward and ridiculous when, with eyes still dazed and not yet accustomed to the darkness, he is compelled, in a law-court or elsewhere, to dispute about the shadows of justice or the images that cast those shadows, and to wrangle over the notions of what is right in the minds of men who have never beheld Justice itself.

It is not at all strange.

No; a sensible man will remember that the eyes may be confused in two ways—by a change from light to darkness or from darkness to light; and he will recognize that the same thing happens to the soul. When he sees it troubled and unable to discern anything clearly, instead of laughing thoughtlessly, he will ask whether, coming from a brighter existence, its unaccustomed vision is obscured by the darkness, in which case he will think its condition enviable and its life a happy one; or whether, emerging from the depths of ignorance, it is dazzled by excess of light. If so, he will rather feel sorry for it; or, if he were inclined to laugh, that would be less ridiculous than to laugh at the soul which has come down from the light.

That is a fair statement.

If this is true, then, we must conclude that education is not what it is said to be by some, who profess to put knowledge into a soul which does not possess it, as if they could put sight into blind eyes. On the contrary, our own account signifies that the soul of every man does possess the power of learning the truth and the organ to see it with; and that, just as one might have to turn the whole body round in order that the eye should see light instead of darkness, so the entire soul must be turned away from this changing world, until its eye can bear to contemplate reality and that supreme splendour which we have called the Good. Hence there may well be an art whose aim would be to effect this very thing, the conversion of the soul, in the readiest way; not to put the power of sight into the soul's eye, which already has it, but to ensure that, instead of looking in the wrong direction, it is turned the way it ought to be.

Yes, it may well be so.

It looks, then, as though wisdom were different from those ordinary virtues, as they are called, which are not far removed from bodily qualities, in that they can be produced by habituation and exercise in a soul which has not possessed them from the first. Wisdom, it seems, is certainly the virtue of some diviner faculty, which never loses its power, though its use for good or harm depends on the direction towards which it is turned. You must have noticed in dishonest men with a reputation for sagacity the shrewd glance of a narrow intelligence piercing the objects to which it is directed. There is nothing wrong with their power of vision, but it has been forced into the service of evil, so that the keener its sight, the more harm it works.

Quite true.

And yet if the growth of a nature like this had been pruned from earliest childhood, cleared of those clinging overgrowths which come of gluttony and all luxurious pleasure and, like leaden weights charged with affinity to this mortal world, hang upon the soul, bending its vision downwards; if, freed from these, the soul were turned round towards true reality, then this same power in these very men would see the truth as keenly as the objects it is turned to now.

Yes, very likely.

Is it not also likely, or indeed certain after what has been said, that a state can never be properly governed either by the uneducated who know nothing of truth or by men who are allowed to spend all their days in the pursuit of culture? The ignorant have no single mark before their eyes at which they must aim in all the conduct of their own lives and of affairs of state; and the others will not engage in action if they can help it, dreaming that, while still alive, they have been translated to the Islands of the Blest.

Quite true.

It is for us, then, as founders of a commonwealth, to bring compulsion to bear on the noblest natures. They must be made to climb the ascent to the vision of Goodness, which we called the highest object of knowledge; and, when they have looked upon it long enough, they must not be allowed, as they now are, to remain on the heights, refusing to come down again to the prisoners or to take any part in their labours and rewards, however much or little these may be worth.

Shall we not be doing them an injustice, if we force on them a worse life than they might have?

You have forgotten again, my friend, that the law is not concerned to make any one class specially happy, but to ensure the welfare of the commonwealth as a whole. By persuasion or constraint it will unite the citizens in harmony, making them share whatever benefits each class can contribute to the common good; and its purpose in forming men of that spirit was not that each should be left to go his own way, but that they should be instrumental in binding the community into one.

True, I had forgotten.

You will see, then, Glaucon, that there will be no real injustice in compelling our philosophers to watch over and care for the other citizens. We can fairly tell them that their compeers in other states may quite reasonably refuse to collaborate: there they have sprung up, like a self-sown plant, in despite of their country's institutions; no one has fostered their growth, and they cannot be expected to show gratitude for a care they have never received. "But," we shall say, "it is not so with you. We have brought you into existence for your country's sake as well as for your own, to be like leaders and king-bees in a hive; you have been better and more thoroughly educated than those others and hence you are more capable of playing your part both as men of thought and as men of action. You must go down, then, each in his turn, to live with the rest and let your eyes grow accustomed to the darkness. You will then see a thousand times better than those who live there always; you will recognize every image for what it is and know what it represents, because you have seen justice, beauty, and goodness in their reality; and so you and we shall find life in our commonwealth no mere dream, as it is in most existing states, where men live fighting one another about shadows and quarrelling for power, as if that were a great prize; whereas in truth government can be at its best and free from dissension only where the destined rulers are least desirous of holding office."

Quite true.

Then will our pupils refuse to listen and to take their turns at sharing in the work of the community, though they may live together for most of their time in a purer air?

No; it is a fair demand, and they are fair-minded men. No doubt, unlike any ruler of the present day, they will think of holding power as an unavoidable necessity.

Yes, my friend; for the truth is that you can have a well-governed society only if you can discover for your future rulers a better way of life than being in office; then only will power be in the hands of men who are rich, not in gold, but in the wealth that brings happiness, a good and wise life. All goes wrong when, starved for lack of anything good in their own lives, men turn to public affairs hoping to snatch from thence the happiness they hunger for. They set about fighting for power, and this internecine conflict ruins them and their country. The life of true philosophy is the only one that looks down upon offices of state; and access to power must be confined to men who are not in love with it; otherwise rivals will start fighting. So whom else can you compel to undertake the guardianship of the commonwealth, if not those who, besides understanding best the principles of government, enjoy a nobler life than the politician's and look for rewards of a different kind?

There is indeed no other choice. . . .

Well, can the knowledge we are demanding ever be attained by people who cannot give a rational account of their statements or make others give an account of theirs?

Once more I should say No.

Here at last, then, we come to the main theme, to be developed in philosophic discussion. It falls within the domain of the intelligible world; but its progress is like that of the power of vision in the released prisoner of our parable. When he had reached the stage of trying to look at the living creatures outside the Cave, then at the stars, and lastly at the Sun himself, he arrived at the highest object in the visible world. So here, the summit of the intelligible world is reached in philosophic discussion by one who aspires, through the discourse of reason unaided by any of the senses, to make his way in every case to the essential reality and perseveres until he has grasped by pure intelligence the very nature of Goodness itself. This journey is what we call Dialectic.

Yes, certainly.

There was also that earlier stage when the prisoner, set free from his chains, turned from the shadows to the images which cast them and to the fire-light, and climbed up out of the cavern into the sunshine. When there, he was still unable to look at the animals and plants and the sunlight; he could only see the shadows of things and their reflections in water, though these, it is true, are works of divine creation and come from real things, not mere shadows of images thrown by the light of the fire, which was itself only an image as compared with the Sun. Now the whole course of study in the arts we have reviewed has the corresponding effect of leading up the noblest faculty of the soul towards the contemplation of the highest of all realities, just as in our allegory the bodily organ which has the clearest perceptions was led up towards the brightest of visible things in the material world.

I agree to what you are saying, Glaucon replied: I find it very hard to accept, but in another way no less hard to deny. However, there will be many other opportunities to reconsider it; so let us assume for the moment that it is true, and go on to develop what you call the main theme as fully as we have treated the prelude. I want you to describe the function of philosophic discussion, into what divisions it falls, and what are its methods; for here, it seems, we have come to the procedure which should lead to the resting-place at our journey's end.

My dear Glaucon, said I, you will not be able to follow me farther, though not for want of willingness on my part. It would mean that, instead of illustrating the truth by an allegory, I should be showing you the truth itself, at least as it appears to me. I cannot be sure whether or not I see it as it really is; but we can be sure that there is some such reality which it concerns us to see. Is not that so?

No doubt.

And also that it can be revealed only to one who is trained in the studies we have discussed, and to him only by the power of dialectic?

That also we can assert.

At any rate, no one will maintain against us that there is any other method of inquiry which systematically attempts in every case to grasp the nature of each thing as it is in itself. The other arts are nearly all concerned with human opinions and desires, or with the production of natural and artificial things, or with the care of them when produced. There remain geometry and those other allied studies which, as we said, do in some measure apprehend reality; but we observe that they cannot yield anything clearer than a dream-like vision of the real so long as they leave the assumptions they employ unquestioned and can give no account of them. If your premiss is something you do not really know and your conclusion and the intermediate steps are a tissue of things you do not really know, your reasoning may be consistent with itself, but how can it ever amount to knowledge?

It cannot.

So, said I, the method of dialectic is the only one which takes this course, doing away with assumptions and travelling up to the first principle of all, so as to make sure of confirmation there. When the eye of the soul is sunk in a veritable slough of barbarous ignorance, this method gently draws it forth and guides it upwards, assisted in this work of conversion by the arts we have enumerated. From force of habit we have several times spoken of these as branches of knowledge; but they need some other name implying something less clear than knowledge, though not so dim as the apprehension of appearances. "Thinking," I believe, was the term we fixed on earlier; but in considering matters of such high importance we shall not quarrel about a name.

Certainly not.

We shall be satisfied, then, with the names we gave earlier to our four divisions: first, knowledge; second, thinking; third, belief; and fourth, imagining. The last two taken together constitute the apprehension of appearances in the world of Becoming; the first two, intelligence concerned with true Being. Finally, as Being is to Becoming, so is intelligence to the apprehension of appearances; and in the same relation again stand knowledge to belief, and thinking to imagining. We had better not discuss the corresponding objects, the intelligible world and the world of appearance, or the twofold division of each of those provinces and the proportion in which the divisions stand. We might be involved in a discussion many times as long as the one we have already had.

Well, I certainly agree on those other points, so far as I can follow you.

And by a master of dialectic do you also mean one who demands an account of the essence of each thing? And would you not say that, in so far as he can render no such account to himself or to others, his intelligence is at fault?

I should.

And does not this apply to the Good? He must be able to distinguish the essential nature of Goodness, isolating it from all other Forms; he must fight his way through all criticisms, determined to examine every step by the standard, not of appearances and opinions, but of reality and truth, and win through to the end without sustaining a fall. If he cannot do this, he will know neither Goodness itself nor any good thing; if he does lay hold upon some semblance of good, it will be only a matter of belief, not of knowledge; and he will dream away his life here in a sleep which has no awakening on this side of that world of Death where he will sleep at last for ever.

I do most earnestly agree with you.

Well then, if you should ever be charged in actual fact with the upbringing and education of these imaginary children of yours, you will not allow them, I suppose, to bear rule in your commonwealth so long as their minds are, as a mathematician might say, irrational quantities, not commensurate with the highest responsibilities. So you will make a law that they must devote themselves especially to the discipline which will make them masters of the technique of asking and answering questions.

Yes, I will, with your collaboration.

May we conclude, then, that our account of the subjects of study is now complete? Dialectic will stand as the coping-stone of the whole structure; there is no other study that deserves to be put above it.

Yes, I agree. . . .

Such, then, being his origin and character, what will his life be like?

I give it up. You must tell me.

I will. When a master passion is enthroned in absolute dominion over every part of the soul, feasting and revelling with courtesans and all such delights will become the order of the day. And every day and night a formidable crop of fresh appetites springs up, whose numerous demands quickly consume whatever income there may be. Soon he will be borrowing and trenching on his capital; and when all resources fail, the lusty brood of appetites will crowd about him clamouring. Goaded on to frenzy by them and above all by that ruling passion to which they serve as a sort of bodyguard, he will look out for any man of property whom he can rob by fraud or violence. Money he must have, no matter how, if he is not to suffer torments.

All that is inevitable.

Now, just as a succession of new pleasures asserted themselves in his soul at the expense of the older ones, so this young man will claim the right to live at his parents' expense and help himself to their property when his own portion is spent. If they resist, he will first try to cheat them; and failing that, he will rob them by force. If the old people still hold out, will any scruple restrain him from behaving like a despot?

I should not have much hope for the parents of such a son.

And yet consider, Adeimantus: his father and mother have been bound to him by the closest ties all his life; and now that they are old and faded, would he really be ready to beat them for the sake of the charms of some new-found mistress or favourite who has no sort of claim on him? Is he going to bring these creatures under the same roof and let them lord it over his parents?

I believe he would.

It is no very enviable lot, then, to give birth to a despotic son.

It is not.

And now suppose that his parents' resources begin to fail, while his appetites for new pleasures have mustered into a great swarm in his soul; he will begin by breaking into someone's house or robbing a traveller by night, and go on to sweep some temple clean of its treasures. Meanwhile, the old approved beliefs about right and wrong which he had as a child will be overpowered by thoughts, once held in subjection, but now emancipated to second that master passion whose bodyguard they form. In his democratic days when he was still under the control of his father and of the laws, they broke loose only in sleep; but now that this passion has set up an absolute dominion, he has become for all his waking life the man he used to be from time to time in his dreams, ready to shed blood or eat forbidden food or do any dreadful deed. The desire that lives in him as sole ruler in a waste of lawless disrule will drive him, as a tyrant would drive his country, into any desperate venture which promises to maintain it with its horde of followers, some of whom evil communication has brought in from without, while others have been released from bondage by the same evil practices within. Is that a fair account of his manner of life? Yes.

If there are a few such characters in a country where most men are law-abiding, they will go elsewhere to join some despot's bodyguard or serve as mercenaries in any war that is toward. In quiet times of peace, they stay at home and commit crimes on a small scale, as thieves, burglars, pickpockets, temple-robbers, kidnappers; or, if they have a ready tongue, they may take to selling their services as informers and false witnesses.

Such crimes will be a small matter, you mean, so long as the criminals are few in number.

Small is a relative term; and all of them put together do not, as they say, come within sight of the degradation and misery of society under a despot. When the number of such criminals and their hangers-on increases and they become aware of their strength, then it is they who, helped by the folly of the common people, create the despot out of that one among their number whose soul is itself under the most tyrannical despotism.

Yes, such a state of mind would naturally be his best qualification.

All goes smoothly if men are ready to submit. But the country may resist; and then, just as he began by calling his father and mother to order, so now he will discipline his once loved fatherland, or motherland as the Cretans call it, and see that it shall live in subjection to the new-found partisans he has called in to enslave it. So this man's desires come to their fulfilment.

Yes, that is true.

In private life, before they gain power, men of this stamp either consort with none but parasites ready to do them any service, or, if they have a favour to beg, they will not hesitate themselves to cringe and posture in simulated friendliness, which soon cools off when their end is gained. So, throughout life, the despotic character has not a friend in the world; he is sometimes master, sometimes slave, but never knows true friendship or freedom. There is no faithfulness in him; and, if we were right in our notion of justice, he is the perfect example of the unjust man.

Certainly.

FRIEDRICH NIETZSCHE

Power and Liberation

Physiologists should think again before postulating the drive to self-preservation as the cardinal drive in an organic being. A living thing desires above all to *vent* its strength—life as such is will to power—: self-preservation is only one of the indirect and most frequent *consequences* of it.—In short, here as everywhere, beware of *superfluous* teleological principles!—such as is the drive to self-preservation (we owe it to Spinoza's inconsistency). For this is a requirement of method, which has essentially to be economy of principles. . . .

Few are made for independence—it is a privilege of the strong. And he who attempts it, having the completest right to it but without being *compelled* to, thereby proves that he is probably not only strong but also daring to the point of recklessness. He ventures into a labyrinth, he multiplies by a thousand the dangers which life as such already brings with it, not the smallest of which is that no one can behold how and where he goes astray, is cut off from others, and is torn to pieces limb from limb by some cave-minotaur of conscience. If such a one is destroyed, it takes place so far from the understanding of men that they neither feel it nor sympathize—and he can no longer go back! He can no longer go back even to the pity of men! . . .

Granted that nothing is "given" as real except our world of desires and passions, that we can rise or sink to no other "reality" than the reality of our drives—for thinking is only the relationship of these drives to one another—: is it not permitted to make the experiment and ask the question whether this which is given does not *suffice* for an understanding even of the so-called mechanical (or "material") world? I do not mean as a deception, an "appearance," an "idea" (in the Berkeleyan and Schopenhaueran sense), but as possessing the same degree of reality as our emotions themselves—as a more primitive form of the world of emotions in which everything still lies locked in mighty unity and then branches out and develops in the organic process (also, as is only fair, is made weaker and more sensitive), as a kind of instinctual life in which all organic functions, together with self-regulation, assimilation, nourishment, excretion, metabolism, are still synthetically bound together—as an *antecedent form* of life?—In the end, it is not merely permitted to make this experiment: it is commanded by the conscience of *method*. Not to assume several kinds of causality so long as the experiment of getting along with one has not been taken to its ultimate limits (—to the point of nonsense, if I may say so): that is a morality of method which one may not repudiate nowadays—it follows "from its definition," as a mathematician would say. In the end, the question is whether we really recognize will as *efficient*, whether we believe in the causality of will: if we do so—and fundamentally belief in *this* is precisely our belief in causality itself—then we *have* to make the experiment of positing causality of will hypothetically as the only one. "Will" can of course operate only on "will"—and not on "matter" (not on "nerves," for example—): enough, one must venture the hypothesis that wherever "effects" are recognized, will is operating upon will—and that all mechanical occurrences, in so far as a force is active in them, are force of will, effects of will.—Granted finally that one succeeded in explaining our entire instinctual life as the development and ramification of *one* basic form of will—as will to power, as is *my* theory—; granted that one could trace all organic functions back to this will to power and could also find in it the solution to the problem of procreation and nourishment—they are *one* problem—one would have acquired the right to define *all* efficient force unequivocally as: *will to power*. The world seen from within, the world described and defined according to its "intelligible character"—it would be "will to power" and nothing else. . . .

One must test oneself to see whether one is destined for independence and command; and one must do so at the proper time. One should not avoid one's tests, although they are perhaps the most dangerous game one could play and are in the end tests which are taken before ourselves and before no other judge. Not to cleave to another person, though he be the one you love most—every person is a prison, also a nook and corner. Not to cleave to a fatherland, though it be the most suffering and in need of help—it is already easier to sever your heart from a victorious fatherland. Not to cleave to a feeling of pity, though it be for higher men into whose rare torment and helplessness chance allowed us to look. Not to cleave to a science, though it lures one with the most precious discoveries seemingly reserved precisely for *us*. Not to cleave to one's own detachment, to that voluptuous remoteness and strangeness of the bird which flies higher and higher so as to see more and more beneath it—the danger which threatens the flier. Not to cleave to our own virtues and become as a whole the victim of some part of us, of our "hospitality" for example, which is the danger of dangers for rich and noble souls who expend themselves prodigally, almost indifferently, and take the virtue of liberality to the point where it becomes a vice. One must know how *to conserve oneself*: the sternest test of independence.

A new species of philosopher is appearing: I venture to baptize these philosophers with a name not without danger in it. As I divine them, as they let themselves be divined—for it pertains to their nature to *want* to remain a riddle in some respects—these philosophers of the future might rightly, but perhaps also wrongly, be described as *attempters*. This name itself is in the end only an attempt and, if you will, a temptation.

Are they new friends of "truth," these coming philosophers? In all probability: for all philosophers have hitherto loved their truths. But certainly they will not be dogmatists. It must offend their pride, and also their taste, if their truth is supposed to be a truth for everyman, which has hitherto been the secret desire and hidden sense of all dogmatic endeavours. "My judgement is *my* judgement: another cannot easily acquire a right to it"—such a philosopher of the future may perhaps say. One has to get rid of the bad taste of wanting to be in agreement with many. "Good" is no longer good when your neighbour takes it into his mouth. And how could there exist a "common good"! The expression is a self-contradiction: what can be common has ever but little value. In the end it must be as it is and has always been: great things are for the great, abysses for the profound, shudders and delicacies for the refined, and, in sum, all rare things for the rare. . . .

He who, prompted by some enigmatic desire, has, like me, long endeavoured to think pessimism through to the bottom and to redeem it from the half-Christian, half-German simplicity and narrowness with which it finally presented itself to this century, namely in the form of the Schopenhaueran philosophy; he who has really gazed with an Asiatic and more than Asiatic eye down into the most world-denying of all possible modes of thought—beyond good and evil had no longer, like Buddha and Schopenhauer, under the spell and illusion of morality—perhaps by that very act, and without really intending to, may have had his eyes opened to the opposite ideal: to the ideal of the most exuberant, most living and most world-affirming man, who has not only learned to get on and treat with all that was and is but who wants to have it again *as it was and is* to all eternity, insatibly calling out *da capo* not only to himself but to the whole piece and play, and not only to a play but fundamentally to him who needs precisely this play—and who makes its necessary: because he needs himself again and again—and makes himself necessary—What? And would this not be—*circulus vitiosus deus?* . . .

The philosopher as *we* understand him, we free spirits—as the man of the most comprehensive responsibility who has the conscience for the collective evolution of mankind: this philosopher will make use of the religions for his work of education and breeding, just as he will make use of existing political and economic conditions. The influence on selection and breeding, that is to say the destructive as well as the creative and formative influence which can be exercised with the aid of the religions, is manifold and various depending on the kind of men placed under their spell and protection. For the strong and independent prepared and predestined for command, in whom the art and reason of a ruling race is incarnated, religion is one more means of overcoming resistance so as to be able to rule: as a bond that unites together ruler and ruled and betrays and hands over to the former the consciences of the latter, all that is hidden and most intimate in them which would like to exclude itself from obedience; and if some natures

of such noble descent incline through lofty spirituality to a more withdrawn and meditative life and reserve to themselves only the most
refined kind of rule (over select disciples or brothers), then religion
can even be used as a means of obtaining peace from the noise and effort of *cruder* modes of government, and cleanliness from the *necessary*
dirt of all politics. Thus did the Brahmins, for example, arrange things:
with the aid of a religious organization they gave themselves the
power of nominating their kings for the people, while keeping and
feeling themselves aside and outside as men of higher and more than
kingly tasks. In the meantime, religion also gives a section of the ruled
guidance and opportunity for preparing itself for future rule and command; that is to say, those slowly rising orders and classes in which
through fortunate marriage customs the strength and joy of the will,
the will to self-mastery is always increasing—religion presents them
with sufficient instigations and temptations to take the road to higher
spirituality, to test the feelings of great self-overcoming, of silence and
solitude—asceticism and puritanism are virtually indispensable means
of education and·ennobling if a race wants to become master over its
origins in the rabble, and work its way up towards future rule. To ordinary men, finally, the great majority, who exist for service and general utility and who *may* exist only for that purpose, religion gives an
invaluable contentment with their nature and station, manifold peace
of heart, an ennobling of obedience, one piece of joy and sorrow more
to share with their fellows, and some transfiguration of the whole
everydayness, the whole lowliness, the whole half-bestial poverty of
their souls. Religion and the religious significance of life sheds sunshine over these perpetual drudges and makes their own sight tolerable to them, it has the effect which an Epicurean philosophy usually
has on sufferers of a higher rank, refreshing, refining, as it were *making the most use of* suffering, ultimately even sanctifying and justifying.
Perhaps nothing in Christianity and Buddhism is so venerable as their
art of teaching even the lowliest to set themselves through piety in an
apparently higher order of things and thus to preserve their contentment with the real order, within which they live hard enough lives—
and necessarily have to! . . .

To refrain from mutual injury, mutual violence, mutual exploitation,
to equate one's own will with that of another: this may in a certain
rough sense become good manners between individuals if the condi-

tions for it are present (namely if their strength and value standards are in fact similar and they both belong to *one* body). As soon as there is a desire to take this principle further, however, and if possible even as the *fundamental principle of society*, it at once reveals itself for what it is: as the will to the *denial* of life, as the principle of dissolution and decay. One has to think this matter thoroughly through to the bottom and resist all sentimental weakness: life itself is *essentially* appropriation, injury, overpowering of the strange and weaker, suppression, severity, imposition of one's own forms, incorporation and, at the least and mildest, exploitation—but why should one always have to employ precisely those words which have from of old been stamped with a slanderous intention? Even that body within which, as was previously assumed, individuals treat one another as equals—this happens in every healthy aristocracy—must, if it is a living and not a decaying body, itself do all that to other bodies which the individuals within it refrain from doing to one another: it will have to be the will to power incarnate, it will want to grow, expand, draw to itself, gain ascendancy—not out of any morality or immorality, but because it *lives*, and because life *is* will to power. On no point, however, is the common European consciousness more reluctant to learn than it is here; everywhere one enthuses, even under scientific disguises, about coming states of society in which there will be "no more exploitation"—that sounds to my ears like promising a life in which there will be no organic functions. "Exploitation" does not pertain to a corrupt or imperfect or primitive society: it pertains to the *essence* of the living thing as a fundamental organic function, it is a consequence of the intrinsic will to power which is precisely the will of life.—Granted this is a novelty as a theory—as a reality it is the *primordial fact* of all history: let us be at least that honest with ourselves!

In a tour of the many finer and coarser moralities which have ruled or still rule on earth I found certain traits regularly recurring together and bound up with one another: until at length two basic types were revealed and a basic distinction emerged. There is *master morality* and *slave morality*—I add at once that in all higher and mixed cultures attempts at mediation between the two are apparent and more frequently confusion and mutual misunderstanding between them, indeed sometimes their harsh juxtaposition—even within the same man, within *one* soul. The moral value-distinctions have arisen either among a ruling order which was pleasurably conscious of its distinction from the ruled—or among the ruled, the slaves and dependants of every degree. In the former case, when it is the rulers who determine the concept "good," it is the exalted, proud states of soul which are considered distinguishing and determine the order of rank. The noble human being separates from himself those natures in which the opposite of such exalted proud states find expression: he despises them. It should be noted at once that in this first type of morality the antithesis "good" and "bad" means the same thing as "noble" and "despicable"—the antithesis "good" and "evil" originates elsewhere. The cowardly, the timid, the petty, and those who think only of narrow utility are despised; as are the mistrustful with their constricted glance, those who abase themselves, the dog-like type of man who lets himself be mistreated, the fawning flatterer, above all the liar—it is a fundamental belief of all aristocrats that the common people are liars. "We who are truthful"—thus did the nobility of ancient Greece designate themselves. It is immediately obvious that designations of moral value were everywhere first applied to *human beings,* and only later and derivatively to *actions:* which is why it is a grave error when moral historians start from such questions as "why has the compassionate action been praised?" The noble type of man feels *himself* to be the determiner of values, he does not need to be approved of, he judges "what harms me is harmful in itself," he knows himself to be that which in general first accords honour to things, he *creates values.* Everything he knows to be part of himself, he honours: such a morality is self-glorification. In the foreground stands the feeling of plenitude, of power which seeks to overflow, the happiness of high tension, the consciousness of a wealth which would like to give away and bestow—the noble human being too aids the unfortunate but not, or almost not, from pity, but more from an urge begotten by superfluity of power. The noble human being honours in himself the man of power, also the man who has power over himself, who understands how to speak and how to keep silent, who enjoys practising severity and harshness upon himself and feels reverence for all that is severe and harsh. "A hard heart has Wotan set in my breast," it says in an old Scandinavian saga: a just expression coming from the soul of a proud Viking. A man of this type is actually proud that he is *not* made for pity: which is why the hero of the saga adds as a warning: "he whose heart is not hard in youth will never have a hard heart." Brave and noble men who think that are at the farthest remove from that morality which sees the mark of the moral precisely in pity or in acting for others or in *désintéressement;* belief in oneself, pride in oneself, a fundamental hostility and irony for "selflessness" belong just as definitely to noble morality as does a mild contempt for and caution against sympathy and the "warm heart."—It is the powerful who *understand* how to honor, that is their art, their realm of invention. Deep reverence for age and the traditional—all law rests on this twofold reverence—belief in and prejudice in favour of ancestors and against descendants, is typical of the morality of the powerful; and when, conversely, men of "modern ideas" believe almost instinctively in "progress" and "the future" and show an increasing lack of respect for age, this reveals clearly enough the ignoble origin of these "ideas." A morality of the rulers is, however, most alien and painful to contemporary taste in the severity of its principle that one has duties only towards one's equals; that toward beings of a lower rank, towards everything alien, one may act as one wishes or "as the heart dictates" and in any case "beyond good and evil"—:it is here that pity and the like can have a place. The capacity for and the duty of protracted gratitude and protracted revenge—both only among one's equals—subtlety in requittal, a refined conception of friendship, a certain need to have enemies (as conduit systems, as it were, for the emotions of envy, quarrelsomeness, arrogance—fundamentally so as to be able to be a good *friend*): all these are typical marks of noble morality which, as previously indicated, is not the morality of "modern ideas" and is therefore hard to enter into today, also hard to unearth and uncover.— It is otherwise with the second type of morality, *slave morality.* Suppose the abused, oppressed, suffering, unfree, those uncertain of themselves and weary should moralize: what would their moral evaluations have in common? Probably a pessimistic mistrust of the entire situation of man will find expression, perhaps a condemnation of man together with his situation. The slave is suspicious of the virtues of the powerful: he is sceptical and mistrustful, *keenly* mistrustful, of everything "good" that is honoured among them—he would like to convince himself that happiness itself is not genuine among them. On the other hand, those qualities which serve to make easier the existence of the suffering will be brought into prominence and flooded with light: here it is that pity, the kind and helping hand, the warm heart, patience, industriousness, humility, friendliness come into honour—for here these are the most useful qualities and virtually the only means of enduring the burden of existence. Slave morality is essentially the morality of utility. Here is the source of the famous antithesis "good" and *"evil"*—power and danger were felt to exist in evil, a certain dreadfulness, subtlety and strength which could not admit of contempt. Thus, according to slave morality the "evil" inspire fear; according to master morality it is precisely the "good" who inspire fear and want to inspire it, while the "bad" man is judged contemptible. The antithesis reaches its height when, consistently with slave morality, a breath of disdain finally also comes to be attached to the "good" of this morality—it may be a slight and benevolent disdain—because within the slaves' way of thinking the good man has in any event to be a *harmless* man: he is good-natured, easy to deceive, perhaps a bit stupid, *un bonhomme*. Wherever slave morality comes to predominate, language exhibits a tendency to bring the words "good" and "stupid" closer to each other.—A final fundamental distinction: the longing for *freedom*, the instinct for the happiness and the refinements of the feeling of freedom, belong just as necessarily to slave morality and morals as the art of reverence and devotion and the enthusiasm for them are the regular symptom of an aristocratic mode of thinking and valuating.—This makes it clear without further ado why love *as passion*—it is our European speciality—absolutely must be of aristocratic origin: it was, as is well known, invented by the poet-knights of Provence, those splendid, inventive men of the *"gai saber"* to whom Europe owes so much and, indeed, almost itself. . . .

To live with a tremendous and proud self-possession; always beyond—. To have and not have one's emotions, one's for and against, at will, to condescend to have them for a few hours; to *seat* oneself on them as on horses, often as on asses—for one has to know how to employ their stupidity as well as their fire. To keep one's three hundred foregrounds; also one's dark glasses: for there are instances where no one may look into our eyes, still less into our "grounds." And to choose for company that cheerful and roguish vice, politeness. And to remain master of one's four virtues, courage, insight, sympathy, solitude. For solitude is with us a virtue: it is a sublime urge and inclination for cleanliness which divines that all contact between man and man—"in society"—must inevitably be unclean. All community makes somehow, somewhere, sometime—"common."

Power and Non-violence

The Doctrine of the Sword

I do believe that, where there is only a choice between cowardice and violence, I would advise violence. Thus when my eldest son asked me what he should have done, had he been present when I was almost fatally assaulted in 1908, whether he should have run away and seen me killed or whether he should have used his physical force which he could and wanted to use, and defended me, I told him that it was his duty to defend me even by using violence. Hence it was that I took part in the Boer War, the so-called Zulu Rebellion and the late War. Hence also do I advocate training in arms for those who believe in the method of violence. I would rather have India resort to arms in order to defend her honour than that she would, in a cowardly manner, become or remain a helpless witness to her own dishonour.

But I believe that non-violence is infinitely superior to violence, forgiveness is more manly than punishment. Forgiveness adorns a soldier. But abstinence is forgiveness only when there is the power to punish; it is meaningless when it pretends to proceed from a helpless creature. A mouse hardly forgives a cat when it allows itself to be torn to pieces by her. I therefore appreciate the sentiment of those who cry out for the condign punishment of General Dyer and his ilk. They would tear him to pieces, if they could. But I do not believe India to be helpless. I do not believe myself to be a helpless creature. Only I want to use India's and my strength for a better purpose.

Let me not be misunderstood. Strength does not come from physical capacity. It comes from an indomitable will. An average Zulu is any way more than a match for an average Englishman in bodily capacity. But he flees from an English boy, because he fears the boy's revolver or those who will use it for him. He fears death and is nerveless in spite of his burly figure. We in India may in a moment realize that one hundred thousand Englishmen need not frighten three hundred million human beings. A definite forgiveness would, therefore, mean a definite recognition of our strength. With enlightened forgiveness must come a mighty wave of strength in us, which would make it impossible for a Dyer and a Frank Johnson to heap affront on India's devoted head. It matters little to me that for the moment I do not drive my point home. We feel too downtrodden not to be angry and revengeful. But I must not refrain from saying that India can gain more by waiving the right of punishment. We have better work to do, a better mission to deliver to the world.

I am not a visionary. I claim to be a practical idealist. The religion of non-violence is not meant merely for the *rishis* and saints. It is meant for the common people as well. Non-violence is the law of our species as violence is the law of the brute. The spirit lies dormant in the brute, and he knows no law but that of physical might. The dignity of man requires obedience to a higher law—to the strength of the spirit.

I have therefore ventured to place before India the ancient law of self-sacrifice. For *satyagraha* and its offshoots, non-cooperation and civil resistance, are nothing but new names for the law of suffering. The *rishis*, who discovered the law of non-violence in the midst of violence, were greater geniuses than Newton. They were themselves greater warriors than Wellington. Having themselves known the use of arms, they realized their uselessness, and taught a weary world that its salvation lay not through violence but through non-violence.

Non-violence in its dynamic condition means conscious suffering. It does not mean meek submission to the will of the evil-doer, but it means putting of one's whole soul against the will of the tyrant. Working under this law of our being, it is possible for a single individual to defy the whole might of an unjust empire to save his honour, his religion, his soul, and lay the foundation for that empire's fall or its regeneration. . . .

Everyone must act on his own responsibility, and interpret the Congress creed to the best of his ability and belief. I have often noticed that weak people have taken shelter under the Congress creed or under my advice, when they have simply, by reason of their coward-ice, been unable to defend their own honour or that of those who were entrusted to their care. I recall the incident that happened near Bettiah when non-cooperation was at its height. Some villagers were looted. They had fled, leaving their wives, children and belongings to the mercy of the looters. When I rebuked them for their cowardice in thus neglecting their charge, they shamelessly pleaded non-violence. I pub-licly denounced their conduct and said that my non-violence fully ac-commodated violence offered by those who did not feel non-violence and who had in their keeping the honour of their womenfolk and little children. Non-violence is not a cover for cowardice, but it is the su-preme virtue of the brave. Exercise of non-violence requires far greater bravery than that of swordsmanship. Cowardice is wholly inconsistent with non-violence. Translation from swordsmanship to non-violence is possible and, at times, even an easy stage. Non-violence, therefore, presupposes ability to strike. It is a conscious deliberate restraint put upon one's desire for vengeance. But vengeance is any day superior to passive, effeminate and helpless submission. Forgiveness is higher still. Vengeance too is weakness. The desire for vengeance comes out of fear of harm, imaginary or real. A dog barks and bites when he fears. A man who fears no one on earth would consider it too trouble-some even to summon up anger against one who is vainly trying to in-jure him. The sun does not wreak vengeance upon little children who throw dust at him. They only harm themselves in the act. . . .

Non-resistance True and False

America is the house of the inter-racial conflict on a vast scale. There are earnest men and women in that land of enterprises who are seek-ing to solve the difficult problem along the lines of non-resistance. One such American friend sends me a paper called *The Inquiry* which contains an interesting discussion on the doctrine of non-resistance. It consists of instances that might possibly be grouped under non-resistancce. I select three samples:

A Chinese student related his experience at the State University from which he was about to graduate. His reception there had been anything but friendly for the most part, although a few men had gone out of their way to befriend him, one of them even inviting the Chinese to his home for a weekend. On the other hand, a fellow student who occupied a room next to his made him-self particularly obnoxious, throwing shoes against his door and indulging in other pranks. The Chinese overheard this student express horror on finding that an American had taken him home to introduce him to his mother and sis-ter, and immediately he made up his mind that he would teach this student to respect him, not for his own sake, but for the sake of his dear motherland.

So he went out of his way to be friendly to his neighbour. Every day he gave him a smiling good morning, though at first he received no response. He ignored every insult, but tried to make himself pleasant and useful. When he knew his neighbour to be hard up he casually invited him to go to a movie with him. Gradually they talked together more often and found they had sev-eral interests in common. After a while this student invited him to his home.

"We have become warm friends," concluded the Chinese. "I have since spent many holidays and week-ends at his home; and on leaving the univer-sity I shall know that one of my fellow students at least will regretfully miss me."

The Secretary of a railroad Young Men's Christian Association brought one evening into the building twelve Danes, working on the railroad who had no place to sleep. The English-speaking men, under the sway of racial antipathy, began to object, and protested against the foreigners being brought in. Among these newcomers, however, was a skilled musician who, while the Americans were presenting their objections to the secretary, began to play up on the accordian. He discoursed sweet music, which soon had its effect. The ire on the faces of the native-born soon began to vanish; the censure died on their lips; their hearts were softened; and that night they sat up late listening to the foreigner playing. (Peter Roberts, *The New Immigration*. The Macmillan Co., 1922, p. 300.)

There is a colony of Japanese in X, California. Several years ago some real es-tate agents sought to sell a considerable amount of land to other Japanese, and the white people were aroused at the thought of a great influx of these people. Meetings were held, and a big sign was put up on the main boulevard which read: "No Japanese wanted here."

The old resident Japanese of X, who had lived on good terms with the white people, being members of their Farmers' Association, went to the white peo-ple, and after consultation finally agreed with them that a further increase in the Japanese population would not be a good thing. The sign was changed to read: "No more Japanese wanted here."

The person who tells this story contends that this action advanced the soli-darity of the community, and improved the relations between the whites and the Japanese in that place, as witness the following:

The Japanese of X, learning that the American church was in financial dif-ficulties, offered to give a definite amount yearly for its support, in addition to carrying on their own Japanese church work.

Now the first easily comes under true non-resistance. The second is more an instance of presence of mind than non-resistance. The third, from the facts as stated, is an instance, if not of cowardice as contended by some of the debators, certainly of selfishness. The resident Japanese population, in order to retain their earthly possessions, agreed to the prohibition of further Japanese immigration. It may have been sound policy. It may have been the only policy advisable. But it was not non-resistance.

Non-resistance is restraint voluntarily undertaken for the good of society. It is, therefore, an intensely active, purifying, inward force. It is often antagonistic to the material good of the non-resister. It may even mean his utter material ruin. It is rooted in internal strength, never weakness. It must be consciously exercised. It therefore presupposes ability to offer physical resistance. In the last instance, therefore, the Japanese would have non-resisted, if they had left all their possessions rather than surrendered the rights of prospective immigrants. They might also have suffered death or lynching without even mental retaliation and thus melted the hearts of their persecutors. It was not victory of truth that without any inconvenience to themselves they were able to retain their property. In terms of non-resistance, their contribution to the American Church in its difficulty was a bribe, by no means a token of goodwill or a free gift.

The acquisition of the spirit of non-resistance is a matter of long training in self-denial and appreciation of the hidden forces within ourselves. It changes one's outlook upon life. It puts different values upon things and upsets previous calculations, and when once it is intensive enough can overtake the whole universe. It is the greatest force because it is the highest expression of the soul. All need not possess the same measure of conscious non-resistance for its full operations. It is enough for one person only to possess it, even as one general is enough to regulate and dispose of the energy of millions of soldiers who enlist under his banner, even though they know not the why and the wherefore of his dispositions. The monkeys of one Rama were enough to confound the innumerable hosts armed from head to foot of the ten-headed Ravana. . . .

It would be cowardly of a neutral country to allow an army to devastate a neighbouring country. But there are two ways in common between soldiers of war and soldiers of non-violence, and if I had been a citizen of Switzerland and a President of the Federal State, what I would have done would be to refuse passage to the invading army by refusing all supplies. Secondly, by re-enacting a Thermopylae in Switzerland, you would have presented a living wall of men and women and children, and inviting the invaders to walk over your corpses. You may say that such a thing is beyond human experience and endurance. I say that it is not so. It was quite possible. Last year in Gujarat women stood *lathi* charges unflinchingly, and in Peshawar thousands stood hails of bullets without resorting to violence. Imagine these men and women staying in front of an army requiring a safe passage to another country. The army would be brutal enough to walk over them, you might say. I would then say, you will still have done your duty by allowing yourself to be annihilated. An army that dares to pass over the corpses of innocent men and women would not be able to repeat that experiment. You may, if you wish, refuse to believe in such courage on the part of the masses of men and women, but then you would have to admit that non-violence is made of sterner stuff. It was never conceived as a weapon of the weak, but of the stoutest hearts.

Q. Is it open to a soldier to fire in the air and avoid violence?

A. A soldier, who having enlisted himself flattered himself that he was avoiding violence by shooting in the air, did no credit to his courage or to his creed of non-violence. In my scheme of things such a man would be held to be guilty of untruth and cowardice both— cowardice in that in order to escape punishment he enlisted, and untruth in that he enlisted to serve as soldier and did not fire as expected. Such a thing discredits the cause of waging war against war. The war-resisters have to be like Caesar's wife—above suspicion. Their strength lies in absolute adherence to the morality of the question. . . .

Five Axioms

Let me lay down five simple axioms of non-violence as I know it:

1. Non-violence implies as complete self-purification as is humanly possible.
2. Man for man the strength of non-violence is in exact proportion to the ability, not the will, of the non-violent person to inflict violence.
3. Non-violence is without exception superior to violence, i.e. the power at the disposal of a non-violent person is always greater than he would have if he was violent.

4. There is no such thing as defeat in non-violence. The end of violence is surest defeat.
5. The ultimate end of non-violence is surest victory—if such a term may be used of non-violence. In reality, where there is no sense of defeat, there is no sense of victory. . . . .

A Talk on Non-violence

Now the talk centered on a discussion which was the main thing that had drawn the distinguished members to Gandhiji.

"Is non-violence from your point of view a form of direct action?" inquired Dr. Thurman. "It is not one form, it is the only form," said Gandhiji. "I do not of course confine the words 'direct action' to their technical meaning. But without a direct active expression of it, non-violence to my mind is meaningless. It is the greatest and the activest force in the world. One cannot be passively non-violent. In fact 'non-violence' is a term I had to coin in order to bring out the root meaning of *ahimsa*. In spite of the negative particle 'non,' it is no negative force. Superficially we are surrounded in life by strife and bloodshed, life living upon life. But some great seer, who ages ago penetrated the center of truth, said: It is not through strife and violence but through non-violence that man can fulfil his destiny and his duty to his fellow creatures. It is a force which is more positive than electricity, and more powerful than even ether. At the centre of non-violence is a force which is self-acting. *Ahimsa* means 'love' in the Pauline sense, and yet something more than the 'love' defined by St. Paul, although I know St. Paul's beautiful definition is good enough for all practical purposes. *Ahimsa* includes the whole creation, and not only human. Besides 'love' in the English language has other connotations, and so I was compelled to use the negative word. But it does not, as I have told you, express a negative force, but a force superior to all the forces put together. One person who can express *ahimsa* in life exercises a force superior to all the forces of brutality."

Q. And is it possible for any individual to achieve this?

Gandhiji: Certainly. If there was any exclusiveness about it, I should reject it at once.

Q. Is any idea of possession foreign to it?

Gandhiji: Yes. It possesses nothing, therefore it possesses everything.

Q. Is it possible for a single human being to resist the persistent invasion of the quality successfully?

Gandhiji: It is possible. Perhaps your question is more universal than you mean. Isn't it possible, you mean to ask, for one single Indian, for instance, to resist the exploitation of 300 million Indians? Or do you mean the onslaught of the whole world against a single individual personally?

Dr. Thurman: Yes, that is one half of the question. I wanted to know if one man can hold the whole violence at bay.

Gandhiji: If he cannot, you must take it that he is not a true representative of *ahimsa*. Supposing I cannot produce a single instance in life of a man who truly converted his adversary, I would then say that it is because no one had yet been found to express *ahimsa* in its fulness.

Q. Then it overrides all other forces?

Gandhiji: Yes, it is the only true force in life.

"Forgive now the weakness of this question," said Dr. Thurman, who was absolutely absorbed in the discussion. "Forgive the weakness, but may I ask how are we to train individuals or communities in this difficult art?"

Gandhiji: There is no royal road, except through living the creed in your life which must be a living sermon. Of course, the expression in one's own life presupposes great study, tremendous perseverance, and thorough cleansing of one's self of all the impurities. If for mastering of the physical sciences you have to devote a whole lifetime, how many lifetimes may be needed for mastering the greatest spiritual force that mankind has known? But why worry even if it means several lifetimes? For, if this is the only permanent thing in life, if this is the only thing that counts, then whatever effort you bestow on mastering it is well spent. Seek ye first the Kingdom of Heaven and everything else shall be added unto you. The Kingdom of Heaven is *ahimsa*.

Mrs. Thurman had restrained herself until now. But she could not go away without asking the question with which, she knew, she would be confronted any day. "How am I to act, supposing my own brother was lynched before my very eyes?"

"There is such a thing as self-immolation," said Gandhiji. "Supposing I was a Negro, and my sister was ravished by a White or lynched by a whole community, what would be my duty?—I ask myself. And the answer comes to me: I must not wish ill to these, but neither must I co-operate with them. It may be that ordinarily I depend on the lynching community for my livelihood. I refuse to co-operate with them, refuse even to touch the food that comes from them, and I refuse to co-operate with even my brother Negroes who tolerate the wrong. That is the self-immolation I mean. I have often in my life resorted to the plan. Of course a mechanical act of starvation will mean nothing. One's faith must remain undimmed whilst life ebbs out minute by minute. But I am a very poor specimen of the practice of non-violence, and my answer may not convince you. But I am striving very hard, and even if I do not succeed fully in this life, my faith will not diminish."

The Power of Acceptance

On Things in Our Power
and Things Not in Our Power

Of our faculties in general you will find that none can take cognizance of itself; none therefore has the power to approve or disapprove its own action. Our grammatical faculty for instance: how far can that take cognizance? Only so far as to distinguish expression. Our musical faculty? Only so far as to distinguish tune. Does any one of these then take cognizance of itself? By no means. If you are writing to your friend, when you want to know what words to write grammar will tell you; but whether you should write to your friend or should not write grammar will not tell you. And in the same way music will tell you about tunes, but whether at this precise moment you should sing and play the lyre or should not sing nor play the lyre it will not tell you. What will tell you then? That faculty which takes cognizance of itself and of all things else. What is this? The reasoning faculty: for this alone of the faculties we have received is created to comprehend even its own nature; that is to say, what it is and what it can do, and with what precious qualities it has come to us, and to comprehend all other faculties as well. For what else is it that tells us that gold is a goodly thing? For the gold does not tell us. Clearly it is the faculty which can deal with our impressions. What else is it which distinguishes the faculties of music, grammar, and the rest, testing their uses and pointing out the due seasons for their use? It is reason and nothing else.

The gods then, as was but right, put in our hands the one blessing that is best of all and master of all, that and nothing else, the power to deal rightly with our impressions, but everything else they did not put in our hands. Was it that they would not? For my part I think that if they could have entrusted us with those other powers as well they would have done so, but they were quite unable. Prisoners on the earth and in an earthly body and among earthly companions, how was it possible that we should not be hindered from the attainment of these powers by these external fetters?

But what says Zeus? "Epictetus, if it were possible I would have made your body and your possessions (those trifles that you prize) free and untrammelled. But as things are—never forget this—this body is not yours, it is but a clever mixture of clay. But since I could not make it free, I gave you a portion in our divinity, this faculty of impulse to act and not to act, of will to get and will to avoid, in a word the faculty which can turn impressions to right use. If you pay heed to this, and put your affairs in its keeping, you will never suffer let nor hindrance, you will not groan, you will blame no man, you will flatter none. What then? Does all this seem but little to you?"

Heaven forbid!

"Are you content then?"

So surely as I hope for the gods' favour.

But, as things are, though we have it in our power to pay heed to one thing and to devote ourselves to one, yet instead of this we prefer to pay heed to many things and to be bound fast to many—our body, our property, brother and friend, child and slave. Inasmuch then as we are bound fast to many things, we are burdened by them and dragged down. That is why, if the weather is bad for sailing, we sit distracted and keep looking continually and ask, "What wind is blowing?" "The north wind." What have we to do with that? "When will the west wind blow?" When it so chooses, good sir, or when Aeolus chooses. For God made Aeolus the master of the winds, not you. What follows? We must make the best of those things that are in our power, and take the rest as nature gives it. What do you mean by "nature"? I mean, God's will.

"What? Am I to be beheaded now, and I alone?"

Why? Would you have had all beheaded, to give you consolation? Will you not stretch out your neck as Lateranus did in Rome when Nero ordered his beheadal? For he stretched out his neck and took the blow, and when the blow dealt him was too weak he shrank up a little and then stretched it out again. Nay more, on a previous occasion, when Nero's freedman Epaphroditus came to him and asked him the cause of his offence, he answered, "If I want to say anything, I will say it to your master."

What then must a man have ready to help him in such emergencies? Surely this: he must ask himself, "What is mine, and what is not mine? What may I do, what may I not do?"

I must die. But must I die groaning? I must be imprisoned. But must I whine as well? I must suffer exile. Can any one then hinder me from going with a smile, and a good courage, and at peace?

"Tell the secret!"

I refuse to tell, for this is in my power.

"But I will chain you."

What say you, fellow? Chain me? My leg you will chain—yes, but my will—no, not even Zeus can conquer that.

"I will imprison you."

My bit of a body, you mean.

"I will behead you."

Why? When did I ever tell you that I was the only man in the world that could not be beheaded?

These are the thoughts that those who pursue philosophy should ponder, these are the lessons they should write down day by day, in these they should exercise themselves.

Thrasea used to say "I had rather be killed to-day than exiled tomorrow." What then did Rufus say to him? "If you choose it as the harder, what is the meaning of your foolish choice? If as the easier, who has given you the easier? Will you not study to be content with what is given you?"

It was in this spirit that Agrippinus used to say—do you know what? "I will not stand in my own way!" News was brought him, "Your trial is on in the Senate!" "Good luck to it, but the fifth hour is come"—this was the hour when he used to take his exercise and have a cold bath—"let us go and take exercise." When he had taken his exercise they came and told him, "You are condemned." "Exile or death?" he asked. "Exile." "And my property?" "It is not confiscated." "Well then, let us go to Aricia and dine."

Here you see the result of training as training should be, of the will to get and will to avoid, so disciplined that nothing can hinder or frustrate them. I must die, must I? If at once, then I am dying: if soon, I dine now, as it is time for dinner, and afterwards when the time comes I will die. And die how? As befits one who gives back what is not his own. . . .

How One Should Behave Towards Tyrants

If a man possesses some advantage, or thinks he does though he does not, he is bound, if he be uneducated, to be puffed up because of it. The tyrant, for instance, says, "I am mightiest of all men."

Well, and what can you give me? Can you enable me to get what I will to get? How can you? Can you avoid what you will to avoid, independent of circumstances? Is your impulse free from error? How can you claim any such power?

Tell me, on shipboard, do you put confidence in yourself or in the man who knows? And in a chariot? Surely in him who knows. How is it in other arts? Exactly the same. What does your power come to then?

"All men pay me attention."

Yes, and I pay attention to my platter and work it and polish it and I fix up a peg for my oil-flask. Does that mean that these are superior to me? No, but they do me some service, and for this reason I pay them attention. Again: do I not pay attention to my ass? Do I not wash his feet? Do I not curry him? Do you not know that every man pays regard to himself, and to you only as to his ass? For who pays regard to you as a man? Show me. Who wishes to become like you? Who regards you as one like Socrates to admire and follow?

"But I can behead you."

Well said. I forgot, of course, one ought to pay you worship as if you were fever or cholera, and raise an altar to you, like the altar to Fever in Rome.

What is it then which disturbs and confounds the multitude? Is it the tyrant and his guards? Nay, God forbid! It is impossible for that which is free by nature to be disturbed or hindered by anything but itself. It is a man's own judgements which disturb him. For when the tyrant says to a man, "I will chain your leg," he that values his leg says, "Nay, have mercy," but he that values his will says, "If it seems more profitable to you, chain it."

"Do you pay no heed?"

No, I pay no heed.

"I will show you that I am master."

How can you? Zeus gave me my freedom. Or do you think that he was likely to let his own son be enslaved? You are master of my dead body, take it.

"Do you mean that when you approach me, you pay no respect to me?"

No, I only pay respect to myself: if you wish me to say that I pay respect to you too, I tell you that I do so, but only as I pay respect to my water-pot.

This is not mere self-love: for it is natural to man, as to other creatures, to do everything for his own sake; for even the sun does everything for its own sake, and in a word so does Zeus himself. But when he would be called "The Rain-giver" and "Fruit-giver" and "Father of men and gods," you see that he cannot win these names or do these works unless he does some good to the world at large: and in general he has so created the nature of the rational animal, that he can attain nothing good for himself, unless he contributes some service to the community. So it turns out that to do everything for his own sake is not unsocial. For what do you expect? Do you expect a man to hold aloof from himself and his own interest? No: we cannot ignore the one principle of action which governs all things—to be at unity with themselves.

What follows? When men's minds harbour wrong opinions on things beyond the will, counting them good and evil, they are bound to pay regard to tyrants. Would that it were only tyrants, and not chamberlains too! How can a man possibly grow wise of a sudden, when Caesar appoints him to the charge of the privy? How is it we straightway say, "Felicio has spoken wisely to me"? I would fain have him deposed from the dung-heap, that he may seem foolish to you again. Epaphroditus had a shoemaker, whom he sold because he was useless: then by some chance he was bought by one of Caesar's officials, and became Caesar's shoemaker. If you could have seen how Epaphroditus honoured him. "How is my good Felicio, I pray you?" Then if some one asked us, "What is your master doing?" the answer was, "He is consulting Felicio about something." What, had he not sold him for useless? Who has suddenly made a wise man of him? This is what comes of honouring anything outside one's will.

He has been honoured with a tribuneship. All who meet him congratulate him; one kisses his eyes, another his neck, his slaves kiss his hands. He comes into his house and finds lamps being lighted. He goes up to the Capitol and offers sacrifice. Who, I ask you, ever offered sacrifice in gratitude for right direction of the will or for impulse in accordance with nature? For we give thanks to the gods for what we think our good!

To-day one spoke to me about the priesthood of Augustus. I told him, "Fellow, leave the thing alone; you will spend a great deal on nothing."

"Well, but those who draw up contracts will record my name."

Can you be there when men read it and say to them, "That is my name," and even supposing you can be there now, what will you do if you die?

"My name will remain."

Write it on a stone and it will remain. But who will remember you outside Nicopolis?

"But I shall wear a golden crown."

If you desire a crown at all, take a crown of roses and wear that: you will look smarter in that. . . .

Concerning Anxiety

When I see a man in a state of anxiety, I say, "What can this man want?" If he did not want something which is not in his power, how could he still be anxious? It is for this reason that one who sings to the lyre is not anxious when he is performing by himself, but when he enters the theatre, even if he has a very good voice and plays well: for he not only wants to perform well, but also to win a great name, and that is beyond his own control.

In fact, where he has knowledge there he has confidence. Bring in any unskilled person you like, and he pays no heed to him. On the other hand he is anxious whenever he has no knowledge and has made no study of the subject. What does this mean? He does not know what "the people" is, nor what its praise is worth: he has learnt to strike the bottom note or the top note, but he does not know what the praise of the multitude is, nor what value it has in life; he has made no study of that. So he is bound to tremble and grow pale.

When I see a man, then, in this state of fear I cannot say that he is no performer with the lyre, but I can say something else of him, and not one thing but many. And first of all I call him a stranger and say, This man does not know where in the world he is; though he has been with us so long, he does not know the laws and customs of the City—what he may do and what he may not do—no, nor has he called in a lawyer at any time to tell him and explain to him what are the requirements of the law. Of course he does not draw up a will without knowing how he ought to draw it up, or without calling in one who knows, nor does he lightly put his seal to a guarantee or give a written security; but he calls in no lawyer when he is exercising the will to get and will to avoid, impulse and intention and purpose. What do I mean by "having no lawyer"? I mean that he does not know that he is wishing to have what is not given him, and wishing not to have what he cannot avoid, and he does not know what is his own and what is not his own. If he did know, he would never feel hindrance or constraint or anxiety; how could he? Does any one fear about things which are not evil?

"No."

Or again about things which are evil but are in his power to prevent?

"Certainly not."

If, then, nothing beyond our will's control is either good or evil, and everything within our will's control depends entirely on ourselves, so that no one can take any such thing away from us or win it for us against our will, what room is left for anxiety? Yet we are anxious for our bit of a body, for our bit of property, for what Caesar will think, but are not anxious at all for what is within us. Am I anxious about not conceiving a false thought? No, for that depends on myself.

Or about indulging an impulse contrary to nature?

No, not about this either. So, when you see a man pale, just as the physician, judging from his colour, says, "This man's spleen is out of order, or that man's liver," so do you say, "This man is disordered in the will to get and the will to avoid, he is not in the right way, he is feverish"; for nothing else changes the complexion and causes a man to tremble and his teeth to chatter.

and droop the knee and sink upon his feet.

[Homer, *Iliad*, XIII, 281]

Concerning Attachment

What happens then if your friends there die?

What else except that mortal men have died? How can you wish at the same time to grow old and not to see the death of any that you love? Do you not know that in the long course of time many events of divers sorts must happen? One man must be overcome by fever, another by a robber, a third by a despot. For such is the nature of the atmosphere about us, and of our companions; cold and heat and unsuitable food, and travel by land, and sea, and winds and manifold perils destroy one man and send another into exile, and another they send on an embassy or as a soldier. Sit still then with your wits dazed at all these things—mourning, unfortunate, miserable, depending on something other than yourself—not one thing or two, but things innumerable.

Is this what your lesson comes to, is this what you learnt in the philosopher's school? Do you not know that life is a soldier's service? One man must keep guard, another go out to reconnoitre, another take the field. It is not possible for all to stay where they are, nor is it better so. But you neglect to fulfil the orders of the general and complain, when some severe order is laid upon you; you do not understand to what a pitiful state you are bringing the army so far as in you lies; you do not see that if all follow your example there will be no one to dig a trench, or raise a palisade, no one to keep night watch or fight in the field, but every one will seem an unserviceable soldier.

Again, if you go as a sailor on shipboard, keep to one place and hold fast to that; if you are called on to climb the mast, refuse, if to run out on the bows, refuse that. Why, what ship's master will put up with you, and not fling you overboard like a useless bit of furniture, a mere hindrance and bad example to the other sailors? So too it is in the world; each man's life is a campaign, and a long and varied one. It is for you to play the soldier's part—do everything at the General's bidding, divining His wishes, if it be possible. For there is no comparison between that General and the ordinary one in power and superiority of character. You are set in an imperial City and not in some humble town; you are always a senator. Do you not know that such a one can attend but little to his own household? He must spend most of his time abroad, in command or under command, or as subordinate to some officer, or as soldier or judge? And yet you tell me you want to be attached like a plant and rooted in the same place?

"Yes, for it is pleasant."

Who denies it? Dainties are pleasant too, and a beautiful woman is a pleasant thing. Your talk is the talk of those who make pleasure their end.

Do you not realize whose language you are using, the language of Epicureans and abandoned creatures? and yet though your actions and your principles are theirs, you quote to us the words of Zeno and Socrates? Fling away from you, as far as may be, these alien properties that you adorn yourself with, and that do not fit you! People of that sort have no wish except to sleep without hindrance or compulsion, and then to get up and yawn at their ease and wash their face, then to write and read at their pleasure, then to talk nonsense and be complimented by their friends, whatever they say, then to go out for a walk and after a little walk to have a bath, then to eat, and then go to sleep—the sort of sleep men of that kind are likely to indulge in—I need say no more—you may judge what it is. . . .

"How then am I to prove myself affectionate?"

In a noble and not a miserable spirit. For it is against all reason to be of an abject and broken spirit and to depend on another and to blame God or man. Prove yourself affectionate, but see that you observe these rules; if this affection of yours, or whatever you call it, is going to make you a miserable slave, it is not for your good to be affectionate. Nay, what prevents you loving a man as one who is mortal and bound to leave you? Did not Socrates love his children? Yes, but as one who is free and bears in mind that the love of the gods stands first, and therefore he failed in none of the duties of a good man, either in his defence, or in assessing his penalty, or earlier still as a member of the council or a soldier in the field. But we abound in every kind of excuse for a mean spirit; with some of us it is a child, with others our mother or our brothers. We ought not to let any one make us miserable, but let every one make us happy, and God above all, Who created us for this. Go to, did Diogenes love no one, he who was so gentle and kind-hearted that he cheerfully took upon him all those troubles and distresses of body for the general good of men? But how did he love? As the servant of Zeus should love, caring for his friends, but submitting himself to God. That was why he alone made the whole world his country, and no special land, and when he was made prisoner he did not long for Athens or for his friends and companions there, but made himself at home with the pirates who took him and tried to make them better, and afterwards when he was sold he lived in Corinth just as he lived before in Athens; yes, and if he had gone away to the Perrhaebians it would have been just the same. That is how freedom is achieved. That is why he said, "Since Antisthenes freed me, I have ceased to be a slave." How did he free him? Hear what he says: "He taught me what is mine and what is not mine; property is not mine, kinsfolk, relations, friends, reputation, familiar places, converse with men—none of these is my own."

What is yours then?

"Power to deal with impressions. He showed me that I possess this beyond all hindrance and compulsion; no one can hamper me, no one can compel me to deal with them otherwise than I will. . . ."

What then is the proper training for this? In the first place, the principal and most important thing, on the very threshold so to speak, is that when you are attached to a thing, not a thing which cannot be taken away but anything like a ewer, or a crystal cup, you should bear in mind what it is, that you may not be disturbed when it is broken. So should it be with persons; if you kiss your child, or brother, or friend, never allow your imagination to range at large, nor allow your exultation to go as far as it will, but pluck it back, keep it in check like those who stand behind generals driving in triumph and remind them that they are men. In like manner you must remind yourself that you love a mortal, and that nothing that you love is your very own; it is given you for the moment, not for ever nor inseparably, but like a fig or a bunch of grapes at the appointed season of the year, and if you long for it in winter you are a fool. So too if you long for your son or your friend, when it is not given you to have him, know that you are longing for a fig in winter time. For as winter is to the fig, so is the whole pressure of the universe to that which it destroys. And therefore in the very moment that you take pleasure in a thing, set before your mind the opposite impressions. What harm is there in whispering to yourself as you kiss your child, "To-morrow you will die," and to your friend in like manner, "To-morrow you or I shall go away, and we shall see one another no more"? . . .

If you always have these thoughts at hand, and make yourself familiar with them and keep them at command, you will never want for one to comfort and strengthen you. For dishonour consists not in having nothing to eat, but in not having reason sufficient to secure you from fear and pain. But if you once win yourself freedom from fear and pain, then tyrants and their guards, and the Emperor's household, will cease to exist for you; you, who have received this high office from Zeus, will not feel the sting of an imperial appointment or of those who offer sacrifice on the Capitol in virtue of their offices.

Only make no display of your office, and boast not yourself in it, but prove it by your conduct; be content, even if no one observes you, to live in true health and happiness.

2

The Desire
for Self-realization

It is attractive to think that things will go well for us if only we do and do well what comes naturally. We appear to have a nature; not to respect it is to go against the grain. Therefore, we suppose that if we discovered what our nature demands, we could gain fulfillment without fail.

We search for this natural self in solitude and in society. We design elaborate life-plans or decide to act impulsively in order to permit our lives to show the imprint of this elusive being. Yet it is difficult to determine who we are and what we truly need.

Some philosophers claim there is no formed or stable self to actualize. Others maintain that it is futile to try to realize the self; it is real already. Yet none can deny that we have needs and potentialities; perhaps the self is the structured unity of these.

But is this structure hierarchical? Or is every part of human nature as good or as important to realize as any other? Is any element more basic or nobler than all the rest? The answers to questions such as these are of immense significance for the long-range plans we make, for daily life, for psychological health. Of equal importance is considering how far we can hope to create or change our nature and to what extent we must discover and simply accept it as given.

A central issue for political thought and social ethics revolves around the relation of the individual to society. Some thinkers maintain that the self is intrinsically independent of social influence. For them, maximal liberty is either a condition or a central element in self-realization. Others argue that we are creatures of our age or class or nation; fulfillment, therefore, is possible only by absorption into the community and identification of our good with that of the social whole.

Yet it is possible that satisfaction comes as a result of the growth of understanding and awareness, independent of both our freedom and our position or possessions. And perhaps self-realization occurs only when persons communicate or treat each other as worthy of respect. Does that mean that it is not a kind of power? The alternatives are many and at every turn we face the nagging question: What must we do and be to be true to ourselves?

ROLLO MAY

The "I Am" Experience

In the hope of making clearer what it means for a person to experience his own being, we shall present an illustration from a case history. This patient, an intelligent woman of twenty-eight, was especially gifted in expressing what was occurring within her. She had come for psychotherapy because of serious anxiety spells in closed places, severe self-doubts, and eruptions of rage which were sometimes uncontrollable. An illegitimate child, she had been brought up by relatives in a small village in the southwestern part of the country. Her mother, in periods of anger, often reminded her as a child of her origin, recounted how she had tried to abort her, and in times of trouble had shouted at the little girl, "If you hadn't been born, we wouldn't have to go through this!" Other relatives had cried at the child, in family quarrels, "Why didn't you kill yourself?" and "You should have been choked the day you were born!" Later, as a young woman, the patient had become well-educated on her own initiative.

In the fourth month of therapy she had the following dream: "I was in a crowd of people. They had no faces; they were like shadows. It seemed like a wilderness of people. Then I saw there was someone in the crowd who had compassion for me." The next session she reported that she had had, in the intervening day, an exceedingly important experience. It is reported here as she wrote it down from memory and notes two years later.

I remember walking that day under the elevated tracks in a slum area, feeling the thought, "I am an illegitimate child." I recall the sweat pouring forth in

127

my anguish in trying to accept that fact. Then I understood what it must feel like to accept, "I am a Negro in the midst of privileged whites," or "I am blind in the midst of people who see." Later on that night I woke up and it came to me this way, "I accept the fact that I am an illegitimate child." *But* "I am not a child anymore." So it is, "I am illegitimate." That is not so either: "I was born illegitimate." Then what is left? What is left is this, "*I Am.*" This *act* of contact and acceptance with "I am," once gotten hold of, gave me (what I think was for me the first time) the experience "Since I Am, I have the right to be."

What is this experience like? It is a primary feeling—it feels like receiving the deed to my house. It is the experience of my own aliveness not caring whether it turns out to be an ion or just a wave. It is like when a very young child I once reached the core of a peach and cracked the pit, not knowing what I would find and then feeling the wonder of finding the inner seed, good to eat in its bitter sweetness. . . . It is like a sailboat in the harbor being given an anchor so that, being made out of earthly things, it can by means of its anchor get in touch again with the earth, the ground from which its wood grew; it can lift its anchor to sail but always at times it can cast its anchor to weather the storm or rest a little. . . . It is my saying to Descartes, "*I Am, therefore* I think, I feel, I do."

It is like an axiom in geometry—never experiencing it would be like going through a geometry course not knowing the first axiom. It is like going into my very own Garden of Eden where I am beyond good and evil and all other human concepts. It is like the experience of the poets of the intuitive world, the mystics, except that instead of the pure feeling of and union with God it is the finding of and the union with my own being. It is like owning Cinderella's shoe and looking all over the world for the foot it will fit and realizing all of a sudden that one's own foot is the only one it will fit. It is a "Matter of Fact" in the etymological sense of the expression. It is like a globe before the mountains and oceans and continents have been drawn on it. It is like a child in grammar finding the *subject* of the verb in a sentence—in this case the subject being one's own life span. It is ceasing to feel like a theory toward one's self. . . .

We shall call this the "I-am" experience. This one phase of a complex case, powerfully and beautifully described above, illustrates the emergence and strengthening of the sense of being in one person. The experience is etched the more sharply in this person because of the more patent threat to her being that she had suffered as an illegitimate child and her poetic articulateness as she looked back on her experience from the vantage point of two years later. I do not believe either of these facts, however, makes her experience different in fundamental quality from what human beings in general, normal or neurotic, go through.

JOHN STUART MILL

Life Plans and Character

As it is useful that while mankind are imperfect there should be different opinions, so it is that there should be different experiments of living; that free scope should be given to varieties of character, short of injury to others; and that the worth of different modes of life should be proved practically, when any one thinks fit to try them. It is desirable, in short, that in things which do not primarily concern others, individuality should assert itself. Where, not the person's own character, but the traditions or customs of other people are the rule of conduct, there is wanting one of the principal ingredients of human happiness, and quite the chief ingredient of individual and social progress.

In maintaining this principle, the greatest difficulty to be encountered does not lie in the appreciation of means toward an acknowledged end, but in the indifference of persons in general to the end itself. If it were felt that the free development of individuality is one of the leading essentials of well-being; that it is not only a co-ordinate element with all that is designated by the terms civilization, instruction, education, culture, but is itself a necessary part and condition of all those things; there would be no danger that liberty should be undervalued, and the adjustment of the boundaries between it and social control would present no extraordinary difficulty. But the evil is, that individual spontaneity is hardly recognized by the common modes of thinking, as having any intrinsic worth, or deserving any regard on its own account. The majority, being satisfied with the ways of mankind as they now are (for it is they who make them what they are), cannot comprehend why those ways should not be good enough for everybody; and what is more, spontaneity forms no part of the ideal of the majority of moral and social reformers, but is rather looked on with jealousy, as a troublesome and perhaps rebellious obstruction to the general acceptance of what these reformers, in their own judgment, think would be best for mankind. Few persons, out of Germany, even comprehend the meaning of the doctrine which Wilhelm Von Humboldt, so eminent both as a *savant* and as a politician, made the text of a treatise—that "the end of man, or that which is prescribed by the eternal or immutable dictates of reason, and not suggested by vague and transient desires, is the highest and most harmonious development of his powers to a complete and consistent whole," that, therefore, the object "towards which every human being must ceaselessly direct his efforts, and on which especially those who design to influence their fellow-men must ever keep their eyes, is the individuality of power and development"; that for this there are two requisites, "freedom, and a variety of situations"; and that from the union of these arise "individual vigour and manifold diversity," which combine themselves in "originality."

Little, however, as people are accustomed to a doctrine like that of Von Humboldt, and surprising as it may be to them to find so high a value attached to individuality, the question, one must nevertheless think, can only be one of degree. No one's idea of excellence in conduct is that people should do absolutely nothing but copy one another. No one would assert that people ought not to put into their mode of life, and into the conduct of their concerns, any impress whatever of their own judgment, or of their own individual character. On the other hand, it would be absurd to pretend that people ought to live as if nothing whatever had been known in the world before they came into it; as if experience had as yet done nothing toward showing that one mode of existence, or of conduct, is preferable to another. Nobody denies that people should be so taught and trained in youth, as to know and benefit by the ascertained results of human experience. But it is the privilege and proper condition of a human being, arrived at the maturity of his faculties, to use and interpret experience in his own way. It is for him to find out what part of recorded experience is properly applicable to his own circumstances and character.

The traditions and customs of other people are, to a certain extent, evidence of what their experience has taught *them;* presumptive evidence, and as such, have a claim to his deference: but, in the first place, their experience may be too narrow; or they may not have interpreted it rightly. Secondly, their interpretation of experience may be correct, but unsuitable to him. Customs are made for customary circumstances, and customary characters: and his circumstances or his character may be uncustomary. Thirdly, though the customs be both good as customs, and suitable to him, yet to conform to custom, merely *as* custom, does not educate or develop in him any of the qualities which are the distinctive endowment of a human being. The human faculties of perception, judgment, discriminative feeling, mental activity, and even moral preference, are exercised only in making a choice. He who does anything because it is the custom, makes no choice. He gains no practice either in discerning or in desiring what is best. The mental and moral, like the muscular powers, are improved only by being used. The faculties are called into no exercise by doing a thing merely because others do it, no more than by believing a thing only because others believe it. If the grounds of an opinion are not conclusive to the person's own reason, his reason cannot be strengthened, but is likely to be weakened by his adopting it: and if the inducements to an act are not such as are consentaneous to his own feelings and character (where affection, or the rights of others, are not concerned) it is so much done toward rendering his feelings and character inert and torpid, instead of active and energetic.

He who lets the world, or his own portion of it, choose his plan of life for him, has no need for any other faculty than the ape-like one of imitation. He who chooses his plan for himself, employs all his faculties. He must use observation to see, reasoning and judgment to foresee, activity to gather materials for decision, discrimination to decide, and when he has decided, firmness and self-control to hold to his deliberate decision. And these qualities he requires and exercises exactly in proportion as the part of his conduct which he determines according to his own judgment and feelings is a large one. It is possible that he might be guided in some good path, and kept out of harm's way, without any of these things. But what will be his comparative worth as a human being? It really is of importance, not only what men do, but also what manner of men they are that do it. Among the works of man, which human life is rightly employed in perfecting and beautifying, the first in importance surely is man himself. Supposing it were possible to get houses built, corn grown, battles fought, causes tried, and even churches erected and prayers said, by machinery—by automatons in human form—it would be a considerable loss to exchange for these automatons even the men and women who at present inhabit the more civilized parts of the world, and who assuredly are but starved specimens of what nature can and will produce. Human nature is not a machine to be built after a model, and set to do exactly the work prescribed for it, but a tree, which requires to grow and develop itself on all sides, according to the tendency of the inward forces which make it a living thing.

It will probably be conceded that it is desirable people should exercise their understandings, and that an intelligent following of custom, or even occasionally an intelligent deviation from custom, is better than a blind and simply mechanical adhesion to it. To a certain extent it is admitted, that our understanding should be our own: but there is not the same willingness to admit that our desires and impulses should be our own likewise; or that to possess impulses of our own, and of any strength, is anything but a peril and a snare. Yet desires and impulses are as much a part of a perfect human being, as beliefs and restraints: and strong impulses are only perilous when not properly balanced; when one set of aims and inclinations is developed into strength, while others, which ought to co-exist with them, remain weak and inactive. It is not because men's desires are strong that they act ill; it is because their consciences are weak. There is no natural connection between strong impulses and a weak conscience. The natural connection is the other way. To say that one person's desires and feelings are stronger and more various than those of another, is merely to say that he has more of the raw material of human nature, and is therefore capable, perhaps of more evil, but certainly of more good. Strong impulses are but another name for energy. Energy may be turned to bad uses; but more good may always be made of an energetic nature, than of an indolent and impassive one. Those who have most natural feeling, are always those whose cultivated feelings may be made the strongest. The same strong susceptibilities which make the personal impulses vivid and powerful, are also the source from whence are generated the most passionate love of virtue, and the sternest self-control. It is through the cultivation of these, that society both does its duty and protects its interests: not by rejecting the stuff of which heroes are made, because it knows not how to make them. A person whose desires and impulses are his own—are the expression of his own nature, as it has been developed and modified by his own culture—is said to have a character. One whose desires and impulses are not his own, has no character, no more than a steam-engine has a character. If, in addition to being his own, his impulses are strong, and are under the government of a strong will, he has an energetic character. Whoever thinks that individuality of desires and impulses should not be encouraged to unfold itself, must maintain that society has no need of strong natures—is not the better for containing many persons who have much character—and that a high general average of energy is not desirable. . . .

Society has now fairly got the better of individuality; and the danger which threatens human nature is not the excess, but the deficiency, of personal impulses and preferences. Things are vastly changed, since the passions of those who were strong by station or by personal endowment were in a state of habitual rebellion against laws and ordinances, and required to be rigorously chained up to enable the persons within their reach to enjoy any particle of security. In our times, from the highest class of society down to the lowest, every one lives as under the eye of a hostile and dreaded censorship. Not only in what concerns others, but in what concerns only themselves, the individual, or the family, do not ask themselves—what do I prefer? or, what would suit my character and disposition? or, what would allow the best and highest in me to have fair play, and enable it to grow and thrive? They ask themselves, what is suitable to my position? what is usually done by persons of my station and pecuniary circumstances? or (worse still) what is usually done by persons of a station and circumstances superior to mine? I do not mean that they choose what is customary, in preference to what suits their own inclination. It does not occur to them to have any inclination, except for what is customary. Thus the mind itself is bowed to the yoke: even in what people do for pleasure, conformity is the first thing thought of: they like in crowds; they exercise choice only among things commonly done: peculiarity of taste, eccentricity of conduct, are shunned equally with crimes: until by dint of not following their own nature, they have no nature to follow: their human capacities are withered and starved: they become incapable of any strong wishes or pleasures, and are generally without either opinions or feelings of home growth, or properly their own. Now is this, or is it not, the desirable condition of human nature? . . .

It is not by wearing down into uniformity all that is individual in themselves, but by cultivating it and calling it forth, within the limits imposed by the rights and interests of others, that human beings become a noble and beautiful object of contemplation; and as the works partake the character of those who do them, by the same process human life also becomes rich, diversified, and animating, furnishing more abundant aliment to high thoughts and elevating feelings, and strengthening the tie which binds every individual to the race, by making the race infinitely better worth belonging to. In proportion to the development of his individuality, each person becomes more valuable to himself, and is therefore capable of being more valuable to others. There is a greater fulness of life about his own existence, and when there is more life in the units there is more in the mass which is composed of them. . . .

Having said that individuality is the same thing with development, and that it is only the cultivation of individuality which produces, or can produce, well-developed human beings, I might here close the argument: for what more or better can be said of any condition of human affairs, than that it brings human beings themselves nearer to the best thing they can be? or what worse can be said of any obstruction to good, than that it prevents this? Doubtless, however, these considerations will not suffice to convince those who most need convincing; and it is necessary further to show, that these developed human beings are of some use to the undeveloped—to point out to those who do not desire liberty, and would not avail themselves of it, that they may be in some intelligible manner rewarded for allowing other people to make use of it without hindrance.

In the first place, then, I would suggest that they might possibly learn something from them. It will not be denied by anybody, that originality is a valuable element in human affairs. There is always need of persons not only to discover new truths, and point out when what were once truths are true no longer, but also to commence new practices, and set the example of more enlightened conduct, and better taste and sense in human life. This cannot well be gainsaid by anybody who does not believe that the world has already attained perfection in all its ways and practices. It is true that this benefit is not capable of being rendered by everybody alike: there are but few persons, in comparison with the whole of mankind, whose experiments, if adopted by others, would be likely to be any improvement on established practice. But these few are the salt of the earth; without them, human life would become a stagnant pool. Not only is it they who introduce good things which did not before exist; it is they who keep the life in those which already existed. If there were nothing new to be done, would human intellect cease to be necessary? Would it be a reason why those who do the old things should forget why they are done, and do them like cattle, not like human beings? There is only too great a tendency in the best beliefs and practices to degenerate into the mechanical; and unless there were a succession of persons whose ever-recurring originality prevents the grounds of those beliefs and practices from becoming merely traditional, such dead matter would not resist the smallest shock from anything really alive, and there would be no reason why civilization should not die out, as in the Byzantine Empire. Persons of genius, it is true, are, and are always likely to be, a small minority; but in order to have them, it is necessary to preserve the soil in which they grow. Genius can only breathe freely in an *atmosphere* of freedom. Persons of genius are, *ex vi termini*, *more* individual than any other people—less capable, consequently, of fitting themselves, without hurtful compression, into any of the small number of molds which society provides in order to save its members the trouble of forming their own character. If from timidity they consent to be forced into one of these molds, and to let all that part of themselves which cannot expand under the pressure reman unexpanded, society will be little the better for their genius. If they are of a strong character, and break their fetters, they become a mark for the society which has not succeeded in reducing them to commonplace, to point at with solemn warning as "wild," "erratic," and the like; much as if one should complain of the Niagara river for not flowing smoothly between its banks like a Dutch canal.

I insist thus emphatically on the importance of genius, and the necessity of allowing it to unfold itself freely both in thought and in practice, being well aware that no one will deny the position in theory, but knowing also that almost every one, in reality, is totally indifferent to it. People think genius a fine thing if it enables a man to write an exciting poem, or paint a picture. But in its true sense, that of originality in thought and action, though no one says that it is not a thing to be admired, nearly all, at heart, think that they can do very well without it. Unhappily this is too natural to be wondered at. Originality is the one thing which unoriginal minds cannot feel the use of. They cannot see what it is to do for them: how should they? If they could see what it would do for them, it would not be originality. The first service which originality has to render them, is that of opening their eyes: which being once fully done, they would have a chance of being themselves original. Meanwhile, recollecting that nothing was ever yet done which someone was not the first to do, and that all good things which exist are the fruits of originality, let them be modest enough to believe that there is something still left for it to accomplish, and assure themselves that they are more in need of originality, the less they are conscious of the want.

In sober truth, whatever homage may be professed, or even paid, to real or supposed mental superiority, the general tendency of things throughout the world is to render mediocrity the ascendant power among mankind. In ancient history, in the middle ages, and in a diminishing degree through the long transition from feudality to the present time, the individual was a power in himself; and if he had either great talents or a high social position, he was a considerable power. At present individuals are lost in the crowd. In politics it is almost a triviality to say that public opinion now rules the world. The only power deserving the name is that of masses, and of governments while they make themselves the organ of the tendencies and instincts of masses. This is as true in the moral and social relations of private life as in public transactions. Those whose opinions go by the name of public opinion, are not always the same sort of public: in America they are the whole white population; in England, chiefly the middle class. But they are always a mass, that is to say, collective mediocrity. And what is a still greater novelty, the mass do not now take their opinions from dignitaries in Church or State, from ostensible leaders, or from books. Their thinking is done for them by men much like themselves, addressing them or speaking in their name, on the spur of the moment, through the newspapers. I am not complaining of all this. I do not assert that anything better is compatible, as a general rule, with the present low state of the human mind. But that does not hinder the government of mediocrity from being mediocre government. No government by a democracy or a numerous aristocracy, either in its political acts or in the opinions, qualities, and tone of mind which it fosters, ever did or could rise above mediocrity, except in so far as the sovereign. Many have let themselves be guided (which in their best times they always have done) by the counsels and influence of a more highly gifted and instructed One or Few. The initiation of all wise or noble things, comes and must come from individuals; generally at first from some one individual. The honor and glory of the average man is that he is capable of following that initiative; that he can respond internally to wise and noble things, and be led to them with his eyes open. I am not countenancing the sort of "hero-worship" which applauds the strong man of genius for forcibly seizing on the government of the world and making it do his bidding in spite of itself. All he can claim is, freedom to point out the way. The power of compelling others into it, is not only inconsistent with the freedom and development of all the rest, but corrupting to the strong man himself. It does seem, however, that when the opinions of masses of merely average men are everywhere become or becoming the dominant power, the counterpoise and corrective to that tendency would be, the more and more pronounced individuality of those who stand on the higher eminences of thought. It is in these circumstances most especially, that exceptional individuals, instead of being deterred, should be encouraged in acting differently from the mass. In other times there was no advantage in their doing so, unless they acted not only differently, but better. In this age the mere example of nonconformity, the mere refusal to bend the knee to custom, is itself a service. Precisely because the tyranny of opinion is such as to make eccentricity a reproach, it is desirable, in order to break through that tyranny, that people should be eccentric. Eccentricity has always abounded when and where strength of character has abounded; and the amount of eccentricity in a society has generally been proportional to the amount of genius, mental vigour, and moral courage which it contained. That so few now dare to be eccentric, marks the chief danger of the time.

I have said that it is important to give the freest scope possible to uncustomary things, in order that it may in time appear which of these are fit to be converted into customs. But independence of action, and disregard of custom are not solely deserving of encouragement for the chance they afford that better modes of action, and customs more worthy of general adoption, may be struck out; nor is it only persons of decided mental superiority who have a just claim to carry on their lives in their own way. There is no reason that all human existences should be constructed on some one, or some small number of patterns. If a person possesses any tolerable amount of common sense and experience, his own mode of laying out his existence is the best, not because it is the best in itself, but because it is his own mode. Human beings are not like sheep; and even sheep are not undistinguishably alike. A man cannot get a coat or a pair of boots to fit him, unless they are either made to his measure, or he has a whole warehouseful to choose from: and is it easier to fit him with a life than with a coat, or are human beings more like one another in their whole physical and spiritual conformation than in the shape of their feet? If it were only that people have diversities of taste, that is reason enough for not attempting to shape them all after one model. But different persons also require different conditions for their spiritual development; and can no more exist healthily in the same moral, than all the variety of plants can in the same physical, atmosphere and climate. The same things which are helps to one person toward the cultivation of his higher nature, are hindrances to another. The same mode of life is a healthy excitement to one, keeping all his faculties of action and enjoyment in their best order, while to another it is a distracting burthen, which suspends or crushes all internal life. Such are the differences among human beings in their sources of pleasure, their susceptibilities of pain, and the operation on them of different physical and moral agencies, that unless there is a corresponding diversity in their modes of life, they neither obtain their fair share of happiness, nor grow up to the mental, moral, and aesthetic stature of which their nature is capable. Why then should tolerance, as far as the public sentiment is concerned, extend only to tastes and modes of life which extort acquiescence by the multitude of their adherents? Nowhere (except in some monastic institutions) is diversity of taste entirely unrecognised; a person may, without blame, either like or dislike rowing, or smoking, or music, or athletic exercises, or chess, or cards, or study, because both those who like each of these things, and those who dislike them, are too numerous to be put down. But the man, and still more the woman, who can be accused either of doing "what nobody does," or of not doing "what everybody does," is the subject of as much depreciatory remark as if he or she had committed some grave moral delinquency. Persons require to possess a title, or some other badge of rank, or of the consideration of people of rank, to be able to indulge somewhat in the luxury of doing as they like without detriment to their estimation. To indulge somewhat, I repeat: for whoever allow themselves much of that indulgence, incur the risk of something worse than disparaging speeches—they are in peril of a commission *de lunatico*, and of having their property taken from them and given to their relations. . . .

The despotism of custom is everywhere the standing hindrance to human advancement, being in unceasing antagonism to that disposition to aim at something better than customary, which is called, according to circumstances, the spirit of liberty, or that of progress or improvement. The spirit of improvement is not always a spirit of liberty, for it may aim at forcing improvements on an unwilling people; and the spirit of liberty, in so far as it resists such attempts, may ally itself locally and temporarily with the opponents of improvement; but the only unfailing and permanent source of improvement is liberty, since by it there are as many possible independent centres of improvement as there are individuals. The progressive principle, however, in either shape, whether as the love of liberty or of improvement, is antagonistic to the sway of Custom, involving at least emancipation from that yoke; and the contest between the two constitutes the chief interest of the history of mankind. . . .

The circumstances which surround different classes and individuals, and shape their characters, are daily becoming more assimilated. Formerly, different ranks, different neighborhoods, different trades and professions, lived in what might be called different worlds; at present, to a great degree in the same. Comparatively speaking, they now read the same things, listen to the same things, see the same things, go to the same places, have their hopes and fears directed to the same objects, have the same rights and liberties, and the same means of asserting them. Great as are the differences of position which remain, they are nothing to those which have ceased. And the assimilation is still proceeding. All the political changes of the age promote it, since they all tend to raise the low and to lower the high. Every extension of education promotes it, because education brings people under common influences, and gives them access to the general stock of facts and sentiments. Improvements in the means of communication promote it, by bringing the inhabitants of distant places into personal contact, and keeping up a rapid flow of changes of residence between one place and another. The increase of commerce and manufactures promotes it, by diffusing more widely the advantages of easy circumstances, and opening all objects of ambition, even the highest, to general competition, whereby the desire of rising becomes no longer the character of a particular class, but of all classes. A more powerful agency than even all these, in bringing about a general similarity among mankind, is the complete establishment, in this and other free countries, of the ascendancy of public opinion in the State. As the various social eminences which enabled persons entrenched on them to disregard the opinion of the multitude, gradually become levelled; as the very idea of resisting the will of the public, when it is positively known that they have a will, disappears more and more from the minds of practical politicians; there ceases to be any social support for non-conformity—any substantive power in society, which, itself opposed to the ascendancy of numbers, is interested in taking under its protection opinions and tendencies at variance with those of the public.

The combination of all these causes forms so great a mass of influences hostile to Individuality, that it is not easy to see how it can stand its ground. It will do so with increasing difficulty, unless the intelligent part of the public can be made to feel its value—to see that it is good there should be differences, even though not for the better, even though, as it may appear to them, some should be for the worse. If the claims of Individuality are ever to be asserted, the time is now, while much is still wanting to complete the enforced assimilation. It is only in the earlier stages that any stand can be successfully made against the encroachment. The demand that all other people shall resemble ourselves, grows by what it feeds on. If resistance waits till life is reduced *nearly* to one uniform type, all deviations from that type will come to be considered impious, immoral, even monstrous and contrary to nature. Mankind speedily become unable to conceive diversity, when they have been for some time unaccustomed to see it.

F. H. BRADLEY

The Social Self

What we have left then is this—the end is the realization of the good will which is superior to ourselves; and again the end is self-realization. Bringing these together we see the end is the realization of ourselves as the will which is above ourselves. And this will (if morality exists) we saw must be "objective," because not dependent on "subjective" liking; and "universal," because not identifiable with any particular, but standing above all actual and possible particulars. Further, though universal it is not abstract since it belongs to its essence that it should be realized, and it has no real existence except in and through its particulars. The good will (for morality) is meaningless, if, whatever else it be, it be not the will of living human beings. It is a concrete universal because it not only is above but is within and throughout its details, and is so far only as they are. It is the life which can live only in and by them, as they are dead unless within it; it is the whole soul which lives so far as the body lives, which makes the body a living body and which without the body is as unreal an abstraction as the body without it. It is an organism and a moral organism; and it is conscious self-realization because only by the will of its self-conscious members can the moral organism give itself reality. It is the self-realization of the whole body because it is one and the same will which lives and acts in the life and action of each. It is the self-realization of each member because each member cannot find the function which makes him himself, apart from the whole to which he belongs;

to be himself he must go beyond himself, to live his life he must live a life which is not *merely* his own, but which, none the less, but on the contrary all the more, is intensely and emphatically his own individuality. Here, and here first, are the contradictions which have beset us solved—here is a universal which can confront our wandering desires with a fixed and stern imperative, but which yet is no unreal form of the mind but a living soul that penetrates and stands fast in the detail of actual existence. It is real, and real for me. It is in its affirmation that I affirm myself, for I am but as a "heart-beat in its system." And I am real in it, for, when I give myself to it, it gives me the fruition of my own personal activity, the accomplished ideal of my life which is happiness. In the realized idea which, superior to me and yet here and now in and by me, affirms itself in a continuous process, we have found the end, we have found self-realization, duty, and happiness in one—yes, we have found ourselves when we have found our station and its duties, our function as an organ in the social organism.

"Mere rhetoric," we shall be told, "a bad metaphysical dream, a stale old story once more warmed up, which cannot hold its own against the logic of facts. That the state was prior to the individual, that the whole was sometimes more than the sum of the parts, was an illusion which preyed on the thinkers of Greece. But that illusion has been traced to its source and dispelled and is in plain words exploded. The family, society, the state, and generally every community of men consists of individuals, and there is nothing in them real except the individuals. Individuals have made them, and make them, by placing themselves and by standing in certain relations. The individuals are real by themselves and it is because of them that the relations are real. They make them, they are real *in* them, not because of them, and they would be just as real *out* of them. The whole is the mere sum of the parts, and the parts are as real away from the whole as they are within the whole. Do you really suppose that the individual would perish if every form of community were destroyed? Do you think that anything real answers to the phrases of universal and organism? Everything is in the organism what it is out, and the universal is a name, the existing fact answering to which is particular persons in such and such relations. To put the matter shortly, the community is the sum of its parts, is made by the addition of parts, and the parts are as real before the addition as after; the relations they stand in do not make them what they are, but are accidental, not essential, to their being; and, as to the whole, if it is not a name for the individuals that compose it, it is a name of nothing actual. These are not metaphysical dreams. They are facts and verifiable facts."

Are they facts? Facts should explain facts; and the view called "individualism" (because the one reality that it believes in is the "individual," in the sense of this, that, and the other particular) should hence be the right explanation. What are the facts here to be explained? They are human communities, the family, society, and the state. Individualism has explained them long ago. They are "collections" held together by force, illusion, or contract. It has told the story of their origin and to its own satisfaction cleared the matter up. Is the explanation satisfactory and verifiable? That would be a bold assertion when historical science has rejected and entirely discredited the individualistic origin of society, and when, if we turn to practice, we find everywhere the state asserting itself as a power which has, and, if need be, asserts the right to make use of and expend the property and person of the individual without regard to his wishes, and which, moreover, may destroy his life in punishment, and put forth other powers such as no theory of contract will explain except by the most palpable fictions, while at the same time no ordinary person calls their morality in question. Both history and practical politics refuse to verify the "facts" of the individualist; and we should find still less to confirm his theory if we examined the family. . . .

To the assertion, then, that selves are "individual" in the sense of exclusive of other selves, we oppose the (equally justified) assertion that this is a mere fancy. We say that, out of theory, no such individual men exist; and we will try to show from fact that, in fact, what we call an individual man is what he is because of and by virtue of community, and that communities are thus not mere names but something real, and can be regarded (if we mean to keep to facts) only as the one in the many.

And to confine the subject and to keep to what is familiar, we will not call to our aid the life of animals, nor early societies, nor the course of history, but we will take men as they are now; we will take ourselves and endeavor to keep wholly to the teaching of experience.

Let us take a man, an Englishman as he is now, and try to point out that apart from what he has in common with others, apart from his sameness with others, he is not an Englishman—nor a man at all; that if you take him as something by himself, he is not what he is. Of course we do not mean to say that he cannot go out of England without disappearing, nor, even if all the rest of the nation perished that he would not survive. What we mean to say is that he is what he is because he is a born and educated social being, and a member of an individual social organism; that if you make abstraction of all this, which is the same in him and in others, what you have left is not an Englishman, nor a man, but some I know not what residuum, which never has existed by itself and does not so exist. If we suppose the world of relations, in which he was born and bred, never to have been, then we suppose the very essence of him not to be; if we take that away, we have taken him away; and hence he now is not an individual, in the sense of owing nothing to the sphere of relations in which he finds himself, but does contain those relations within himself as belonging to his very being; he is what he is, in brief, so far as he is what others also are. . . .

So far, . . . we have seen that the "individual" apart from the community is an abstraction. It is not anything real and hence not anything that we can realize, however much we may wish to do so. We have seen that I am myself by sharing with others, by including in my essence relations to them, the relations of the social state. If I wish to realize my true being I must therefore realize something beyond my being as a mere this or that, for my true being has in it a life which is not the life of any mere particular, and so must be called a universal life.

What is it then that I am to realize? We have said it in "my station and its duties." To know what a man is (as we have seen) you must not take him in isolation. He is one of a people, he was born in a family, he lives in a certain society, in a certain state. What he has to do depends on what his place is, what his function is, and that all comes from his station in the organism. Are there then such organisms in which he lives, and if so, what is their nature? Here we come to questions which must be answered in full by any complete system of Ethics, but which we cannot enter on. We must content ourselves by pointing out that there are such facts as the family, then in a middle position a man's own profession and society, and, over all, the larger community of the state. Leaving out of sight the question of a society wider than the state, we must say that a man's life with its moral duties is in the main filled up by his station in that system of wholes which the state is, and that this, partly by its laws and institutions and still more by its spirit, gives him the life which he does live and ought to live. That objective institutions exist is of course an obvious fact; and it is a fact which every day is becoming plainer that these institutions are organic, and further, that they are moral. . . .

The non-theoretical person, if he be not immoral, is at peace with reality. . . . He sees evils which cannot discourage him, since they point to the strength of the life which can endure such parasites and flourish in spite of them. . . . He sees the true account of the state (which holds it to be neither mere force nor convention, but the moral organism, the real identity of might and right) unknown or "refuted," laughed at and despised, but he sees the state every day in its practice refute every other doctrine, and do with the moral approval of all what the explicit theory of scarcely one will morally justify. He sees instincts are better and stronger than so-called "principles." He sees in the hour of need what are called "rights" laughed at, "freedom," the liberty to do what one pleases, tramped on, the claims of the individual trodden under foot, and theories burst like cobwebs. And he sees, as of old, the heart of a nation rise high and beat in the breast of each one of her citizens till her safety and her honor are dearer to each than life, till to those who live her shame and sorrow, if such is allotted, outweigh their loss, and death seems a little thing to those who go for her to their common and nameless grave. And he knows that what is stronger than death is hate or love, hate here for love's sake, and that love does not fear death because already it is the death into life of what our philosophers tell us is the only life and reality.

Yes, the state is not put together, but it lives; it is not a heap nor a machine; it is no mere extravagance when a poet talks of a nation's soul. It is the objective mind which is subjective and self-conscious in its citizens—it feels and knows itself in the heart of each. It speaks the word of command and gives the field of accomplishment, and in the activity of obedience it has and bestows individual life and satisfaction and happiness. . . .

The belief in this real moral organism is the one solution of ethical problems. It breaks down the antithesis of despotism and individualism; it denies them, while it preserves the truth of both. The truth of individualism is saved, because unless we have intense life and self-consciousness in the members of the state, the whole state is ossified. The truth of despotism is saved, because unless the member realizes the whole by and in himself, he fails to reach his own individuality. Considered in the main, the best communities are those which have the best men for their members, and the best men are the members of the best communities. Circle as this is, it is not a vicious circle. The two problems of the best man and best state are two sides, two distinguishable aspects of the one problem, how to realize in human nature the perfect unity of homogeneity and specification; and when we see that each of these without the other is unreal, then we see that (speaking in general) the welfare of the state and the welfare of its individuals are questions which it is mistaken and ruinous to separate. Personal morality and political and social institutions cannot exist apart, and (in general) the better the one the better the other. The community is moral because it realizes personal morality; personal morality is moral because and in so far as it realizes the moral whole. . . .

The next point we come to is the question, How do I get to know in particular what is right and wrong? and here again we find a strangely erroneous preconception. It is thought that moral philosophy has to accomplish this task for us, and the conclusion lies near at hand that any system which will not do this is worthless. Well, we first remark, and with some confidence, that there cannot be a moral philosophy which will tell us what in particular we are to do, and also that it is not the business of philosophy to do so. All philosophy has to do is "to understand what is," and moral philosophy has to understand morals which exist, not to make them or give directions for making them. Such a notion is simply ludicrous. Philosophy in general has not to anticipate the discoveries of the particular sciences nor the evolution of history; the philosophy of religion has not to make a new religion or teach an old one, but simply to understand the religious consciousness; and aesthetic has not to produce works of fine art, but to theorize the beautiful which it finds; political philosophy has not to play tricks with the state, but to understand it; and ethics has not to make the world moral, but to reduce to theory the morality current in the world. If we want it to do anything more, so much the worse for us; for it cannot possibly construct new morality, and, even if it could to any extent codify what exists (a point on which I do not enter), yet it surely is clear that in cases of collision of duties it would not help you to know what to do. Who would go to a learned theologian, as such, in a practical religious difficulty; to a system of aesthetic for suggestions on the handling of an artistic theme; to a physiologist, as such, for a diagnosis and prescription; to a political philosopher in practical politics; or to a psychologist in an intrigue of any kind? All these persons no doubt *might* be the best to go to, but that would not be because they were the best theorists, but because they were more. In short, the view which thinks moral philosophy is to supply us with particular moral prescriptions confuses science with art, and confuses, besides, reflective with intuitive judgment. That which tells us what in particular is right and wrong is not reflection but intuition. . . .

If a man is to know what is right, he should have imbibed by precept, and still more by example, the spirit of his community, its general and special beliefs as to right and wrong. . . . What is moral *in any particular given case* is seldom doubtful. Society pronounces beforehand; or, after some one course has been taken, it can say whether it was right or not; though society cannot generalize much, and, if asked to reflect, is helpless and becomes incoherent. But I do not say there are no cases where the morally minded man has to doubt; most certainly such do arise, though not so many as some people think, far fewer than some would be glad to think. A very large number arise from reflection, which wants to act from an explicit principle, and so begins to abstract and divide, and, thus becoming one-sided, makes the relative absolute. Apart from this, however, collisions must take place, and here there is no guide whatever but the intuitive judgment of oneself or others.[1]

This intuition must not be confounded with what is sometimes mis-called "conscience." It is not mere individual opinion or caprice. It presupposes the morality of the community as its basis, and is subject to the approval thereof. Here, if anywhere, the idea of universal and impersonal morality is realized. . . . "Conscience" is the antipodes of this. It wants you to have no law but yourself, and to be better than the world. But this tells you that, if you could be as good as your world, you would be better than most likely you are, and that to wish to be better than the world is to be already on the threshold of immorality. . . .

1. I may remark on this (after Erdmann, and I suppose Plato) that collisions of duties are avoided mostly by each man keeping to his own immediate duties, and not trying to see from the point of view of other stations than his own.

Let us be clear. What is that wish to be better, and to make the world better, which is on the threshold of immorality? What is the "world" in this sense? It is the morality already existing ready to hand in laws, institutions, social usages, moral opinions and feelings. This is the element in which the young are brought up. It has given moral content to themselves and it is the only source of such content. It is not wrong, it is a duty, to take the best that there is, and to live up to the best. It is not wrong, it is a duty, standing on the basis of the existing, and in harmony with its general spirit, to try and make not only oneself but also the world better, or rather, and in preference, one's own world better. But it is another thing, starting from oneself, from ideals in one's head, to set oneself and them against the moral world. The moral world with its social institutions, etc., is a fact; it is real; our "ideals" are not real. "But we will make them real." We should consider what we are, and what the world is. We should learn to see the great moral fact in the world, and to reflect on the likelihood of our private "ideal" being anything more than an abstraction, which, because an abstraction, is all the better fitted for our heads, and all the worse fitted for actual existence.

We should consider whether the encouraging oneself in having opinions of one's own, in the sense of thinking differently from the world on moral subjects, be not, in any person other than a heaven-born prophet, sheer self-conceit. And though the disease may spend itself in the harmless and even entertaining sillinesses by which we are advised to assert our social "individuality," yet still the having theories of one's own in the face of the world is not far from having practice in the same direction; and if the latter is (as it often must be) immorality, the former has certainly but stopped at the threshold.

But the moral organism is strong against both. The person anxious to throw off the yoke of custom and develop his "individuality" in startling directions, passes as a rule into the common Philistine, and learns that Philistinism is after all a good thing. And the licentious young man, anxious for pleasure at any price, who, without troubling himself about "principles," does put into practice the principles of the former person, finds after all that the self within him can be satisfied only with that from whence it came. And some fine morning the dream is gone, the enchanted bower is a hideous phantasm, and the despised and common reality has become the ideal.

We have thus seen the community to be the real moral idea, to be stronger than the theories and the practice of its members against it, and to give us self-realization. And this is indeed limitation; it bids us say farewell to visions of superhuman morality, to ideal societies, and to practical "ideals" generally. But perhaps the unlimited is not the perfect nor the true ideal. And, leaving "ideals" out of sight, it is quite clear that if anybody wants to realize himself as a perfect man without trying to be a perfect member of his country and all his smaller communities, he makes what all sane persons would admit to be a great mistake. There is no more fatal enemy than theories which are not also facts; and when people inveigh against the vulgar antithesis of the two, they themselves should accept their own doctrine, and give up the harboring of theories of what should be and is not. Until they do that, the vulgar are in the right; for a theory of that which (only) is to be, is a theory of that which in fact is not, and that I suppose is only a theory.

Attaining Individualism Through Socialism

It is clear, then, that no Authoritarian Socialism will do. For while under the present system a very large number of people can lead lives of a certain amount of freedom and expression and happiness, under an industrial-barrack system, or a system of economic tyranny, nobody would be able to have any such freedom at all. It is to be regretted that a portion of our community should be practically in slavery, but to propose to solve the problem by enslaving the entire community is childish. Every man must be left quite free to choose his own work. No form of compulsion must be exercised over him. If there is, his work will not be good for him, will not be good in itself and will not be good for others. And by work I simply mean activity of any kind.

I hardly think that any Socialist, nowadays, would seriously propose that an inspector should call every morning at each house to see that each citizen rose up and did manual labour for eight hours. Humanity has got beyond that stage, and reserves such a form of life for the people whom, in a very arbitrary manner, it chooses to call criminals. But I confess that many of the socialistic views that I have come across seem to me to be tainted with ideas of authority, if not of actual compulsion. Of course, authority and compulsion are out of the question. All association must be quite voluntary. It is only in voluntary associations that man is fine.

But it may be asked how Individualism, which is now more or less dependent on the existence of private property for its development, will benefit by the abolition of such private property. The answer is very simple. It is true that, under existing conditions, a few men who have had private means of their own, such as Byron, Shelley, Browning, Victor Hugo, Baudelaire and others, have been able to realize their personality, more or less completely. Not one of these men ever did a single day's work for hire. They were relieved from poverty. They had an immense advantage. The question is whether it would be for the good of Individualism that such an advantage should be taken away. Let us suppose that it is taken away. What happens then to Individualism? How will it benefit?

It will benefit in this way. Under the new conditions Individualism will be far freer, far finer and far more intensified than it is now. I am not talking of the great imaginatively realized Individualism of such poets as I have mentioned, but of the great actual Individualism latent and potential in mankind generally. For the recognition of private property has really harmed Individualism, and obscured it, by confusing a man with what he possesses. It has led Individualism entirely astray. It has made gain, not growth, its aim. So that man thought that the important thing was to have, and did not know that the important thing is to be. The true perfection of man lies, not in what man has, but in what man is. Private property has crushed true Individualism, and set up an Individualism that is false. It has debarred one part of the community from being individual by starving them. It has debarred the other part of the community from being individual by putting them on the wrong road, and encumbering them. Indeed, so completely has man's personality been absorbed by his possessions that the English law has always treated offences against a man's property with far more severity than offences against his person, and property is still the test of complete citizenship. The industry necessary for the making of money is also very demoralizing. In a community like ours, where property confers immense distinction, social position, honour, respect, titles and other pleasant things of the kind, man, being naturally ambitious, makes it his aim to accumulate this property, and goes on wearily and tediously accumulating it long after he has got far more than he wants, or can use, or enjoy, or perhaps even know of. Man will kill himself by overwork in order to secure property, and really, considering the enormous advantages that property brings, one is hardly surprised. One's regret is that society should be constructed on such a basis that man has been forced into a groove in which he cannot freely develop what is wonderful, and fascinating, and delightful in him—in which, in fact, he misses the true pleasure and joy of living. He is also, under existing conditions, very insecure. An enormously wealthy merchant may be—often is—at every moment of his life at the mercy of things that are not under his control. If the wind blows an extra point or so, or the weather suddenly changes, or some trivial thing happens, his ship may go down, his speculations may go wrong and he finds himself a poor man, with his social position quite gone. Now, nothing should be able to harm a man except himself. Nothing should be able to rob a man at all. What a man really has, is what is in him. What is outside of him should be a matter of no importance.

With the abolition of private property, then, we shall have true, beautiful, healthy Individualism. Nobody will waste his life in accumulating things, and the symbols for things. One will live. To live is the rarest thing in the world. Most people exist, that is all.

It is a question whether we have ever seen the full expression of a personality, except on the imaginative plane of art. In action, we never have.

It will be a marvellous thing—the true personality of man—when we see it. It will grow naturally and simply, flowerlike, or as a tree grows. It will not be at discord. It will never argue or dispute. It will not prove things. It will know everything. And yet it will not busy itself about knowledge. It will have wisdom. Its value will not be measured by material things. It will have nothing. And yet it will have everything, and whatever one takes from it, it will still have, so rich will it be. It will not be always meddling with others, or asking them to be like itself. It will love them because they will be different. And yet while it will not meddle with others, it will help all, as a beautiful thing helps us, by being what it is. The personality of man will be very wonderful. It will be as wonderful as the personality of a child.

Individualism, then, is what through Socialism we are to attain. As a natural result the State must give up all idea of government. It must give it up because, as a wise man once said many centuries before Christ, there is such a thing as leaving mankind alone; there is no such thing as governing mankind. All modes of government are failures. Despotism is unjust to everybody, including the despot, who was probably made for better things. Oligarchies are unjust to the many, and ochlocracies are unjust to the few. High hopes were once formed of democracy; but democracy means simply the bludgeoning of the people by the people for the people. It has been found out. I must say that it was high time, for all authority is quite degrading. It degrades those who exercise it, and degrades those over whom it is exercised. When it is violently, grossly and cruelly used, it produces a good effect, by creating, or at any rate bringing out, the spirit of revolt and Individualism that is to kill it. When it is used with a certain amount of kindness, and accompanied by prizes and rewards, it is dreadfully demoralizing. People, in that case, are less conscious of the horrible pressure that is being put on them, and so go through their lives in a sort of coarse comfort, like petted animals, without ever realizing that they are probably thinking other people's thoughts, living by other people's standards, wearing practically what one may call other people's second-hand clothes and never being themselves for a single moment. "He who would be free," says a fine thinker, "must not conform." And authority, by bribing people to conform, produces a very gross kind of overfed barbarism amongst us.

Now as the State is not to govern, it may be asked what the State is to do. The State is to be a voluntary association that will organize labor, and be the manufacturer and distributor of necessary commodities. The State is to make what is useful. The individual is to make what is beautiful. And as I have mentioned the word labour, I cannot help saying that a great deal of nonsense is being written and talked nowadays about the dignity of manual labour. There is nothing necessarily dignified about manual labour at all, and most of it is absolutely degrading. It is mentally and morally injurious to man to do anything in which he does not find pleasure, and many forms of labour are quite pleasureless activities, and should be regarded as such. To sweep a slushy crossing for eight hours on a day when the east wind is blowing is a disgusting occupation. To sweep it with mental, moral or physical dignity seems to me to be impossible. To sweep it with joy would be appalling. Man is made for something better than disturbing dirt. All work of that kind should be done by a machine.

And I have no doubt that it will be so. Up to the present, man has been, to a certain extent, the slave of machinery, and there is something tragic in the fact that as soon as man had invented a machine to do his work he began to starve. This, however, is, of course, the result of our property system and our system of competition. One man owns a machine which does the work of five hundred men. Five hundred men are, in consequence, thrown out of employment, and, having no work to do, become hungry and take to thieving. The one man secures the produce of the machine and keeps it, and has five hundred times as much as he should have, and probably, which is of much more importance, a great deal more than he really wants. Were that machine the property of all, everybody would benefit by it. It would be an immense advantage to the community. All unintellectual labour, all monotonous, dull labour, all labour that deals with dreadful things, and involves unpleasant conditions, must be done by machinery. Machinery must work for us in coal mines, and do all sanitary services, and be the stoker of steamers, and clean the streets, and run messages on wet days, and do anything that is tedious or distressing. At present machinery competes against man. Under proper conditions machinery will serve man. There is no doubt at all that this is the future of machinery; and just as trees grow while the country gentleman is asleep, so while Humanity will be amusing itself, or enjoying cultivated leisure—which, and not labour, is the aim of man—or making beautiful things, or reading beautiful things, or simply contemplating the world with admiration and delight, machinery will be doing all the necessary and unpleasant work. The fact is, that civilization requires slaves. The Greeks were quite right there. Unless there are slaves to do the ugly, horrible, uninteresting work, culture and contemplation become almost impossible. Human slavery is wrong, insecure and demoralizing. On mechanical slavery, on the slavery of the machine, the future of the world depends. And when scientific men are no longer called upon to go down to a depressing East End and distribute bad cocoa and worse blankets to starving people, they will have delightful leisure in which to devise wonderful and marvellous things for their own joy and the joy of everyone else. There will be great storages of force for every city, and for every house if required, and this force man will convert into heat, light or motion, according to his needs. Is this Utopian? A map of the world that does not include Utopia is not worth even glancing at, for it leaves out the one country at which Humanity is always landing. And when Humanity lands there, it looks out and, seeing a better country, sets sail. Progress is the realization of Utopias.

H. RASHDALL

Self-realization

With the psychological doctrine that some form of personal good is the object of every desire (thought that good need not be pleasure) I have already dealt. It seems to be open to exactly the same objections as those urged by its supporters against psychological Hedonism, into a refined form of which the doctrine of self-realization shows a strong tendency to degenerate. I shall here therefore confine myself to the purely ethical aspect of this fascinating formula—"Self-realization is the end of life."

In order to subject the doctrine to any profitable criticism, it seems necessary to attempt the by no means easy task of distinguishing the various possible senses in which this watchword seems to be used by its devotees. The formula would probably have proved less attractive, had these various senses been distinguished by those to whom it presents itself as a "short and easy way" out of all ethical perplexities.

1. Firstly, then, we may suppose that the upholder of self-realization means exactly what he says. If he does, it seems easy to show that what he is committing himself to is mere self-contradictory nonsense. To realize means to make real. You cannot make real what is real already, and the self must certainly be regarded as real before we are invited to set about realizing it.[1] Nor is the task to which we are invited

---

1. It is of course possible to hold that the self is not real in an ultimate metaphysical sense, but in that sense it is hard to see how it can be made more real than it is, unless "real" is used as a mere synonym of "good."

rendered easier when we are assured that the self, which is to become something that it was not, is out of time, and consequently (one might have supposed) insusceptible of change.

2. But of course if will be said that what is actually meant by self-realization is the realization of some potentiality or capacity of the self which is at present unrealized. In this sense no doubt it is true enough that Morality must consist in some kind of self-realization. But to say so is to say something "generally admitted indeed but obscure," as Aristotle would have put it. In this sense the formula gives us just no information at all. For whatever you do or abstain from doing, if you only sit still or go to sleep, you must still be realizing some one of your capacities: since nobody can by any possibility do anything which he was not first capable of doing. Morality is self-realization beyond a doubt, but then so is immorality. The precious formula leaves out the whole differentia of Morality; and it is a differentia presumably which we are in search of when we ask, "What is Morality?" and are solemnly told, "It is doing or being something which you are capable of doing or being."

3. It may be maintained that Morality is the realization of *all* the capacities of human nature. But this is impossible, since one capacity can only be realized by the non-realization or sacrifice of some other capacity. There can be no self-realization without self-sacrifice. The good man and the bad alike realize one element or capacity of their nature, and sacrifice another. The whole question is which capacity is to be realized and which is to be sacrificed. And as to this our formula gives us just no information.

4. Or more vaguely self-realization may be interpreted to mean an equal, all-round development of one's whole nature—physical, intellectual, emotional. To such a view I should object that, interpreted strictly and literally, it is just as impracticable as the last. It is impossible for the most gifted person to become a first-rate Musician without much less completely realizing any capacity he has of becoming a first-rate Painter. It is impossible to become really learned in one subject without remaining ignorant of many others: impossible to develope one's athletic capacities to the full without starving and stunting the intellect, impossible (as a simple matter of Physiology) to carry to its highest point the cultivation of one's intellectual faculties without some sacrifice of physical efficiency. There is a similar collision between the demands of intellectual cultivation and those of practical

work. Up to a certain point it is extremely desirable no doubt that every man should seek to improve his mind, and also to engage in some sort of practical, social activity. There is no practical work, except that which is purely mechanical, which will not be the better done for a little study of some kind or other: and, even where a man's ordinary work in life is most purely practical, he has, or ought to have, a life of practical citizenship outside his daily task which will be enriched and enlarged by some kind of intellectual cultivation. It is scarcely possible to exaggerate the extent for instance to which the efficiency of the clerical or of the scholastic profession would be increased if every clergyman and every schoolmaster, however much absorbed in the work of his profession, were to devote a few hours a week to serious study. And equally valuable to the intellectual man is a certain measure of practical experience—equally valuable, at least in many cases, even in the interests of his purely intellectual work. Familiar illustrations are to be found in the value to Hume of his diplomatic appointment, the value to Macaulay and Grote (as is acknowledged by the critics of a nation which has little experience in free political life) of their parliamentary careers, the value to Gibbon even of a few months' home service in the Hampshire militia. And, even in spheres of intellectual labour less connected with practice than the writing of History, a literary life may gain something from more active occupations. Up to a certain point it is no doubt desirable that a man should endeavour to develope different sides of his nature: but that point is soon reached. Beyond that point there must come the inevitable sacrifice—of body to mind or of mind to body, of learning or speculative insight to practical efficiency or of practical efficiency to learning or insight.

It is the same within the intellectual sphere itself. There too the law of sacrifice prevails. Up to a certain point no doubt the man who is a mere specialist will be a bad specialist, but that point is soon reached. Charles Darwin found that the cultivation of reasoning power and observation had extinguished his once keen imagination and aesthetic sensibility. And yet who would wish—whether in the interests of the world or in the interests of what was best worthy of development in Charles Darwin's own nature—that his work should have been spoiled in order that one of the three hours which was the maximum working day his health allowed should have been absorbed by politics or philanthropy? Who would decide that the origin of species should have been undiscovered, in order that the man who might have discovered it should retain the power of enjoying Wordsworth? This notion of an equal, all-round, "harmonious" development is thus a sheer impossibility, excluded by the very constitution of human nature, and incompatible with the welfare of human society. And, in so far as some approximation to such an ideal of life is possible, it involves a very apotheosis of mediocrity, ineffectiveness, dilettantism.

And there is a more formidable objection to come. If the ideal of self-realization is to be logically carried out, it must involve the cultivation of a man's capacity for what vulgar prejudice calls Immorality as well as of his capacity for Morality. It is quite arbitrary to exclude certain kinds of activity as "bad," because what we are in search of was some definition of the good in conduct, and we were told that it was the development of all his capacities. Mr. Bradley would really appear not to shrink from the full acceptance of this corollary:

> This double effort of the mind to enlarge by all means its domain, to widen in every way both the world of knowledge and the realm of practice, shows us merely two sides of that single impulse to self-realization, which most of us are agreed to find so mystical. But, mystical or intelligible, we must bow to its sway, for escape is impossible.[2]

"To widen in every direction the sphere of knowledge." That may, in the abstract, be accepted. It would perhaps be hypercritical to suggest that there are some things not worth knowing, that it would be an unprofitable employment to count the grains of sand upon the sea-shore, and that even the pursuit of knowledge must be governed and controlled by a certain selection based upon an ideal comparison of values, which is the work of the practical Reason. And again it might be well to remember that there are things of which (with Mill) we may say that "it is necessary to be aware of them; but to live in their contemplation makes it scarcely possible to keep up in oneself a high tone of mind. The imagination and feelings become tuned to a lower pitch; degrading instead of elevating associations become connected with the daily objects and incidents of life, and give their colour to the thoughts, just as associations of sensuality do in those who indulge freely in that sort of contemplations"[3]—a reminder which, in view of Mr. Bradley's plea for the apparently unlimited

2. *The Principles of Logic*, p. 452.
3. *Three Essays on Religion*, p. 248.

"freedom of Art," might seem to be not wholly irrelevant. But to "widen in every direction the sphere of practice"! In the name of common sense, would not an occasional incursion into the higher branches of crime vary the sameness of Virtue and the dull monotony of Goodness? Is not a life compounded of good and evil "wider" than an experience which includes only good? Could the attempt to widen "in every direction" the sphere of practice end otherwise than in a prison or a lunatic asylum—if not in both? A German thinker has urged that the failure of most Moral Philosophers may be set down to the fact that as a class, they have been rather exceptionally respectable men: the Moral Philosopher should have experience both of Virtue and vice. If "wideness" is to be a sole criterion of practice, one does not see why this catholicity of experience should be confined to professional Moral Philosophers.

5. One possible interpretation of our formula remains. Self-realization may mean the realization of a man's highest capacities by the sacrifice of the lower. No doubt, in a sense every school of Moral Philosophy which allows of the distinction between a "higher" and a "lower" at all would admit that Morality does mean the sacrifice of the lower to the higher—though it might be objected that this ideal, taken literally, is too ascetic: the lower capacities of human nature have a certain value: they ought to be realized to a certain extent—to be subordinated, not "sacrificed," except in so far as their realization is inconsistent with that of the higher. But then there is nothing of all this in the word "self-realization." And even with the gloss that "self-realization" means realization of the "true" or "higher" self, it tells us just nothing at all about the question what this true self-realization is. In fact the formula which is presented to us as the key to the ethical problem of the end of life, turns out on examination to mean merely "The end of life is the end of life." No doubt it has been said that every attempt to define Morality must have the appearance of moving in a circle. In a sense that may be the case. The moral cannot be defined in terms of the non-moral. But then that is just what our formula attempts to do, and that is just the source of its futility. Moreover, when the word "self-realization" is presented to us, not merely as an account of the end, but also as the immediate criterion for the individual's conduct, it is open to the objection that it says exactly nothing about the fundamental question of Ethics—the question of the relation of my end to that of others.

6. This last difficulty would be removed if, with Mr. Bradley in one of his phases (a phase difficult to reconcile with the definition given above), we contend that the self which is realized in Morality, actually includes in itself all the selves in whom I feel an interest:

> If my self which I aim at is the realization in me of a moral world which is a system of selves, an organism in which I am a member, and in whose life I live—then I cannot aim at my own well-being without aiming at that of others. The others are not mere means to me, but are involved in my essence.[4]

Now to the adoption of self-realization in this sense as an answer to the ethical problem I should object (a) that the interpretation is not the one which is naturally suggested by that term. If the end of life is (in part or in whole) to attain the ends of others besides myself, that is a most important truth which should surely be emphasized in any answer, however summary, to the question, "What is the end of life?"; and not left to be understood in a formula which takes no explicit account of it. (b) We are as far off as ever from knowing what the "realization" of the other selves, which is included in the realization of mine, really is. (c) The proposition that I cannot attain my end without promoting the end of others is at all events an intelligible proposition. Not so, I respectfully submit, the proposition that "others are involved in my essence." Such an assertion seems to me to ignore the very essence of selfhood, which excludes an absorption or inclusion in other selves, however closely related to us. Of course, Mr. Bradley will reply that we cannot distinguish a thing from its relations. And yet Mr. Bradley has himself taught us—no one more effectively—that there cannot be relations without something to relate. No doubt a *thing*, which does not exist for itself, but only in and for a mind, cannot even in thought be abstracted from its relations: the thing is made what it is by its intelligible relations, if we include in its relations the content which it has for a mind other than itself. But this is not so with a self. Unquestionably there can be no subject without an object; the very nature of a subject is constituted by its knowledge of such and such objects. The objects that it knows are part of the self; in the view of a thorough-going Idealism, indeed, the subject and its experiences make up one spiritual being. But, all the same, of such a spiritual being it is not true that it is made what it is by its relation to other spiritual beings in the same way as a mere thing, which exists for

4. *Ethical Studies*, p. 105.

others and not for itself, is made what it is by its relations. The *thing* has no *esse* except to be felt, thought, experienced; the way it enters into the experience of minds is the only sort of being it possesses. On the other hand, the "esse" of the soul is to think, to feel, to experience. This thinking, feeling, experiencing does undoubtedly include relations to other selves; but such relations are not the whole of its being. The experiences of a soul may be *like* those of another soul: they may be caused by and dependent upon the experiences of another soul. But the experiences of one soul cannot be or become identical with the experience of another soul: the content of two consciousnesses may be the same—the universal abstracted from the particular, but not the reality: neither, therefore, can the good of one soul or self be the good of another, or be included in or be part of the good of another. Hence, if we are to avoid a mysticism which frankly takes leave of intelligibility, we cannot include any realization of the capacities of others in our conception of self-realization, however essential to such realization the good of others may be. If all that is meant is that other selves may be ends to me, not mere means, that is precisely the point which is usually disguised, if it is not denied, by those who employ the formula "self-realization." The tendency of the phrase is to represent all moral conduct as motived by a desire for my own good, into which consideration of others can only enter as means to the realization of my end. Even if there be a more ultimate metaphysical sense in which my self and others are really the same self, that is not in the sense with which we have to do with selves in Ethics: in Ethics at least we are concerned with the relations between a plurality of selves.

Further defence of this last objection would carry us more deeply into the metaphysical region than it would be in place to go at present. But I trust that what has been said will be enough to suggest that there is nothing to be gained by the use of this ambiguous, mysterious term. It tells us nothing important, nothing that could not be better expressed in some other way. It is an attempt to evade the real problems of Morality instead of answering them. That is sufficiently indicated by the fact that it is equally popular with writers whose real ethical ideals are as wide apart as the poles—with the school of the late Professor Green and with the school of Mr. Bradley, with those whose ideal is austere to the point of Asceticism and with those by whom a large part of what the plain man calls Morality is regarded as an exploded superstition. For some people it has the attraction of a vague,

imposing technicality, acting like "that comfortable word Mesopo-
tamia" upon the mind of the pious old woman. With others it is a
mere cover for a more or less refined Hedonism. What they really
mean is "the end of life is to have a good time," but they do not quite
like to say so because there is a vulgar prejudice against that view; and
besides, in academic circles there is a general consensus that Hedonism is unphilosophical.

ABRAHAM MASLOW

The Experience and Psychology of Self-realization

Deficiency Motivation and Growth Motivation

The concept "basic need" can be defined in terms of the questions which it answers and the operations which uncovered it. My original question was about psychopathogenesis. "What makes people neurotic?" My answer (a modification of and, I think, an improvement upon the analytic one) was, in brief, that neurosis seemed at its core, and in its beginning, to be a deficiency disease; that it was born out of being deprived of certain satisfactions which I called needs in the same sense that water and amino acids and calcium are needs, namely that their absence produces illness. Most neuroses involved, along with other complex determinants, ungratified wishes for safety, for belongingness and identification, for close love relationships and for respect and prestige. My "data" were gathered through twelve years of psychotherapeutic work and research and twenty years of personality study. One obvious control research (done at the same time and in the same operation) was on the effect of replacement therapy which showed, with many complexities, that when these deficiencies were eliminated, sicknesses tended to disappear.

These conclusions, which are now in effect shared by most clinicians, therapists, and child psychologists (many of them would not phrase it as I have) make it more possible year by year to define need, in a natural, easy, spontaneous way, as a generalization of actual experiential data (rather than by fiat, arbitrarily and prematurely, *prior* to the accumulation of knowledge rather than subsequent to it simply for the sake of greater objectivity).

The long-run deficiency characteristics are then the following. It is a basic or instinctoid need if

1. its absence breeds illness,
2. its presence prevents illness,
3. its restoration cures illness,
4. under certain (very complex) free choice situations, it is preferred by the deprived person over other satisfactions,
5. it is found to be inactive, at a low ebb, or functionally absent in the healthy person.

Two additional characteristics are subjective ones, namely, conscious or unconscious yearning and desire, and feeling of lack or deficiency, as of something missing on the one hand, and, on the other, palatability. ("It tastes good.") . . .

It is these needs which are essentially deficits in the organism, empty holes, so to' speak, which must be filled up for health's sake, and furthermore must be filled from without by human beings *other* than the subject, that I shall call deficits or deficiency needs for purposes of this exposition and to set them in contrast to another and very different kind of motivation.

It would not occur to anyone to question the statement that we "need" iodine or vitamin C. I remind you that the evidence that we "need" love is of exactly the same type.

In recent years more and more psychologists have found themselves compelled to postulate some tendency to growth or self-perfection to supplement the concepts of equilibrium, homeostasis, tension-reduction, defense and other conserving motivations. This was so for various reasons.

1. *Psychotherapy.* The pressure toward health makes therapy possible. It is an absolute *sine qua non.* If there were no such trend, therapy would be inexplicable to the extent that it goes beyond the building of defenses against pain and anxiety.

2. *Brain-injured soldiers.* Goldstein's work is well known to all. He found it necessary to invent the concept of self-actualization to explain the reorganization of the person's capacities after injury.

3. *Psychoanalysis.* Some analysts, notably Fromm and Horney, have found it impossible to understand even neuroses unless one postulates that they are a distorted version of an impulse toward growth, toward perfection of development, toward the fulfillment of the person's possibilities.

4. *Creativeness.* Much light is being thrown on the general subject of creativeness by the study of healthy growing and grown people, especially when contrasted with sick people. Especially does the theory of art and art education call for a concept of growth and spontaneity.

5. *Child Psychology.* Observation of children shows more and more clearly that healthy children *enjoy* growing and moving forward, gaining new skills, capacities and powers. This is in flat contradiction to that version of Freudian theory which conceives of every child as hanging on desperately to each adjustment that it achieves and to each state of rest or equilibrium. According to this theory, the reluctant and conservative child has continually to be kicked upstairs, out of its comfortable, preferred state of rest *into* a new frightening situation. . . .

This present treatment, however, derives mostly from a direct study of psychologically healthy individuals. This was undertaken not only for reasons of intrinsic and personal interest but also to supply a firmer foundation for the theory of therapy, of pathology and therefore of values. The true goals of education, of family training, of psychotherapy, of self-development, it seems to me, can be discovered only by such a direct attack. The end product of growth teaches us much about the processes of growth. . . .

So far as motivational status is concerned, healthy people have sufficiently gratified their basic needs for safety, belongingness, love, respect and self-esteem so that they are motivated primarily by trends to self-actualization (defined as ongoing actualization of potentials, capacities and talents, as fulfillment of mission (or call, fate, destiny, or vocation), as a fuller knowledge of, and acceptance of, the person's own intrinsic nature, as an unceasing trend toward unity, integration or synergy within the person).

Much to be preferred to this generalized definition would be a descriptive and operational one which I have already published. These healthy people are there defined by describing their clinically observed characteristics. These are:

1. Superior perception of reality.
2. Increased acceptance of self, of others and of nature.
3. Increased spontaneity.
4. Increase in problem-centering.
5. Increased detachment and desire for privacy.
6. Increased autonomy, and resistance to enculturation.
7. Greater freshness of appreciation, and richness of emotional reaction.
8. Higher frequency of peak experiences.
9. Increased identification with the human species.
10. Changed (the clinician would say, improved) interpersonal relations.
11. More democratic character structure.
12. Greatly increased creativeness.
13. Certain changes in the value system.

Furthermore, in this book are described also the limitations imposed upon the definition by unavoidable shortcomings in sampling and in availability of data.

One major difficulty with this conception as so far presented is its somewhat static character. Self-actualization, since I have studied it mostly in older people, tends to be seen as an ultimate or final state of affairs, a far goal, rather than a dynamic process, active throughout life, Being, rather than Becoming.

If we define growth as the various processes which bring the person toward ultimate self-actualization, then this conforms better with the observed fact that it is going on *all* the time in the life history. It discourages also the stepwise, *all* or none, saltatory conception of motivational progression toward self-actualization in which the basic needs are completely gratified, one by one, before the next higher one emerges into consciousness. Growth is seen then not only as progressive gratification of basic needs to the point where they "disappear," but also in the form of specific growth motivations over and above these basic needs, e.g., talents, capacities, creative tendencies, constitutional potentialities. We are thereby helped also to realize that basic needs and self-actualization do not contradict each other any more than do childhood and maturity. One passes into the other and is a necessary prerequisite for it.

The differentiation between these growth-needs and basic needs which we shall explore here is a consequence of the clinical perception of qualitative differences between the motivational lives of self-actualizers and of other people. These differences, listed below, are fairly well though not perfectly described by the names deficiency-needs and growth-needs. For instance, not all physiological needs are deficits, e.g., sex, elimination, sleep and rest.

In any case, the psychological life of the person, in many of its aspects, is lived out differently when he is deficiency-need-gratification-bent and when he is growth-dominated or "meta-motivated" or growth-motivated or self-actualizing. The following differences make this clear.

1. Attitude Toward Impulse: Impulse-rejection and Impulse-acceptance

Practically all historical and contemporary theories of motivation unite in regarding needs, drives and motivating states in general as annoying, irritating, unpleasant, undesirable, as something to get rid of. Motivated behavior, goal seeking, consummatory responses are all techniques for reducing these discomforts. This attitude is very explicitly assumed in such widely used descriptions of motivation as need reduction, tension reduction, drive reduction, and anxiety reduction.

This approach is understandable in animal psychology and in the behaviorism which is so heavily based upon work with animals. It may be that animals have *only* deficiency needs. Whether or not this turns out to be so, in any case we have treated animals *as if* this were so for the sake of objectivity. A goal object has to be something outside the animal organism so that we can measure the effort put out by the animal in achieving this goal.

It is also understandable that the Freudian psychology should be built upon the same attitude toward motivation that impulses are dangerous and to be fought. After all, this whole psychology is based upon experience with sick people, people who in fact suffer from bad experiences with their needs, and with their gratifications and frustrations. It is no wonder that such people should fear or even loathe their impulses which have made so much trouble for them and which they handle so badly, and that a usual way of handling them is repression.

This derogation of desire and need has, of course, been a constant theme throughout the history of philosophy, theology and psychology. The Stoics, most hedonists, practically all theologians, many political philosophers and most economic theorists have united in affirming the fact that good or happiness or pleasure is essentially the consequence of amelioration of this unpleasant state-of-affairs of wanting, of desiring, of needing.

To put it as succinctly as possible, these people all find desire or impulse to be a nuisance or even a threat and therefore will try generally to get rid of it, to deny it or to avoid it.

This contention is sometimes an accurate report of what is the case. The physiological needs, the needs for safety, for love, for respect, for information are in fact often nuisances for many people, psychic troublemakers, and problem-creators, especially for those who have had unsuccessful experiences at gratifying them and for those who cannot now count on gratification.

Even with these deficiencies, however, the case is very badly overdrawn: one can accept and enjoy one's needs and welcome them to consciousness if (a) past experience with them has been rewarding, and (b) if present and future gratification can be counted on. For example, if one has in general enjoyed food and if good food is now available, the emergence of appetite into consciousness is welcomed instead of dreaded. ("The trouble with eating is that it kills my appetite.") Something like this is true for thirst, for sleepiness, for sex, for dependency needs and for love needs. However, a far more powerful refutation of the "need-is-a-nuisance" theory is found in the recently merging awareness of, and concern with, growth (self-actualization) motivation.

The multitude of idiosyncratic motives which come under the head of "self-actualization" can hardly be listed since each person has different talents, capacities, potentialities. But some characteristics are general to all of them. And one is that these impulses are desired and welcomed, are enjoyable and pleasant, that the person wants more of them rather than less, and that if they constitute tensions, they are *pleasurable* tensions. The creator ordinarily welcomes his creative impulses, the talented person enjoys using and expanding his talents.

It is simply inaccurate to speak in such instances of tension-reduction, implying thereby the getting rid of an annoying state. For these states are not annoying.

2. Differential Effects of Gratification

Almost always associated with negative attitudes toward the need is the conception that the primary aim of the organism is to get rid of the annoying need and thereby to achieve a cessation of tension, an equilibrium, a homeostasis, a quiescence, a state of rest, a lack of pain.

The drive or need presses toward its own elimination. Its only striving is toward cessation, toward getting rid of itself, toward a state of not wanting. Pushed to its logical extreme, we wind up with Freud's death-instinct. . . .

However, when we examine people who are predominantly growth-motivated, the coming-to-rest conception of motivation becomes completely useless. In such people gratification breeds increased rather than decreased motivation, heightened rather than lessened excitement. The appetites become intensified and heightened. They grow upon themselves and instead of wanting less and less, such a person wants more and more of, for instance, education. The person rather than coming to rest becomes more active. The appetite for growth is whetted rather than allayed by gratification. Growth is, *in itself*, a rewarding and exciting process, e.g., the fulfilling of yearnings and ambitions, like that of being a good doctor; the acquisition of admired skills, like playing the violin or being a good carpenter; the steady increase of understanding about people or about the universe, or about oneself; the development of creativeness in whatever field, or, most important, simply the ambition to be a good human being.

Wertheimer long ago stressed another aspect of this same differentiation by claiming, in a seeming paradox, that true goal-seeking activity took up less than 10% of his time. Activity can be enjoyed either intrinsically, for its own sake, or else have worth and value only because it is instrumental in bringing about a desired gratification. In the latter case it loses its value and is no longer pleasurable when it is no longer successful or efficient. More frequently, it is simply *not enjoyed at all*, but only the goal is enjoyed. This is similar to that attitude toward life which values it less for its own sake than because one goes to Heaven at the end of it. The observation upon which this generalization is based is that self-actualizing people enjoy life in general and in practically all its aspects, while most other people enjoy only stray moments of triumph, of achievement or of climax or peak experience.

Partly this intrinsic validity of living comes from the pleasurableness inherent in growing and in being grown. But it also comes from the ability of healthy people to transform means-activity into end-experience, so that even instrumental activity is enjoyed as if it were end activity. Growth motivation may be long-term in character. Most of a lifetime may be involved in becoming a good psychologist or a good artist. All equilibrium or homeostasis or rest theories deal only with short-term episodes, each of which has nothing to do with each other. Allport particularly has stressed this point. Planfulness and looking into the future, he points out, are of the central stuff or healthy human nature. He agrees that "Deficit motives do, in fact, call for the reduction of tension and restoration of equilibrium. Growth motives, on the other hand, maintain tension in the interest of distant and often unattainable goals. As such they distinguish human from animal becoming, and adult from infant becoming."

3. Clinical and Personological Effects of Gratification

Deficit-need gratifications and growth-need gratifications have differential subjective and objective effects upon the personality. If I may phrase what I am groping for here in a generalized way, it is this: satisfying deficiencies avoids illness; growth satisfactions produce positive health. I must grant that this will be difficult to pin down for research purposes at this time. And yet there is a real *clinical* difference between fending off threat or attack and positive triumph and achievement, between protecting, defending and preserving oneself and reaching out for fulfillment, for excitement and for enlargement. I have tried to express this as a contrast between living fully and *preparing* to live fully, between growing up and being grown. . . .

4. Different Kinds of Pleasure

Erich Fromm has made an interesting and important effort to distinguish higher from lower pleasures, as have so many others before him. This is a crucial necessity for breaking through subjective ethical relativity and is a prerequisite for a scientific value theory.

He distinguishes scarcity-pleasure from abundance-pleasure, the "lower" pleasure of satiation of a need from the "higher" pleasure of production, creation and growth of insight. The glut, the relaxation, and the loss of tension that follows deficiency-satiation can at best be called "relief" by contrast with the *Funktions-lust*, the ecstasy, the serenity that one experiences when functioning easily, perfectly and at the peak of one's powers—in overdrive, so to speak.

"Relief," depending so strongly on something that disappears, is itself more likely to disappear. It must be less stable, less enduring, less constant than the pleasure accompanying growth, which can go on forever.

5. *Attainable (Episodic) and Unattainable Goal States*

Deficiency-need gratification tends to be episodic and climactic. The most frequent schema here begins with an instigating, motivating state which sets off motivated behavior designed to achieve a goal-state, which, mounting gradually and steadily in desire and excitement, finally reaches a peak in a moment of success and consummation. From this peak curve of desire, excitement and pleasure fall rapidly to a plateau of quiet tension-release, and lack of motivation.

This schema, though not universally applicable, in any case contrasts very sharply with the situation in growth-motivation, for here, characteristically, there is no climax or consummation, no orgasmic moment, no end-state, even no goal if this be defined climactically. Growth is instead a continued, more or less steady upward or forward development. The more one gets, the more one wants, so that this kind of wanting is endless and can never be attained or satisfied.

It is for this reason that the usual separation between instigation, goal-seeking behavior, the goal object and the accompanying effect breaks down completely. The behaving is itself the goal, and to differentiate the goal of growth from the instigation to growth is impossible. They too are the same.

6. *Species-wide Goals and Idiosyncratic Goals*

The deficit-needs are shared by all members of the human species and to some extent by other species as well. Self-actualization is idiosyncratic since every person is different. The deficits, i.e., the species requirements, must ordinarily be fairly well satisfied before real individuality can develop fully.

Just as all trees need sun, water, and foods from the environment, so do all people need safety, love and status from *their* environment.

However, in both cases this is just where real development of individuality can begin, for once satiated with these elementary, species-wide necessities, each tree and each person proceeds to develop in his own style, uniquely, using these necessities for his own private purposes. In a very meaningful sense, development then becomes more determined from within rather than from without.

7. Dependence on, and Independence of, the Environment

The needs for safety, belongingness, love relations and for respect can be satisfied only by other people, i.e., only from outside the person. This means considerable dependence on the environment. A person in this dependent position cannot really be said to be governing himself, or in control of his own fate. He *must* be beholden to the sources of supply of needed gratifications. Their wishes, their whims, their rules and laws govern him and must be appeased lest he jeopardize his sources of supply. He *must* be, to an extent, "other-directed," and *must* be sensitive to other people's approval, affection and good will. This is the same as saying that he must adapt and adjust by being flexible and responsive and by changing himself to fit the external situation. *He* is the dependent variable; the environment is the fixed, independent variable.

Because of this, the deficiency-motivated man must be more afraid of the environment, since there is always the possibility that it may fail or disappoint him. We now know that this kind of anxious dependence breeds hostility as well. All of which adds up to a lack of freedom, more or less, depending on the good fortune or bad fortune of the individual.

In contrast, the self-actualizing individual, by definition gratified in his basic needs, is far less dependent, far less beholden, far more autonomous and self-directed. Far from needing other people, growth-motivated people may actually be hampered by them. I have already reported their special liking for privacy, for detachment and for meditativeness.

Such people become far more self-sufficient and self-contained. The determinants which govern them are now primarily inner ones, rather than social or environmental. They are the laws of their own inner nature, their potentialities and capacities, their talents, their latent resources, their creative impulses, their needs to know themselves and to become more and more integrated and unified, more and more aware of what they really are, of what they really want, of what their call or vocation or fate is to be.

Since they depend less on other people, they are less ambivalent about them, less anxious and also less hostile, less needful of their praise and their affection. They are less anxious for honors, prestige and rewards.

Autonomy or relative independence of environment means also relative independence of adverse external circumstances, such as ill fortune, hard knocks, tragedy, stress, deprivation. As Allport has stressed, the notion of the human being as essentially reactive, the S-R man, we might call him, who is set into motion by external stimuli, becomes completely ridiculous and untenable for self-actualizing people. The sources of *their* actions are more internal than reactive. This *relative* independence of the outside world and its wishes and pressures, does not mean of course, lack of intercourse with it or respect for its "demand-character." It means only that in these contacts, the self-actualizer's wishes and plans are the primary determiners, rather than stresses from the environment. This I have called psychological freedom, contrasting it with geographical freedom.

Allport's expressive contrast between "opportunistic" and "propriate" determination of behavior parallels closely our outer-determined, inner-determined opposition. It reminds us also of the uniform agreement among biological theorists in considering increasing autonomy and independence of environmental stimuli as *the* defining characteristics of full individuality, of true freedom, of the whole evolutionary process.

8. Interested and Disinterested
Interpersonal Relations

In essence, the deficit-motivated man is far more dependent upon other people than is the man who is predominantly growth-motivated. He is more "interested," more needful, more attached, more desirous.

This dependency colors and limits interpersonal relations. To see people primarily as need-gratifiers or as sources of supply is an abstractive act. They are seen not as wholes, as complicated, unique individuals, but rather from the point of view of usefulness. What in them is not related to the perceiver's needs is either overlooked al-

together, or else bores, irritates, or threatens. This parallels our relations with cows, horses, and sheep, as well as with waiters, taxicab
drivers, porters, policemen or others whom we *use*.

Fully disinterested, desireless, objective and holistic perception of
another human being becomes possible only when nothing is needed
from him, only when *he* is not needed. Idiographic, aesthetic perception of the whole person is far more possible for self-actualizing people (or in moments of self-actualization), and furthermore approval,
admiration, and love are based less upon gratitude for usefulness and
more upon the objective, intrinsic qualities of the perceived person.
He is admired for objectively admirable qualities rather than because
he flatters or praises. He is loved because he is love-worthy rather
than because he gives out love. This is what will be discussed below
as unneeding love, e.g., for Abraham Lincoln.

One characteristic of "interested" and need-gratifying relations to
other people is that to a very large extent these need-gratifying persons are interchangeable. Since, for instance, the adolescent girl needs
admiration per se, it therefore makes little difference who supplies
this admiration; one admiration-supplier is about as good as another.
So also for the love-supplier or the safety-supplier.

Disinterested, unrewarded, useless, desireless perception of the
other as unique, as independent, as end-in-himself—in other words,
as a person rather than as a tool—is the more difficult, the more
hungry the perceiver is for deficit satisfaction. A "high-ceiling" interpersonal psychology, i.e., an understanding of the highest possible
development of human relationships, cannot base itself on deficit
theory of motivation.

9. Ego-centering and Ego-transcendence

We are confronted with a difficult paradox when we attempt to describe the complex attitude toward the self or ego of the growth-ori-
ented, self-actualized person. It is just this person, in whom ego-
strength is at its height, who most easily forgets or transcends the ego,
who can be most problem-centered, most self-forgetful, most spontaneous in his activities, most homonomous, to use Angyal's term. In
such people, absorption in perceiving, in doing, in enjoying, in creating can be very complete, very integrated and very pure.

This ability to center upon the world rather than to be self-conscious, egocentric and gratification-oriented becomes the more difficult the more need-deficits the person has. The more growth-motivated the person is the more problem-centered can he be, and the more he can leave self-consciousness behind him as he deals with the objective world.

10. Interpersonal Psychotherapy and Intrapersonal Psychology

A major characteristic of people who seek psychotherapy is a former and/or present deficiency of basic-need gratification. Neurosis can be seen as a deficiency-disease. Because this is so, a basic necessity for cure is supplying what has been lacking or making it possible for the patient to do this himself. Since these supplies come from other people, ordinary therapy *must* be interpersonal.

But this fact has been badly over-generalized. It is true that people whose deficiency needs have been gratified and who are primarily growth-motivated are by no means exempt from conflict, unhappiness, anxiety, and confusion. In such moments they too are apt to seek help and may very well turn to interpersonal therapy. And yet it is unwise to forget that frequently the problems and the conflicts of the growth-motivated person are solved by himself by turning inward in a meditative way, i.e., self-searching, rather than seeking for help from someone. Even in principle, many of the tasks of self-actualization are largely intrapersonal, such as the making of plans, the discovery of self, the selection of potentialities to develop, the construction of a life-outlook. . . .

11. Instrumental Learning and Personality Change

So-called learning theory in this country has based itself almost entirely on deficit-motivation with goal objects usually external to the organism, i.e., learning the best way to satisfy a need. For this reason, among others, our psychology of learning is a limited body of knowledge, useful only in small areas of life and of real interest only to other "learning theorists."

This is of little help in solving the problem of growth and self-actualization. Here the techniques of repeatedly acquiring from the outside world satisfactions of motivational deficiencies are much less needed. Associative learning and canalizations give way more to perceptual learning, to the increase of insight and understanding, to knowledge of self and to the steady growth of personality, i.e., increased synergy, integration and inner consistency. Change becomes much less an acquisition of habits or associations one by one, and much more a total change of the total person, i.e., a new person rather than the same person with some habits added like new external possessions.

This kind of character-change-learning means changing a very complex, highly integrated, holistic organism, which in turn means that many impacts will make no change at all because more and more such impacts will be rejected as the person becomes more stable and more autonomous.

The most important learning experiences reported to me by my subjects were very frequently single life experiences such as tragedies, deaths, traumata, conversions, and sudden insights, which forced change in the life-outlook of the person and consequently in everything that he did. (Of course the so-called "working through" of the tragedy or of the insight took place over a longer period of time but this, too, was not primarily a matter of associative learning.)

To the extent that growth consists in peeling away inhibitions and constraints and then permitting the person to "be himself," to emit behavior—"radiantly," as it were—rather than to repeat it, to allow his inner nature to express itself, to this extent the behavior of self-actualizers is unlearned, created and released rather than acquired, expressive rather than coping. . . .

Needing Love and Unneeding Love

The love need as ordinarily studied is a deficit need. It is a hole which has to be filled, an emptiness into which love is poured. If this healing necessity is not available, severe pathology results; if it *is* available at the right time, in the right quantities and with proper style, then pathology is averted. Intermediate states of pathology and health follow upon intermediate states of thwarting or satiation. If the pathology is not too severe and if it is caught early enough, replacement therapy can cure. That is to say the sickness, "love-hunger," can be cured in certain cases by making up the pathological deficiency. Love hunger is a deficiency disease, like salt hunger or the avitaminoses.

The healthy person, not having this deficiency, does not need to receive love except in steady, small, maintenance doses and he may even do without these for periods of time. But if motivation is entirely a matter of satisfying deficits and thus getting rid of needs, then a contradiction appears. Satisfaction of the need should cause it to disappear, which is to say that people who have stood in satisfying love relationships are precisely the people who should be *less* likely to give and to receive love! But clinical study of healthier people, who have been love-need-satiated, show that although they need less to *receive* love, they are more able to *give* love. In this sense, they are *more* loving people.

This finding in itself exposes the limitation of ordinary (deficiency-need-centered) motivation theory and indicates the necessity for "metamotivation theory" (or growth-motivation or self-actualization theory).

I have already described in a preliminary fashion the contrasting dynamics of B-love (love for the Being of another person, unneeding love, unselfish love) and D-love (deficiency-love, love need, selfish love). At this point, I wish only to use these two contrasting groups of people to exemplify and illustrate some of the generalizations made above.

1. B-love is welcomed into consciousness, and is completely enjoyed. Since it is non-possessive, and is admiring rather than needing, it makes no trouble and is practically always pleasure-giving.

2. It can never be sated; it may be enjoyed without end. It usually grows greater rather than disappearing. It is intrinsically enjoyable. It is end rather than means.

3. The B-love experience is often described as being the same as, and having the same effects as the aesthetic experience or the mystic experience.

4. The therapeutic and psychogogic effects of experiencing B-love are very profound and widespread. Similar are the characterological effects of the relatively pure love of a healthy mother for her baby, or the perfect love of their God that some mystics have described.

5. B-love is, beyond the shadow of a doubt, a richer, "higher," more valuable subjective experience than D-love (which all B-lovers have also previously experienced). This preference is also reported by my other older, more average subjects, many of whom experi-

ence both kinds of love simultaneously in varying combinations.

6. D-love *can* be gratified. The concept "gratification" hardly applies at all to admiration-love for another person's admiration-worthiness and love-worthiness.

7. In B-love there is a minimum of anxiety-hostility. For all practical human purposes, it may even be considered to be absent. There *can*, of course, be anxiety-for-the-other. In D-love one must always expect some degree of anxiety-hostility.

8. B-lovers are more independent of each other, more autonomous, less jealous or threatened, less needful, more individual, more disinterested, but also simultaneously more eager to help the other toward self-actualization, more proud of his triumphs, more altruistic, generous and fostering.

9. The truest, most penetrating perception of the other is made possible by B-love. It is as much a cognitive as an emotional-conative reaction, as I have already emphasized. So impressive is this, and so often validated by other people's later experience, that, far from accepting the common platitude that love makes people blind, I become more and more inclined to think of the *opposite* as true, namely that non-love makes us blind.

10. Finally, I may say that B-love, in a profound but testable sense, creates the partner. It gives him a self-image, it gives him self-acceptance, a feeling of love-worthiness, all of which permit him to grow. It is a real question whether the full development of the human being is possible without it.

Cognition of Being in the Peak-experiences

Self-actualizing people, those who have come to a high level of maturation, health, and self-fulfillment, have so much to teach us that sometimes they seem almost like a different breed of human beings. But, because it is so new, the exploration of the highest reaches of human nature and of its ultimate possibilities and aspirations is a difficult and tortuous task. It has involved for me the continuous destruction of cherished axioms, the perpetual coping with seeming paradoxes, contradictions and vaguenesses and the occasional collapse around my ears of long established, firmly believed in and seemingly unassailable laws of psychology. Often these have turned out to be no laws at all but only rules for living in a state of mild and chronic

psycho-pathology and fearfulness, of stunting and crippling and im-
maturity which we don't notice because most others have this same
disease that we have. . . .

This chapter is an attempt to generalize in a single description some
of these basic cognitive happenings in the B-love experience, the
parental experience, the mystic, or oceanic, or nature expérience, the
aesthetic perception, the creative moment, the therapeutic or intellectual insight, the orgasmic experience, certain forms of athletic fulfillment, etc. These and other moments of highest happiness and fulfillment I shall call the peak-experiences. . . .

B-Cognition in Peak-experiences

I shall present one by one now in a condensed summary, the characteristics of the cognition found in the generalized peak-experience,
using the term "cognition" in an extremely broad sense.

1. In *B-cognition the experience or the object tends to be seen as a
whole, as a complete unit, detached from relations, from possible usefulness, from expediency, and from purpose.* It is seen as if it were all there
was in the universe, as if it were all of Being, synonymous with the
universe.

This contrasts with D-cognition, which includes most human cognitive experiences. These experiences are partial and incomplete in ways
that will be described below.

We are reminded here of the absolute idealism of the 19th century,
in which all of the universe was conceived to be a unit. Since this
unity could never be encompassed or perceived or cognized by a limited human being, all actual human cognitions were perceived as necessarily *part* of Being, and never conceivably the whole of it.

2. *When there is a B-cognition, the percept is exclusively and fully attended to.* This may be called "total attention"—see also Schachtel.
What I am trying to describe here is very much akin to fascination or
complete absorption. In such attention the figure becomes *all* figure
and the ground, in effect, disappears, or at least is not importantly
perceived. It is as if the figure were isolated for the time being from all
else, as if the world were forgotten, as if the percept had become for
the moment the whole of Being.

Since the whole of Being is being perceived, all those laws obtain which would hold if the whole of the cosmos could be encompassed at once.

This kind of perception is in sharp contrast to normal perception. Here the object is attended to simultaneously with attention to all else that is relevant. It is seen imbedded in its relationships with everything else in the world, and as *part* of the world. Normal figure-ground relationships hold, i.e., both the ground and the figure are attended to, although in different ways. Furthermore, in ordinary cognition, the object is seen not so much *per se* but as a member of a class, as an instance in a larger category. This kind of perception I have described as "rubricizing," and again would point out that this is not so much a full perception of all aspects of the objects or person being perceived, as it is a kind of taxonomy, a classifying, a ticketing off into one file cabinet or another.

To a far greater degree than we ordinarily realize, cognition involves also placing on a continuum. It involves a kind of automatic comparing or judging or evaluating. It implies higher than, less than, better than, taller than, etc.

B-cognition may be called non-comparing cognition or non-evaluating or non-judging cognition. I mean this in the sense in which Dorothy Lee has described the way in which certain primitive peoples differ from us in their perceptions.

A person can be seen *per se,* in himself and by himself. He can be seen uniquely and idiosyncratically, as if he were the sole member of his class. This is what we mean by perception of the unique individual, and this is, of course, what all clinicians try to achieve. But it is a very difficult task, far more difficult than we are ordinarily willing to admit. However, it *can* happen, if only transiently, and it *does* happen characteristically in the peak-experience. The healthy mother, perceiving her infant in love, approaches to this kind of perception of the uniqueness of the person. Her baby is not quite like anybody else in the world. It is marvelous, perfect, and fascinating (at least to the extent that she is able to detach herself from Gesell's norms and comparisons with neighbors' children).

Concrete perceiving of the whole of the object implies, also, that it is seen with "care." Contrariwise, "caring" for the object will produce the sustained attention, the repeated examination that is so necessary for perception of all aspects of the object. The caring minuteness with which a mother will gaze upon her infant again and again, or the lover at his beloved, or the connoisseur at his painting will surely produce a more complete perception than the usual casual rubricizing which passes illegitimately for perception. We may expect richness of detail and a many-sided awareness of the object from this kind of absorbed, fascinated, fully attending cognition. This contrasts with the product of casual observation which gives only the bare bones of the experience, an object which is seen in only some of its aspects in a selective way and from a point of view of "importance" and "unimportance." (Is there any "unimportant" part of a painting, a baby, or a beloved?)

3. While it is true that all human perception is in part a product of the human being and is his creation to an extent, we can yet make some differentiation between the perception of *external objects as relevant to human concerns and as irrelevant to human concerns*. Self-actualizing people are more able to perceive the world as if it were independent not only of them but also of human beings in general. This also tends to be true of the average human being in his highest moments, i.e., in his peak experiences. He can then more readily look upon nature as if it were there in itself and for itself, and not simply as if it were a human playground put there for human purposes. He can more easily refrain from projecting human purposes upon it. In a word, he can see it in its own Being ("endness") rather than as something to be used, or something to be afraid of, or to be reacted to in some other human way.

As one example, let us take the microscope which can reveal through histological slides either a world of *per se* beauty or else a world of threat, danger and pathology. A section of cancer seen through a microscope, if only we can forget that it is a cancer, can be seen as a beautiful and intricate and awe-inspiring organization. A mosquito is a wondrous object if seen as an end-in-itself. Viruses under the electron microscope are fascinating objects (or, at least, they *can* be if we can only forget their human relevance).

B-cognition, because it makes human-irrelevance more possible, enables us thereby to see more truly the nature of the object in itself.

4. One difference between B-cognition and average cognition which is now emerging in my studies, but of which I am as yet uncertain, is that repeated *B-cognizing seems to make the perception richer*. The re-

peated, fascinated, experiencing of a face that we love or a painting that we admire makes us like it more, and permits us to see more and more of it in various senses. This we may call intra-object richness.

But this so far contrasts rather sharply with the more usual effects of repeated experiencing, i.e., boredom, familiarization effects, loss of attention and the like. I have found to my own satisfaction (although I have not tried to prove it) that repeated exposures to what I consider a good painting will make the painting look *more* beautiful to people preselected as perceptive and sensitive, while repeated exposures to what I consider a bad painting will make it look *less* beautiful. The same seems to be true for good people and bad people, cruel or mean ones for instance. Seeing the good ones repeatedly seems to make them look better. Seeing the bad ones repeatedly tends to make them look worse.

In this more usual kind of perception, where so frequently the initial perception is simply a classification into useful or not useful, dangerous or not dangerous, repeated looking makes it become more and more empty. The task of normal perception which is so frequently anxiety-based or D-motivation-determined, is fulfilled in the first viewing. *Need*-to-perceive then disappears, and thereafter the object or person, now that it has been catalogued, is simply no longer perceived. Poverty shows up in repeated experiencing; so, also, does richness. Furthermore, not only does poverty of the percept show up in repeated looking, but also the poverty of the beholder.

One of the main mechanisms by which love produces a profounder perception of the intrinsic qualities of the love object than does non-love is that love involves fascination with the love-object, and therefore repeated and intent and searching looking, seeing with "care." Lovers can see potentialities in each other that other people are blind to. Customarily we say "Love is blind," but we must now make room for the possibility that love may be under certain circumstances more perceptive than non-love. Of course this implies that it is possible in some sense to perceive potentialities which are not yet actual. This is not as difficult a research problem as it sounds. The Rorschach test in the hands of an expert is also a perception of potentialities which are not yet actualized. This is a testable hypothesis in principle.

5. American psychology, or more broadly, Western psychology, in what I consider to be an ethnocentric way, assumes that human needs,

fears and interests must always be determinants of perception. . . .

My findings indicate that in the normal perceptions of self-actualizing people and in the more occasional peak experiences of average
people, *perception can be relatively ego-transcending, self-forgetful, ego-
less.* It can be unmotivated, impersonal, desireless, unselfish, not *needing,* detached. It can be object-centered rather than ego-centered. That
is to say, that the perceptual experience can be organized around the
object as a centering point rather than being based upon the ego. It is
as if they were perceiving something that had independent reality of
its own, and was not dependent upon the beholder. It is possible in
the aesthetic experience or the love experience to become so absorbed
and "poured into" the object that the self, in a very real sense, disappears. Some writers on aesthetics, mysticism, on motherhood and
on love, e.g., Sorokin, have gone so far as to say that in the peak experience we may even speak of identification of the perceiver and the
perceived, a fusion of what was two into a new and larger whole, a
super-ordinate unit. This could remind us of some of the definitions of
empathy and of identification, and, of course, opens up the possibilities of research in this direction.

6. *The peak-experience is felt as a self-validating, self-justifying moment
which carries its own intrinsic value with it.* That is to say it is an end in
itself, what we may call an end-experience rather than a means-ex-
perience. It is felt to be so valuable an experience, so great a revelation, that even to attempt to justify it takes away from its dignity and
worth. This is universally attested to by my subjects as they report
their love experiences, their mystic experiences, their aesthetic experiences, their creative experiences, and their bursts of insight. Particularly with the moment of insight in the therapeutic situation does this
become obvious. By virtue of the very fact that the person defends
himself against the insight, it is therefore by definition painful to accept. Its breaking through into consciousness is sometimes crushing to
the person. And yet, in spite of this fact, it is universally reported to
be worth while, desirable and wanted in the long run. Seeing is better
than being blind, even when seeing hurts. It is a case in which the intrinsic self-justifying, self-validating worth of the experience makes
the pain worthwhile. Numerous writers on aesthetics, religion, creativeness and love uniformly describe these experiences not only as
valuable intrinsically, but also as *so* valuable that they make life worth

while by their occasional occurrence. The mystics have always affirmed this great value of the great mystic experience which may come
only two or three times in a lifetime.

The contrast is very sharp with the ordinary experiences of life,
especially in the West, and, most especially, for American psychologists. Behavior is so identified with means to ends that by many
writers the words "behavior" and "instrumental behavior" are taken
as synonymous. Everything is done for the sake of some further goal,
in order to achieve something else. The apotheosis of this attitude is
reached by John Dewey in his theory of value, in which he finds no
ends at all but only means to ends. Even this statement is not quite accurate because it implies the existence of ends. Rather to be quite accurate he implies that means are means to other means, which in turn
are means, and so on ad infinitum.

The peak-experiences of pure delight are for my subjects among the
ultimate goals of living and the ultimate validations and justifications
for it. That the psychologist should by-pass them or even be officially
unaware of their existence, or what is even worse, in the objectivistic
psychologies, deny a priori the possibility of their existence as objects
for scientific study, is incomprehensible.

7. *In all the common peak-experiences which I have studied, there is a
very characteristic disorientation in time and space.* It would be accurate
to say that in these moments the person is outside of time and space
subjectively. In the creative furor, the poet or artist becomes oblivious
of his surroundings, and of the passage of time. It is impossible for
him when he wakes up to judge how much time has passed.
Frequently he has to shake his head as if emerging from a daze to
rediscover where he is.

But more than this is the frequent report, especially by lovers, of the
complete loss of extension in time. Not only does time pass in their ecstasies with a frightening rapidity so that a day may pass as if it were
a minute but also a minute so intensely lived may feel like a day or a
year. It is as if they had, in a way, some place in another world in
which time simultaneously stood still and moved with great rapidity.
For our ordinary categories, this is of course a paradox and a contradiction. And yet this is what is reported and it is therefore a fact that
we must take account of. I see no reason why this kind of experiencing

of time should not be amenable to experimental research. The judgment of the passing of time in peak-experience must be very inaccurate. So, also, must consciousness of surroundings be much less accurate than in normal living.

8.   The implications of my findings for a psychology of values are very puzzling and yet so uniform that it is necessary not only to report them but also to try somehow to understand them. To start at the end first, *the peak-experience is only good and desirable, and is never experienced as evil or undesirable.* The experience is intrinsically valid; the experience is perfect, complete and needs nothing else. It is sufficient to itself. It is felt as being intrinsically necessary and inevitable. It is just as good as it *should* be. It is reacted to with awe, wonder, amazement, humility and even reverence, exaltation and piety. The word sacred is occasionally used to describe the person's reaction to it. It is delightful and "amusing" in a Being sense.

The philosophical implications here are tremendous. If, for the sake of argument, we accept the thesis that in peak-experience the nature of reality itself *may* be seen more clearly and its essence penetrated more profoundly, then this is almost the same as saying what so many philosophers and theologians have affirmed, that the whole of Being, when seen at its best and from an Olympian point of view, is only neutral or good, and that evil or pain or threat is only a partial phenomenon, a product of not seeing the world whole and unified, and of seeing it from a self-centered or from too low a point of view. (Of course this is not a denial of evil or pain or death but rather a reconciliation with it, an understanding of its necessity.) . . .

These B-values, so far as I can make out at this point, are—

1. wholeness; (unity; integration; tendency to one-ness; interconnectedness; simplicity; organization; structure; dichotomy-transcendence; order);
2. perfection; (necessity; just-right-ness; just-so-ness; inevitability; suitability; justice; completeness; "oughtness");
3. completion; (ending; finality; justice; "it's finished") fulfillment; *finis* and *telos*; destiny; fate);
4. justice; (fairness; orderliness; lawfulness; "oughtness");
5. aliveness; (process; non-deadness; spontaneity; self-regulation; full-functioning);

6. richness; (differentiation, complexity; intricacy);

7. simplicity; (honesty; nakedness; essentiality; abstract, essential, skeletal structure);

8. beauty; (rightness; form; aliveness; simplicity; richness; wholeness; perfection; completion; uniqueness; honesty);

9. goodness; (rightness; desirability; oughtness; justice; benevolence; honesty);

10. uniqueness; (idiosyncrasy; individuality; non-comparability; novelty);

11. effortlessness; (ease; lack of strain, striving or difficulty; grace; perfect, beautiful functioning);

12. playfulness; (fun; joy; amusement; gaiety; humor; exuberance; effortlessness);

13. truth; honesty; reality; (nakedness; simplicity; richness; oughtness; beauty; pure, clean and unadulterated; completeness; essentiality).

14. self-sufficiency; (autonomy; independence; not-needing-other-than-itself-in-order-to-be-itself; self-determining; environment-transcendence; separateness; living by its own laws).

These are obviously *not* mutually exclusive. They are not separate or distinct, but overlay or fuse with each other. Ultimately they are all *facets* of Being rather than *parts* of it. Various of these aspects will come to the foreground of cognition depending on the operation which has revealed it, e.g., perceiving the beautiful person or the beautiful painting, experiencing perfect sex and/or perfect love, insight, creativeness, parturition, etc. . . .

This finding, if it turns out to be correct, is in direct and flat contradiction to one of the basic axioms that guides all scientific thought, namely, that the more objective and impersonal perception becomes, the more detached it becomes from value. Fact and value have almost always (by intellectuals) been considered to be antonyms and mutually exclusive. But perhaps the opposite is true, for when we examine the most ego-detached, objective, motivationless, passive cognition, we find that it claims to perceive values directly, that values cannot be shorn away from reality and that the most profound perceptions of "facts" causes the "is" and the "ought" to fuse. In these moments reality is tinged with wonder, admiration, awe and approval i.e., with value. . . .

9. *The emotional reaction in the peak experience has a special flavor of wonder, of awe, of reverence, of humility and surrender before the experience as before something great.* This sometimes has a touch of fear (although pleasant fear) of being overwhelmed. My subjects report this in such phrases as "This is too much for me." "It is more than I can bear." "It is too wonderful." The experience may have a certain poignancy and piercing quality which may bring either tears or laughter or both, and which may be paradoxically akin to pain, although this is a desirable pain which is often described as "sweet." This may go so far as to involve thoughts of death in a peculiar way. Not only my subjects but many writers on the various peak experiences have made the parallel with the experience of dying, that is, an eager dying. A typical phrase might be: "This is too wonderful. I don't know how I can bear it. I could die now and it would be all right." Perhaps this is in part a hanging on to the experience and a reluctance to go down from this peak into the valley of ordinary existence. Perhaps it is in part, also, an aspect of the profound sense of humility, smallness, unworthiness before the enormity of the experience. . . .

10. There are substantial differences between the cognition that abstracts and categorizes and the fresh cognition of the concrete, the raw and the particular. This is the sense in which I shall use the terms abstract and concrete. They are not very different from Goldstein's terms. Most of our cognitions (attendings, perceivings, rememberings, thinkings and learnings) are abstract rather than concrete. That is, we mostly categorize, schematize, classify and abstract in our cognitive life. We do not so much cognize the nature of the world as it actually is, as we do the organization of our own inner world outlook. Most of experience is filtered through our system of categories, constructs and rubrics, as Schachtel has also pointed out in his classical paper on "Childhood Amnesia and the Problem of Memory." I was led to this differentiation by my studies of self-actualizing people, *finding in them simultaneously the ability to abstract without giving up concreteness and the ability to be concrete without giving up abstractness.* This adds a little to Goldstein's description because I found not only a reduction to the concrete but also what we might call a reduction to the abstract, i.e., a loss of ability to cognize the concrete. Since then I have found this same exceptional ability to perceive in good artists and clinicians as well, even though not self-actualizing. More recently I find this same

ability in ordinary people in their peak moments. They are then more able to grasp the percept in its own concrete, idiosyncratic nature. . . .

Let us take for example the perception of a painting or of a person. In order to perceive them fully we must fight our tendency to classify, to compare, to evaluate, to need, to use. The moment that we say this man is, e.g., a foreigner, in that moment we have classified him, performed an abstracting act and, to some extent, cut ourselves off from the possibility of seeing him as a unique and whole human being, different from any other one in the whole world. In the moment that we approach the painting on the wall to read the name of the artist, we have cut ourselves off from the possibility of seeing it with complete freshness in its own uniqueness. To a certain extent then, what we call *knowing*, i.e., the placing of an experience in a system of concepts or words or relations, cuts off the possibility of full cognizing. Herbert Read has pointed out that the child has the "innocent eye," the ability to see something as if he were seeing it for the first time (frequently he *is* seeing it for the first time). He can then stare at it in wonder, examining all aspects of it, taking in all its attributes, since for the child in this situation, no attribute of a strange object is any more important than any other attribute. He does not organize it; he simply stares at it. He savors the qualities of the experience. In the similar situation for the adult, to the extent that we can prevent ourselves from only abstracting, naming, placing, comparing, relating, to that extent will we be able to see more and more aspects of the many-sidedness of the person or of the painting. Particularly I must underline the ability to perceive the ineffable, that which cannot be put into words. Trying to force it into words changes it, and makes it something other than it is, something else *like* it, something similar, and yet something different than *it* itself. . . .

11. *At the higher levels of human maturation, many dichotomies, polarities, and conflicts are fused, transcended or resolved.* Self-actualizing people are simultaneously selfish and unselfish, Dionysian and Apollonian, individual and social, rational and irrational, fused with others and detached from others, and so on. What I had thought to be straight-line continua, whose extremes were polar to each other and as far apart as possible, turned out to be rather like circles or spirals, in which the polar extremes came together into a fused unity. So also do I

find this as a strong tendency in the full cognition of the object. The more we understand the whole of Being, the more we can tolerate the simultaneous existence and perception of inconsistencies, of oppositions and of flat contradictions. These seem to be products of partial cognition, and fade away with cognition of the whole. The neurotic person seen from a godlike vantage point, can then be seen as a wonderful, intricate, even beautiful unity of process. What we normally see as conflict and contradiction and dissociation can then be perceived as inevitable, necessary, even fated. That is to say if he can be fully understood, then everything falls into its necessary place and he can be aesthetically perceived and appreciated. All his conflicts and splits turn out to have a kind of sense or wisdom. Even the concepts of sickness and of health may fuse and blur when we see the symptom as a pressure toward health, or see the neurosis as the healthiest possible solution at the moment to the problems of the individual. . . .

12. *One aspect of the peak-experience is a complete, though momentary, loss of fear, anxiety, inhibition, defense and control, a giving up of renunciation, delay and restraint.* The fear of disintegration and dissolution, the fear of being overwhelmed by the "instincts," the fear of death and of insanity, the fear of giving in to unbridled pleasure and emotion, all tend to disappear or go into abeyance for the time being. This too implies a greater openness of perception since fear distorts.

It may be thought of as pure gratification, pure expression, pure elation or joy. But since it is "in the world," it represents a kind of fusion of the Freudian "pleasure principle" and "reality principle." It is therefore still another instance of the resolution of ordinarily dichotomous concepts at higher levels of psychological functioning.

We may therefore expect to find a certain "permeability" in people who have such experiences commonly, a closeness and openness to the unconscious, and a relative lack of fear of it.

GABRIEL MARCEL

Self-realization:
A Mystery, not a Problem

Everything really comes down to the distinction between what we have and what we are. But it is extraordinarily hard to express this in conceptual terms, though it must be possible to do so. What we *have* obviously presents an appearance of externality to ourselves. But it is not an absolute externality. In principle, what we *have* are things (or what can be compared to things, precisely in so far as this comparison is possible). I can only *have*, in the strict sense of the word, something whose existence is, up to a certain point, independent of me. In other words, what I have is added to me; and the fact that it is possessed by me is added to the other properties, qualities, etc., belonging to the thing I have. I only have what I can in some manner and within certain limits dispose of; in other words, in so far as I can be considered as a force, a being endowed with powers. We can only transmit what we have.

Here, then, is one approach, but it is not the only one. I cannot, for instance, concentrate my attention on what is properly called *my* body—as distinct from the body-as-object considered by physiologists—without coming once more upon this almost impenetrable notion of having. And yet, can I, with real accuracy, say that my body is something which I have? In the first place, can my body as such be called a thing? If I treat it as a thing, what is this "I" which so treats it? "In the last analysis," I wrote in the *Journal Métaphysique* (p. 252), "we end up with the formula: My body is (an object), I am—nothing. Idealism has one further resource: it can declare that I am the act which posits the objective reality of my body. But is not this a mere sleight-of-hand? I fear so. The difference between this sort of idealism and

190

pure materialism amounts almost to nothing." But we can go much deeper than this. In particular, we can show the consequences of such a mode of representation or imagination for our attitude towards death or suicide.

Surely killing ourselves is disposing of our bodies (or lives) as though they are something we *have,* as though they are things. And surely this is an implicit admission that we belong to ourselves? But almost unfathomable perplexities then assail us: what is the self? What is this mysterious relation between the self and ourself? It is surely clear that the relation is quite a different thing for the man who refuses to kill himself, because he does not recognise a right to do so, since he does not belong to himself. Beneath this apparently negligible difference of formulae, may we not perceive a kind of gulf which we cannot fill in, and can only explore a step at a time? . . .

We should first notice that the philosophers seem to have always shown a sort of implicit mistrust towards the notion of having (I say "notion," but we must ask whether this is a suitable expression, and I really think it is not). It looks as if the philosophers had on the whole turned away from having, as if it were an impure idea, essentially incapable of being made precise.

The essential ambiguity of having should certainly be underlined from the very beginning. But I think that we cannot, at present, exempt ourselves from going on to the inquiry I am suggesting today. I was prosecuting this inquiry when I first came across Herr Gunter Stern's book *Uber das Haben* (published at Bonn by Cohen, 1928). I will content myself with quoting these few lines:

We have a body. We have. . . . In ordinary talk we are perfectly clear about what we mean by this. And yet nobody has thought of turning his attention upon what, in common parlance, is intended by the word "have"; no one has attended to it as a complex of relations, and asked himself in what having consists, simply as having.

I should like to start with the clearest examples I can, where having is plainly in its strongest and most exact sense. There are other cases where this sense (or perhaps we should more properly call it this emphasis) is weakened almost to vanishing point. Such limiting cases can and should be practically neglected (having headaches, for instance, having need, etc.—the absence of the article is a revealing sign here). In cases of the first type, however, that is, in significant cases, it seems that we are right to distinguish two kinds, so long as we do not forget afterwards to ask ourselves about the relations between them. Having-as-possession can itself develop varieties that are very different, and arranged, as it were, in a hierarchy. But the possessive index is as clearly marked when I say, "I have a bicycle," as it is when I assert, "I have my own views on that," or even when I say (and this takes us in a slightly different direction), "I have time to do so-and-so." We will provisionally set aside having-as-implication. In all having-as-possession there does seem to be a certain content. That is too definite a word. Call it a certain *quid* relating to a certain *qui* who is treated as a center of inherence or apprehension. I purposely abstain from the use of the word subject, because of the special meanings, whether logical or epistemological, which it connotes: whereas it is our task—and difficult for this very reason—to try to blaze a trail for ourselves across territory outside the realms either of logic or of the theory of knowledge.

Notice that the *qui* is from the first taken as in some degree transcendent to the *quid*. By transcendent I just mean that there is a difference of level or degree between the two of them, but I make no attempt to pronounce on the nature of that difference. It is as clear when I say, "I have a bicycle," or "Paul has a bicycle," as when I say "James has very original ideas about that."

This is all perfectly simple. The position becomes more complicated when we observe that any assertion about having seems to be somehow built on the model of a kind of prototypical statement, where the *qui* is no other than *myself*. It looks as if having is only felt in its full force, and given its full weight, when it is within "I have." If a "you have" or a "he has" is possible, it is only possible in virtue of a kind of transference, and such a transference cannot be made without losing something in the process.

This can be made somewhat clearer if we think of the relation which plainly joins possession to power, at any rate where the possession is actual and literal. Power is something which I experience by exercising it or by resisting it—after all, it comes to the same thing.

I should be told here that having is often apt to reduce itself to the fact of containing. But even if we admit that this is so, the important point must still be made, that the containing itself cannot be defined in purely spatial terms. It seems to me always to imply the idea of a potentiality. To contain is to enclose; but to enclose is to prevent, to resist, and to oppose the tendency of the content towards spreading, spilling out, and escaping.

And so I think that the objection, if it is one, turns, on a closer examination, against the man who makes it.

At the heart of having, then, we can discern a kind of *suppressed* dynamic, and suppression is certainly the key-word here. It is this which lights up what I call the transcendence of the *qui*. It is significant that the relation embodied in having is, grammatically, found to be intransitive. The verb "to have" is only used in the passive in exceptional and specialised ways. It is as though we saw passing before us a kind of irreversible progress from the *qui* towards the *quid*. Let me add that we are not here concerned with a mere step taken by the subject reflecting upon having. No, the progress seems to be carried out by the *qui* itself: it seems to be within the *qui*. Here we must pause for a moment, as we are drawing close to the central point.

We can only express ourselves in terms of *having* when we are moving on a level where, in whatever manner and whatever degree of transposition, the contrast between within and without retains a meaning. . . .

The characteristic of a possession is being sh[o]wable. There is a strict parallel between having drawings by X in one's portfolios, which can be sh[o]wn to this or that visitor, and having ideas or opinion on this or that question.

This act of sh[o]wing may take place or unfold before another or before one's-self. The curious thing is that analysis will reveal to us that this difference is devoid of meaning. In so far as I sh[o]w my own views to myself, I myself become someone else. That, I suppose, is the metaphysical basis for the possibility of expression. I can only express myself in so far as I can become someone else to myself.

And now we see the transition take place from the first formula to the second one: we can only express ourselves in terms of having, when we are moving on the level implying reference to another taken as another. There is no contradiction between this formula and my remarks just now on "I have." The statement "I have" can only be made over against *another* which is felt to be other.

In so far as I conceive myself as having in myself, or more exactly, as mine, certain characteristics, certain trappings, I consider myself from the point of view of another—but I do not separate myself from this other except after having first implicitly identified myself with him.

When I say, for instance, "I have my own opinion about that" I imply, "My opinion is not everybody's"; but I can only exclude or reject everybody's opinion if I have first, by a momentary fiction, assimilated it and made it mine.

Having, therefore, is not found in the scale of purely interior relations, far from it. It would there be meaningless. It is found, rather, in a scale where externality and internality can no longer be really separated, any more than height and depth of musical tone. And here, I think, it is the tension between them that is important.

We must now return to having-as-possession in its strict sense. Take the simplest case, possession of any object whatever, say a picture. From one point of view we should say that this object is exterior to its possessor. It is spatially distinct from him, and their destinies are also different. And yet this is only a superficial view. The stronger the emphasis placed on having and possession, the less permissible is it to harp upon this externality. It is absolutely certain that there is a link between the *qui* and the *quid*, and that this link is not simply an external conjunction. But in so far as this *quid* is a thing, and consequently subject to the changes and chances proper to things, it may be lost or destroyed. So it becomes, or is in danger of becoming, the centre of a kind of whirlpool of fears and anxieties, thus expressing exactly the tension which is an essential part of the order of having.

It may be said that I can easily be indifferent to the fate of this or that object in my possession. But in that case, I should say that the possession is only nominal, or again, residual.

It is, on the other hand, very important to notice that having already exists, in a most profound sense, in desire or in covetousness. To desire is in a manner to have without having. That is why there is a kind of suffering or burning which is an essential part of desire. It is really the expression of a sort of contradiction; it expresses the friction inseparable from an untenable position. There is also an absolute balance between covetousness and the pain I feel at the idea that I am going to lose what I have, what I thought I had, and what I have no longer. But if this is so, then it seems (a point we had noticed before) that having in some way depends upon time. Here again we shall find ourselves confronted with a kind of mysterious polarity.

There is certainly a twofold permanency in having: there is the permanency of the *qui*, and the permanency of the *quid*. But this permanency is, of its very nature, threatened. It is willed, or at least wished, and it slips from our grasp. The threat is the hold exerted by the other *qua* other, the other which may be the world itself, and before which I so painfully feel that I am I. I hug to myself this thing which may be torn from me, and I desperately try to incorporate it in myself, to form myself and it into a single and dissoluble complex. A desperate, hopeless struggle. . . .

Normally, or (if you prefer it) usually, I find myself confronted with things: and some of these things have a relationship with me which is at once peculiar and mysterious. These things are not *only external:* it is as though there were a connecting corridor between them and me; they reach me, one might say, underground. In exact proportion as I am attached to these things, they are seen to exercise a power over me which my attachment confers upon them, and which grows as the attachment grows. There is one particular thing which really stands first among them, or which enjoys an absolute priority, in this respect, over them—my body. The tyranny it exercises over me depends, by no means completely, but to a considerable degree, upon the attachment I have for it. But—and this is the most paradoxical feature of the situation—I seem, in the last resort, to be annihilating myself in this attachment, by sinking myself in this body to which I cling. It seems that my body literally devours me, and it is the same with all the other possessions which are somehow attached or hung upon my body. So that in the last analysis—and this is a new point of view—Having as such seems to have a tendency to destroy and lose itself in the very thing it began by possessing, but which now absorbs the master who thought he controlled it. It seems that it is of the very nature of my body, or of my instruments in so far as I treat them as possessions, that they should tend to blot me out, although it is I who possess them.

But if I think again, I shall see that this kind of dialectic is only possible if it starts from an act of desertion which makes it possible. And this observation at once opens up the way to a whole new region.

And yet, what difficulties we find! What an array of possible objections! In particular, could it not be said, "In so far as you treat the instrument as pure instrument, it has no power over you. You control it yourself and it does not react upon you." This is perfectly true. But there is a division or interval, hardly measurable by thought, between having something, and controlling or using it: and the danger we are speaking of lies in this division or interval. Spengler, in the very remarkable book he has just published on *The Decisive Years* and the state of the world today, somewhere notices the distinction that I am getting at here. In speaking of investments or shares in companies, he emphasises the difference between pure having (*das blosse Haben*), and the responsible work of direction which falls to the head of the under-taking. Elsewhere he insists upon the contrast between money, treated as an abstract, in the mass (*Wertmenge*), and real property (*Besitz*), in a piece of land, for example. There is something in this to throw indirect light upon the difficult piece of thinking which I am now trying to explain. "Our possessions eat us up," I said just now: and it is truer of us, strangely enough, when we are in a state of inertia in face of objects which are themselves inert, but falser when we are more vitally and actively bound up with something serving as the immediate subject-matter of a personal creative act, a subject-matter perpetually renewed. (It may be the garden of the keen gardener, the farm of a farmer, the violin of a musician, or the laboratory of a scientist.) In all these cases, we may say, having tends, not to be destroyed, but to be sublimated and changed into being.

Wherever there is pure creation, having as such is transcended or etherialised within the creative act: the duality of possessor and possessed is lost in a living reality. This demands the most concrete illustration we can think of, and not mere examples taken from the category of material possessions. I am thinking in particular of such pseudo-possessions as *my ideas and opinions*. In this case, the word "have" takes on a meaning which is at once positive and threatening. The more I treat my own ideas, or even my convictions, as something *belonging* to me—and so as something I am proud of (unconsciously perhaps) as I might be proud of my greenhouse or my stables—the more surely will these ideas and opinions tend, by their very inertia (or my inertia towards them, which comes to the same thing) to exercise a tyrannical power over me; that is the principle of fanaticism in all its shapes. What happens in the case of the fanatic, and in other cases too, it seems, is a sort of unjustified alienation of the subject— the use of the term is unavoidable here—in face of the thing, whatever it may be. That, in my opinion, is the difference between the ideologist, on the one hand, and the thinker or artist on the other. The ideologist is one of the most dangerous of all human types, because he is unconsciously enslaved to a part of himself which has mortified, and this slavery is bound to manifest itself outwardly as tyranny.

There, by the way, may be seen a connection which deserves serious and separate examination. The thinker, on the other hand, is continually on guard against this alienation, this possible fossilising of his thought. He lives in a continual state of creativity, and the whole of his thought is always being called in question from one minute to the next. . . .

We can see what is to be understood by the uncharacterisable. I said that, underlying our mental picture of things, as subjects possessing predicates or characteristics, there must be a transference. It seems plain to me that the distinction between the thing and its characteristics cannot have any metaphysical bearing: it is, shall we say, purely phenomenal. Notice, too, that characteristics can only be asserted in an order which admits of the use of the word "also." The characteristic is picked out from others; but at the same time, we cannot say that the thing is a collection of characteristics. Characteristics cannot be juxtaposed, and we do not juxtapose them except in so far as we ignore their specifying function and treat them as units or homogeneous entities; but that is a fiction which does not bear examination. I can, strictly speaking, treat an apple, a bullet, a key, and a ball of string as objects of the same nature, and as a sum of units. But it is quite different with the smell of a flower and its colour, or the consistency, flavour and digestibility of a dish. In so far, then, as characterisation consists in enumerating properties, placing one beside the other, it is an absolutely external proceeding; it misleads us, and never, in any circumstances, gives us the least opportunity of reaching the heart of that reality which we are trying to characterise. But, speaking philosophically, the really important point to recognise is that characterisation implies a certain setting of myself in front of the other, and (if I may say so) a sort of radical banishment or cutting-off of me from it. I myself bring about this banishment, by myself implicitly coming to a *halt,* separating myself, and treating myself (though I probably am not conscious of so doing) as a thing bounded by its outlines. It is only in relation to this implicitly limited *thing* that I can place whatever I am trying to characterise.

It is plain that the will to characterise implies, in the man who is exerting it, a belief at once sincere and illusory that he can make abstraction from himself *qua* himself. The Leibnizian idea of *characteristica universalis* shows us how far this *pretension* can go. But I am inclined to think that we forget how untenable, metaphysically speaking, is the position of a thought which believes that it can place itself over against things in order to grasp them. It can certainly develop a system of taking its bearings by things, a system of increasing and even infinite complexity: but its aim is to let the essence of things go.

To say that reality is perhaps uncharacterisable is certainly to make an ambiguous and apparently contradictory pronouncement, and we must be careful not to interpret it in a way which conforms with the principles of present-day agnosticism. This means:—If I adopt that attitude to Reality, which all efforts to characterise it would presuppose, I at once cease to apprehend it *qua* Reality: it slips away from my eyes, leaving me face to face with no more than its ghost. I am deceived by the inevitable coherence of this ghost, and so sink into self-satisfaction and pride, when in fact I ought rather to be attacked by doubts of the soundness of my undertaking.

Characterisation is a certain kind of possession, or claim to possession, of that which cannot be possessed. It is the construction of a little abstract effigy, a *model* as English physicists call it, of a reality which will not lend itself to these deceptive pretences, except in the most superficial way. Reality will only play this game with us in so far as we cut ourselves off from it, and consequently are guilty of self-desertion.

I think, therefore, that as we raise ourselves towards Reality, and approach it more nearly, we find that it cannot be compared with an object placed before us on which we can take bearings: and we find, too, that we are ourselves actually changed in the process. . . . If Being is more uncharacterisable (i.e. more unpossessable and more transcendent in every way) in proportion as it has more Being, then the attributes can do no more than express and translate, in terms that are completely inadequate, the fact that Absolute Being is as a whole rebellious to descriptions which will never fit anything but what has less Being. They will only fit an object before which we can place ourselves, reducing ourselves, to some extent, to its measure, and reducing it to ours. God can only be given to me as Absolute Presence in worship; any idea I form of Him is only an abstract expression or intellectualisation of the Presence. I must never fail to remember this, when I try to handle such thoughts; otherwise the thoughts will suffer distortion in my sacrilegious hands.

And so we come at last to what is for me the essential distinction— the central point of my essay on *The Ontological Mystery*, to be published in a few days—the distinction between problem and mystery, already presupposed in the paper you have just heard.

I venture to read now a passage from a paper delivered last year to the Marseilles Philosophical Society. It will appear in a few days from now as the appendix to a play, *le Monde Cassé*.

In turning my attention to what one usually thinks of as ontological problems, such as Does Being exist? What is Being? etc., I came to observe that I cannot think about these problems without seeing a new gulf open beneath my feet, namely, This I, I who ask questions about being, can I be sure that I exist? What qualifications have I for pursuing these inquiries? If I do not exist, how can I hope to bring them to a conclusion? Even admitting that I do exist, how can I be assured that I do? In spite of the thought which comes first into my head, I do not think that Descartes' *cogito* can be of any help to us here. The *cogito*, as I have written elsewhere, is at the mere threshold of validity; the subject of the *cogito* is the epistemological subject. Cartesianism implies a severance, which may be fatal anyhow, between intellect and life; the result is a depreciation of the one, and an exaltation of the other, both arbitrary. There is here an inevitable rhythm only too familiar to us, for which we are bound to find an explanation. It would certainly not be proper to deny the legitimacy of making distinctions of order within the unity of a living subject, who *thinks* and strives to *think of himself*. But the ontological problem can only arise beyond such distinctions, and for the living being grasped in his full unity and vitality.

This leads us to ask what conditions are involved in the idea of working out a problem. Wherever a problem is found, I am working upon data placed before me; but at the same time, the general state of affairs authorises me to carry on as if I had no need to trouble myself with this Me who is at work: he is here simply presupposed. It is, as we have just seen, quite a different matter when the inquiry is about Being. Here the ontological status of the questioner becomes of the highest importance. Could it be said, then, that I am involving myself in an infinite regress? No, for by the very act of so conceiving the regress, I am placing myself above it. I am recognising that the whole reflexive process remains within a certain assertion which I *am*—rather than *which I pronounce*—an assertion of which I am the place, and not the subject. Thereby we advance into the realm of the metaproblematic, that is, of mystery. A mystery is a problem which encroaches upon its own data and invades them, and so is transcended *qua* problem.

It seems clear to me that the realm of having is identical with the realm of the problematic—and at the same time, of course, with the realm where technics can be used. The metaproblematic is in fact metatechnical. Every technic presupposes a group of previously made abstractions which are the condition of its working; it is powerless where fullblooded Being is in question. This point might be drawn

out in several directions. At the root of having, as also at the root of
the problem or the technic, there lies a certain specialisation or specification of the self, and this is connected with that partial alienation of
the self which I mentioned earlier. Anything in the nature of interests,
whatever the interests are, can be treated with relative ease as a sphere
or district with fixed boundaries. And further, I can, to a great extent,
treat my own life as capable of being administered by another or by
myself (myself here meaning the not-other). I can administer anything
which admits the comparison, however indirect, with a fortune or
possession. But it is quite different when the category of having can
no longer be applied, for then I can no longer talk of administration in
any sense, and so cannot speak of autonomy. Take, for example, the
realm of literary or artistic talents. To a certain extent a talent may be
administered, when its possessor has taken the measure of it, when
his talent resides in him as a possession. But for genius, properly so-
called, the idea of such administration is a complete contradiction; for
it is of the essence of genius to be always outrunning itself and spilling over in all directions. A man *is* a genius, but *has* talent (the expression "to *have* genius" is literally meaningless). I really think that the
idea of autonomy, whatever we may have thought of it, is bound up
with a kind of reduction or particularisation of the subject. The more I
enter into the whole of an activity with the whole of myself, the less
legitimate it is to say that I am autonomous. In this sense, the philosopher is less autonomous than the scientist, and the scientist less autonomous than the technician. The man who is most autonomous is,
in a certain sense, most fully involved. Only this nonautonomy of the
philosopher or the great artist is not heteronomy any more than love is
hetero-centricity. It is rooted in Being, at a point either short of self or
beyond self, and in a sphere which transcends all possible possession;
the sphere, indeed, which I reach in contemplation or worship. And,
in my view, this means that such nonautonomy is very freedom.

MARTIN BUBER

The I-You Beyond the Self

The world is twofold for man in accordance with his twofold attitude.

The attitude of man is twofold in accordance with the two basic words he can speak.

The basic words are not single words but word pairs.

One basic word is the word pair I-You.

The other basic word is the word pair I-It; but this basic word is not changed when He or She takes the place of It.

Thus the I of man is also twofold.

For the I of the basic word I-You is different from that in the basic word I-It.

Basic words do not state something that might exist outside them; by being spoken they establish a mode of existence.

Basic words are spoken with one's being.

When one says You, the I of the word pair I-You is said, too.

When one says It, the I of the word pair I-It is said, too.

The basic word I-You can only be spoken with one's whole being.

The basic word I-It can never be spoken with one's whole being.

There is no I as such but only the I of the basic word I-You and the I of the basic word I-It.

When a man says I, he means one or the other. The I he means is present when he says I. And when he says You or It, the I of one or the other basic word is also present.

Being I and saying I are the same. Saying I and saying one of the two basic words are the same.

Whoever speaks one of the basic words enters into the word and stands in it.

The life of a human being does not exist merely in the sphere of goal-directed verbs. It does not consist merely of activities that have something for their object.

I perceive something. I feel something. I imagine something. I want something. I sense something. I think something. The life of a human being does not consist merely of all this and its like.

All this and its like is the basis of the realm of It.

But the realm of You has another basis.

Whoever says You does not have something for his object. For wherever there is something there is also another something; every It borders on other Its; It is only by virtue of bordering on others. But where You is said there is no something. You has no borders.

Whoever says You does not have something; he has nothing. But he stands in relation.

We are told that man experiences his world. What does this mean?

Man goes over the surfaces of things and experiences them. He brings back from them some knowledge of their condition—an experience. He experiences what there is to things.

But it is not experiences alone that bring the world to man.

For what they bring to him is only a world that consists of It and It and It, of He and He and She and She and It.

I experience something.

All this is not changed by adding "inner" experiences to the "external" ones, in line with the non-eternal distinction that is born of mankind's craving to take the edge off the mystery of death. Inner things like external things, things among things!

I experience something.

And all this is not changed by adding "mysterious" experiences to "manifest" ones, self-confident in the wisdom that recognizes a secret compartment in things, reserved for the initiated, and holds the key. O mysteriousness without mystery, O piling up of information! It, it, it!

Those who experience do not participate in the world. For the experience is "in them" and not between them and the world.

The world does not participate in experience. It allows itself to be experienced, but it is not concerned, for it contributes nothing, and nothing happens to it.

The world as experience belongs to the basic word I-It.

The basic word I-You establishes the world of relation.

Three are the spheres in which the world of relation arises.

The first: life with nature. Here the relation vibrates in the dark and remains below language. The creatures stir across from us, but they are unable to come to us, and the You we say to them sticks to the threshold of language.

The second: life with men. Here the relation is manifest and enters language. We can give and receive the You.

The third: life with spiritual beings. Here the relation is wrapped in a cloud but reveals itself, it lacks but creates language. We hear no You and yet feel addressed; we answer—creating, thinking, acting: with our being we speak the basic word, unable to say You with our mouth.

But how can we incorporate into the world of the basic word what lies outside language?

In every sphere, through everything that becomes present to us, we gaze toward the train of the eternal You; in each we perceive a breath of it; in every You we address the eternal You, in every sphere according to its manner.

I contemplate a tree.

I can accept it as a picture: a rigid pillar in a flood of light, or splashes of green traversed by the gentleness of the blue silver ground.

I can feel it as movement: the flowing veins around the sturdy, striving core, the sucking of the roots, the breathing of the leaves, the infinite commerce with earth and air—and the growing itself in its darkness.

I can assign it to a species and observe it as an instance, with an eye to its construction and its way of life.

I can overcome its uniqueness and form so rigorously that I recognize it only as an expression of the law—those laws according to which a constant opposition of forces is continually adjusted, or those laws according to which the elements mix and separate.

I can dissolve it into a number, into a pure relation between numbers, and eternalize it.

Throughout all of this the tree remains my object and has its place and its time span, its kind and condition.

But it can also happen, if will and grace are joined, that as I contemplate the tree I am drawn into a relation, and the tree ceases to be an It. The power of exclusiveness has seized me.

This does not require me to forego any of the modes of contemplation. There is nothing that I must not see in order to see, and there is no knowledge that I must forget. Rather is everything, picture and movement, species and instance, law and number included and inseparably fused.

Whatever belongs to the tree is included: its form and its mechanics, its colors and its chemistry, its conversation with the elements and its conversation with the stars—all this in its entirety.

The tree is no impression, no play of my imagination, no aspect of a mood; it confronts me bodily and has to deal with me as I must deal with it—only differently.

One should not try to dilute the meaning of the relation: relation is reciprocity.

Does the tree then have consciousness, similar to our own? I have no experience of that. But thinking that you have brought this off in your own case, must you again divide the indivisible? What I encounter is neither the soul of a tree nor a dryad, but the tree itself.

When I confront a human being as my You and speak the basic word I-You to him, then he is nothing among things nor does he consist of things.

He is no longer He or She, limited by other Hes and Shes, a dot in the world grid of space and time, nor a condition that can be experienced and described, a loose bundle of named qualities. Neighborless and seamless, he is You and fills the firmament. Not as if there were nothing but he; but everything else lives in *his* light.

Even as a melody is not composed of tones, nor a verse of words, nor a statue of lines—one must pull and tear to turn a unity into a multiplicity—so it is with the human being to whom I say You. I can abstract from him the color of his hair or the color of his speech or the color of his graciousness; I have to do this again and again; but immediately he is no longer You.

And even as prayer is not in time but time in prayer, the sacrifice not in space but space in the sacrifice—and whoever reverses the relation annuls the reality—I do not find the human being to whom I say You in any Sometime and Somewhere. I can place him there and have to do this again and again, but immediately he becomes a He or a She, an It, and no longer remains my You.

As long as the firmament of the You is spread over me, the tempests of causality cower at my heels, and the whirl of doom congeals.

The human being to whom I say You I do not experience. But I stand in relation to him, in the sacred basic word. Only when I step out of this do I experience him again. Experience is remoteness from You.

The relation can obtain even if the human being to whom I say You does not hear it in his experience. For You is more than It knows. You does more, and more happens to it, than It knows. No deception reaches this far: here is the cradle of actual life.

This is the eternal origin of art that a human being confronts a form that wants to become a work through him. Not a figment of his soul but something that appears to the soul and demands the soul's creative power. What is required is a deed that a man does with his whole being: if he commits it and speaks with his being the basic word to the form that appears, then the creative power is released and the work comes into being.

The deed involves a sacrifice and a risk. The sacrifice: infinite possibility is surrendered on the altar of the form; all that but a moment ago floated playfully through one's perspective has to be exterminated; none of it may penetrate into the work; the exclusiveness of such a confrontation demands this. The risk: the basic word can only be spoken with one's whole being; whoever commits himself may not hold back part of himself; and the work does not permit me, as a tree or man might, to seek relaxation in the It-world; it is imperious: if I do not serve it properly, it breaks, or it breaks me.

The form that confronts me I cannot experience nor describe; I can only actualize it. And yet I see it, radiant in the splendor of the confrontation, far more clearly than all clarity of the experienced world.

Not as a thing among the "internal" things, not as a figment of the "imagination," but as what is present. Tested for its objectivity, the form is not "there" at all; but what can equal its presence? And it is an actual relation: it acts on me as I act on it.

Such work is creation, inventing is finding. Forming is discovery. As I actualize, I uncover. I lead the form across—into the world of It. The created work is a thing among things and can be experienced and described as an aggregate of qualities. But the receptive beholder may be bodily confronted now and again.

—One can understand how the It-world, left to itself, untouched and unthawed by the emergence of any You, should become alienated and turn into an incubus; but how does it happen that, as you say, the I of man is deactualized? Whether it lives in relation or outside it, the I remains assured of itself in its self-consciousness, which is a strong thread of gold on which the changing states are strung. Whether I say, "I see you" or "I see the tree," seeing may not be equally actual in both cases, but the I is equally actual in both.

—Let us examine, let us examine ourselves to see whether this is so. The linguistic form proves nothing. After all, many a spoken You really means an It to which one merely says You from habit, thoughtlessly. And many a spoken It really means a You whose presence one may remember with one's whole being, although one is far away. Similarly, there are innumerable occasions when I is only an indispensable pronoun, only a necessary abbreviation for "This one there who is speaking." But self-consciousness? If one sentence truly intends the You of a relation and the other one the It of an experience, and if the I in both sentences is thus intended in truth, do both sentences issue from the same self-consciousness?

The I of the basic word I-You is different from that of the basic word I-It.

The I of the basic word I-It appears as an ego and becomes conscious of itself as a subject (of experience and use).

The I of the basic word I-You appears as a person and becomes conscious of itself as subjectivity (without any dependent genetive).

Egos appear by setting themselves apart from other egos.

Persons appear by entering into relation to other persons.

One is the spiritual form of natural differentiation, the other that of natural association.

The purpose of setting oneself apart is to experience and use, and the purpose of that is "living"—which means dying one human life long.

The purpose of relation is the relation itself—touching the You. For as soon as we touch a You, we are touched by a breath of eternal life.

Whoever stands in relation, participates in an actuality; that is, in a being that is neither merely a part of him nor merely outside him. All actuality is an activity in which I participate without being able to appropriate it. Where there is no participation, there is no actuality. Where there is self-appropriation, there is no actuality. The more directly the You is touched, the more perfect is the participation.

The I is actual through its participation in actuality. The more perfect the participation is, the more actual the I becomes.

But the I that steps out of the event of the relation into detachment and the self-consciousness accompanying that, does not lose its actuality. Participation remains in it as a living potentiality. To use words that originally refer to the highest relation but may also be applied to all others: the seed remains in him. This is the realm of subjectivity in which the I apprehends simultaneously its association and its detachment. Genuine subjectivity can be understood only dynamically, as the vibration of the I in its lonely truth. This is also the place where the desire for ever higher and more unconditional relation and for perfect participation in being arises and keeps rising. In subjectivity the spiritual substance of the person matures.

The person becomes conscious of himself as participating in being, as being-with, and thus as a being. The ego becomes conscious of himself as being this way and not that. The person says, "I am"; the ego says, "That is how I am." "Know thyself" means to the person: know yourself as being. To the ego it means: know your being-that-way. By setting himself apart from others, the ego moves away from being.

This does not mean that the person "gives up" his being-that-way, his being different; only, this is not the decisive perspective but merely the necessary and meaningful form of being. The ego, on the other hand, wallows in his being-that-way—or rather for the most part in the fiction of his being-that-way—a fiction that he has devised for himself. For at bottom self-knowledge usually means to him the fabrication of an effective apparition of the self that has the power to deceive him ever more thoroughly; and through the contemplation and veneration of this apparition one seeks the semblance of knowledge of one's own being-that-way, while actual knowledge of it would lead one to self-destruction—or rebirth.

The person beholds his self; the ego occupies himself with his My: my manner, my race, my works, my genius.

The ego does not participate in any actuality nor does he gain any. He sets himself apart from everything else and tries to possess as much as possible by means of experience and use. This is *his* dynamics: setting himself apart and taking possession—and the object is always It, that which is not actual. He knows himself as a subject, but this subject can appropriate as much as it wants to, it will never gain any substance: it remains like a point, functional, that which experiences, that which uses, nothing more. All of its extensive and multifarious being-that-way, all of its eager "individuality" cannot help it to gain any substance.

There are not two kinds of human beings, but there are two poles of humanity.

No human being is pure person, and none is pure ego; none is entirely actual, none entirely lacking in actuality. Each lives in a twofold I. But some men are so person-oriented that one may call them persons, while others are so ego-oriented that one may call them egos. Between these and those true history takes place.

The more a human being, the more humanity is dominated by the ego, the more does the I fall prey to inactuality. In such ages the person in the human being and in humanity comes to lead a subterranean, hidden, as it were invalid existence—until it is summoned.

—What is that: self-contradiction?

—When man does not test the *a priori* of relation in the world, working out and actualizing the innate You in what he encounters, it turns inside. Then it unfolds through the unnatural, impossible object, the I—which is to say that it unfolds where there is no room for it to unfold. Thus the confrontation within the self comes into being, and this cannot be relation, presence, the current of reciprocity, but only self-contradiction. Some men may try to interpret this as a relation, perhaps one that is religious, in order to extricate themselves from the horror of their *Doppelgänger:* they are bound to keep rediscovering the deception of any such interpretation. Here is the edge of life. What is unfulfilled has here escaped into the mad delusion of some fulfillment;

now it gropes around in the labyrinth and gets lost ever more profoundly.

At times when man is overcome by the horror of the alienation between I and world, it occurs to him that something might be done. Imagine that at some dreadful midnight you lie there, tormented by a waking dream: the bulwarks have crumbled and the abysses scream, and you realize in the midst of this agony that life is still there and I must merely get through to it—but how? how? Thus feels man in the hours when he collects himself: overcome by horror, pondering, without direction. And yet he may know the right direction, deep down in the unloved knowledge of the depths—the direction of return that leads through sacrifice. But he rejects this knowledge; what is "mystical" cannot endure the artificial midnight sun. He summons thought in which he places, quite rightly, much confidence: thought is supposed to fix everything. After all, it is the lofty art of thought that it can paint a reliable and practically credible picture of the world. Thus man says to his thought: "Look at the dreadful shape that lies over there with those cruel eyes—is she not the one with whom I played long ago? Do you remember how she used to laugh at me with these eyes and how good they were then? And now look at my wretched I—I'll admit it to you: it is empty, and whatever I put into myself, experience as well as use, does not penetrate to this cavern. Won't you fix things between her and me so that she relents and I get well again?" And thought, ever obliging and skillful, paints with its accustomed speed a series—nay, two series of pictures on the right and the left wall. Here is (or rather: happens, for the world pictures of thought are reliable motion pictures) the universe. From the whirl of the stars emerges the small earth, from the teeming on earth emerges small man, and now history carries him forth through the ages, to persevere in rebuilding the anthills of the cultures that crumble under its steps. Beneath this series of pictures is written: "One and all." On the other wall happens the soul. A female figure spins the orbits of all stars and the life of all creatures and the whole of world history; all is spun with a single thread and is no longer called stars and creatures and world but feelings and representations or even living experiences and states of the soul. And beneath this series of pictures is written: "One and all."

Henceforth, when man is for once overcome by the horror of alienation and the world fills him with anxiety, he looks up (right or left, as the case may be) and sees a picture. Then he sees that the I is contained in the world, and that there really is no I, and thus the world cannot harm the I, and he calms down; or he sees that the world is contained in the I, and that there really is no world, and thus the world cannot harm the I, and he calms down. And when man is overcome again by the horror of alienation and the I fills him with anxiety, he looks up and sees a picture; and whichever he sees, it does not matter, either the empty I is stuffed full of world or it is submerged in the flood of the world, and he calms down.

But the moment will come, and it is near, when man, overcome by horror, looks up and in a flash sees both pictures at once. And he is seized by a deeper horror.

Every actual relationship to another being in the world is exclusive. Its You is freed and steps forth to confront us in its uniqueness. It fills the firmament—not as if there were nothing else, but everything else lives in *its* light. As long as the presence of the relationship endures, this world-wideness cannot be infringed. But as soon as a You becomes an It, the world-wideness of the relationship appears as an injustice against the world, and its exclusiveness as an exclusion of the universe.

In the relation to God, unconditional exclusiveness and unconditional inclusiveness are one. For those who enter into the absolute relationship, nothing particular retains any importance—neither things nor beings, neither earth nor heaven—but everything is included in the relationship. For entering into the pure relationship does not involve ignoring everything but seeing everything in the You, not renouncing the world but placing it upon its proper ground. Looking away from the world is no help toward God; staring at the world is no help either; but whoever beholds the world in him stands in his presence. "World here, God there"—that is It-talk; and "God in the world"—that, too, is It-talk; but leaving out nothing, leaving nothing behind, to comprehend all—all the world—in comprehending the You, giving the world its due and truth, to have nothing besides God but to grasp everything in him, that is the perfect relationship.

One does not find God if one remains in the world; one does not find God if one leaves the world. Whoever goes forth to his You with his whole being and carries to it all the being of the world, finds him whom one cannot seek.

Of course, God is "the wholly other"; but he is also the wholly same: the wholly present. Of course, he is the *mysterium tremendum* that appears and overwhelms; but he is also the mystery of the obvious that is closer to me than my own I.

When you fathom the life of things and of conditionality, you reach the indissoluble; when you dispute the life of things and of conditionality, you wind up before the nothing; when you consecrate life you encounter the living God.

Of these three spheres one is distinguished: life with men. Here language is perfected as a sequence and becomes speech and reply. Only here does the word, formed in language, encounter its reply. Only here does the basic word go back and forth in the same shape; that of the address and that of the reply are alive in the same tongue; I and You do not only stand in a relationship but also in firm honesty. The moments of relation are joined here, and only here, through the element of language in which they are immersed. Here that which confronts us has developed the full actuality of the You. Here alone beholding and being beheld, recognizing and being recognized, loving and being loved exist as an actuality that cannot be lost.

This is the main portal into whose inclusive opening the two side portals lead.

"When a man is intimate with his wife, the longing of the eternal hills wafts about them."

The relation to a human being is the proper metaphor for the relation to God—as genuine address is here accorded a genuine answer. But in God's answer all, the All, reveals itself as language.

—But isn't solitude, too, a portal? Does it not happen sometimes in the stillest lonesomeness that we unexpectedly behold? Cannot intercourse with oneself change mysteriously into intercourse with mystery? Indeed, is not only he that is no longer attached to any being worthy of confronting being? "Come, lonesome one to the lonesome," Simeon, the New Theologian, addresses his God.

—There are two kinds of lonesomeness, depending on what it turns away from. If lonesomeness means detaching oneself from experiencing and using things, then this is always required to achieve any act of relation, not only the supreme one. But if lonesomeness means the absence of relation: if other beings have forsaken us after we had spoken the true You to them, we will be accepted by God; but not if we ourselves have forsaken other beings. Only he that is full of covetousness to use them is *attached* to some of them; he that lives in the strength of the presence can only be associated with them. The latter, however— he alone is ready for God. For he alone counters God's actuality with a human actuality.

And again there are two kinds of lonesomeness, depending on what it turns to. If lonesomeness is the place of purification which even the associate needs before he enters the holy of holies, but which he also needs in the midst of his trials, between his unavoidable failures and his ascent to prove himself—that is how we are constituted. But if it is the castle of separation where man conducts a dialogue with himself, not in order to test himself and master himself for what awaits him but in his enjoyment of the configuration of his own soul—that is the spirit's lapse into mere spirituality. And this becomes truly abysmal when self-deception reaches the point where one thinks that one has God within and speaks to him. But as surely as God embraces us and dwells in us, we never have him within. And we speak to him only when all speech has ceased within.

What is it that is eternal: the primal phenomenon, present in the here and now, of what we call revelation? It is man's emerging from the moment of the supreme encounter, being no longer the same as he was when entering into it. The moment of encounter is not a "living experience" that stirs in the receptive soul and blissfully rounds itself out: something happens to man. At times it is like feeling a breath and at times like a wrestling match; no matter: something happens. The man who steps out of the essential act of pure relation has something More in his being, something new has grown there of which he did not know before and for whose origin he lacks any suitable words. Wherever the scientific world orientation in its legitimate desire for a causal chain without gaps may place the origin of what is new here: for us, being concerned with the actual contemplation of the actual, no subconscious and no other psychic apparatus will do. Actually, we receive what we did not have before, in such a manner that we know: it has been given to us. In the language of the Bible: "Those who wait for God will receive strength in exchange." In the language of Nietzsche who is still faithful to actuality in his report: "One accepts, one does not ask who gives."

Man receives, and what he receives is not a "content" but a presence, a presence as strength. This presence and strength includes three elements that are not separate but may nevertheless be contemplated as three. First, the whole abundance of actual reciprocity, of being admitted, of being associated while one is altogether unable to indicate what that is like with which one is associated, nor does association make life any easier for us—it makes life heavier but heavy with meaning. And this is second: the inexpressible confirmation of meaning. It is guaranteed. Nothing, nothing can henceforth be meaningless. The question about the meaning of life has vanished. But if it were still there, it would not require an answer. You do not know how to point to or define the meaning, you lack any formula or image for it, and yet it is more certain for you than the sensations of your senses. What could it intend with us, what does it desire from us, being revealed and surreptitious? It does not wish to be interpreted by us—for that we lack the ability—only to be done by us. This comes third: it is not the meaning of "another life" but that of this our life, not that of a "beyond" but of this our world, and it wants to be demonstrated by us in this life and this world. The meaning can be received but not experienced; it cannot be experienced, but it can be done; and this is what it intends with us. The guarantee does not wish to remain shut up within me, it wants to be born into the world by me. But even as the meaning itself cannot be transferred or expressed as a universally valid and generally acceptable piece of knowledge, putting it to the proof in action cannot be handed on as a valid ought; it is not prescribed, not inscribed on a table that could be put up over everybody's head. The meaning we receive can be put to the proof in action only by each person in the uniqueness of his being and in the uniqueness of his life. No prescription can lead us to the encounter, and none leads from it. Only the acceptance of the presence is required to come to it or, in a new sense, to go from it. As we have nothing but a You on our lips when we enter the encounter, it is with this on our lips that we are released from it into the world.

That before which we live, that in which we live, that out of which and into which we live, the mystery—has remained what it was. It has become present for us, and through its presence it has made itself

known to us as salvation; we have "known" it, but we have no knowledge of it that might diminish or extenuate its mysteriousness. We
have come close to God, but no closer to an unriddling, unveiling of
being. We have felt salvation but no "solution." We cannot go to
others with what we have received, saying: This is what needs to be
known, this is what needs to be done. We can only go and put to the
proof in action. And even this is not what we "ought to" do: rather we
can—we cannot do otherwise.

This is the eternal revelation which is present in the here and now. I
neither know of nor believe in any revelation that is not the same in
its primal phenomenon. I do not believe in God's naming himself or
in God's defining himself before man. The word of revelation is: I am
there as whoever I am there. That which reveals is that which reveals.
That which has being is there, nothing more. The eternal source of
strength flows, the eternal touch is waiting, the eternal voice sounds,
nothing more.

By its very nature the eternal You cannot become an It; because by its
very nature it cannot be placed within measure and limit, not even
within the measure of the immeasurable and the limit of the unlimited; because by its very nature cannot be grasped as a sum of qualities, not even as an infinite sum of qualities that have been raised to
transcendence; because it is not to be found either in or outside the
world; because it cannot be experienced; because it cannot be
thought; because we transgress against it, against that which has
being, if we say: "I believe that he is"—even "he" is still a metaphor,
while "you" is not.

And yet we reduce the eternal You ever again to an It, to something,
turning God into a thing, in accordance with our nature. Not capri-
ciously. The history of God as a thing, the way of the God-thing
through religion and its marginal forms, through its illuminations and
eclipses, the times when it heightened and when it destroyed life, the
way from the living God and back to him again, the metamorphoses of
the present, of embedment in forms, of objectification, of conceptualization, dissolution, and renewal are one way, are *the* way.

The asserted knowledge and the posited action of the religions—
whence do they come? The presence and strength of revelation (for all
of them necessarily invoke some sort of revelation, whether verbal,
natural, or psychic—there are, strictly speaking, only revealed re-

ligions), the presence and strength that man received through revelation—how do they become a "content"?

The explanation has two levels. The exoteric, psychic level is known when man is considered by himself, apart from history. The esoteric, factual one, the primal phenomenon of religion, when we afterward place him in history again. Both belong together.

Man desires to have God; he desires to have God continually in space and time. He is loath to be satisfied with the inexpressible confirmation of the meaning; he wants to see it spread out as something that one can take out and handle again and again—a continuum unbroken in space and time that insures life for him at every point and moment.

Life's rhythm of pure relation, the alternation of actuality and a latency in which only our strength to relate and hence also the presence, but not the primal presence, wanes, does not suffice man's thirst for continuity. He thirsts for something spread out in time, for duration. Thus God becomes an object of faith. Originally, faith fills the temporal gaps between the acts of relation; gradually, it becomes a substitute for these acts. The ever new movement of being through concentration and going forth is supplanted by coming to rest in an It in which one has faith. The trust-in-spite-of-all of the fighter who knows the remoteness and nearness of God is transformed ever more completely into the profiteer's assurance that nothing can happen to him because he has the faith that there is One who would not permit anything to happen to him.

The life-structure of the pure relation, the "lonesomeness" of the I before the You, the law that man, however he may include the world in his encounter, can still go forth only as a person to encounter God—all this also does not satisfy man's thirst for continuity. He thirsts for something spread out in space, for the representation in which the community of the faithful is united with its God. Thus God becomes a cult object. The cult, too, originally supplements the acts of relation, by fitting the living prayer, the immediate You-saying into a spatial context of great plastic power and connecting it with the life of the senses. And the cult, too, gradually becomes a substitute, as the personal prayer is no longer supported but rather pushed aside by communal prayer; and as the essential deed simply does not permit any rules, it is supplanted by devotions that follow rules.

In truth, however, the pure relation can be built up into spatio-temporal continuity only by becoming embodied in the whole stuff of life. It cannot be preserved but only put to the proof in action; it can only be done, poured into life. Man can do justice to the relation to God that has been given to him only by actualizing God in the world in accordance with his ability and the measure of each day, daily. This is the only genuine guarantee of continuity. The genuine guarantee of duration is that the pure relation can be fulfilled as the beings become You, as they are elevated to the You, so that the holy basic word sounds through all of them. Thus the time of human life is formed into an abundance of actuality; and although human life cannot and ought not to overcome the It-relation, it then becomes so permeated by relation that this gains a radiant and penetrating constancy in it. The moments of supreme encounter are no mere flashes of lightning in the dark but like a rising moon in a clear starry night. And thus the genuine guarantee of spatial constancy consists in this that men's relations to their true You, being radii that lead from all I-points to the center, create a circle. Not the periphery, not the community comes first, but the radii, the common relation to the center. That alone assures the genuine existence of a community.

The anchoring of time in a relation-oriented life of salvation and the anchoring of space in a community unified by a common center: only when both of these come to be and only as long as both continue to be, a human cosmos comes to be and continues to be around the invisible altar, grasped in the spirit out of the world stuff of the eon.

The encounter with God does not come to man in order that he may henceforth attend to God but in order that he may prove its meaning in action in the world. All revelation is a calling and a mission. But again and again man shuns actualization and bends back toward the revealer: he would rather attend to God than to the world. Now that he has bent back, however, he is no longer confronted by a You; he can do nothing but place a divine It in the realm of things, believe that he knows about God as an It, and talk about him. Even as the egomaniac does not live anything directly, whether it be a perception or an affection, but reflects on his perceiving or affectionate I and thus misses the truth of the process, thus the theomaniac (who, incidentally, can get along very well with the egomaniac in the very same soul) will not let the gift take full effect but reflects instead on that which gives, and misses both.

3

Seeking Happiness

Many persons agree that what they want most in life is happiness. Yet this agreement is perhaps only an agreement on words. For there are widely differing views of what makes people happy. To some, happiness means the freedom and the power to do what they want. To others, it is having their wishes fulfilled. Yet others cannot think of happiness apart from the meaning they find in life or from the responsibilities their commitments entail.

Some philosophers who have reflected on this diversity of opinions think that the central and unifying thread in all forms of happiness is the feeling of pleasure or satisfaction we desire. But we can all remember times when life seemed intensely meaningful or when we were deeply at peace with ourselves and yet suffered great physical pain. Moreover, some people who have everything they want feel dissatisfied or unhappy. Surely, then, feeling good is an important part of happiness but is not all of it: we must always be careful to distinguish *feeling* happy from truly *being* happy.

A number of thinkers maintain that happiness is simply a sequence of desires rapidly followed by satisfactions. They think it would be best to have all our wishes granted without our having to do anything. Yet instant satisfaction yields boredom, not happiness. As a result, some of those who think that what we want is to have our desires met find happiness empty and without allure. A simple life close to nature, needing and wanting as little as possible, may be better after all. Best of all, perhaps, is a life of activity in which we look for no ulterior rewards; one in which our exertions are justified by their value and by the joy we take in them. Yet, attractive as the simple and the active lives may be, it is unrealistic to maintain that health, social position, and money have no bearing on our chance at happiness.

If happiness consists of the development of our faculties, it is really the same as self-realization. If it involves activities, as it surely must, it requires a measure of power and control. The key may be to find the proper proportion of active doing and passive enjoyment in our lives. And even so, happiness may not come unless, in addition to striving to get what we want, we also learn to like what we get, or else learn how not to strive at all.

H. D. THOREAU

Happiness Is Natural Simplicity

Where I Lived, and What I Lived For

At a certain season of our life we are accustomed to consider every spot as the possible site of a house. I have thus surveyed the country on every side within a dozen miles of where I live. In imagination I have bought all the farms in succession, for all were to be bought, and I knew their price. I walked over each farmer's premises, tasted his wild apples, discoursed on husbandry with him, took his farm at his price, at any price, mortgaging it to him in my mind; even put a higher price on it,—took everything but a deed of it,—took his word for his deed, for I dearly love to talk,—cultivated it, and him too to some extent, I trust, and withdrew when I had enjoyed it long enough, leaving him to carry it on. This experience entitled me to be regarded as a sort of real-estate broker by my friends. Wherever I sat, there I might live, and the landscape radiated from me accordingly. What is a house but a *sedes*, a seat?—better if a country seat. I discovered many a site for a house not likely to be soon improved, which some might have thought too far from the village, but to my eyes the village was too far from it. Well, there I might live, I said; and there I did live, for an hour, a summer and a winter life; saw how I could let the years run off, buffet the winter through, and see the spring come in. The future inhabitants of this region, wherever they may place their houses, may be sure that they have been anticipated. An afternoon sufficed to lay out the land into orchard, wood-lot, and pasture, and to decide what fine oaks or pines should be left to stand before the door, and whence each blasted tree could be seen to the best advantage; and then I let it lie, fallow perchance, for a man is rich in proportion to the number of things which he can afford to let alone.

My imagination carried me so far that I even had the refusal of several farms,—the refusal was all I wanted,—but I never got my fingers burned by actual possession. The nearest that I came to actual possession was when I bought the Hollowell place, and had begun to sort my seeds, and collected materials with which to make a wheelbarrow to carry it on or off with: but before the owner gave me a deed of it, his wife—every man has such a wife—changed her mind and wished to keep it, and he offered me ten dollars to release him. Now, to speak the truth, I had but ten cents in the world, and it surpassed my arithmetic to tell, if I was that man who had ten cents, or who had a farm, or ten dollars, or all together. However, I let him keep the ten dollars and the farm too, for I had carried it far enough; or rather, to be generous, I sold him the farm for just what I gave for it, and, as he was not a rich man, made him a present of ten dollars, and still had my ten cents, and seeds, and materials for a wheelbarrow left. I found thus that I had been a rich man without any damage to my poverty. But I retained the landscape, and I have since annually carried off what it yielded without a wheelbarrow. With respect to landscapes,—

> I am monarch of all I survey,
> My right there is none to dispute.

I have frequently seen a poet withdraw, having enjoyed the most valuable part of a farm, while the crusty farmer supposed that he had got a few wild apples only. Why, the owner does not know it for many years when a poet has put his farm in rhyme, the most admirable kind of invisible fence, has fairly impounded it, milked it, skimmed it, and got all the cream, and left the farmer only the skimmed milk.

The real attractions of the Hollowell farm, to me, were: its complete retirement, being about two miles from the village, half a mile from the nearest neighbor, and separated from the highway by a broad field; its bounding on the river, which the owner said protected it by its fogs from frosts in the spring, though that was nothing to me; the gray color and ruinous state of the house and barn, and the dilapidated fences, which put such an interval between me and the last occupant; the hollow and lichen-covered apple tree, gnawed by rabbits, showing what kind of neighbors I should have; but above all, the recollection I had of it from my earliest voyages up the river, when the house was concealed behind a dense grove of red-maples, through which I heard the house-dog bark. I was in haste to buy it, before the proprietor finished getting out some rocks, cutting down the hollow apple trees, and grubbing up some young birches which had sprung up in the pasture, or in short, had made any more of his improvements. To enjoy these advantages I was ready to carry it on; like Atlas, to take the world on my shoulders,—I never heard what compensation he received for that,—and do all those things which had no other motive or excuse but that I might pay for it and be unmolested in my possession of it; for I knew all the while that it would yield the most abundant crop of the kind I wanted, if I could only afford to let it alone. But it turned out as I have said.

All that I could say, then, with respect to farming on a large scale—I have always cultivated a garden—was, that I had had my seeds ready. Many think that seeds improve with age. I have no doubt that time discriminates between the good and the bad; and when at last I shall plant, I shall be less likely to be disappointed. But I would say to my fellows, once for all, As long as possible live free and uncommitted. It makes but little difference whether you are committed to a farm or the county jail. . . .

Every morning was a cheerful invitation to make my life of equal simplicity, and I may say innocence, with Nature herself. I have been as sincere a worshipper of Aurora as the Greeks. I got up early and bathed in the pond; that was a religious exercise, and one of the best things which I did. They say that characters were engraven on the bathing tub of King Tching-thang to this effect: "Renew thyself completely each day; do it again, and again, and forever again." I can understand that. Morning brings back the heroic ages. I was as much affected by the faint hum of a mosquito making its invisible and unimaginable tour through my apartment at earliest dawn, when I was sitting with door and windows open, as I could be by any trumpet that ever sang of fame. It was Homer's requiem; itself an Iliad and Odyssey in the air, singing its own wrath and wanderings. There was something cosmical about it; a standing advertisement, till forbidden, of the everlasting vigor and fertility of the world. The morning, which is the most memorable season of the day, is the awakening hour. Then there is least somnolence in us; and for an hour, at least, some part of us awakes which slumbers all the rest of the day and night. Little is to be expected of that day, if it can be called a day, to which we are not awakened by our Genius, but by the mechanical nudgings of some servitor, are not awakened by our own newly acquired force and aspirations from within, accompanied by the undulations of celestial music, instead of factory bells, and fragrance filling the air—to a higher life than we fell asleep from; and thus the darkness bear its fruit, and prove itself to be good, no less than the light. That man who does not believe that each day contains an earlier, more sacred, and auroral hour than he has yet profaned, has despaired of life, and is pursuing a descending and darkening way. After a partial cessation of his sensuous life, the soul of man, or its organs rather, are reinvigorated each day, and his Genius tries again what noble life it can make. All memorable events, I should say, transpire in morning time and in a morning atmosphere. The Vedas say, "All intelligences awake with the morning." Poetry and art, and the fairest and most memorable of the actions of men, date from such an hour. All poets and heroes, like Memnon, are the children of Aurora, and emit their music at sunrise. To him whose elastic and vigorous thought keeps pace with the sun, the day is a perpetual morning. It matters not what the clocks say or the attitudes and labors of men. Morning is when I am awake and there is a dawn in me. Moral reform is the effort to throw off sleep. Why is it that men give so poor an account of their day if they have not been slumbering? They are not such poor calculators. If they had not been overcome with drowsiness, they would have performed something. The millions are awake enough for physical labor; but only one in a million is awake enough for effective intellectual exertion, only one in a hundred millions to a poetic or divine life. To be awake is to be alive. I have never yet met a man who was quite awake. How could I have looked him in the face?

We must learn to reawaken and keep ourselves awake, not by mechanical aids, but by an infinite expectation of the dawn, which does not forsake us in our soundest sleep. I know of no more encouraging fact than the unquestionable ability of man to elevate his life by a conscious endeavor. It is something to be able to paint a particular picture, or to carve a statue, and so to make a few objects beautiful; but it is far more glorious to carve and paint the very atmosphere and medium through which we look, which morally we can do. To affect the quality of the day, that is the highest of arts. Every man is tasked to make his life, even in its details, worthy of the contemplation of his most elevated and critical hour. If we refused, or rather used up, such paltry information as we get, the oracles would distinctly inform us how this might be done.

I went to the woods because I wished to live deliberately, to front only the essential facts of life, and see if I could not learn what it had to teach, and not, when I came to die, discover that I had not lived. I did not wish to live what was not life, living is so dear; nor did I wish to practice resignation, unless it was quite necessary. I wanted to live deep and suck out all the marrow of life, to live so sturdily and Spartan-like as to put to rout all that was not life, to cut a broad swath and shave close, to drive life into a corner, and reduce it to its lowest terms, and, if it proved to be mean, why then to get the whole and genuine meanness of it, and publish its meanness to the world; or if it were sublime, to know it by experience, and be able to give a true account of it in my next excursion. For most men, it appears to me, are in a strange uncertainty about it, whether it is of the devil or of God, and have *somewhat hastily* concluded that it is the chief end of man here to "glorify God and enjoy him forever."

Still we live meanly, like ants; though the fable tells us that we were long ago changed into men; like pygmies we fight with cranes; it is error upon error, and clout upon clout, and our best virtue has for its occasion a superfluous and evitable wretchedness. Our life is frittered away by detail. An honest man has hardly need to count more than his ten fingers, or in extreme cases he may add his ten toes, and lump the rest. Simplicity, simplicity, simplicity! I say, let your affairs be as two or three, and not a hundred or a thousand; instead of a million count half a dozen, and keep your accounts on your thumb-nail. In the midst of this chopping sea of civilized life, such are the clouds and storms and quicksands and thousand-and-one items to be allowed for, that a man has to live, if he would not founder and go to the bottom and not make his port at all, by dead reckoning, and he must be a great calculator indeed who succeeds. Simplify, simplify. Instead of three meals a day, if it be necessary eat but one; instead of a hundred dishes, five; and reduce other things in proportion. Our life is like a German Confederacy, made up of petty states, with its boundary forever fluctuating, so that even a German cannot tell you how it is bounded at any moment. The nation itself, with all its so-called internal improvements, which, by the way are all external and superficial, is just such an unwieldly and overgrown establishment, cluttered with furniture and tripped up by its own traps, ruined by luxury and heedless expense, by want of calculation and a worthy aim, as the million households in the land; and the only cure for it, as for them, is in a rigid economy, a stern and more than Spartan simplicity of life and elevation of purpose. It lives too fast. Men think that it is essential that the *Nation* have commerce, and export ice, and talk through a telegraph, and ride thirty miles an hour, without a doubt, whether *they* do or not; but whether we should live like baboons or like men, is a little uncertain. If we do not get out sleepers, and forge rails, and devote days and nights to the work, but go to tinkering upon our *lives* to improve *them*, who will build railroads? And if railroads are not built, how shall we get to heaven in season? But if we stay at home and mind our business, who will want railroads? We do not ride on the railroad; it rides upon us. Did you ever think what those sleepers are that underlie the railroad? Each one is a man, an Irishman, or a Yankee man. The rails are laid on them, and they are covered with sand, and the cars run smoothly over them. They are sound sleepers, I assure you. And every few years a new lot is laid down and run over; so that, if some have the pleasure of riding on a rail, others have the misfortune to be ridden upon. And when they run over a man that is walking in his sleep, a supernumerary sleeper in the wrong position, and wake him up, they suddenly stop the cars, and make a hue and cry about it, as if this were an exception. I am glad to know that it takes a gang of men for every five miles to keep the sleepers down and level in their beds as it is, for this is a sign that they may sometime get up again.

Why should we live with such hurry and waste of life? We are determined to be starved before we are hungry. Men say that a stitch in time saves nine, and so they take a thousand stitches today to save nine tomorrow. As for *work*, we haven't any of any consequence. We have the Saint Vitus' dance, and cannot possibly keep our heads still. If I should only give a few pulls at the parish bell-rope, as for a fire, that is, without setting the bell, there is hardly a man on his farm in the outskirts of Concord, notwithstanding that press of engagements which was his excuse so many times this morning, nor a boy, nor a woman, I might almost say, but would forsake all and follow that sound, not mainly to save property from the flames, but, if we will confess the truth, much more to see it burn, since burn it must, and we, be it known, did not set it on fire,—or to see it put out, and have a hand in it, if that is done as handsomely; yes, even if it were the parish church itself. Hardly a man takes a half-hour's nap after dinner, but when he wakes he holds up his head and asks, "What's the news?" as if the rest of mankind had stood his sentinels. Some give directions to be waked every half-hour, doubtless for no other purpose; and then, to pay for it, they tell what they have dreamed. After a night's sleep the news is as indispensable as the breakfast. "Pray tell me anything new that has happened to a man anywhere on this globe,"—and he reads it over his coffee and rolls, that a man has had his eyes gouged out this morning on the Wachito River; never dreaming the while that he lives in the dark unfathomed mammoth cave of this world, and has but the rudiment of an eye himself.

For my part, I could easily do without the post office. I think that there are very few important communications made through it. To speak critically, I never received more than one or two letters in my life—I wrote this some years ago—that were worth the postage. The penny-post is, commonly, an institution through which you seriously offer a man that penny for his thoughts which is so often safely offered in jest. And I am sure that I never read any memorable news in a newspaper. If we read of one man robbed, or murdered, or killed by accident, or one house burned, or one vessel wrecked, or one steamboat blown up, or one cow run over on the Western Railroad, or one mad dog killed, or one lot of grasshoppers in the winter,—we never need read of another. One is enough. If you are acquainted with the principle, what do you care for a myriad instances and applications? To a philosopher all *news*, as it is called, is gossip, and they who edit and read it are old women over their tea. Yet not a few are greedy after this gossip. There was such a rush, as I hear, the other day at one of the offices to learn the foreign news by the last arrival, that several large squares of plate glass belonging to the establishment were broken by the pressure,—news which I seriously think a ready wit might write a twelvemonth, or twelve years, beforehand with sufficient accuracy. As for Spain, for instance, if you know how to throw in Don Carlos and the Infanta, and Don Pedro and Seville and Granada, from time to time in the right proportions,—they may have changed the names a little since I saw the papers,—and serve up a bullfight when other entertainments fail, it will be true to the letter, and give us as good an idea of the exact state or ruin of things in Spain as the most succinct and lucid reports under this head in the newspapers: and as for England, almost the last significant scrap of news from that quarter was the revolution of 1649; and if you have learned the history of her crops for an average year, you never need attend to that thing again, unless your speculations are of a merely pecuniary character. If one may judge who rarely looks into the newspapers, nothing new does ever happen in foreign parts, a French revolution not excepted.

What news! how much more important to know what that is which was never old! "Kieou-he-yu (great dignitary of the state of Wei) sent a man to Khoung-tseu to know his news. Khoung-tseu caused the messenger to be seated near him, and questioned him in these terms: What is your master doing? The messenger answered with respect: My master desires to diminish the number of his faults, but he cannot come to the end of them. The messenger being gone, the philosopher remarked: What a worthy messenger! What a worthy messenger!" The preacher, instead of vexing the ears of drowsy farmers on their day of rest at the end of the week,—for Sunday is the fit conclusion of an ill-spent week, and not the fresh and brave beginning of a new one,— with this one other draggle-tail of a sermon, should shout with thundering voice, "Pause! Avast! Why so seeming fast, but deadly slow?"

Shams and delusions are esteemed for soundest truths, while reality is fabulous. If men would steadily observe realities only, and not allow themselves to be deluded, life, to compare it with such things as we know, would be like a fairy tale and the Arabian Nights' Entertainments. If we respected only what is inevitable and has a right to be, music and poetry would resound along the streets. When we are unhurried and wise, we perceive that only great and worthy things have any permanent and absolute existence, that petty fears and petty pleasures are but the shadow of the reality. This is always exhilarating and sublime. By closing the eyes and slumbering, and consenting to be deceived by shows, men establish and confirm their daily life of routine and habit everywhere, which still is built on purely illusory foundations. Children, who play life, discern its true law and relations more clearly than men, who fail to live it worthily, but who think that they are wiser by experience, that is, by failure. I have read in a Hindoo book, that "there was a king's son, who, being expelled in infancy from his native city, was brought up by a forester, and, growing up to maturity in that state, imagined himself to belong to the barbarous race with which he lived. One of his father's ministers having discovered him, revealed to him what he was, and the misconception of his character was removed, and he knew himself to be a prince. So soul," continues the Hindoo philosopher, "from the circumstances in which it is placed, mistakes its own character, until the truth is revealed to it by some holy teacher, and then it knows itself to be *Brahme*." I perceive that we inhabitants of New England live this mean life that we do because our vision does not penetrate the surface of things. We think that this *is* which *appears* to be. If a man should walk through this town and see only the reality, where, think you, would the "Milldam" go to? If he should give us an account of the realities he beheld there, we should not recognize the place in his description. Look at a meeting-house, or a court-house, or a jail, or a shop, or a dwelling-house, and say what that thing really is before a true gaze, and they would all go to pieces in your account of them. Men esteem truth remote, in the outskirts of the system, behind the farthest star, before Adam and after the last man. In eternity there is indeed something true and sublime. But all these times and places and occasions are now and here. God himself culminates in the present moment, and will never be more divine in the lapse of all the ages. And we are enabled to apprehend at all what is sublime and noble only by the perpetual instilling and drenching of the reality that surrounds us. The universe constantly and obediently answers to our conceptions; whether we travel fast or slow, the track is laid for us. Let us spend our lives in conceiving them. The poet or the artist never yet had so fair and noble a design but some of his posterity at least could accomplish it.

Let us spend one day as deliberately as Nature, and not be thrown off the track by every nutshell and mosquito's wing that falls on the rails. Let us rise early and fast, or break fast, gently and without perturbation; let company come and let company go, let the bells ring and the children cry,—determined to make a day of it. Why should we knock under and go with the stream? Let us not be upset and overwhelmed in that terrible rapid and whirlpool called a dinner, situated in the meridian shallows. Weather this danger and you are safe, for the rest of the way is down hill. With unrelaxed nerves, with morning vigor, sail by it, looking another way, tied to the mast like Ulysses. If the engine whistles, let it whistle till it is hoarse for its pains. If the bell rings, why should we run? We will consider what kind of music they are like. Let us settle ourselves, and work and wedge our feet downward through the mud and slush of opinion, and prejudice, and tradition, and delusion, and appearance, that alluvion which covers the globe, through Paris and London, through New York and Boston and Concord, through Church and State, through poetry and philosophy and religion, till we come to a hard bottom and rocks in place, which we can call *reality*, and say, This is, and no mistake; and then begin, having a point d'appui, below freshet and frost and fire, a place where you might found a wall or a state, or set a lamp-post safely, or perhaps a gauge, not a Nilometer, but a Realometer, that future ages might know how deep a freshet of shams and appearances had gathered from time to time. If you stand right fronting and face to face to a fact, you will see the sun glimmer on both its surfaces, as if it were a scimiter, and feel its sweet edge dividing you through the heart and marrow, and so you will happily conclude your mortal career. Be it life or death, we crave only reality. If we are really dying, let us hear the rattle in our throats and feel cold in the extremities; if we are alive, let us go about our business.

Time is but the stream I go a-fishing in. I drink at it; but while I drink I see the sandy bottom and detect how shallow it is. Its thin current slides away, but eternity remains. I would drink deeper; fish in the sky, whose bottom is pebbly with stars. I cannot count one. I know not the first letter of the alphabet. I have always been regretting that I was not as wise as the day I was born. The intellect is a cleaver; it discerns and rifts its way into the secret of things. I do not wish to be any more busy with my hands than is necessary. My head is hands and feet. I feel all my best faculties concentrated in it. My instinct tells me that my head is an organ for burrowing, as some creatures use their snout and fore paws, and with it I would mine and burrow my way through these hills. I think that the richest vein is somewhere hereabouts; so by the divining-rod and thin rising vapors I judge; and here I will begin to mine.

ARISTOTLE

The Good For Human Beings

Let us again return to the good we are seeking, and ask what it can be. It seems different in different actions and arts; it is different in medicine, in strategy, and in the other arts likewise. What then is the good of each? Surely that for whose sake everything else is done. In medicine this is health, in strategy victory, in architecture a house, in any other sphere something else, and in every action and pursuit the end; for it is for the sake of this that all men do whatever else they do. Therefore, if there is an end for all that we do, this will be the good achievable by action, and if there are more than one, these will be the goods achievable by action.

So the argument has by a different course reached the same point; but we must try to state this even more clearly. Since there are evidently more than one end, and we choose some of these (e.g. wealth, flutes, and in general instruments) for the sake of something else, clearly not all ends are final ends; but the chief good is evidently something final. Therefore, if there is only one final end, this will be what we are seeking, and if there are more than one, the most final of these will be what we are seeking. Now we call that which is in itself worthy of pursuit more final than that which is worthy of pursuit for the sake of something else, and that which is never desirable for the sake of something else more final than the things that are desirable both in themselves and for the sake of that other thing, and therefore we call final without qualification that which is always desirable in itself and never for the sake of something else.

Now such a thing happiness, above all else, is held to be; for this we choose always for itself and never for the sake of something else, but honor, pleasure, reason, and every virtue we choose indeed for themselves (for if nothing resulted from them we should still choose each of them), but we choose them also for the sake of happiness, judging that by means of them we shall be happy. Happiness, on the other hand, no one chooses for the sake of these, nor, in general, for anything other than itself.

From the point of view of self-sufficiency the same result seems to follow; for the final good is thought to be self-sufficient. Now by self-sufficient we do not mean that which is sufficient for a man by himself, for one who lives a solitary life, but also for parents, children, wife, and in general for his friends and fellow citizens, since man is born for citizenship. But some limit must be set to this; for if we extend our requirement to ancestors and descendants and friends' friends we are in for an infinite series. Let us examine this question, however, on another occasion; the self-sufficient we now define as that which when isolated makes life desirable and lacking in nothing; and such we think happiness to be; and further we think it most desirable of all things, without being counted as one good thing among others—if it were so counted it would clearly be made more desirable by the addition of even the least of goods; for that which is added becomes an excess of goods, and of goods the greater is always more desirable. Happiness, then, is something final and self-sufficient, and is the end of action.

Presumably, however, to say that happiness is the chief good seems a platitude, and a clearer account of what it is is still desired. This might perhaps be given, if we could first ascertain the function of man. For just as for a flute-player, a sculptor, or any artist, and, in general, for all things that have a function or activity, the good and the "well" is thought to reside in the function, so would it seem to be for man, if he has a function. Have the carpenter, then, and the tanner certain functions or activities, and has man none? Is he born without a function? Or as eye, hand, foot, and in general each of the parts evidently has a function, may one lay it down that man similarly has a function apart from all these? What then can this be? Life seems to be common even to plants, but we are seeking what is peculiar to man. Let us exclude, therefore, the life of nutrition and growth. Next there would be a life of perception, but *it* also seems to be common even to the horse, the ox, and every animal. There remains, then, an active life of the element that has a rational principle; of this, one part has such a principle in the sense of being obedient to one, the other in the sense of possessing one and exercising thought. And, as "life of the rational element" also has two meanings, we must state that life in the sense of activity is what we mean; for this seems to be the more proper sense of the term. Now if the function of man is an activity of soul which follows or implies a rational principle, and if we say "a so-and-so" and "a good so-and-so" have a function which is the same in kind, e.g. a lyre-player and a good lyre-player, and so without qualification in all cases, eminence in respect of goodness being added to the name of the function (for the function of a lyre-player is to play the lyre, and that of a good lyre-player is to do so well): if this is the case, [and we state the function of man to be a certain kind of life, and this to be an activity or actions of the soul implying a rational principle, and the function of a good man to be the good and noble performance of these, and if any action is well performed when it is performed in accordance with the appropriate excellence: if this is the case,] human good turns out to be activity of soul in accordance with virtue, and if there are more than one virtue, in accordance with the best and most complete.

But we must add "in a complete life." For one swallow does not make a summer, nor does one day; and so too one day, or a short time, does not make a man blessed and happy.

Let this serve as an outline of the good; for we must presumably first sketch it roughly, and then later fill in the details. But it would seem that any one is capable of carrying on and articulating what has once been well outlined, and that time is a good discoverer or partner in such a work; to which facts the advances of the arts are due; for any one can add what is lacking. And we must also remember what has been said before, and not look for precision in all things alike, but in each class of things such precision as accords with the subject-matter, and so much as is appropriate to the inquiry. For a carpenter and a geometer investigate the right angle in different ways; the former does so in so far as the right angle is useful for his work, while the latter inquires what it is or what sort of thing it is; for he is a spectator of the truth. We must act in the same way, then, in all other matters as well, that our main task may not be subordinated to minor questions. Nor must we demand the cause in all matters alike; it is enough in some cases that the *fact* be well established, as in the case of the first principles; the fact is the primary thing or first principle. Now of first principles we see some by induction, some by perception, some by a certain habituation, and others too in other ways. But each set of principles we must try to investigate in the natural way, and we must take pains to state them definitely, since they have a great influence on what follows. For the beginning is thought to be more than half of the whole, and many of the questions we ask are cleared up by it.

We must consider it, however, in the light not only of our conclusion and our premisses, but also of what is commonly said about it; for with a true view all the data harmonize, but with a false one the facts soon clash. Now goods have been divided into three classes, and some are described as external, others as relating to soul or to body; we call those that relate to soul most properly and truly goods, and psychical actions and activities we class as relating to soul. Therefore our account must be sound, at least according to this view, which is an old one and agreed on by philosophers. It is correct also in that we identify the end with certain actions and activities; for thus it falls among goods of the soul and not among external goods. Another belief which harmonizes with our account is that the happy man lives well and does well; for we have practically defined happiness as a sort of good life and good action. The characteristics that are looked for in happiness seem also, all of them, to belong to what we have defined happiness as being. For some identify happiness with virtue, some with practical wisdom, others with a kind of philosophic wisdom, others with these, or one of these, accompanied by pleasure or not without pleasure; while others include also external prosperity. Now some of these views have been held by many men and men of old, others by a few eminent persons; and it is not probable that either of these should be entirely mistaken, but rather that they should be right in at least some one respect or even in most respects.

With those who identify happiness with virtue or some one virtue our account is in harmony; for to virtue belongs virtuous activity. But it makes, perhaps, no small difference whether we place the chief good in possession or in use, in state of mind or in activity. For the state of mind may exist without producing any good result, as in a man who is asleep or in some other way quite inactive, but the activity cannot; for one who has the activity will of necessity be acting, and acting well. And as in the Olympic Games it is not the most beautiful and the strongest that are crowned but those who compete (for it is some of these that are victorious), so those who act win, and rightly win, the noble and good things in life.   °

Their life is also in itself pleasant. For pleasure is a state of *soul,* and to each man that which he is said to be a lover of is pleasant; e.g. not only is a horse pleasant to the lover of horses, and a spectacle to the lover of sights, but also in the same way just acts are pleasant to the lover of justice and in general virtuous acts to the lover of virtue. Now for most men their pleasures are in conflict with one another because these are not by nature pleasant, but the lovers of what is noble find pleasant the things that are by nature pleasant; and virtuous actions are such, so that these are pleasant for such men as well as in their own nature. Their life, therefore, has no further need of pleasure as a sort of adventitious charm, but has its pleasure in itself. For, besides what we have said, the man who does not rejoice in noble actions is not even good; since no one would call a man just who did not enjoy acting justly, nor any man liberal who did not enjoy liberal actions; and similarly in all other cases. If this is so, virtuous actions must be in themselves pleasant. But they are also *good* and *noble,* and have each of these attributes in the highest degree, since the good man judges well about these attributes; his judgment is such as we have described. Happiness then is the best, noblest, and most pleasant thing in the world, and these attributes are not severed as in the inscription at Delos—

> Most noble is that which is justest, and best is health;
> But pleasantest is it to win what we love.

For all these properties belong to the best activities; and these, or one—the best—of these, we identify with happiness.

Yet evidently, as we said, it needs the external goods as well; for it is impossible, or not easy, to do noble acts without the proper equipment. In many actions we use friends and riches and political power as instruments; and there are some things the lack of which takes the lustre from happiness, as good birth, goodly children, beauty; for the man who is very ugly in appearance or ill-born or solitary and child-less is not very likely to be happy, and perhaps a man would be still less likely if he had thoroughly bad children or friends or had lost good children or friends by death. As we said, then, happiness seems

to need this sort of prosperity in additon; for which reason some identify happiness with good fortune, though others identify it with virtue.

For this reason also the question is asked, whether happiness is to be
acquired by learning or by habituation or some other sort of training,
or comes in virtue of some divine providence or again by chance. Now
if there is *any* gift of the gods to men, it is reasonable that happiness
should be god-given, and most surely god-given of all human things
inasmuch as it is the best. But this question would perhaps be more
appropriate to another inquiry; happiness seems, however, even if it
is not god-sent but comes as a result of virtue and some process of
learning or training, to be among the most god-like things; for that
which is the prize and end of virtue seems to be the best thing in the
world, and something godlike and blessed.

It will also on this view be very generally shared; for all who are not
maimed as regards their potentiality for virtue may win it by a certain
kind of study and care. But if it is better to be happy thus than by
chance, it is reasonable that the facts should be so, since everything
that depends on the action of nature is by nature as good as it can be,
and similarly everything that depends on art or any rational cause,
and especially if it depends on the best of all causes. To entrust to
chance what is greatest and most noble would be a very defective arrangement.

The answer to the question we are asking is plain also from the definition of happiness; for it has been said to be a virtuous activity of
soul, of a certain kind. Of the remaining goods, some must necessarily
pre-exist as conditions of happiness, and others are naturally co-
operative and useful as instruments. And this will be found to agree
with what we said at the outset; for we stated the end of political
science to be the best end, and political science spends most of its
pains on making the citizens to be of a certain character, viz. good and
capable of noble acts.

It is natural, then, that we call neither ox nor horse nor any other of
the animals happy; for none of them is capable of sharing in such activity. For this reason also a boy is not happy; for he is not yet capable
of such acts, owing to his age; and boys who are called happy are
being congratulated by reason of the hopes we have for them. For
there is required, as we said, not only complete virtue but also a

complete life, since many changes occur in life, and all manner of chances, and the most prosperous may fall into great misfortunes in old age, as is told of Priam in the Trojan Cycle; and one who has experienced such chances and has ended wretchedly no one calls happy.

Must no one at all, then, be called happy while he lives; must we, as Solon says, see the end? Even if we are to lay down this doctrine, is it also the case that a man *is* happy when he is *dead?* Or is not this quite absurd, especially for us who say that happiness is an activity? But if we do not call the dead man happy, and if Solon does not mean this, but that one can then safely *call* a man blessed as being at last beyond evils and misfortunes, this also affords matter for discussion; for both evil and good are thought to exist for a dead man, as much as for one who is alive but not aware of them; e.g. honors and dishonors and the good or bad fortunes of children and in general of descendants. And this also presents a problem; for though a man has lived happily up to old age and has had a death worthy of his life, many reverses may befall his descendants—some of them may be good and attain the life they deserve, while with others the opposite may be the case; and clearly too the degrees of relationship between them and their ancestors may vary indefinitely. It would be odd, then, if the dead man were to share in these changes and become at one time happy, at another wretched; while it would also be odd if the fortunes of the descendants did not for *some* time have *some* effect on the happiness of their ancestors.

But we must return to our first difficulty; for perhaps by a consideration of it our present problem might be solved. Now if we must see the end and only then call a man happy, not as being happy but as having been so before, surely this is a paradox, that when he is happy the attribute that belongs to him is not to be truly predicated of him because we do not wish to call living men happy, on account of the changes that may befall them, and because we have assumed happiness to be something permanent and by no means easily changed, while a single man may suffer many turns of fortune's wheel. For clearly if we were to keep pace with his fortunes, we should often call the same man happy and again wretched, making the happy man out to be a "chameleon and insecurely based." Or is this keeping pace with his fortunes quite wrong? Success or failure in life does not depend on these, but human life, as we said, needs these as mere additions, while virtuous activities or their opposites are what constitute happiness or the reverse.

The question we have now discussed confirms our definition. For no function of man has so much permanence as virtuous activities (these are thought to be more durable even than knowledge of the sciences), and of these themselves the most valuable are more durable because those who are happy spend their life most readily and most continuously in these; for this seems to be the reason why we do not forget them. The attribute in question, then, will belong to the happy man, and he will be happy throughout his life; for always, or by preference to everything else, he will be engaged in virtuous action and contemplation, and he will bear the chances of life most nobly and altogether decorously, if he is "truly good" and "foursquare beyond reproach."

IMMANUEL KANT

You Must Be Well Occupied
To Be Happy

It is by his activities and not by enjoyment that man feels that he is alive. The busier we are the more we feel that we live and the more conscious we are of life. In idleness we not only feel that life is fleeting but we also feel lifeless. Activity is part of life's sustenance. We find any empty space of time disagreeable. What then makes time agreeable to us? The pleasures of life do not fill time full, but leave it empty. The human mind abhors an empty time, and is bored and disgusted with it. The present may, indeed, seem full to us, but if we have filled it with play, etc., the appearance of fullness will be confined to the present. Memory will find it empty. For if we have done nothing in life except waste our time and we review in retrospect the span of our life, we are puzzled to know how it has passed so quickly; we have done so little in it. Time can be filled up only by action. Only when occupied are we conscious that we live; indulgence gives us a feeling of insufficiency; for what is life? Life is the faculty of spontaneous activity, the awareness of all our human powers. Occupation gives us this awareness, and the more we feel our powers the more we feel that we are alive. Feeling is but the capacity to be aware of impressions; in feeling we are passive, or only so far active as to make awareness possible. But the more active he is, the more conscious a man is of his life; he can remember it the more, because there is much to remember; and at death he feels the more that he has had fullness of life. To have had one's fill of life is not to be weary of it. Mere enjoyment leads to weariness of life; but to die having had fullness of life is possible only after a life of action, and after we have made such full and busy use of our life that at its end we are not sorry that we have lived. He who has so lived has had fullness of life; he who has done nothing, grows weary of life; he does not seem to have lived; he is bored and would fain begin to live when it is time to die. We must, therefore, fill out our span of life with activities, and we shall not then complain that whilst each period of time has been long, when we look upon the past, the time as a whole has been all too short. This is the lament of people who do nothing; the hours drag and seem long to them because they have nothing to do; but in retrospect time seems to have fled, and they do not know what has become of it. But not so with the busy man; for him the hours are short and pass all too quickly whilst he is occupied; he wonders how they have passed until he looks back and sees how much he has managed to do in the time. Man must, therefore, by constant practice preserve his life-force, that is, his energies; his worth must be measured by what he does. Laziness reduces the degree of life. Unless man feels within him an impulse to activity, he will not even trouble to make a beginning; and since then all moral precepts are in vain, it must be the condition of all other duties that we should be energetic and zealous, show vigor and resolution in difficult tasks, and shun procrastination. Vigour is the reverse of indolence.

All occupation is either play or work. To have no occupation is a vice; it is better to be occupied in play than not to be occupied at all; for by play we at least sustain our energies. But if a man has no occupation whatever, he loses some of his life-force, and by degrees grows indolent. After a while he finds it difficult to regain his former energy of mind.

Without occupation man cannot live happily. If he earns his bread, he eats it with greater pleasure than when it is doled out to him. When mail-day is over, the businessman goes eagerly to the theater, and is more pleased and contented than if there had been no mail-day. Man feels more contented after heavy work than when he has done no work; for by work he has set his powers in motion; he, therefore, feels them better, and his mind is on that account more alive to pleasure. But when a man does nothing, he does not feel his life and his powers, and he is not disposed to pleasure.

Rest must be distinguished from idleness. There is something to be said for a life of rest if it comes at the end of an active life. When a man has laid down the duties of his station in the world after a busy life, he has the right to rest from the general labors of the world and from the common routine, but there is no reason why he should not find private occupations. Then his rest is the tranquility of the sage. The rest enjoyed by the aged is no laziness, but refreshment after labor. In order to rest man must have been occupied; he who has done nothing cannot rest. Rest cannot be properly enjoyed except after occupation. After a busy day we enjoy a restful sleep; rest is not so pleasant to the man who has done nothing.

ARTHUR SCHOPENHAUER

Happiness Is Not Worth Having

Nothing comforts us so effectually as the consideration of what has happened from the standpoint of necessity, from which all accidents appear as tools in the hand of an over-ruling fate, and we therefore recognise the evil that has come to us as inevitably produced by the conflict of inner and outer circumstances; in other words, fatalism. We really only complain and storm so long as we hope either to affect others or to excite ourselves to unheard-of efforts. But children and grown-up people know very well to yield contentedly as soon as they clearly see that it absolutely cannot be otherwise. We are like the entrapped elephants, that rage and struggle for many days, till they see that it is useless, and then suddenly offer their necks quietly to the yoke, tamed for ever. We are like King David, who, as long as his son still lived, unceasingly importuned Jehovah with prayers, and behaved himself as if in despair; but as soon as his son was dead, thought no longer about it. Hence it arises that innumerable permanent ills, such as lameness, poverty, low estate, ugliness, a disagreeable dwelling-place, are borne with indifference by innumerable persons, and are no longer felt, like healed wounds, just because these persons know that inward or outward necessity renders it impossible that any change can take place in these things; while those who are more fortunate cannot understand how such misfortunes can be borne. Now as with outward necessity, so also with inward; nothing reconciles so thoroughly as a distinct knowledge of it. If we have once for all distinctly recognised not only our good qualities and our strength, but also our defects and weakness, established our aim accordingly, and rest satisfied concerning what cannot be attained, we thus escape in the surest way, as far as our individuality permits, the bitterest of all sorrows, discontentment with ourselves, which is the inevitable result of ignorance of our own individuality, of false conceit and the audacity that proceeds from it.

At every grade that is enlightened by knowledge, the will appears as an individual. The human individual finds himself as finite in infinite space and time, and consequently as a vanishing quantity compared with them. He is projected into them, and, on account of their unlimited nature, he has always a merely relative, never absolute *when* and *where* of his existence; for his place and duration are finite parts of what is infinite and boundless. His real existence is only in the present, whose unchecked flight into the past is a constant transition into death, a constant dying. For his past life, apart from its possible consequences for the present, and the testimony regarding the will that is expressed in it, is now entirely done with, dead, and no longer anything; and, therefore, it must be, as a matter of reason, indifferent to him whether the content of that past was pain or pleasure. But the present is always passing through his hands into the past; the future is quite uncertain and always short. Thus his existence, even when we consider only its formal side, is a constant hurrying of the present into the dead past, a constant dying. But if we look at it from the physical side; it is clear that, as our walking is admittedly merely a constantly prevented falling, the life of our body is only a constantly prevented dying, an ever-postponed death: finally, in the same way, the activity of our mind is a constantly deferred ennui. Every breath we draw wards off the death that is constantly intruding upon us. In this way we fight with it every moment, and again, at longer intervals, through every meal we eat, every sleep we take, every time we warm ourselves, &c. In the end, death must conquer, for we became subject to him through birth, and he only plays for a little while with his prey before he swallows it up. We pursue our life, however, with great interest and much solicitude as long as possible, as we blow out a soap-bubble as long and as large as possible, although we know perfectly well that it will burst.

We saw that the inner being of unconscious nature is a constant striving without end and without rest. And this appears to us much more distinctly when we consider the nature of brutes and man. Willing and striving is its whole being, which may be very well compared to an unquenchable thirst. But the basis of all willing is need, deficiency, and thus pain. Consequently, the nature of brutes and man is subject to pain originally and through its very being. If, on the other hand, it lacks objects of desire, because it is at once deprived of them by a too easy satisfaction, a terrible void and ennui comes over it, i.e., its being and existence itself becomes an unbearable burden to it. Thus its life swings like a pendulum backwards and forwards between pain and ennui. This has also had to express itself very oddly in this way; after man had transferred all pain and torments to hell, there then remained nothing over for heaven but ennui.

But the constant striving which constitutes the inner nature of every manifestation of will obtains its primary and most general foundation at the higher grades of objectification, from the fact that here the will manifests itself as a living body, with the iron command to nourish it; and what gives strength to this command is just that this body is nothing but the objectified will to live itself. Man, as the most complete objectification of that will, is in like measure also the most necessitous of all beings: he is through and through concrete willing and needing; he is a concretion of a thousand necessities. With these he stands upon the earth, left to himself, uncertain about everything except his own need and misery. Consequently the care for the maintenance of that existence under exacting demands, which are renewed every day, occupies, as a rule, the whole of human life. To this is directly related the second claim, that of the propagation of the species. At the same time he is threatened from all sides by the most different kinds of dangers, from which it requires constant watchfulness to escape. With cautious steps and casting anxious glances round him he pursues his path, for a thousand accidents and a thousand enemies lie in wait for him. Thus he went while yet a savage, thus he goes in civilised life; there is no security for him. The life of the great majority is only a constant struggle for this existence itself, with the certainty of losing it at last. But what enables them to endure this wearisome battle is not so much the love of life as the fear of death, which yet stands in the background as inevitable, and may come upon them at any moment. Life itself is a sea, full of rocks and whirlpools, which man avoids with the greatest care and solicitude, although he knows that even if he succeeds in getting through with all his efforts and skill, he yet by doing so comes nearer at every step to the greatest, the total, inevitable, and irremediable shipwreck, death; nay, even steers right upon it: this is the final goal of the laborious voyage, and worse for him than all the rocks from which he has escaped.

Now it is well worth observing that, on the one hand, the suffering and misery of life may easily increase to such an extent that death itself, in the flight from which the whole of life consists, becomes desirable, and we hasten towards it voluntarily; and again, on the other hand, that as soon as want and suffering permit rest to a man, ennui is at once so near that he necessarily requires diversion. The striving after existence is what occupies all living things and maintains them in motion. But when existence is assured, then they know not what to do with it; thus the second thing that sets them in motion is the effort to get free from the burden of existence, to make it cease to be felt, "to kill time," i.e., to escape from ennui. Accordingly, we see that almost all men who are secure from want and care, now that at last they have thrown off all other burdens, become a burden to themselves, and regard as a gain every hour they succeed in getting through, and thus every diminution of the very life which, till then, they have employed all their powers to maintain as long as possible. Ennui is by no means an evil to be lightly esteemed; in the end it depicts on the countenance real despair. It makes beings who love each other so little as men do, seek each other eagerly, and thus becomes the source of social intercourse. Moreover, even from motives of policy, public precautions are everywhere taken against it, as against other universal calamities. For this evil may drive men to the greatest excesses, just as much as its opposite extreme, famine: the people require *panem et circenses* ("bread and circuses"). The strict penitentiary system of Philadelphia makes use of ennui alone as a means of punishment, through solitary confinement and idleness, and it is found so terrible that it has even led prisoners to commit suicide. As want is the constant scourge of the people, so ennui is that of the fashionable world. In middle-class life ennui is represented by the Sunday, and want by the six week-days.

Thus between desiring and attaining all human life flows on throughout. The wish is, in its nature, pain; the attainment soon begets satiety: the end was only apparent; possession takes away the charm; the wish, the need, presents itself under a new form; when it does not, then follows desolateness, emptiness, ennui, against which the conflict is just as painful as against want. That wish and satisfac-

tion should follow each other neither too quickly nor too slowly reduces the suffering, which both occasion to the smallest amount, and
constitutes the happiest life. For that which we might otherwise call
the most beautiful part of life, its purest joy, if it were only because it
lifts us out of real existence and transforms us into disinterested spectators of it—that is, pure knowledge, which is foreign to all willing,
the pleasure of the beautiful, the true delight in art—this is granted
only to a very few, because it demands rare talents, and to these few
only as a passing dream. And then, even these few, on account of
their higher intellectual power, are made susceptible of far greater suffering than duller minds can ever feel, and are also placed in lonely
isolation by a nature which is obviously different from that of others;
thus here also accounts are squared. But to the great majority of men
purely intellectual pleasures are not accessible. They are almost quite
incapable of the joys which lie in pure knowledge. They are entirely
given up to willing. If, therefore, anything is to win their sympathy,
to be *interesting* to them, it must (as is implied in the meaning of the
word) in some way excite their *will*, even if it is only through a distant
and merely problematical relation to it; the will must not be left altogether out of the question, for their existence lies far more in willing
than in knowing,—action and reaction is their one element. We may
find in trifles and everyday occurrences the naïve expressions of this
quality. Thus, for example, at any place worth seeing they may visit,
they write their names, in order thus to react, to affect the place since
it does not affect them. Again, when they see a strange rare animal,
they cannot easily confine themselves to merely observing it; they
must rouse it, tease it, play with it, merely to experience action and reaction; but this need for excitement of the will manifests itself very
specially in the discovery and support of cardplaying, which is quite
peculiarly the expression of the miserable side of humanity.

All satisfaction, or what is commonly called happiness, is always really and essentially only *negative*, and never positive. It is not an original gratification coming to us of itself, but must always be the satisfaction of a wish. The wish, i.e., some want, is the condition which
precedes every pleasure. But with the satisfaction the wish and therefore the pleasure cease. Thus the satisfaction or the pleasing can never
be more than the deliverance from a pain, from a want; for such is not
only every actual, open sorrow, but every desire, the importunity of
which disturbs our peace, and, indeed, the deadening ennui also that

makes life a burden to us. It is, however, so hard to attain or achieve anything; difficulties and troubles without end are opposed to every purpose, and at every step hindrances accumulate. But when finally everything is overcome and attained, nothing can ever be gained but deliverance from some sorrow or desire, so that we find ourselves just in the same position as we occupied before this sorrow or desire appeared. All that is even directly given us is merely the want, i.e., the pain. The satisfaction and the pleasure we can only know indirectly through the remembrance of the preceding suffering and want, which ceases with its appearance. Hence it arises that we are not properly conscious of the blessings and advantages we actually possess, nor do we prize them, but think of them merely as a matter of course, for they gratify us only negatively by restraining suffering. Only when we have lost them do we become sensible of their value; for the want, the privation, the sorrow, is the positive, communicating itself directly to us. Thus also we are pleased by the remembrance of past need, sickness, want, and such like, because this is the only means of enjoying the present blessings. And, further, it cannot be denied that in this respect, and from this standpoint of egoism, which is the form of the will to live, the sight or the description of the sufferings of others affords us satisfaction and pleasure. Yet we shall see farther on that this kind of pleasure, through knowledge of our own well-being obtained in this way, lies very near the source of real, positive wickedness.

That all happiness is only of a negative not a positive nature, that just on this account it cannot be lasting satisfaction and gratification, but merely delivers us from some pain or want which must be followed either by a new pain, or by languor, empty longing, and ennui; this finds support in art, that true mirror of the world and life, and especially in poetry. Every epic and dramatic poem can only represent a struggle, an effort, and fight for happiness, never enduring and complete happiness itself. It conducts its heroes through a thousand difficulties and dangers to the goal; as soon as this is reached, it hastens to let the curtain fall; for now there would remain nothing for it to do but to show that the glittering goal in which the hero expected to find happiness had only disappointed him, and that after its attainment he was no better off than before. Because a genuine enduring happiness is not possible, it cannot be the subject of art. Certainly the aim of the idyll is the description of such a happiness, but one also sees that the idyll as such cannot continue. The poet always finds that it either becomes epical in his hands, and in this case it is a very in-significant epic, made up of trifling sorrows, trifling delights, and trifling efforts—this is the commonest cause—or else it becomes a merely descriptive poem, describing the beauty of nature, i.e., pure knowing free from will, which certainly, as a matter of fact, is the only pure happiness, which is neither preceded by suffering or want, nor necessarily followed by repentance, sorrow, emptiness, or satiety; but this happiness cannot fill the whole life, but is only possible at mo-ments. What we see in poetry we find again in music; in the melodies of which we have recognised the universal expression of the inmost history of the self-conscious will, the most secret life, longing, suffer-ing, and delight; the ebb and flow of the human heart. Melody is always a deviation from the keynote through a thousand capricious wanderings, even to the most painful discord, and then a final return to the keynote which expresses the satisfaction and appeasing of the will, but with which nothing more can then be done, and the continu-ance of which any longer would only be a wearisome and unmeaning monotony corresponding to ennui.

JOHN LACHS

To Have and To Be

In an incident Aesop did not record, three animals were lamenting their fate. "If only I had more to eat," said the pig, and he imagined himself buried under an avalanche of fragrant victuals. "If only I had shorter hours and less work," complained the ass as he rubbed his aching back. "If only people had more things and I greater skill to steal them," whispered the fox for he did not want to be found out.

The God Zeus, known for his cruel sense of humor, heard their complaints and decided to grant the animals what they desired. The pig's larder was overflowing with food: he had so much that he had to ask the fox to store some of it for him. But soon the pig could no longer enjoy these good things. Eating too much had caused indigestion and he could not even think of cooking or of food. The ass's workday was reduced; his master bought a small truck to do his heavy work. But soon, instead of concentrating on all the important things he had said he would do, the ass fell asleep and spent his day in a stupor. The fox did not fall asleep, but once the initial glory and excitement of plucking defenseless chickens had abated, he grew indifferent to the charm of pillage. He was bored.

The fable has, of course, no moral for anyone who thinks that boredom, stupor and the glut that comes of overconsumption are integral parts of a good and human life. No good has ever come of the fanatic claim that only one's own ideas are right and only one's own values authentic: if there is anyone who wishes to adopt the fabled pig's desires or share the fox's fate, I will be glad to have him try. The ultimate test of living by the right values is satisfaction or equilibrium, and satisfaction is an individual matter. It is possible that undisciplined consumption is the good of some, while others find happiness in the indulgence of their orgiastic passions. Nothing could be farther from my intention than to censure such behavior. Nature continues to laugh in the face of those stern moralists who strain to set bounds to the plasticity of man.

I will, then, not condemn a way of life, and I will not categorically reject the set of values which it embodies. Nor will I recommend the universal acceptance of another, possibly quite dissimilar, set of principles or aims. I will restrict myself to a critical appraisal of some of the values by which some men in our society live, and for which too many may be willing to die. A critical approach need not lead to criticism: it is merely the dispassionate attitude of the investigator who attempts, in this instance, to determine the value of certain values. As sympathy can only be aroused in men who share a certain concern and possess imagination, values can only be discerned by persons whose natures coincide and who are endowed with sagacity and insight. For this reason, my conclusions will have no validity at all save for those whose nature—being similar to mine—prescribes for them a similar way of life, who are able to achieve the self-knowledge that is required to recognize this, and eventually perhaps to muster the courage to carry it out.

If the values of the pig, the fox or the ass satisfy you, I will not argue: surely, nature will out. Your satisfaction implies that in truth you are a human pig, or a human fox, or an ass. But what of the rest of us who live amidst the ruins of values that were our fathers'? Tossed in an ocean of conflicting obligations and alien pressures, many of us survive by makeshift, impermanent adjustments: we live without settled principles, without a private attitude to life, without a planned pattern to our being. We are not trained to divine the demands of our individual nature, and as a consequence many of us lack the inner unity that is the unmistakable feature of a *person*. There is nothing mysterious about this inner unity. Morality is a kind of hygiene: it is a cleanliness and unpromiscuity of mind. As the child learns the simple facts of animal hygiene—to eat only that which nourishes and to reject whatever does not agree with his nature—the adult has to learn, sometimes through tragic experiences, the importance of acting by a single principle and living by a single plan, assimilating and dismissing as his nature commands. A healthy conscience is but the inner demand for consistency which makes one's life the history of a person instead of a disconnected series of events.

There is a current fallacy whose prevalence I do not feel called upon to discuss. This specious but unuttered principle is best expressed in the phrase "To live is to make a living." All the values of our Consumer Age are implicit in this phrase. "To make a living," of course, means to earn enough to be able to purchase the goods necessary for life. But what are the goods necessary for life? According to what I shall, for short, call the Consumer's Fallacy about the Ends of Human Life, enough food to avoid hunger, and enough shelter and clothing to keep warm, are not enough to *live* in the full sense of that word. Implicit in the Consumer's Fallacy is the claim that we do not even begin to *live* until we have the right or approved kind of food bought in a good store, fashionable clothing, and a cave as good as our neighbors'. This, of course, is only the beginning. For there are characteristically human needs, such as the need for fast cars, the need for heartshaped bathtubs, and the need for the envy of one's fellows. We *live* when we have as many of these and other goods as our fortune will allow or our stratagems create.

The possession and the use of manufactured physical objects have become primary and fundamental facts in our culture and in our lives. They have penetrated our thought to such an extent that the attitudes appropriate to ownership and use have come to serve as the model for our attitudes to the world at large and to other human beings in it. Our attitude to almost every thing we have or wish for is the attitude of a consumer. We use not only cars and washing machines, but also reputation and the goodwill of our neighbors. We possess not only typewriters and television sets, but also security and the loyalty of our children. It is, of course, natural for the human mind to reify the intangible: to substitute images for attitudes and concrete objects for abstract relations. But when such conceptual aids cease to be merely that and begin to penetrate our mental life and to govern our actions, when human beings begin to be considered physical objects and human feelings things to be consumed, the result is that the good life becomes a life filled with goods, and our attempt to live it culminates in a rage of possessiveness.

At the basis of the Consumer's Fallacy is the supposition that a man is what he has: the happiness is a function of the goods we possess and the things we consume, that it is the result of urges satisfied. Thus Hobbes, an early exponent of the Consumer's Fallacy writes:

Continual success in obtaining those things which a man from time to time desires, that is to say, continual prospering, is what men call FELICITY.[1]

If this is true, the introduction of mass advertising and of credit buying are the two greatest steps ever taken to promote the happiness of man. Advertizers create new desires, and consumer credit makes it possible for these desires to be readily satisfied. The unbroken cycle of desires and satisfactions guaranteed amounts to that "continual prospering" which men call "felicity." Continual success, which is happiness, is the share of the American who desires, purchases and consumes in proportion to the installment payments he can meet. And lest my point be misunderstood: what is purchased need not be a manufactured object, it may be love, and the installment payment need not be a sum of money, it may be time to listen to a woman's troubles, or a promise of security.

If Hobbes and his contemporary soul-mates are right and happiness is but the satisfaction of desires on the basis of wisdom in trading, I wonder why so many Americans, shrewd businessmen at work as well as in their private life, remain unhappy. If Hobbes's analysis were correct, the successful consumption of physical objects and of human emotions should suffice to make us happy. How is it then, that so many of us are successful as owners and consumers, even as consumers of human feelings, but unsuccessful as men? The answer to this question is not to be found by an examination of the means we utilize to achieve our ends: it resides, instead, in the nature and inadequacy of our current ends. Similarly, the cure for human dissatisfaction is not by concentrating on increasing our possessions, nor again by concentrating on combating the natural urge to have, but by relegating possession and consumption to their rightful and limited place in a comprehensive scheme of human values.

The Consumer's Fallacy and the accompanying tendency to treat human feelings as commodities and human beings as serviceable objects, is closely connected with our current veneration of progress. Progress is a kind of motion: it is motion in the direction of some

1. Thomas Hobbes, *Leviathan* (London, 1943), p. 30.

desirable goal. What differentiates progress from mere movement or change is its directionality. Direction, in turn, implies a fixed point of reference: some state of affairs for which we strive, an objective that is deemed worthwhile. I do not wish to assail the apologists of progress on the issue of mistaken standards: that some of the objectives in terms of which we measure our "progress" are insignificant or worthless is too obvious to require emphasis. It is as easy to suppose as it is barbarous to assert that the possession of two radios per family or the development of wash-and-wear, warm-yet-light, no-ironing-needed under-wear is the yardstick by which human advance is to be judged. My immediate concern here is not with such mistakes, but with two even more fundamental errors which the indiscriminate veneration of progress promotes.

The first blunder is best expressed in the scandalous slogan "Progress is our most important product." Progress, in fact, is a movement not a product, and its sole importance derives from the importance and the value of its goal. No progress is valuable in and of itself; only the end of progress is of any worth, and it is only by reference to this end that a change may be called "progressive." The value of progress is, in this way, entirely derivative: it is wholly dependent on the value of the fixed objective at which progress aims. This single reflection should eliminate the mistake of supposing that progress can or ought to go on indefinitely or, in other words, that progress can be its own end. Like all forms of transit, progress aims at a destination not at its own self-propagation: its object is a state where progress will no longer be because its goal will have been achieved. I am, of course, not denying that progress is a "good thing" in some sense of that ambiguous phrase. But good things are of two sorts: those which we want for their own sake or as ends, and those which we want for the sake of other things or as means. Comfort and pleasure may be things we want in and of themselves: if they are such *ends*, they are valuable. Coal and electrical generators are a *means* to these ends. They help to bring about our comfort and pleasure and while not intrinsically valuable, they are at least useful. Now progress is at best useful; it is not intrinsically valuable. It is good as a means but not as an end: it must have an end or objective other than itself. Hence progress can never be the goal of progress and no progress can be indefinitely sustained. Progress makes no sense at all without the possibility of fulfilment or attainment, and the more fervently we desire the attainment of our goal, the more we look forward to the time when progress, having got us our aim, will have ceased to be.

The sharp separation of progress from its goal is the source of the second mistake to which I alluded. We believe that it is important to progress and pride ourselves on being a "progressive" nation. We tend to overlook the fact that progress is not a term of unqualified commendation. Progress is movement in the direction of that which we do not have and which, at the same time, it would be good to have. Its existence implies a current lack along with the hope of future consummation. For this reason, any society committed to progress is at once also committed to the future, and whoever is committed to the future ceases to live in the present. But it is impossible to live in anything but the present. The person who attempts to live in the future ends up by not living at all: his present is saturated with a heavy sense of impermanence, worthlessness and longing for the morrow. His concentration on what is yet to come blinds him to the satisfactions that are possible now. His desire to come closer to his goal makes his present a chamber of horrors: by hastening the passage of the days he wishes·his life away. And not only is his longing agonized, after such fierce desire each attainment is an anticlimax. Unreleased emotion paints in hues reality can never match. The object of desire once possessed is only a pale replica of what it was to be.

The meaning of life is not to be found in the future and the characteristically human malady of trying to find it there leads only to disappointment and despair. Caught between the incompleteness of striving and the essential insufficiency of the possessions which flow from desire and hard work, the future-directed man lives with a pervasive sense of insecurity, anxiety, defeat. The paradigm is the grotesque figure of the man who works so hard to provide for his retirement that he dies of a heart-attack when he is forty-two. I will call the belief, fostered by our veneration of progress, that the means and the end must be distinct and separated by time, the Fallacy of Separation. The combination of the attitudes of ownership and use implicit in the Consumer's Fallacy with this Fallacy of Separation issues in disastrous effects on the attempt to lead the good life.

The Fallacy of Separation is so deep-seated in our thinking that it is difficult for us to conceive and almost impossible to admit that means and end may coincide. But this admission is the foundation of all sound ethics and, accordingly, it is found on the first page of Aristotle's great work on the subject. There Aristotle says:

A certain difference is found among ends; some are activities, others are products apart from the actions that produce them.[2]

As a result of our commitment to the future and of our interest in "products apart from the actions that produce them," the concept of *activity* has been virtually lost to Western civilization. An activity is a deed, any deed, that is performed for its own sake. It is an action done not as a means to obtaining some ulterior end or producing some product. Let me make my point with unceremonious simplicity: to engage in activity is to keep doing things without getting anywhere. But why should we wish to get anywhere if we are satisfied with whatever we are doing? The desire to get somewhere, our everlasting restlessness, betrays a sense of dissatisfaction with what we have and what we do and what we are. If we find something worth doing, it is reasonable to enjoy doing it and to ask for no more. If we are satisfied with what we do and are, it becomes unnecessary to look to the future and hope for improvement and progress.

Because the concept of activity is alien to us today, we tend to think that whenever change ceases, stagnation sets in. If this were true, no one would be more stagnant than the Christian God, who is free of desire and eternally changeless. However, to be without the striving that characterizes the infantile romantic mind is not necessarily to be static or inert. Striving might come to an end not only out of exhaustion or disgust, but also because the condition of all striving, the separation of means and end, of creative act and created product, is eliminated. Activity is not the sequestered sleep of the impotent: it is, instead, achievement unfailing and instantaneous, because in it alone the human act is its own reason for existence. I readily admit that all activity is useless, and hasten to add that this uselessness of activity is the best indication of its great value. The useful merely *produces* good things without being one. Activity, on the other hand, is good in and of itself. Too often our actions are useful to bring about ends that are worthless. When these actions cease to point beyond themselves, like poisoned arrows, when they begin to function as ultimate ends, they

2. Aristotle, *Nicomachean Ethics*, 1094a 3–5.

acquire a worth that places them in the category of what is useless but because of its intrinsic value also priceless.

If the good life is a happy life, the pig, the fox and the ass are guilty of two fundamental errors. The first is an error of attitudes, the second an error of aims. The Consumer's Fallacy prompted the animals to extend the attitudes of ownership, use and consumption to areas, such as leisure, happiness and the emotions of human persons, in which they are inappropriate. The Fallacy of Separation prompted the unfelicitous beasts to look for aims and goals that are other than activities, for products of the human act instead of the enjoyment of the act for what it is. In short, the pig, the fox and the ass all wished to *have* and not to *do*. But human beings are built to be bustling engines: they are agents and only action can satisfy them. Possession is not action, it is a passive state and as such at best a substitute for activity.

There is no clearer instance of a possession that functions as an activity-substitute than what is now commonly called a "status-symbol." To *be* a developed person is to engage in characteristic activity. Nothing is more difficult than this, since it involves self-knowledge, spontaneous action and self-control. Thus the majority of us settle for less, while we wish to appear as if we had not compromised. If we cannot *be* someone, we can do the next best and *appear to be:* and this is done by acquiring the possessions that seem to go with being a man of distinction or a developed individual. On the level of the popular mind the confusion is even clearer. Each status symbol reveals an attempt to substitute having for being, ownership for activity, possessions for character: each is a visible manifestation of our endeavor to be someone by having what he has.

A question spontaneously arises in my mind, and I am sure it has already arisen in yours. What cure can we prescribe for the three beasts? My answer to this is as simple as it is disarming. I cannot prescribe a cure for animals. If satisfaction attends their life, I congratulate them: if they do not interfere with mine, I will at least tolerate them. But how could I prescribe a mode of life for forms of life that are as alien from mine as oysters are from migratory mice? I can only speak for myself and for anyone else whose similar nature demands a similar fulfilment.

For us my counsel is to be. Life itself is an activity, and we should not approach it with the attitude of the devourer of experiences or with a possessive violence. We must develop attitudes appropriate to activity, to self-contained, self-validating human action: nothing short of this can make a life happy, spontaneous, and free. Finally, we must engage in appropriate activity. Which activities are appropriate for us is determined by our nature and may be discovered by self-knowledge. The two rules of the personal hygiene of the mind are to know oneself and to concentrate on the exercise of human powers for its own sake and not for its products or its usefulness. By knowing ourselves we will do the right things, by concentrating on the exercise of human powers for its own sake we will do them for the right reason. In this way, each moment of life acquires meaning and inalienable value. In this way, death cannot cut us off or leave our lives dismembered. For under these conditions each moment of existence shines like a total crystal: each is an appropriate, meaningful, and completed human act.

ERICH FROMM

Loving and Being Happy

To love somebody is the actualization and concentration of the power of love. The basic affirmation contained in love is directed toward the beloved person as an incarnation of essentially human qualities. Love of one person implies love of man as such. The kind of "division of labor," as William James calls it, by which one loves one's family but is without feeling for the "stranger," is a sign of a basic inability to love. Love of man is not, as is frequently supposed, an abstraction coming after the love for a specific person, but it is its premise, although genetically it is acquired in loving specific individuals.

From this it follows that my own self must be as much an object of my love as another person. *The affirmation of one's own life, happiness, growth, freedom is rooted in one's capacity to love,* i.e., in care, respect, responsibility, and knowledge. If an individual is able to love productively, he loves himself too; if he can love *only* others, he cannot love at all.

Granted that love for oneself and for others in principle is conjunctive, how do we explain selfishness, which obviously excludes any genuine concern for others? The *selfish* person is interested only in himself, wants everything for himself, feels no pleasure in giving, but only in taking. The world outside is looked at only from the standpoint of what he can get out of it; he lacks interest in the needs of others, and respect for their dignity and integrity. He can see nothing but himself; he judges everyone and everything from its usefulness to him; he is basically unable to love. Does not this prove that concern for others and concern for oneself are unavoidable alternatives? This would be so if selfishness and self-love were identical. But that assumption is the very fallacy which has led to so many mistaken conclusions concerning our problem. *Selfishness and self-love, far from being identical, are actually opposites.* The selfish person does not love himself too much but too little; in fact he hates himself. This lack of fondness and care for himself, which is only one expression of his lack of productiveness, leaves him empty and frustrated. He is necessarily unhappy and anxiously concerned to snatch from life the satisfactions which he blocks himself from attaining. He seems to care too much for himself, but actually he only makes an unsuccessful attempt to cover up and compensate for his failure to care for his real self. Freud holds that the selfish person is narcissistic, as if he had withdrawn his love from others and turned it toward his own person. *It is true that selfish persons are incapable of loving others, but they are not capable of loving themselves either.*

It is easier to understand selfishness by comparing it with greedy concern for others, as we find it, for instance, in an oversolicitous mother. While she consciously believes that she is particularly fond of her child, she has actually a deeply repressed hostility toward the object of her concern. She is overconcerned not because she loves the child too much, but because she has to compensate for her lack of capacity to love him at all.

This theory of the nature of selfishness is borne out by psychoanalytic experience with neurotic "unselfishness," a symptom of neurosis observed in not a few people who usually are troubled not by this symptom but by others connected with it, like depression, tiredness, inability to work, failure in love relationships, and so on. Not only is unselfishness not felt as a "symptom"; it is often the one redeeming character trait on which such people pride themselves. The "unselfish" person "does not want anything for himself"; he "lives only for others," is proud that he does not consider himself important. He is puzzled to find that in spite of his unselfishness he is unhappy, and that his relationships to those closest to him are unsatisfactory. Analytic work shows that his unselfishness is not something apart from his other symptoms but one of them, in fact often the most important one; that he is paralyzed in his capacity to love or to enjoy anything; that he is pervaded by hostility toward life and that behind the façade of unselfishness a subtle but not less intense self-centeredness is hidden. This person can be cured only if his unselfishness too is interpreted as a symptom along with the others, so that his lack of productiveness, which is at the root of both his unselfishness *and* his other troubles, can be corrected.

The nature of unselfishness becomes particularly apparent in its effect on others, and most frequently in our culture in the effect the "unselfish" mother has on her children. She believes that by her unselfishness her children will experience what it means to be loved and to learn, in turn, what it means to love. The effect of her unselfishness, however, does not at all correspond to her expectations. The children do not show the happiness of persons who are convinced that they are loved; they are anxious, tense, afraid of the mother's disapproval and anxious to live up to her expectations. Usually, they are affected by their mother's hidden hostility toward life, which they sense rather than recognize clearly, and eventually they become imbued with it themselves. Altogether, the effect of the "unselfish" mother is not too different from that of the selfish one; indeed, it is often worse, because the mother's unselfishness prevents the children from criticizing her. They are put under the obligation not to disappoint her; they are taught, under the mask of virtue, dislike for life. If one has a chance to study the effect of a mother with genuine self-love, one can see that there is nothing more conducive to giving a child the experience of what love, joy and happiness are than being loved by a mother who loves herself.

These ideas on self-love cannot be summarized better than by quoting Meister Eckhart on this topic: "If you love yourself, you love everybody else as you do yourself. As long as you love another person less than you love yourself, you will not really succeed in loving yourself, but if you love all alike, including yourself, you will love them as one person and that person is both God and man. Thus he is a great and righteous person who, loving himself, loves all others equally. . . ."

Modern man is alienated from himself, from his fellow men, and from nature. He has been transformed into a commodity, experiences his life forces as an investment which must bring him the maximum profit obtainable under existing market conditions. Human relations are essentially those of alienated automatons, each basing his security on staying close to the herd, and not being different in thought, feeling or action. While everybody tries to be as close as possible to the rest, everybody remains utterly alone, pervaded by the deep sense of insecurity, anxiety and guilt which always results when human separateness cannot be overcome. Our civilization offers many palliatives which help people to be consciously unaware of this aloneness: first of all the strict routine of bureaucratized, mechanical work, which helps people to remain unaware of their most fundamental human desires, of the longing for transcendence and unity. Inasmuch as the routine alone does not succeed in this, man overcomes his unconscious despair by the routine of amusement, the passive consumption of sounds and sights offered by the amusement industry; furthermore by the satisfaction of buying ever new things, and soon exchanging them for others. Modern man is actually close to the picture Huxley describes in his *Brave New World:* well fed, well clad, satisifed sexually, yet without self, without any except the most superficial contact with his fellow men, guided by the slogans which Huxley formulated so succinctly, such as: "When the individual feels, the community reels"; or "Never put off till tomorrow the fun you can have today," or, as the crowning statement: "Everybody is happy nowadays." Man's happiness today consists in "having fun." Having fun lies in the satisfaction of consuming and "taking in" commodities, sights, food, drinks, cigarettes, people, lectures, books, movies—all are consumed, swallowed. The world is one great object for our appetite, a big apple, a big bottle, a big breast; we are the sucklers, the eternally expectant ones, the hopeful ones—and the eternally disappointed ones. Our character is geared to exchange and to receive, to barter and to consume; everything, spiritual as well as material objects, becomes an object of exchange and of consumption.

The situation as far as love is concerned corresponds, as it has to by necessity, to this social character of modern man. Automatons cannot love; they can exchange their "personality packages" and hope for a fair bargain. One of the most significant expressions of love, and especially of marriage with this alienated structure, is the idea of the "team." In any number of articles on happy marriage, the ideal described is that of the smoothly functioning team. This description is not too different from the idea of a smoothly functioning employee; he should be "reasonably independent," co-operative, tolerant, and at the same time ambitious and aggressive. Thus, the marriage counselor tells us, the husband should "understand" his wife and be helpful. He should comment favorably on her new dress, and on a tasty dish. She, in turn, should understand when he comes home tired and disgruntled, she should listen attentively when he talks about his business troubles, should not be angry but understanding when he forgets her birthday. All this kind of relationship amounts to is the well-oiled relationship between two persons who remain strangers all their lives, who never arrive at a "central relationship," but who treat each other with courtesy and who attempt to make each other feel better.

In this concept of love and marriage the main emphasis is on finding a refuge from an otherwise unbearable sense of aloneness. In "love" one has found, at last, a haven from aloneness. One forms an alliance of two against the world, and this egoism à deux is mistaken for love and intimacy.

The emphasis on team spirit, mutual tolerance and so forth is a relatively recent development. It was preceded, in the years after the First World War, by a concept of love in which mutual sexual satisfaction was supposed to be the basis for satisfactory love relations, and especially for a happy marriage. It was believed that the reasons for the frequent unhappiness in marriage were to be found in that the marriage partners had not made a correct "sexual adjustment"; the reason for this fault was seen in the ignorance regarding "correct" sexual behavior, hence in the faulty sexual technique of one or both partners. In order to "cure" this fault, and to help the unfortunate couples who could not love each other, many books gave instructions and counsel concerning the correct sexual behavior, and promised implicity or explicity that happiness and love would follow. The underlying idea was that love is the child of sexual pleasure, and that if two people learn how to satisfy each other sexually, they will love each other. It fitted the general illusion of the time to assume that using the right techniques is the solution not only to technical problems of industrial production, but of all human problems as well. One ignored the fact that the contrary of the underlying assumption is true.

Love is not the result of adequate sexual satisfaction, but sexual happiness—even the knowledge of the so-called sexual technique—is the result of love. If aside from everyday observation this thesis needed to be proved, such proof can be found in ample material of psychoanalytic data. The study of the most frequent sexual problems—frigidity in women, and the more or less severe forms of psychic impotence in men—shows that the cause does not lie in a lack of knowledge of the right technique, but in the inhibitions which make it impossible to love. Fear of or hatred for the other sex are at the bottom of those difficulties which prevent a person from giving himself completely, from acting spontaneously, from trusting the sexual partner in the immediacy and directness of physical closeness. If a sexually inhibited person can emerge from fear or hate, and hence become capable of loving, his or her sexual problems are solved. If not, no amount of knowledge about sexual techniques will help.

But while the data of psychoanalytic therapy point to the fallacy of the idea that knowledge of the correct sexual technique leads to sexual happiness and love, the underlying assumption that love is the concomitant of mutual sexual satisfaction was largely influenced by the theories of Freud. For Freud, love was basically a sexual phenomenon. "Man having found by experience that sexual (genital) love afforded him his greatest gratification, so that it became in fact a prototype of all happiness to him, must have been thereby impelled to seek his happiness further along the path of sexual relations, to make genital eroticism the central point of his life."[1] The experience of brotherly love is, for Freud, an outcome of sexual desire, but with the sexual instinct being transformed into an impulse with "inhibited aim." "Love with an inhibited aim was indeed originally full of sensual love, and in man's unconscious mind is so still."[2] As far as the feeling of fusion, of oneness ("oceanic feeling"), which is the essence of mystical experience and the root of the most intense sense of union with one other person or with one's fellow men, is concerned, it was interpreted by Freud as a pathological phenomenon, as a regression to a state of an early "limitless narcissism."[3]

It is only one step further that for Freud love is in itself an irrational phenomenon. The difference between irrational love, and love as an expression of the mature personality does not exist for him. He pointed out in a paper on transference love,[4] that transference love is essentially not different from the "normal" phenomenon of love. Falling in love always verges on the abnormal, is always accompanied by blindness to reality, compulsiveness, and is a transference from love

1. S. Freud, *Civilization and Its Discontents*, translated by J. Riviere, The Hogarth Press, Ltd., London, 1953, p. 69.
2. *Ibid.*, p. 69.
3. *Ibid.*, p. 21.
4. Freud, *Gesamte Werke*, London, 1940–52, Vol. X.

objects of childhood. Love as a rational phenomenon, as the crowning achievement of maturity, was, to Freud, no subject matter for investigation, since it had no real existence.

However, it would be a mistake to overestimate the influence of Freud's ideas on the concept that love is the result of sexual attraction, or rather that it is the *same* as sexual satisfaction, reflected in conscious feeling. Essentially the causal nexus proceeds the other way around. Freud's ideas were partly influenced by the spirit of the nineteenth century; partly they became popular through the prevailing spirit of the years after the First World War. Some of the factors which influenced both the popular and the Freudian concepts were, first, the reaction against the strict mores of the Victorian age. The second factor determining Freud's theories lies in the prevailing concept of man, which is based on the structure of capitalism. In order to prove that capitalism corresponded to the natural needs of man, one had to show that man was by nature competitive and full of mutual hostility. While economists "proved" this in terms of the insatiable desire for economic gain, and the Darwinists in terms of the biological law of the survival of the fittest, Freud came to the same result by the assumption that man is driven by a limitless desire for the sexual conquest of all women, and that only the pressure of society prevented man from acting on his desires. As a result men are necessarily jealous of each other, and this mutual jealousy and competition would continue even if all social and economic reasons for it would disappear.

Eventually, Freud was largely influenced in his thinking by the type of materialism prevalent in the nineteenth century. One believed that the substratum of all mental phenomena was to be found in physiological phenomena; hence, love, hate, ambition, jealousy were explained by Freud as so many outcomes of various forms of the sexual instinct. He did not see that the basic reality lies in the totality of human existence, first of all in the human situation common to all men, and secondly in the practice of life determined by the specific structure of society. (The decisive step beyond this type of materialism was taken by Marx in his "historical materialism," in which not the body, nor an instinct like the need for food or possession, serves as the key to the understanding of man, but the total life process of man, his "practice of life"). According to Freud, the full and uninhibited satisfaction of all instinctual desires would create mental health and happiness. But the obvious clinical facts demonstrate that men—and women—who devote their lives to unrestricted sexual satisfaction do not attain happiness, and very often suffer from severe neurotic conflicts or symptoms. The complete satisfaction of all instinctual needs is not only not a basis for happiness, it does not even guarantee sanity. Yet Freud's idea could only have become so popular in the period after the First World War because of the changes which had occurred in the spirit of capitalism, from the emphasis on saving to that on spending, from self-frustration as a means for economic success to consumption as the basis for an ever-widening market, and as the main satisfaction for the anxious, automatized individual. Not to postpone the satisfaction of any desire became the main tendency in the sphere of sex as well as in that of all material consumption.

MEDARD BOSS

Coming To Be Happy: East and West

None of the leading scholars and great wise men of India I had the pleasure of meeting ever failed to point out with special emphasis one thing: all the Indian philosophical systems that matter have always been concerned with the same two problems. They dealt with the fact of the endless suffering that people had to endure and the equally undeniable fact of man's powerful longing for release from suffering and for happiness. Owing to the strict focusing of their thought on these two vital circumstances of our life, the Indian philosophers became veritable pioneers of the ways to salvation. At the same time, they never elevated the intellectual investigation of the truth as their ultimate aim, as did Western philosophers, but regarded it as merely one of the possible provisional means of producing a release from suffering.

If what I had heard from such authoritative spokesmen was the case, the Indian philosophies were nothing more than spiritual prescriptions against human suffering in all its forms. Then we should call them psychotherapies rather than philosophies, if the Indians had ever believed in the existence of a "psyche." Instead, Indian thought always understood man as an essentially luminating "Atman-being," belonging directly to "Brahman," the hidden matrix of all appearing, being, vanishing and non-being. Indian philosophy sees in this conception not only the truth about the basic nature of man but also the only effective therapeutics to ensure genuine cures and lasting salvation. Therefore—aside from the always despised materialists—it is the common aim of all Indian schools of philosophy to explore ways and means fully to elucidate this truth in terms of an experience that encompasses man as a whole. Thus it would be more appropriate to call the Indian philosophies "elucidation therapies." And yet this other name removes them only apparently from the methods of treatment called "psychotherapies" in the West. In reality, it brings the two therapies, Eastern and Western, so close to each other that their point of contact becomes visible at once. For had not Freud very early discovered that the criterion setting his psychoanalytical method apart from all other medical therapies is the simultaneous occurrence of illuminating insight into the hidden nature of a neurotic disturbance and of therapeutic liberation from this suffering? Could he not also sum up the principle behind his method of treatment in the words: where "id" was, let there be "ego"? And ever since Freud, have not all Western psychotherapies worthy of the name endeavoured to make patients themselves see into their unveiled nature, to make them transparent to themselves? It does not matter how various in kind are all the secondary, theoretical superstructures erected above these therapies. But where could there ever be an elucidation (lux = light), a transparency, a shining-through, without light and a light-giving source?

However, no matter how closely Eastern philosophies and Western psychotherapies agree, the *degree* of illuminating power that the Western psychotherapies are as a rule capable of attaining struck me as so insufficient that I began to look for assistance in the Indian tradition. I had a unique experience at the very beginning of my Indian stay; it drove home the point that our psychotherapeutic methods needed urgent improvement of their capacity to illuminate. I had made friends with the family of an Indian philosophy professor, a very perceptive and learned man. He had felt a need to supplement his mastery of ancient Indian teachings with a knowledge of European psychology and psychotherapy. To employ his own words, he hoped that, thus equipped, he could render more individual assistance to patients than before. Therefore he had come to Europe for two years and had successfully completed a course of study at a psychotherapeutic institute. Nevertheless, since his return to India he himself had been complaining—and his family concurred—that he had been made much more unhappy by learning about Western psychotherapy. Whereas formerly he had accepted the vicissitudes of life, like illnesses in the family, with great calmness, now every trifle made him nervous, restless and pessimistic. Now he always thought he had to do this or that at once, and he made everything worse with his haste. He had forgotten how to wait patiently, and had become harder and more loveless. Obviously, from his training in Western psychotherapy, he had learned to see himself as a "psyche," i.e. a balanced system of mental functions, libidinous dynamisms and archetypical structures and forces within the psychic realm of a subject. Now he had to find his way through the bustle and tumult of an external world, based on nothing but a fundamentally unknowable, anonymous, id-like "unconscious". He had lost so much of his former Indian wisdom and poised calm that his confidence-inspiring realization of his participation in all-encompassing, sustaining "Brahman" had shrunk to a fragile dependence on individual authority figures and their psychological notions. I learned all this not only from his waking behaviour but also from the troublesome dreams which had begun to torment him towards the end of his psychoanalytical training, and which still bothered him here in India. It does not matter which school of psychoanalysis this was. Any Western psychology would have involved this Indian philosopher in the same difficulties. Nevertheless, there is little doubt that the same psychotherapy would have been of the greatest use to many a hardened, ego-obsessed European or American. But my friend had previously been living in the vastness of Indian thinking and feeling, and Western psychotherapy seemed to him like a prison demoralizing him with its narrowness.

Still less encouraging were my first experiences with European and American people who had gone in wholeheartedly for Eastern wisdom. Even before my Indian trip I had met patients who had had to pay with a severe mental illness for their newly acquired acquaintance with the Indian tradition. Their attempts to sink into meditation in the Indian fashion and to yield themselves up to "Brahman" had unleashed in them a schizophrenic chaos. The first thing the doctor had to do was to divert their attention from all Indian ideas and to bring them back into their native world with the aid of occupational therapy.

In India itself I met altogether eight European and American people who had entered upon one of the Indian ways of salvation. They were living either in a retreat in the mountains or had joined the ashram of a holy man and donned the Indian monk's or nun's garb along with the corresponding ascetic discipline. With one exception, however, they had remained in the depths of their hearts self-willed, envious and intolerant Occidentals. They had merely inflated their very limited egos with Indian formulas of wisdom instead of with large bank accounts or other means to power. Clear evidence of this.was their ungenerous contempt for Western culture and for Christian beliefs. The human magnanimity of their Indian teachers did not appear to have left any traces on them as yet.

The misfortune that had befallen my Indian philosopher friend was a clear warning against trying to force a person at peace in an Eastern wisdom into the framework of a Western psychological theory. On the other hand, these experiences with Occidentals taught me to keep all Indian knowledge about the nature of man far removed from my future therapeutic work.

And yet there were the exalted figures of the sages and holy men themselves, each one of them a living example of the possibility of human growth and maturity and of the attainment of an imperturbable inner peace, a joyous freedom from guilt and a purified, selfless goodness and calmness. The means and aims of our Western psychotherapy struck me as quite inadequate in comparison with the teachings and the behaviour of these masters. Of course, our psychologies furnish students with easily assimilable psychological formulas and concepts. Their obvious handiness nourishes our belief that they give us something really solid, something we can rely on. They make us forget that they are for the most part only intellectual reductions of the nature of man to unreal abstractions.

However, the aims behind a rightly understood training analysis, as required by every serious school of psychotherapy in the West, coincide in many respects with the instructions of the Indian sages. But compared with the degree of self-purification expected by the latter, even the best Western training analysis is not much more than an introductory course. Above all, Western psychotherapies had previously taught me never to expect more from my patients than the possibility that they might grow into a conscious appropriation of all their vital capacities and become able to live with their fellow-men in a spirit of mature love. But there was no hope that a person would actually get rid of his "shadow" by means of psychotherapy. The therapist had to be satisfied if a patient under analysis became aware of his aggressive, destructive, animal drives. For in that way he at least got control of them. They could no longer emerge from repression and with their false pretences wreak their havoc in the shape of pathological symptoms, and treacherously disturb the natural goodness in man. Yet, at best, we all had to live out our lives consciously in the presence of the dark and evil forces of our natures.

Nevertheless, the Indian sages seem to have worked the miracle of truly freeing themselves from evil. I was forced to the conclusion that in them there is nothing at all evil, covetous, destructive, fearful, guilty or dark, to be consciously controlled and unconsciously repressed. No matter how carefully I observed the waking lives of the holy men, no matter how ready they were to tell me about their dreams, I could not detect in the best of them a trace of a selfish action or any kind of repressed or consciously concealed shadow life. They seemed to me to consist of pure love, which had long since redeemed in them all hate and desire. Yet such a liberation and such unclouded bliss—they had always taught me—presupposed "Vairagya," the renunciation of all self-seeking attachment to things and to people. "Vairagya" did not need to have anything to do with a bodily withdrawal.

Whenever I listened to the Indian sages, I always asked myself whether I would not have to overhaul my whole psychotherapeutic knowledge or give it up entirely.

I was so perplexed by the contradictory experiences of my Indian journey that finally my tormenting doubts overcame me in the presence of my Kashmiri teacher. He could see my trouble in my face, broke off in the middle of a sentence and went on: "Do not think you would have to apply in some way, in your profession, what you have learned in India, or derive from it a new psychotherapeutic technique. You had better not say anything at all to your patients about it. Don't make the slightest change in your psychological technique of free association and in your analysis of resistance. I told you, when you described for me the basic principles of Western psychoanalysis, that from time immemorial Indian teachers too imposed on their pupils a corresponding 'training-analysis,' a realization of their own desires and passions. Of course, what you call psychotherapy and psychoanalysis are only preliminary treatments. They may be doubly necessary, indispensable and tedious for Occidentals. People in the West have for centuries been disciplined in their consciousness of a self-contained personality, in their overemphasis on rational, conceptual thinking and in their divisive idea of the sinfulness of the bodily and instinc-tual side. And yet, at bottom, no person anywhere in the world will attain to truly profound and restorative knowledge unless he has freed himself from all false ideas about himself and from any attachment to immature childish needs. How should one obtain the strength of spirit to overcome one's ego-attachment and the vision of the ordinary man—and grow into the much more encompassing state of conscious-ness called 'Samadhi,' complete enlightenment, unless one had con-scious control of all one's vital capacities? If, however, a man attempts this before he has attained the necessary maturity and freedom, he will surely break down, fall into confusion or become exalted.

"Tell all whom it may concern that the attainment of truth by medi-tation does not presuppose a weak, unprepared mind, but an espe-cially mature frame of mind and a powerful consciousness capable of comprehending all human capacities. Meditation should never be mis-understood as a retreat or a regression to a pre-individual state. A per-son who truly meditates becomes not less but more than what you call a 'personality.' He develops a vision that transcends everything indi-vidual. He never gives up his so-called ego-consciousness in order to drift in a state of self-dissolution, but in order to attain the state of a much profounder and more comprehensive consciousness. That is no child's game. The wise men of India had always warned against all 'wild' meditation experiments and repeatedly stressed the necessity of a proper introduction and guidance by an experienced teacher. In this they are also in accord with you, since, as you tell me, you are familiar too with the dangers of a 'wild' psychoanalysis and with the necessity of a careful training in this field."

Thus, without being asked to do so, this man had largely resolved my confusion. I now understood the regrettable events that made Oc-cidentals in contact with the Indian tradition either self-willed, senti-mental phantasts or confused schizophrenics. Their mental structure was obviously too restricted, too hardened; and its basis was too nar-row, weak and fragile to enable them to integrate such insights. They would all have greatly needed psychoanalysis first, which the master had understood as a preliminary treatment.

However, had not the wise man at the same time explained the situ-ation in a way that decidedly put me in my place? Had he not spoken out clearly enough against any attempt of a Western psychotherapist to overstep the bounds of just such a "preliminary treatment," when he advised me to keep silent about all my Indian experiences, and would not hear of any change in my previous psychotherapeutic methods?

To make sure, I asked again: "Then, my whole Indian journey can at best expand my own horizon a little, but can not benefit my patients in any way? Is my relationship to them really to remain as it was before?"

"Externally, of course," was the reply of the master. "The outward aspects of your work will hardly change. For the best thing you can do as a conscientious doctor is quietly to assimilate your Indian experiences. If these have impinged deeply enough, everything else will follow of itself. Your patients will sense that your actions are becoming meaningful in and for themselves. Do you remember how I asked you to lie flat on the floor here one evening after we had first met? How tense you were, as if you could not trust these thick boards and the rock underneath to hold you up, as if even in lying you had to hold yourself together by an effort of sheer will in order not to perish! But how should a person who does not trust his own basis and does not dare to yield to it have the calmness and strength to give aid to others who need it?

"However, some people can experience in the last fibres of their being, by tireless concentration and contemplation of the true nature of all phenomena, their immediate participation in 'Brahman,' the one ineffable but most real of all givens. With such people, every single action, no matter how slight or how close to all previous actions, every word takes on a new, fuller and more beneficent significance. For an unshakable confidence is radiated by everything such a person does or leaves undone. It is the primordial trust in what is inconceivable by conceptual understanding, incalculable by all calculations, in which all things are rooted. Even though all this is still a deeply veiled mystery to you, it will one day dawn on your intellect as that great beginning which, though incalculable, is never just the contrary of a calculable order, merely chaos, but is always what sustains all chaos and order together.

"Many another pre-condition of a fruitful psychotherapy will be automatically established if you are prepared to make the effort of tireless, open, still and concentrated listening to what goes on within, to the root-melody of all being—instead of a 'straining of the intellect,' to employ your own term. You would never again fall prey to a superficial fascination with any kind of psychotherapeutic techniques or psychological theories. Neither would you, of course, despise psychotherapeutic devices and think you are entitled to do without them and replace them by sentimentality. You would only use psychotherapeutic equipment like all other inventions of technology, in freedom, rejoice in its good effects and so be able to play with it, without taking it for something ultimate. At the same time, you would be immune to all the pathological cramps of an eternal compulsion, obligation and will to determine everything yourself. You would know that true human progress occurs only when every will to progress has vanished and a relaxed waiting and ability-to-let-be has replaced it. When all the phenomena of the world and all their interrelationships become transparent in their deepest nature and hidden perfection to you as a truly aware person—no matter how tormenting and destructive they may appear to a rigid and constricted intellect—then you will be able to enjoy an unperturbed and liberating happiness. Only then would you never again feel yourself to be torn into an ego, into menacing anonymous drives and into a hostile conscience. You would, rather, be able to understand all your psychic possibilities as related articulations of one and the same comprehensive root-being.

"Out of the same understanding, a genuine healer also sees everything that happens in his patients as stemming from the same origin as his own life, constantly pervading it and actually constituting it. Therefore he is open to and capable of an acceptance of the Other that is unlimited because, from his viewpoint, there are no longer any barriers between an *I* and a *Thou* and the ultimate ground. But, then, these barriers have never been erected *in such a way* that there ever would be the danger of an entangling and merging of two small subjects, for example, a mutual mindless infatuation. Rather, the barriers are overcome in such a way that the true healer helps the other person to become increasingly aware of the essential native root-nature common to both of them, until, in its light, a time comes when all pathological distortions and constrictions vanish spontaneously."

Then the master was silent. Like my previous Indian teachers, he had also early requested me to look him straight in the eyes, as often and as long as possible. That helped understanding, promoted mutual access to the essential human core in each of us and cut through the superficial cultural and social masks that we all wear. Here, too, I over-

came my Western shyness, my fear of offending by such unabashed
staring. In this intimate contact with the master I gained for a while
the great peace that simply allows all things to come to pass. This
simple thing was the certainty that what our psychotherapy needs
above all is a change in the psychotherapists. If our science of mental
health is to become more effective, psychotherapists will have to balance their knowledge of psychological concepts and techniques with a
contemplative awareness. This will have to be an awareness that exercises itself day after day in quiet openness; it must address the inexpressible origin of all that is, of the healthy and the sick and also of all
psychotherapeutic interventions. Then psychiatrists, in their own
way, will be able to help people who are becoming increasingly alienated from their roots. They will then be able to restore to these people
that sense of nest-warmth that is more protective and sustaining than
all the institutions and techniques that have ever been devised. . . .

I spent the days that followed almost entirely in the ashram and in
the immediate presence of the master. Mornings and afternoons the
wise man's pupils would throng about him for two, three or four
hours on end. They would render homage to him, at times with rev-
erential silence, and at other times with chanting and music. Then the
sage would again encourage individual disciples along the path of
spiritual purification. I was never refused admittance to the master's
consecrated meditation room, where I was allowed to sit with them
all, although association with a casteless person like me was presumably not conducive to their spiritual welfare. When I looked about
from one of these worshipful visages to the other, gazing up in profound and rapt reverence and awe at their master, it often seemed to
me as if a scene of worshipping angels and saints by Fra Angelico had
come to life. Among living people I had never before encountered
such consummate purity. For many days, to be sure, my critical intellect resisted the idea of seeing anything more in the behaviour of
the disciples than a rather embarrassing deification of a human being
and in the honoured one himself anything more than a benevolent,
yet by no means extraordinary man. Also, it struck me as suspicious
that a human being could countenance such a deification of himself.
Was not a considerable portion of residual vanity and craving for
power seeking to express itself in this way? Or did such a master simply understand the spiritual inadequacy of lesser souls, who were
capable of seeing into the realm of the divine only by way of a palpa-

ble intermediary? Did he expose himself to worship only for the sake of the others, who needed him, without allowing himself to be affected by it in the slightest? Yes, the latter must be the true explanation. How, otherwise, would I have come to sense with ever deepening conviction, day after day, what an unheard of, unsullied, blissful peace was emanated from the mere physical presence of the master? But precisely this was the decisive criterion mentioned repeatedly by reliable and experienced informants; by it alone the true holy men could be swiftly distinguished from the false ones. The entire being of this master was unmistakably purified into a state of perfect selflessness and all-embracing love. No word of his, no glance, no gesture, no action betrayed to me even the slightest bondage to egoistic needs, no matter how tirelessly and critically I kept his comportment under observation during all my fourteen days with him. It was also obvious that this spirit possessed a radiating power which reduced to silence in the people about him all petty desires for recognition, ambitious rivalries, and self-centered motives in general. Even the sexual difference between his male and female disciples was no longer a problem in the atmosphere of this ashram. All fretful cares about the future gave way to irrepressible gaiety and high spirits in the face of this knowledge of the last and profoundest mysteries betrayed and at the same time retained by his eyes. These eyes of his seemed to shine forth from some inner source of light. Even physical hunger ceased its clamorings. I almost entirely forgot about eating, so abundantly was I provided with spiritual nourishment, in group instruction, in long talks alone with the master, and still more by his mere presence.

4

Knowing Truth and Being True

Perhaps no desire is as powerful and insatiable as that for truth. For accurate knowledge is widely supposed to be a condition of success in all our other searches. Power requires an understanding of circumstances and instrumentalities, and self-realization is impossible without knowledge of the self. If we could grasp the nature of man and the structure of spirituality, happiness and transcendence would be our prize. Some people even believe that sufficient knowledge could extend human life indefinitely, or at least enable us to live better as we prepare for death.

The increase of knowledge has brought us great benefits. We have gained a measure of control over hunger and disease. We have made human life more comfortable and more secure. Through foresightful interventions we have converted much that used to be viewed as fate—such as reproduction and job or station in life—into matters of choice. When we see the immense power of knowledge, it is natural to suppose that what we need to solve all our problems is an even broader and more thorough grasp of truths about the world. Some philosophers have gone so far as to maintain that wickedness itself is curable by information; on the assumption that no one would choose the wrong thing knowingly, they concluded that evil is always bred by ignorance.

Yet we find that the growth of information does not solve our deepest problems. We could devise a scientific life based on accurate knowledge that might maximize the good we do for society or for ourselves. But such a life would necessitate a great loss in freedom and feeling. For knowledge and truth are rarely effective on their own, and rational habits require immense self-control and sacrifice. Moreover, objective truth may be insufficient as a basis for living. It reveals little about moral values and leaves altogether out of account the spiritual and perhaps unspeakable cravings of the heart.

Our search for accurate, factual information presupposes that the truth is there independently of us, ready to be known. This assumption of an objective, discoverable reality is fruitful in terms of practical results, but it is not easy to prove or justify. It may well be that all our knowledge is structured by the concepts we employ, by our cognitive apparatus, by our projects or our purposes. If so, knowers and the world they know are inextricably bound together.

We have seen how philosophical reflection challenges claims to knowledge. It should not be surprising, therefore, to find that although we know a great deal, we lack a clear grasp of the role and limits, even of the nature of truth. What is truth? Does it lead to happiness? Is it a condition of knowledge, a product of human self-creation, an intensity of will, or the selfless disclosure of things?

HERBERT SPENCER

The Life Based on Science

Before devoting years to some subject which fashion or fancy suggests, it is surely wise to weigh with great care the worth of the results, as compared with the worth of various alternative results which the same years might bring if otherwise applied.

In education, then, this is the question of questions, which it is high time we discussed in some methodic way. The first in importance, though the last to be considered, is the problem—how to decide among the conflicting claims of various subjects on our attention. Before there can be a rational *curriculum*, we must settle which things it most concerns us to know; or, to use a word of Bacon's, now unfortunately obsolete—we must determine the relative values of knowledges.

To this end, a measure of value is the first requisite. And happily, respecting the true measure of value, as expressed in general terms, there can be no dispute. Every one in contending for the worth of any particular order of information, does so by showing its bearing upon some part of life. In reply to the question, "Of what use is it?" the mathematician, linguist, naturalist, or philosopher, explains the way in which his learning beneficially influences action—saves from evil or secures good—conduces to happiness. When the teacher of writing has pointed out how great an aid writing is to success in business— that is, to the obtainment of sustenance—that is, to satisfactory living; he is held to have proved his case. And when the collector of dead facts (say a numismatist) fails to make clear any appreciable effects which these facts can produce on human welfare, he is obliged to admit that they are comparatively valueless. And then, either directly or by implication, appeal to this as the ultimate test.

How to live?—that is the essential question for us. Not how to live in the mere material sense only, but in the widest sense. The general problem which comprehends every special problem is—the right ruling of conduct in all directions under all circumstances. In what way to treat the body; in what way to treat the mind; in what way to manage our affairs; in what way to bring up a family; in what way to behave as a citizen; in what way to utilize all those sources of happiness which nature supplies—how to use all our faculties to the greatest advantage of ourselves and others—how to live completely? And this being the great thing needful for us to learn, is, by consequence, the great thing which education has to teach. To prepare us for complete living is the function which education has to discharge; and the only rational mode of judging of any educational course is, to judge in what degree it discharges such function.

This test, never used in its entirety, but rarely even partially used, and used then in a vague, half conscious way, has to be applied consciously, methodically, and throughout all cases. It behooves us to set before ourselves, and ever to keep clearly in view, complete living as the end to be achieved; so that in bringing up our children we may choose subjects and methods of instruction, with deliberate reference to this end. Not only ought we to cease from the mere unthinking adoption of the current fashion in education, which has no better warrant than any other fashion; but we must also rise above that rude, empirical style of judging displayed by those more intelligent people who do bestow some care in overseeing the cultivation of their children's minds. It must not suffice simply to *think* that such or such information will be useful in after life, or that this kind of knowledge is of more practical value than that; but we must seek out some process of estimating their respective values, so that as far as possible we may positively *know* which are most deserving of attention. . . .

If any one doubts the importance of an acquaintance with the fundamental principles of physiology as a means to complete living, let him look around and see how many men and women he can find in middle or later life who are thoroughly well. Occasionally only do we meet with an example of vigorous health continued to old age; hourly do we meet with examples of acute disorder, chronic ailment, general debility, premature decrepitude. Scarcely is there one to whom you put the question, who has not, in the course of his life, brought upon himself illnesses which a little knowledge would have saved him from. Here is a case of heart disease consequent on a rheumatic fever that followed reckless exposure. There is a case of eyes spoiled for life by overstudy. Yesterday the account was of one whose long-enduring lameness was brought on by continuing, spite of the pain, to use a knee after it had been slightly injured. And today we are told of another who has had to lie by for years, because he did not know that the palpitation he suffered from resulted from overtaxed brain. Now we hear of an irremediable injury that followed some silly feat of strength; and, again, of a constitution that has never recovered from the effects of excessive work needlessly undertaken. . . .

Hence, knowledge which subserves direct self-preservation by preventing this loss of health, is of primary importance. We do not contend that possession of such knowledge would by any means wholly remedy the evil. For it is clear that in our present phase of civilization men's necessities often compel them to transgress. And it is further clear that, even in the absence of such compulsion, their inclinations would frequently lead them, spite of their knowledge, to sacrifice future good to present gratification. But we do contend that the right knowledge impressed in the right way would effect much; and we further contend that as the laws of health must be recognised before they can be fully conformed to, the imparting of such knowledge must precede a more rational living—come when that may. We infer that as vigorous health and its accompanying high spirits are larger elements of happiness than any other things whatever, the teaching how to maintain them is a teaching that yields in moment to no other whatever. . . .

We need not insist on the value of that knowledge which aids indirect self-preservation by facilitating the gaining of a livelihood. . . .

For, leaving out only some very small classes, what are all men employed in? They are employed in the production, preparation, and distribution of commodities. And on what does efficiency in the production, preparation, and distribution of commodities depend? It depends on the use of methods fitted to the respective natures of these commodities; it depends on an adequate knowledge of their physical, chemical, or vital properties, as the case may be; that is, it depends on

Science. This order of knowledge, which is in great part ignored in our school courses, is the order of knowledge underlying the right performance of all those processes by which civilized life is made possible. . . .

For all the higher arts of construction, some acquaintance with Mathematics is indispensable. The village carpenter, who, lacking rational instruction, lays out his work by empirical rules learnt in his apprenticeship, equally with the builder of a Britannia Bridge, makes hourly reference to the laws of quantitative relations. The surveyor on whose survey the land is purchased; the architect in designing a mansion to be built on it; the builder in preparing his estimates; his foreman in laying out the foundations; the masons in cutting the stones; and the various artisans who put up the fittings; are all guided by geometrical truths. Railway-making is regulated from beginning to end by mathematics: alike in the preparation of plans and sections; in staking out the line; in the mensuration of cuttings and embankments; in the designing, estimating, and building of bridges, culverts, viaducts, tunnels, stations. And similarly with the harbours, docks, piers, and various engineering and architectural works that fringe the coasts and overspread the face of the country; as well as the mines that run underneath it. Out of geometry, too, as applied to astronomy, the art of navigation has grown; and so, by this science, has been made possible that enormous foreign commerce which supports a large part of our population, and supplies us with many necessaries and most of our luxuries. And now-a-days even the farmer, for the correct laying out of his drains, has recourse to the level—that is, to geometrical principles. When from those divisions of mathematics which deal with *space*, and *number*, some small smattering of which is given in schools, we turn to that other division which deals with *force*, of which even a smattering is scarcely ever given, we meet with another large class of activities which this science presides over. . . .

Pass next to Physics. Joined with mathematics, it has given us the steam-engine, which does the work of millions of labourers. That section of physics which deals with the laws of heat, has taught us how to economise fuel in our various industries; how to increase the produce of our smelting furnaces by substituting the hot for the cold blast; how to ventilate our mines; how to prevent explosions by using the safety-lamp; and, through the thermometer, how to regulate innumerable processes. That division which has the phenomena of light for its subject, gives eyes to the old and the myopic; aids through the microscope in detecting diseases and adulterations; and by improved lighthouses prevents shipwrecks. . . .

Still more numerous are the bearings of Chemistry on those activities by which men obtain the means of living. The bleacher, the dyer, the calico-printer, are severally occupied in processes that are well or ill done according as they do or do not conform to chemical laws. The economical reduction from their ores of copper, tin, zinc, lead, silver, iron, are in a great measure questions of chemistry. Sugar-refining, gas-making, soap-boiling, gunpowder manufacture, are operations all partly chemical; as are also those by which are produced glass and procelain. . . .

And then the science of life—Biology: does not this, too, bear fundamentally upon these processes of indirect self-preservation? With what we ordinarily call manufactures, it has, indeed, little connexion; but with the all-essential manufacture—that of food—it is inseperably connected. As agriculture must conform its methods to the phenomena of vegetable and animal life, it follows necessarily that the science of these phenomena is the rational basis of agriculture. Various biological truths have indeed been empirically established and acted upon by farmers while yet there has been no conception of them as science: such as that particular manures are suited to particular plants; that crops of certain kinds unfit the soil for other crops; that horses cannot do good work on poor food; that such and such diseases of cattle and sheep are caused by such and such conditions. These, and the everyday knowledge which the agriculturist gains by experience respecting the right management of plants and animals, constitute his stock of biological facts; on the largeness of which greatly depends his success. And as these biological facts, scanty, indefinite, rudimentary, though they are, aid him so essentially; judge what must be the value to him of such facts when they become positive, definite, and exhaustive. Indeed, even now we may see the benefits that rational biology is conferring on him. . . .

Yet one more science have we to note as bearing directly on industrial success—the Science of Society. Without knowing it, men who daily look at the state of the money-market, glance over prices current, discuss the probable crops of corn, cotton, sugar, wool, silk, weigh the chances of war, and from all those data decide on their mercantile operations, are students of social science: empirical and blundering students it may be; but still, students who gain the prizes or are plucked of their profits, according as they do or do not reach the right conclusion. Not only the manufacturer and the merchant must guide their transactions by calculations of supply and demand, based on numerous facts, and tacitly recognising sundry general principles of social action; but even the retailer must do the like: his prosperity very greatly depending upon the correctness of his judgments respecting the future wholesale prices and the future rates of consumption. Manifestly, all who take part in the entangled commercial activities of a community, are vitally interested in understanding the laws according to which those activities vary.

Thus, to all such as are occupied in the production, exchange, or distribution of commodities, acquaintance with science in some of its departments, is of fundamental importance. Whoever is immediately or remotely implicated in any form of industry (and few are not) has a direct interest in understanding something of the mathematical, physical, and chemical properties of things; perhaps, also, has a direct interest in biology; and certainly has in sociology. Whether he does or does not succeed well in that indirect self-preservation which we call getting a good livelihood, depends in a great degree on his knowledge of one or more of these sciences: not, it may be, a rational knowledge; but still a knowledge, though empirical. For what we call learning a business, really implies learning the science involved in it; though not perhaps under the name of science. . . .

We come now to the third great division of human activities—a division for which no preparation whatever is made. If by some strange chance not a vestige of us descended to the remote future save a pile of our school-books or some college examination papers, we may imagine how puzzled an antiquary of the period would be on finding in them no indication that the learners were ever likely to be parents. "This must have been the *curriculum* for their celibates," we may fancy him concluding. "I perceive here an elaborate preparation for many things: especially for reading the books of extinct nations and of co-existing nations (from which indeed it seems clear that these people had very little worth reading in their own tongue); but I find no reference whatever to the bringing up of children. They could not have been so absurd as to omit all training for this gravest of responsibilities. Evidently then, this was the school course of one of their monastic orders."

Seriously, is it not an astonishing fact, that though on the treatment of offspring depend their lives or deaths, and their moral welfare or ruin; yet not one word of instruction on the treatment of offspring is ever given to those who will hereafter be parents? Is it not monstrous that the fate of a new generation should be left to the chances of unreasoning custom, impulse, fancy—joined with the suggestions of ignorant nurses and the prejudiced counsel of grandmothers? If a merchant commenced business without any knowledge of arithmetic and book-keeping, we should exclaim at his folly, and look for disastrous consequences. Or if, before studying anatomy, a man set up as a surgical operator, we should wonder at his audacity and pity his patients. But that parents should begin the difficult task of rearing children without ever having given a thought to the principles—physical, moral, or intellectual—which ought to guide them, excites neither surprise at the actors nor pity for their victims. . . .

Grant that the phenomena of intelligence conform to laws; grant that the evolution of intelligence in a child also conforms to laws; and it follows inevitably that education can be rightly guided only by a knowledge of these laws. To suppose that you can properly regulate this process of forming and accumulating ideas, without understanding the nature of the process, is absurd. How widely, then, must teaching as it is, differ from teaching as it should be; when hardly any parents, and but few teachers, know anything about psychology. . . .

The training of children—physical, moral, and intellectual—is dreadfully defective. And in great measure it is so, because parents are devoid of that knowledge by which this training can alone be rightly guided. What is to be expected when one of the most intricate of problems is undertaken by those who have given scarcely a thought to the principles on which its solution depends? For shoe-making or house-building, for the management of a ship or a locomotive-engine, a long apprenticeship is needful. Is it, then, that the unfolding of a human being in body and mind, is so comparatively simple a process, that any one may superintend and regulate it with no preparation whatever? If not—if the process is with one exception more complex than any in Nature, and the task of administering to it one of surpassing difficulty; is it not madness to make no provision for such a task? Better sacrifice accomplishments than omit this all-essential instruction. . . .

Thus we see that for regulating the third great division of human activities, a knowledge of the laws of life is the one thing needful. Some acquaintance with the first principles of physiology and the elementary truths of psychology is indispensable for the right bringing up of children. . . .

From the parental functions let us pass now to the functions of the citizen. We have here to inquire what knowledge best fits a man for the discharge of these functions. . . .

Without an acquaintance with the general truths of biology and psychology, rational interpretation of social phenomena is impossible. Only in proportion as men obtain a certain rude, empirical knowledge of human nature, are they enabled to understand even the simplest facts of social life: as, for instance, the relation between supply and demand. And if not even the most elementary truths of sociology can be reached until some knowledge is obtained of how men generally think, feel, and act under given circumstances; then it is manifest that there can be nothing like a wide comprehension of sociology, unless through a competent knowledge of man in all his faculties, bodily and mental. Consider the matter in the abstract, and this conclusion is self-evident. Thus:—Society is made up of individuals; all that is done in society is done by the combined actions of individuals; and therefore, in individual actions only can be found the solutions of social phenomena. But the actions of individuals depend on the laws of their natures; and their actions cannot be understood until these laws are understood. These laws, however, when reduced to their simplest expression, are found to depend on the laws of body and mind in general. Hence it necessarily follows, that biology and psychology are indispensable as interpreters of sociology. Or, to state the conclusions still more simply:—all social phenomena are phenomena of life—are the most complex manifestations of life—are ultimately dependent on the laws of life—and can be understood only when the laws of life are understood. Thus, then, we see that for the regulation of this fourth division of human activities, we are, as before, dependent on Science. . . .

And now we come to that remaining division of human life which includes the relaxations, pleasures, and amusements filling leisure hours. After considering what training best fits for self-preservation, for the obtainment of sustenance, for the discharge of parental duties, and for the regulation of social and political conduct; we have now to consider what training best fits for the miscellaneous ends not in-cluded in these—for the enjoyments of Nature, of Literature, and of the Fine Arts, in all their forms. Postponing them as we do to things that bear more vitally upon human welfare; and bringing everything, as we have, to the test of actual value; it will perhaps be inferred that we are inclined to slight these less essential things. No greater mistake could be made, however. We yield to none in the value we attach to aesthetic culture and its pleasures. Without painting, sculpture, music, poetry, and the emotions produced by natural beauty of every kind, life would lose half its charm. So far from thinking that the train-ing and gratification of the tastes are unimportant, we believe the time will come when they will occupy a much larger share of human life than now. When the forces of Nature have been fully conquered to man's use—when the means of production have been brought to per-fection—when labour has been economized to the highest degree—when education has been so systematized that a preparation for the more essential activities may be made with comparative rapidity—and when, consequently, there is a great increase of spare time; then will the poetry, both of Art and Nature, rightly fill a large space in the minds of all.

But it is one thing to admit that aesthetic culture is in a high degree conducive to human happiness; and another thing to admit that it is a fundamental requisite to human happiness. However important it may be, it must yield precedence to those kinds of culture which bear more directly upon the duties of life. As before hinted, literature and the fine arts are made possible by those activities which make individ-ual and social life possible; and manifestly, that which is made pos-sible, must be postponed to that which makes it possible. A florist cul-tivates a plant for the sake of its flower; and regards the roots and leaves as of value, chiefly because they are instrumental in producing the flower. But while, as an ultimate product, the flower is the thing to which everything else is subordinate, the florist very well knows that the root and leaves are intrinsically of greater importance; because on them the evolution of the flower depends. He bestows every care in rearing a healthy plant; and knows it would be folly if, in his anxiety to obtain the flower, he were to neglect the plant. Similarly in the case before us. Architecture, sculpture, painting, music, poetry, &c., may be truly called the efflorescence of civilized life. But even supposing them to be of such transcendent worth as to subordinate the civilized life out of which they grow (which can hardly be asserted), it will still be admitted that the production of a healthy civilized life must be the first consideration; and that the knowledge conducing to this must occupy the highest place. . . .

Unexpected as the assertion may be, it is nevertheless true, that the highest Art of every kind is based upon Science—that without Science there can be neither perfect production nor full appreciation. Science, in that limited technical acceptation current in society, may not have been possessed by many artists of high repute; but acute observers as they have been, they have always possessed a stock of those empirical generalizations which constitute science in its lowest phase; and they have habitually fallen far below perfection, partly because their generalizations were comparatively few and inaccurate. That science necessarily underlies the fine arts, becomes manifest à priori, when we remember that art-products are all more or less representative of objective or subjective phenomena; that they can be true only in proportion as they conform to the laws of these phenomena; and that before they can thus conform the artist must know what these laws are. . . .

Youths preparing for the practice of sculpture, have to acquaint themselves with the bones and muscles of the human frame in their distribution, attachments, and movements. This is a portion of science; and it has been found needful to impart it for the prevention of those many errors which sculptors who do not possess it commit. For the prevention of other mistakes, a knowledge of mechanical principles is requisite. . . .

In painting, the necessity for scientific knowledge, empirical if not rational, is still more conspicuous. In what consists the grotesqueness of Chinese pictures, unless in their utter disregard of the laws of appearances—in their absurd linear perspective, and their want of aerial perspective? In what are the drawings of a child so faulty, if not in a similar absence of truth—an absence arising, in great part, from ignorance of the way in which the aspects of things vary with the conditions? . . .

To say that music, too, has need of scientific aid will seem still more surprising. Yet it is demonstrable that music is but an idealization of the natural language of emotion; and that consequently, music must be good or bad according as it conforms to the laws of this natural language. The various inflections of voice which accompany feelings of different kinds and intensities, have been shown to be the germs out of which music is developed. It has been further shown, that these inflections and cadences are not accidental or arbitrary; but that they are determined by certain general principles of vital action; and that their expressiveness depends on this. Whence it follows that musical phrases and the melodies built of them, can be effective only when they are in harmony with these general principles. . . .

Even in poetry the same thing holds. Like music, poetry has its root in those natural modes of expression which accompany deep feeling. Its rhythm, its strong and numerous metaphors, its hyperboles, its violent inversions, are simply exaggerations of the traits of excited speech. To be good, therefore, poetry must pay respect to those laws of nervous action which excited speech obeys. . . .

Not only is it that the artist, of whatever kind, cannot produce a truthful work without he understands the laws of the phenomena he represents; but it is that he must also understand how the minds of spectators or listeners will be affected by the several peculiarities of his work—a question in psychology. What impression any given art-product generates, manifestly depends upon the mental natures of those to whom it is presented; and as all mental natures have certain general principles in common, there must result certain corresponding general principles on which alone art-products can be successfully framed. These general principles cannot be fully understood and applied, unless the artist sees how they follow from the laws of mind. To ask whether the composition of a picture is good, is really to ask how the perceptions and feelings of observers will be affected by it. To ask whether a drama is well constructed, is to ask whether its situations are so arranged as duly to consult the power of attention of an audience, and duly to avoid overtaxing any one class of feelings. Equally in arranging the leading divisions of a poem or fictions, and in combining the words of a single sentence, the goodness of the effect depends upon the skill with which the mental energies and susceptibilities of the reader are economized. Every artist, in the course of his education and after-life, accumulates a stock of maxims by which his practice is regulated. Trace such maxims to their roots, and you find they inevitably lead you down to psychological principles. And only when the artist rationally understands these psychological principles and their various corollaries, can he work in harmony with them. . . .

And now let us not overlook the further great fact, that not only does science underlie sculpture, painting, music, poetry, but that science is itself poetic. The current opinion that science and poetry are opposed is a delusion. It is doubtless true that as states of consciousness, cognition and emotion tend to exclude each other. And it is doubtless also true that an extreme activity of the reflective powers tends to deaden the feelings; while an extreme activity of the feelings tends to deaden the reflective powers: in which sense, indeed, all orders of activity are antagonistic to each other. But it is not true that the facts of science are unpoetical; or that the cultivation of science is necessarily unfriendly to the exercise of imagination or the love of the beautiful. On the contrary science opens up realms of poetry where to the unscientific all is a blank. Those engaged in scientific researches constantly show us that they realize not less vividly, but more vividly, than others, the poetry of their subjects. . . . Think you that what is carelessly looked upon by the uninitiated as a mere snow-flake, does not suggest higher associations to one who has seen through a microscope the wondrously varied and elegant forms of snow-crystals? Think you that the rounded rock marked with parallel scratches calls up as much poetry in an ignorant mind as in the mind of a geologist, who knows that over this rock a glacier slid a million years ago? The truth is, that those who have never entered upon scientific pursuits know not a tithe of the poetry by which they are surrounded. . . .

Lastly we have to assert—and the assertion will, we doubt not, cause extreme surprise—that the discipline of science is superior to that of our ordinary education, because of the *religious* culture that it gives. Of course we do not here use the words scientific and religious in their ordinary limited acceptations; but in their widest and highest acceptations. Doubtless, to the superstitions that pass under the name of religion, science is antagonistic; but not to the essential religion which these superstitions merely hide. Doubtless, too, in much of the science that is current, there is a pervading spirit of irreligion; but not in that true science which has passed beyond the superficial into the profound. . . .

So far from science being irreligious, as many think, it is the neglect of science that is irreligious—it is the refusal to study the surrounding creation that is irreligious. . . . Devotion to science, is a tacit worship—a tacit recognition of worth in the things studied; and by implication in their Cause. It is not a mere lip-homage, but a homage expressed in actions—not a mere professed respect, but a respect proved by the sacrifice of time, thought, and labor.

Nor is it thus only that true science is essentially religious. It is religious, too, inasmuch as it generates a profound respect for, and an implicit faith in, those uniform laws which underlie all things. By accumulated experiences the man of science acquires a thorough belief in the unchanging relations of phenomena—in the invariable connexion of cause and consequence—in the necessity of good or evil results. Instead of the rewards and punishments of traditional belief, which men vaguely hope they may gain, or escape, spite of their disobedience; he finds that there are rewards and punishments in the ordained constitution of things, and that the evil results of disobedience are inevitable. He sees that the laws to which we must submit are not only inexorable but beneficent. . . .

Thus to the question with which we set out—What knowledge is of most worth?—the uniform reply is—Science. This is the verdict on all the counts. For direct self-preservation, or the maintenance of life and health, the all-important knowledge is—Science. For that indirect self-preservation which we call gaining a livelihood, the knowledge of greatest value is—Science. For the due discharge of parental functions, the proper guidance is to be found only in—Science. For that interpretation of national life, past and present, without which the citizen cannot rightly regulate his conduct, the indispensable key is—Science. Alike for the most perfect production and highest enjoyment of art in all its forms, the needful preparation is still—Science. And for purposes of discipline—intellectual, moral, religious—the most efficient study is, once more—Science. The question which at first seemed so perplexed, has become, in the course of our inquiry, comparatively simple. We have not to estimate the degrees of importance of different orders of human activity, and different studies as severally fitting us for them; since we find that the study of Science, in its most comprehensive meaning, is the best preparation for all these orders of activity. We have not to decide between the claims of knowledge of great though conventional value, and knowledge of less though intrinsic value; seeing that the knowledge which we find to be of most value in all other respects, is intrinsically most valuable: its worth is not dependent upon opinion, but is as fixed as is the relation of man to the surrounding world. Necessary and eternal as are its truths, all Science concerns all mankind for all time. Equally at present, and in the remotest future, must it be of incalculable importance for the regulation of their conduct, that men should understand the science of life, physical, mental, and social; and that they should understand all other science as a key to the science of life.

And yet the knowledge which is of such transcendent value is that which, in our age of boasted education, receives the least attention. While this which we call civilization could never have arisen had it not been for science; science forms scarcely an appreciable element in what men consider civilized training. Though to the progress of science we owe it, that millions find support where once there was food only for thousands; yet of these millions but a few thousands pay any respect to that which has made their existence possible. Though this increasing knowledge of the properties and relations of things has not only enabled wandering tribes to grow into populous nations, but has given to the countless members of those populous nations comforts and pleasures which their few naked ancestors never even conceived, or could have believed, yet is this kind of knowledge only now receiving a grudging recognition in our highest educational institutions. To the slowly growing acquaintance with the uniform co-existences and sequences of phenomena—to the establishment of invariable laws, we owe our emancipation from the grossest superstitions. But for science we should be still worshipping fetishes; or, with hecatombs of victims, propitiating diabolical deities. And yet this science, which, in place of the most degrading conceptions of things, has given us some insight into the grandeurs of creation, is written against in our theologies and frowned upon from our pulpits.

Paraphrasing an Eastern fable, we may say that in the family of knowledges, Science is the household drudge, who, in obscurity, hides unrecognised perfections. To her has been committed all the work; by her skill, intelligence, and devotion, have all the conveniences and gratifications been obtained; and while ceaselessly occupied ministering to the rest, she has been kept in the background, that her haughty sisters might flaunt their fripperies in the eyes of the world. The parallel holds yet further. For we are fast coming to the dénouement, when the positions will be changed; and while these haughty sisters sink into merited neglect, Science, proclaimed as highest alike in worth and beauty, will reign supreme.

C. S. PEIRCE

Never Block the Way
of Inquiry

If we endeavour to form our conceptions upon history and life, we
remark three classes of men. The first consists of those for whom the
chief thing is the qualities of feelings. These men create art. The second consists of the practical men, who carry on the business of the
world. They respect nothing but power, and respect power only so far
as it [is] exercised. The third class consists of men to whom nothing
seems great but reason. If force interests them, it is not in its exertion,
but in that it has a reason and a law. For men of the first class, nature
is a picture; for men of the second class, it is an opportunity; for men
of the third class, it is a cosmos, so admirable, that to penetrate to its
ways seems to them the only thing that makes life worth living. These
are the men whom we see possessed by a passion to learn, just as
other men have a passion to teach and to disseminate their influence.
If they do not give themselves over completely to their passion to
learn, it is because they exercise self-control. Those are natural scientific men; and they are the only men that have any real success in scientific research.

If we are to define science, not in the sense of stuffing it into an artificial pigeon-hole where it may be found again by some insignificant
mark, but in the sense of characterizing it as a living historic entity,
we must conceive it as that about which such men as I have described
busy themselves. As such, it does not consist so much in *knowing*, nor
even in "organized knowledge," as it does in diligent inquiry into

truth for truth's sake, without any sort of axe to grind, nor for the sake of the delight of contemplating it, but from an impulse to penetrate into the reason of things. This is the sense in which this book is entitled a History of *Science*. Science and philosophy seem to have been changed in their cradles. For it is not knowing, but the love of learning, that characterizes the scientific man; while the "philosopher" is a man with a system which he thinks embodies all that is best worth knowing. If a man burns to learn and sets himself to comparing his ideas with experimental results in order that he may correct those ideas, every scientific man will recognize him as a brother, no matter how small his knowledge may be.

But if a man occupies himself with investigating the truth of some question for some ulterior purpose, such as to make money, or to amend his life, or to benefit his fellows, he may be ever so much better than a scientific man, if you will—to discuss that would be aside from the question—but he is not a scientific man. For example, there are numbers of chemists who occupy themselves exclusively with the study of dyestuffs. They discover facts that are useful to scientific chemistry; but they do not rank as genuine scientific men. The genuine scientific chemist cares just as much to learn about erbium—the extreme rarity of which renders it commercially unimportant—as he does about iron. He is more eager to learn about erbium if the knowledge of it would do more to complete his conception of the Periodic Law, which expresses the mutual relations of the elements.

When a man desires ardently to know the truth, his first effort will be to imagine what that truth can be. He cannot prosecute his pursuit long without finding that imagination unbridled is sure to carry him off the track. Yet nevertheless, it remains true that there is, after all, nothing but imagination that can ever supply him an inkling of the truth. He can stare stupidly at phenomena; but in the absence of imagination they will not connect themselves together in any rational way. Just as for Peter Bell a cowslip was nothing but a cowslip, so for thousands of men a falling apple was nothing but a falling apple; and to compare it to the moon would by them be deemed "fanciful."

It is not too much to say that next after the passion to learn there is no quality so indispensable to the successful prosecution of science as imagination. Find me a people whose early medicine is not mixed up with magic and incantations, and I will find you a people devoid of all scientific ability. There is no magic in the medical Papyrus Ebers. The stolid Egyptian saw nothing in disease but derangement of the affected organ. There never was any true Egyptian science.

There are, no doubt, kinds of imagination of no value in science, mere artistic imagination, mere dreaming of opportunities for gain. The scientific imagination dreams of explanations and laws.

A scientific man must be single-minded and sincere with himself. Otherwise, his love of truth will melt away, at once. He can, therefore, hardly be otherwise than an honest, fair-minded man. True, a few naturalists have been accused of purloining specimens; and some men have been far from judicial in advocating their theories. Both of these faults must be exceedingly deleterious to their scientific ability. But on the whole, scientific men have been the best of men. It is quite natural, therefore, that a young man who might develop into a scientific man should be a well-conducted person.

Yet in more ways than one an exaggerated regard for morality is unfavorable to scientific progress. I shall present only one of those ways. It will no doubt shock some persons that I should speak of morality as involving an element which can become bad. To them good conduct and moral conduct are one and the same—and they will accuse me of hostility to morality. I regard morality as highly necessary; but it is a means to good life, not necessarily coextensive with good conduct. Morality consists in the folklore of right conduct. A man is brought up to think he ought to behave in certain ways. If he behaves otherwise, he is uncomfortable. His conscience pricks him. That system of morals is the traditional wisdom of ages of experience. If a man cuts loose from it, he will become the victim of his passions. It is not safe for him even to reason about it, except in a purely speculative way. Hence, morality is essentially conservative. Good morals and good manners are identical except that tradition attaches less importance to the latter. The gentleman is imbued with conservatism. This conservatism is a habit, and it is the law of habit that it tends to spread and extend itself over more and more of the life. In this way, conservatism about morals leads to conservatism about manners and finally conservatism about opinions of a speculative kind. Besides, to distinguish between speculative and practical opinions is the mark of the most cultivated intellects. Go down below this level and you come across reformers and rationalists at every turn—people who propose to remodel the ten commandments on modern science. Hence it is that morality leads to a conservatism which any new view, or even any free inquiry, no matter how purely speculative, shocks. The whole moral weight of such a community will be cast against science. To inquire into nature is for a Turk very unbecoming to a good Moslem; just as the family of Tycho Brahe regarded his pursuit of astronomy as unbecoming to a nobleman. (See Thomas Nash in *Pierce Pennilesse* for the character of a Danish nobleman.)

This tendency is necessarily greatly exaggerated in a country when the "gentleman," or recognized exponent of good manners, is appointed to that place as the most learned man. For them the inquiring spirit cannot say the gentlemen are a lot of ignorant fools. To the moral weight cast against progress in science is added the weight of superior learning. Wherever there is a large class of academic professors who are provided with good incomes and looked up to as gentlemen, scientific inquiry must languish. Wherever the bureaucrats are the more learned class, the case will be still worse. . . .

Upon this first, and in one sense this sole, rule of reason, that in order to learn you must desire to learn, and in so desiring not be satisfied with what you already incline to think, there follows one corollary which itself deserves to be inscribed upon every wall of the city of philosophy:

Do not block the way of inquiry.

Although it is better to be methodical in our investigations, and to consider the economics of research, yet there is no positive sin against logic in *trying* any theory which may come into our heads, so long as it is adopted in such a sense as to permit the investigation to go on unimpeded and undiscouraged. On the other hand, to set up a philosophy which barricades the road of further advance toward the truth is the one unpardonable offence in reasoning, as it is also the one to which metaphysicians have in all ages shown themselves the most addicted.

Let me call your attention to four familiar shapes in which this venomous error assails our knowledge.

The first is the shape of absolute assertion. That we can be sure of nothing in science is an ancient truth. The Academy taught it. Yet science has been infested with overconfident assertion, especially on the part of the third-rate and fourth-rate men, who had been more concerned with teaching than with learning, at all times. No doubt some of the geometries still teach as a self-evident truth the proposition that if two straight lines in one plane meet a third straight line so as to make the sum of the internal angles on one side less than two right angles those two lines will meet on that side if sufficiently prolonged. Euclid, whose logic was more careful, only reckoned this proposition as a *Postulate*, or arbitrary Hypothesis. Yet even he places among his axioms the proposition that a part is less than its whole, and falls into several conflicts with our most modern geometry in consequence. But why need we stop to consider cases where some subtilty of thought is required to see that the assertion is not warranted when every book which applies philosophy to the conduct of life lays down as positive certainty propositions which it is quite as easy to doubt as to believe?

The second bar which philosophers often set up across the roadway of inquiry lies in maintaining that this, that, and the other never can be known. When Auguste Comte was pressed to specify any matter of positive fact to the knowledge of which no man could by any possibility attain, he instanced the knowledge of the chemical composition of the fixed stars; and you may see his answer set down in the *Philosophie positive.* But the ink was scarcely dry upon the printed page before the spectroscope was discovered and that which he had deemed absolutely unknowable was well on the way of getting ascertained. It is easy enough to mention a question the answer to which is not known to me today. But to aver that that answer will not be known tomorrow is somewhat risky; for oftentimes it is precisely the least expected truth which is turned up under the ploughshare of research. And when it comes to positive assertion that the truth never will be found out, that, in the light of the history of our time, seems to me more hazardous than the venture of Andrée.

The third philosophical stratagem for cutting off inquiry consists in maintaining that this, that, or the other element of science is basic, ultimate, independent of aught else, and utterly inexplicable—not so much from any defect in our knowing as because there is nothing beneath it to know. The only type of reasoning by which such a conclusion could possibly be reached is *retroduction*. Now nothing justifies a retroductive inference except its affording an explanation of the facts.

It is, however, no explanation at all of a fact to pronounce it *inexplicable*. That, therefore, is a conclusion which no reasoning can ever justify or excuse.

The last philosophical obstacle to the advance of knowledge which I intend to mention is the holding that this or that law or truth has found its last and perfect formulation—and especially that the ordinary and usual course of nature never can be broken through. "Stones do not fall from heaven," said Laplace, although they had been falling upon inhabited ground every day from the earliest times. But there is no kind of inference which can lend the slightest probability to any such absolute denial of an unusual phenomenon.

All positive reasoning is of the nature of judging the proportion of something in a whole collection by the proportion found in a sample. Accordingly, there are three things to which we can never hope to attain by reasoning, namely, absolute certainty, absolute exactitude, absolute universality. We cannot be absolutely certain that our conclusions are even approximately true; for the sample may be utterly unlike the unsampled part of the collection. We cannot pretend to be even probably exact; because the sample consists of but a finite number of instances and only admits special values of the proportion sought. Finally, even if we could ascertain with absolute certainty and exactness that the ratio of sinful men to all men was as 1 to 1; still among the *infinite* generations of men there would be room for any finite number of sinless men without violating the proportion. The case is the same with a seven-legged calf.

Now if exactitude, certitude, and universality are not to be attained by reasoning, there is certainly no other means by which they can be reached.

Somebody will suggest *revelation*. There are scientists and people influenced by science who laugh at revelation; and certainly science has taught us to look at testimony in such a light that the whole theological doctrine of the "Evidences" seems pretty weak. However, I do not think it is philosophical to reject the possibility of a revelation. Still, granting that, I declare as a logician that revealed truths—that is, truths which have nothing in their favour but revelations made to a few individuals—constitute by far the most uncertain class of truths there are. There is here no question of universality; for revelation is itself sporadic and miraculous. There is no question of mathematical exactitude; for no revelation makes any pretension to that character. But it does pretend to be *certain;* and against that there are three conclusive objections. First, we never can be absolutely certain that any given deliverance really is inspired; for that can only be established by reasoning. We cannot even prove it with any very high degree of probability. Second, even if it is inspired, we cannot be sure, or nearly sure, that the statement is true. We know that one of the commandments was in one of the Bibles printed with[out] a *not* in it. All inspired matter has been subject to human distortion or coloring. Besides we cannot penetrate the counsels of the most High, or lay down anything as a principle that would govern his conduct. We do not know his inscrutable purposes, nor can we comprehend his plans. We cannot tell but he might see fit to inspire his servants with errors. In the third place, a truth which rests on the authority of inspiration only is of a somewhat incomprehensible nature; and we never can be sure that we rightly comprehend it. As there is no way of evading these difficulties, I say that revelation, far from affording us any certainty, gives results less certain than other sources of information. This would be so even if revelation were much plainer than it is.

But, it will be said, you forget the laws which are known to us a priori, the axioms of geometry, the principles of logic, the maxims of *causality,* and the like. Those are absolutely certain, without exception and exact. To this I reply that it seems to me there is the most positive historic proof that innate truths are particularly uncertain and mixed up with error, and therefore a fortiori not without exception. This historical proof is, of course, not infallible; but it is very strong. Therefore, I ask *how do you know* that a priori truth is certain, exceptionless, and exact? You cannot know it by *reasoning.* For that would be subject to uncertainty and inexactitude. Then, it must amount to this that you know it a priori; that is, you take a priori judgments at their own valuation, without criticism or credentials. That is barring the gate of inquiry.

Ah! but it will be said, you forget direct experience. Direct experience is neither certain nor uncertain, because it affirms nothing—it just *is.* There are delusions, hallucinations, dreams. But there is no mistake that such things really do appear, and direct experience means simply the appearance. It involves no error, because it testifies to nothing but its own appearance. For the same reason, it affords no certainty. It is not *exact*, because it leaves much vague; though it is not *inexact* either; that is, it has no false exactitude.

All this is true of direct experience at its first presentation. But when it comes up to be criticized it is past, itself, and is represented by *memory*. Now the deceptions and inexactitude of memory are proverbial.

. . . On the whole, then, we cannot in any way reach perfect certitude nor exactitude. We never can be absolutely sure of anything, nor can we with any probability ascertain the exact value of any measure or general ratio.

This is my conclusion, after many years study of the logic of science; and it is the conclusion which others, of very different cast of mind, have come to, likewise. I believe I may say there is no tenable opinion regarding human knowledge which does not legitimately lead to this corollary. Certainly there is nothing new in it; and many of the greatest minds of all time have held it for true.

Indeed, most everybody will admit it until he begins to see what is involved in the admission—and then most people will draw back. It will not be admitted by persons utterly incapable of philosophical reflection. It will not be fully admitted by masterful minds developed exclusively in the direction of action and accustomed to claim practical infallibility in matters of business. These men will admit the incurable fallibility of all opinions readily enough; only, they will always make exception of their own. The doctrine of fallibilism will also be denied by those who fear its consequences for science, for religion, and for morality. But I will take leave to say to these highly conservative gentlemen that however competent they may be to direct the affairs of a church or other corporation, they had better not try to manage science in that way. Conservatism—in the sense of a dread of consequences—is altogether out of place in science—which has on the contrary always been forwarded by radicals and radicalism, in the sense of the eagerness to carry consequences to their extremes. Not the radicalism that is cocksure, however, but the *radicalism that tries experiments*. Indeed, it is precisely among men animated by the spirit of science that the doctrine of fallibilism will find supporters.

Still, even such a man as that may well ask whether I propose to say that it is not quite certain that twice two are four—and that it is even not probably quite exact! But it would be quite misunderstanding the doctrine of fallibilism to suppose that it means that twice two is probably not exactly four. As I have already remarked, it is not my purpose to doubt that people can usually *count* with accuracy. Nor does fallibilism say that men cannot attain a sure knowledge of the creations of their own minds. It neither affirms nor denies that. It only says that people cannot attain absolute certainty concerning questions of fact. Numbers are merely a system of names devised by men for the purpose of counting. It is a matter of real fact to say that in a certain room there are two persons. It is a matter of fact to say that each person has two eyes. It is a matter of fact to say that there are four eyes in the room. But to say that *if* there are two persons and each person has two eyes there *will be* four eyes is not a statement of fact, but a statement about the system of numbers which is our own creation.

GEORGE SANTAYANA
Loving Truth

The love of truth is often mentioned, the hatred of truth hardly ever, yet the latter is the commoner. People say they love the truth when they pursue it, and they pursue it when unknown: not therefore because of any felt affinity to it in their souls, but probably because they need information for practical purposes, or to solve some conventional riddle. Where known, on the contrary, truth is almost always dismissed or disguised, because the aspect of it is hateful. And this apart from any devilish perversity in the natural man, or accidental vices that may fear the light. On the contrary, the cause is rather the natural man's innocence and courage in thinking himself the measure of all things. Life imposes selfish interests and subjective views on every inhabitant of earth: and in hugging these interests and these views the man hugs what he initially assumes to be the truth and the right. So that aversion from the real truth, a sort of antecedent hatred of it as contrary to presumption, is interwoven into the very fabric of thought.

Images and feelings do not arise without a certain vital enthusiasm in forming or affirming them. To enjoy them is in some sense to hypostatize them and set them up as models to which other images and feelings should conform. A child will protest and be inwardly wounded if a story once told him is told differently the second time. His little soul has accepted that world, and needs to build upon it undisturbed. Sensation, which makes the foreground of what is called experience, is thus raised by innocent faith to the level of truth. And

false these images and feelings would not be, if they provoked no assertions about further objects. They would compose the ingredients of
a true biography, although perhaps, when the circumstances are considered, the biography of a dupe.

Now love is a passion, and we might expect it not to be aroused at
all by intellectual objects, such as truth, or theory purporting to be
true: and yet the bitterest feuds, in families and nations, often turn on
the love or hatred of particular beliefs, attacked or defended for the
most fantastic reasons. Both sides may perhaps say that they are fighting for the truth; but evidently it is not any circumstantial evidence
that supports the claims of the opposed ideas to be veridical; nor is
there often much intrinsic beauty in those ideas. The theological notion of the Trinity was little affected by that iota for which nevertheless blood flowed in the streets of Byzantium; yet the metaphysical
dignity of the Virgin Mary was involved, and nobody should be suffered to question the truth of a devout image so fondly lodged in the
mind.

In such a case the passion concerned is not the love of truth, but a
natural joy in thinking freely, and the self-assertion of each mind
against all others. If meantime any attention is paid to the truth at all,
it is only indirectly, in that the ideal authority of truth is recognized,
whilst, by an absurd contradiction, its verdict is dictated to it by violence. The truth is needed, but not respected, not loved but raped; and
that barbarous outrage to the truth in the concrete is still a sort of
homage to truth as the coveted sanction of fancy. . . .

There is no *reason* why we should love the truth. There is no *reason*
why we should love anything. There are only causes that, according to
the routine of nature, bring about the love of various things on
various occasions. As a matter of fact, nature breeds life, and life is everywhere aflame with love, and with its opposite; and there is also no
reason why this spiritual passion—spiritual because it engages and
colours the spirit—should stop short at bodily concerns or social affairs, and should not extend to all the relations radiating from bodily
life into the realms of truth and of essence. This radiation, as I call it,
is in itself passive and merely formal, yet physical organization must
take account of it if life is to prosper; and this tension of life towards
the eventual, the distant, the past and the future is what becomes conscious and bursts into actuality in spirit. Spirit is a child of truth. Matter in any one of its moments and in any one of its atoms offers no

foothold for consciousness: but let certain tropes and cycles be established in the movement of matter, let certain kinds of matter cohere and pulse together in an organism, and behold, consciousness has arisen. Now tropes, cycles, organisms, and pulsations, with all the laws of nature, are units proper to the realm of truth; units that bridge the flux of existence and are suspended over it, as truth and spirit also are suspended. So that in conceiving and loving the truth spirit is not indulging in any caprice; it is surveying with pleasure the soil and the broad reaches of its native country.

Nor is love too warm a term for the sense of this radical affinity. There is cosmic justification for such a passion. Love is, biologically, an emotion proper to generation: and generation, in the cosmos at large, is the same thing as genesis or flux. Love, ever since Hesiod and Empedocles, has therefore been the poetic name for the instability and fecundity of transitive existence everywhere; life passing, and passing joyfully, from each phase to the next, and from one individual to another. Yet this joyful procreation of things is also tragic, because as Lucretius says, nothing is born save by the death of something else. In loving, in breeding, and in bringing up the young we make an unconscious sacrifice of ourselves to posterity. Such is the dominance of love in the realm of matter, where progression is, as it were, horizontal, and the thing generated continues and repeats the nature of its parents. But where the transmitted form is organic, and spirit inhabits it, life and love have also a vertical direction and a synthetic power, such that in precipitating the future, the present evokes some image of the past, and some notion of the outlying realities by which the present and the future are being controlled. In other words, life, in propagating itself, has also generated knowledge, and has become aware of the truth.

This by-product or hypostasis of organic life is also tragic, like physical reproduction, and accepts death; but instead of surrendering one life for another of the same kind and on the same level, we now surmount or disregard physical life altogether, in order to define its form and consider its achievements. This consideration or definition of nature is itself a work of nature, occurring in time and requiring material organs. It therefore partakes of the joy proper to all vital functions in their perfection. The beauty of truth is loved as naturally as the beauty of women, and our ideas are cherished like our children. Enthusiasm and inspiration (which are other names of love addressed to the truth) have no less warmth and breed no less heroism than the love of home or of country.

Thus spirit is born and chooses its aims in sympathy with the movement of organic life, and is simply that movement become emotion and idea. For this radical reason spirit cannot be an independent power coming from nowhere to direct or accelerate animal action. We do not look about us because we love the truth, but we love the truth because we look about us. Were it merely a question of keeping alive or of controlling matter, business would actually be expedited if besides Occam's razor we used, so to speak, Occam's glasses, and reduced our visions of things to pointer-readings, releasing appropriate reactions on our part without further rhetoric. Ignorance, when not materially dangerous, simplifies the fighting mind and is an economic advantage. It renders courage absolute and disturbs no comfortable or harmless illusions. Nature, however, being spontaneous and free, with no end of time before her, despises such thrift and is initially lavish and all-consenting. Her indefinite passive fertility is committed to no antecedent prejudices or desires. She adopts her laws and types unwittingly, as they avail to establish themselves; and they leave untouched her original potentialities. They may become, indeed, positive occasions for playful complications far outrunning those special terms and eluding their measure. Such a complication life seems to us to be in respect to mechanism, and consciousness in respect to life. In these cases the new fruit, while having an underivable character proper to itself, will draw all its existential sap from the tree on which it is grafted. Life requires food, warmth and air, yet is none of those things but an organization accruing to them; and spirit feeds on the life of the psyche, while establishing tangential and transcendent interests of its own. When feeling (a form of spirit evoked by organic processes in the body) becomes perception and begins to describe the objects that arouse feeling, spirit is already launched upon the pursuit of truth, an ideal reality altogether transcending the level of the psyche and of her world. When, moreover, the eye and the intellect have adequately surveyed the scene, or gathered the event observed into a dramatic unity, the organ of spirit is satisfied. It is satisfied in the very act by which a truth is discerned; so that by nature this discernment is a joy to the spirit, and the truth automatically conceived becomes an object of love for its own sake.

The vital and fundamentally physical quality of this love of truth appears clearly when it is thwarted. We see daily in young children and in impatient reformers how nothing is more hateful to a passionate being than obstruction, nothing more precious than liberty. The psyche will have her way in the first place, let the result be what it will. Indeed, the primitive horror of being stifled, of being held down and prevented from moving, is doubtless what lends its magic to the word liberty: any idea of what we might do with our liberty when we got it would have no such power. To be checked in our natural actions before we initiate them produces melancholy: to be checked in the middle of them produces rage. This intolerableness of suppression extends to the movement of our thoughts. It was in the act of spinning fine long threads of relationship that nature first evoked spirit: that web must not be torn, and nature demands that spirit should think the truth. We cannot endure to be cheated, to be deluded, even to suspect that we are deceiving ourselves. We may be incurious about remote truths, if our intellect is lazy; but at least we would not stultify what intellect we have by believing things positively false. Therefore when authority or public opinion would hold us down to some manifest error, however harmless and metaphysical, our impetuous souls resent the outrage. It is not the calm truth that calls for witnesses: martyrs usually die for some new error. It is the martyrs that cannot endure in themselves the arrest of the heart upon thoughts that the heart despises. No matter how tragic or arid the truth may be, the spirit follows and loves it, as the eye follows the light.

Automatic as the love of truth is, and internal as is the joy of discovering and holding the truth, this love has nothing narcissistic about it. It is as far as possible from being joy in the luster or harmony of one's ideas. It is a clean, healthy, sacrificial love. In the form of childish curiosity it is turned from the beginning towards alien things, engaging the impulse to explore, to dissect, and to dare. The element of courage, united with submission and humility, belongs to the love of truth even in its ultimate reaches. Truth, in spite of what Platonists and poets may say, is not at all the same as beauty. Truth does not arrange or idealize its subject-facts. It can eliminate nothing. It can transfigure nothing, except by merely lifting it bodily from the plane of existence and exhibiting it, not as a present lure or as a disaster for some native ambition, but as a comedy or tragedy seen as a whole and liberating the spirit that understands it. In other words, truth is a moral, not an aesthetic good. The possession of it is not free intuition, but knowledge necessary to a man's moral integrity and intellectual peace.

That conventional truths, as exhibited to the senses, or in historical narrative or scientific exposition, may often be impressive aesthetically goes without saying: but it is not this aesthetic quality that makes their truth or satisfies the intellect. If truth at first entertains, as falsehood does also, it very soon sobers and rebukes. It is tragic even in comedy, since it looks to the end of every career and every achievement. The very movement of instinctive exploration that discloses truth, thereby discloses also the relativity, limits, and fugitiveness of this exploration. It shows life under the form of eternity, which is the form of death. Life thereby becomes an offering, a prayer, a sacrifice offered up to the eternal; and though there may be incense in that sacrifice, there is also blood.

ERICH FROMM

Is Truth Founded in Loving?

To respect a person is not possible without *knowing* him; care and responsibility would be blind if they were not guided by knowledge. Knowledge would be empty if it were not motivated by concern. There are many layers of knowledge; the knowledge which is an aspect of love is one which does not stay at the periphery, but penetrates to the core. It is possible only when I can transcend the concern for myself and see the other person in his own terms. I may know, for instance, that a person is angry, even if he does not show it overtly; but I may know him more deeply than that; then I know that he is anxious, and worried; that he feels lonely, that he feels guilty. Then I know that his anger is only the manifestation of something deeper, and I see him as anxious and embarrassed, that is, as the suffering person, rather than as the angry one.

Knowledge has one more, and a more fundamental, relation to the problem of love. The basic need to fuse with another person so as to transcend the prison of one's separateness is closely related to another specifically human desire, that to know the "secret of man." While life in its merely biological aspects is a miracle and a secret, man in his human aspects is an unfathomable secret to himself—and to his fellow man. We know ourselves, and yet even with all the efforts we may make, we do not know ourselves. We know our fellow man, and yet we do not know him, because we are not a thing, and our fellow man is not a thing. The further we reach into the depth of our being, or someone else's being, the more the goal of knowledge eludes us. Yet we cannot help desiring to penetrate into the secret of man's soul, into the innermost nucleus which is "he."

There is one way, a desperate one, to know the secret: it is that of complete power over another person; the power which makes him do what we want, feel what we want, think what we want; which transforms him into a thing, our thing, our possession. The ultimate degree of this attempt to know lies in the extremes of sadism, the desire and ability to make a human being suffer; to torture him, to force him to betray his secret in his suffering. In this craving for penetrating man's secret, his and hence our own, lies an essential motivation for the depth and intensity of cruelty and destructiveness. In a very succinct way this idea has been expressed by Isaac Babel. He quotes a fellow officer in the Russian civil war, who has just stamped his former master to death, as saying: "With shooting—I'll put it this way—with shooting you only get rid of a chap. . . . With shooting you'll never get at the soul, to where it is in a fellow and how it shows itself. But I don't spare myself, and I've more than once trampled an enemy for over an hour. You see, I want to get to know what life really is, what life's like down our way."

In children we often see this path to knowledge quite overtly. The child takes something apart, breaks it up in order to know it; or it takes an animal apart; cruelly tears off the wings of a butterfly in order to know it, to force its secret. The cruelty itself is motivated by something deeper: the wish to know the secret of things and of life.

The other path to knowing "the secret" is love. Love is active penetration of the other person, in which my desire to know is stilled by union. In the act of fusion I know you, I know myself, I know everybody—and I "know" nothing. I know in the only way knowledge of that which is alive is possible for man—by experience of union—not by any knowledge our thought can give. Sadism is motivated by the wish to know the secret, yet I remain as ignorant as I was before. I have torn the other being apart limb from limb, yet all I have done is to destroy him. Love is the only way of knowledge, which in the act of union answers my quest. In the act of loving, of giving myself, in the act of penetrating the other person, I find myself, I discover myself, I discover us both, I discover man.

The longing to know ourselves and to know our fellow man has been expressed in the Delphic motto "Know thyself." It is the mainspring of all psychology. But inasmuch as the desire is to know all of man, his innermost secret, the desire can never be fulfilled in knowledge of the ordinary kind, in knowledge only by thought. Even if we knew a thousand times more of ourselves, we would never reach bottom. We would still remain an enigma to ourselves, as our fellow man would remain an enigma to us. The only way of full knowledge lies in the *act* of love: this act transcends thought, it transcends words. It is the daring plunge into the experience of union. However, knowledge in thought, that is psychological knowledge, is a necessary condition for full knowledge in the act of love. I have to know the other person and myself objectively, in order to be able to see his reality, or rather, to overcome the illusions, the irrationally distorted picture I have of him. Only if I know a human being objectively, can I know him in his ultimate essence, in the act of love.

The problem of knowing man is parallel to the religious problem of knowing God. In conventional Western theology the attempt is made to know God by thought, to make statements *about* God. It is assumed that I can know God in my thought. In mysticism, which is the consequent outcome of monotheism (as I shall try to show later on), the attempt is given up to know God by thought, and it is replaced by the experience of union with God in which there is no more room—and no need—for knowledge *about* God.

The experience of union, with man, or religiously speaking, with God, is by no means irrational. On the contrary, it is as Albert Schweitzer has pointed out, the consequence of rationalism, its most daring and radical consequence. It is based on our knowledge of the fundamental, and not accidental, limitations of our knowledge. It is the knowledge that we shall never "grasp" the secret of man and of the universe, but that we can know, nevertheless, in the act of love. Psychology as a science has its limitations, and, as the logical consequence of theology is mysticism, so the ultimate consequence of psychology is love.

Care, responsibility, respect and knowledge are mutually interdependent. They are a syndrome of attitudes which are to be found in the mature person; that is, in the person who develops his own powers productively, who only wants to have that which he has worked for, who has given up narcissistic dreams of omniscience and omnipotence, who has acquired humility based on the inner strength which only genuine productive activity can give.

FRIEDRICH NIETZSCHE

Is Truth Strength of Will?
Is Falseness Founded in Weakness?

The will to truth which will still tempt us to many a venture, that famous truthfulness of which all philosophers so far have spoken with respect—what questions has this will to truth not laid before us! What strange, wicked, questionable questions! That is a long story even now—and yet it seems as if it had scarcely begun. Is it any wonder that we should finally become suspicious, lose patience, and turn away impatiently? that we should finally learn from this Sphinx to ask questions, too? *Who* is it really that puts questions to us here? *What* in us really wants "truth"?

Indeed we came to a long halt at the question about the cause of this will—until we finally came to a complete stop before a still more basic question. We asked about the *value* of this will. Suppose we want truth: *why not rather* untruth? and uncertainty? even ignorance?

The problem of the value of truth came before us—or was it we who came before the problem? Who of us is Oedipus here? Who the Sphinx? It is a rendezvous, it seems, of questions and question marks.

And though it scarcely seems credible, it finally almost seems to us as if the problem had never even been put so far—as if we were the first to see it, fix it with our eyes, and *risk* it. For it does involve a risk, and perhaps there is none that is greater.

"How *could* anything originate out of its opposite? for example, truth out of error? or the will to truth out of the will to deception? or selfless deeds out of selfishness? or the pure and sunlike gaze of the sage out of lust? Such origins are impossible; whoever dreams of them is a fool, indeed worse; the things of the highest value must have another *peculiar* origin—they cannot be derived from this transitory, seductive, deceptive, paltry world, from this turmoil of delusion and lust. Rather from the lap of Being, the intransitory, the hidden god, the 'thing-in-itself'—there must be their basis, and nowhere else."

This way of judging constitutes the typical prejudgment and prejudice which give away the metaphysicians of all ages; this kind of valuation looms in the background of all their logical procedures; it is on account of this "faith" that they trouble themselves about "knowledge," about something that is finally baptized solemnly as "the truth." The fundamental faith of the metaphysicians is *the faith in opposite values.* It has not even occurred to the most cautious among them that one might have a doubt right here at the threshold where it was surely most necessary—even if they vowed to themselves, *"de omnibus dubitandum."* [1]

For one may doubt, first, whether there are any opposites at all, and secondly whether these popular valuations and opposite values on which the metaphysicians put their seal, are not perhaps merely foreground estimates, only provisional perspectives, perhaps even from some nook, perhaps from below, frog perspectives, as it were, to borrow an expression painters use. For all the value that the true, the truthful, the selfless may deserve, it would still be possible that a higher and more fundamental value for life might have to be ascribed to deception, selfishness, and lust. It might even be possible that what constitutes the value of these good and revered things is precisely that they are insidiously related, tied to, and involved with these wicked, seemingly opposite things—maybe even one with them in essence. Maybe!

But who has the will to concern himself with such dangerous maybes? For that, one really has to wait for the advent of a new species of philosophers, such as have somehow another and converse taste and propensity from those we have known so far—philosophers of the dangerous "maybe" in every sense.

And in all seriousness: I see such new philosophers coming up.

1. "All is to be doubted." Descartes.

After having looked long enough between the philosopher's lines and fingers, I say to myself: by far the greater part of conscious thinking must still be included among instinctive activities, and that goes even for philosophical thinking. We have to relearn here, as one has had to relearn about heredity and what is "innate." As the act of birth deserves no consideration in the whole process and procedure of heredity, so "being conscious" is not in any decisive sense the *opposite* of what is instinctive: most of the conscious thinking of a philosopher is secretly guided and forced into certain channels by his instincts.

Behind all logic and its seeming sovereignty of movement, too, there stand valuations or, more clearly, physiological demands for the preservation of a certain type of life. For example, that the definite should be worth more than the indefinite, and mere appearance worth less than "truth"—such estimates might be, in spite of their regulative importance for *us,* nevertheless mere foreground estimates, a certain kind of *niaiserie*[2] which may be necessary for the preservation of just such beings as we are. Supposing, that is, that not just man is the "measure of things"—

The falseness of a judgment is for us not necessarily an objection to a judgment; in this respect our new language may sound strangest. The question is to what extent it is life-promoting, life-preserving, species-preserving, perhaps even species-cultivating. And we are fundamentally inclined to claim that the falsest judgments (which include the synthetic judgments *a priori*) are the most indispensable for us; that without accepting the fictions of logic, without measuring reality against the purely invented world of the unconditional and self-identical, without a constant falsification of the world by means of numbers, man could not live—that renouncing false judgments would mean renouncing life and a denial of life. To recognize untruth as a condition of life—that certainly means resisting accustomed value feelings in a dangerous way; and a philosophy that risks this would by that token alone place itself beyond good and evil.

What provokes one to look at all philosophers half suspiciously, half mockingly, is not that one discovers again and again how innocent

---

2. Folly, stupidity, silliness: one of Nietzsche's favorite French words.

they are—how often and how easily they make mistakes and go astray; in short, their childishness and childlikeness—but they are not honest enough in their work, although they all make a lot of virtuous noise when the problem of truthfulness is touched even remotely. They all pose as if they had discovered and reached their real opinions through the self-development of a cold, pure, divinely unconcerned dialectic (as opposed to the mystics of every rank, who are more honest and doltish—and talk of "inspiration"); while at bottom it is an assumption, a hunch, indeed a kind of "inspiration"—most often a desire of the heart that has been filtered and made abstract—that they defend with reasons they have sought after the fact. They are all advocates who resent that name, and for the most part even wily spokesmen for their prejudices which they baptize "truths"—and *very* far from having the courage of the conscience that admits this, precisely this, to itself; very far from having the good taste of the courage which also lets this be known, whether to warn an enemy or friend, or, from exuberance, to mock itself.

The equally stiff and decorous Tartuffery of the old Kant as he lures us on the dialectical bypaths that lead to his "categorical imperative"—really lead astray and seduce—this spectacle makes us smile, as we are fastidious and find it quite amusing to watch closely the subtle tricks of old moralists and preachers of morals. Or consider the hocus-pocus of mathematical form with which Spinoza clad his philosophy—really "the love of *his* wisdom," to render that word fairly and squarely—in mail and mask, to strike terror at the very outset into the heart of any assailant who should dare to glance at that invincible maiden and Pallas Athena: how much personal timidity and vulnerability this masquerade of a sick hermit betrays!

Gradually it has become clear to me what every great philosophy so far has been: namely, the personal confession of its author and a kind of involuntary and unconscious memoir; also that the moral (or immoral) intentions in every philosophy constituted the real germ of life from which the whole plant had grown.

Indeed, if one would explain how the abstrusest metaphysical claims of a philosopher really came about, it is always well (and wise) to ask first: at what morality does all this (does *he*) aim? Accordingly, I do not believe that a "drive to knowledge" is the father of philosophy; but rather that another drive has, here as elsewhere, employed understanding (and misunderstanding) as a mere instrument. But anyone who considers the basic drives of man to see to what extent they may have been at play just here as *inspiring* spirits (or demons and kobolds) will find that all of them have done philosophy at some time—and that every single one of them would like only too well to represent just *itself* as the ultimate purpose of existence and the legitimate *master* of all the other drives. For every drive wants to be master—and it attempts to philosophize in *that spirit.*

To be sure: among scholars who are really scientific men, things may be different—"better," if you like—there you may really find something like a drive for knowledge, some small, independent clockwork that, once well wound, works on vigorously *without* any essential participation from all the other drives of the scholar. The real "interests" of the scholar therefore lie usually somewhere else—say, in his family, or in making money, or in politics. Indeed, it is almost a matter of total indifference whether his little machine is placed at this or that spot in science, and whether the "promising" young worker turns himself into a good philologist or an expert on fungi or a chemist: it does not *characterize* him that he becomes this or that. In the philosopher, conversely, there is nothing whatever that is impersonal, and above all, his morality bears decided and decisive witness to *who he is*—that is, in what order of rank the innermost drives of his nature stand in relation to each other. . . .

The eagerness and subtlety—I might even say, shrewdness—with which the problem of "the real and the apparent world" is today attacked all over Europe makes one think and wonder; and anyone who hears nothing in the background except a "will to truth," certainly does not have the best of ears. In rare and isolated instances it may really be the case that such a will to truth, some extravagant and adventurous courage, a metaphysician's ambition to hold a hopeless position, may participate and ultimately prefer even a handful of "certainty" to a whole carload of beautiful possibilities; there may actually be puritanical fanatics of conscience who prefer even a certain nothing to an uncertain something to lie down on—and die. But this is nihilism and the sign of a despairing, mortally weary soul—however courageous the gestures of such a virtue may look.

It seems, however, to be otherwise with stronger and livelier thinkers who are still eager for life. When they side *against* appearance, and speak of "perspective," with a new arrogance; when they rank the credibility of their own bodies about as low as the credibility of the visual evidence that "the earth stands still," and thus, apparently in good humor, let their securest possession go (for in what does one at present believe more firmly than in one's body?)—who knows if they are not trying at bottom to win back something that was formerly an even *securer* possession, something of the ancient domain of the faith of former times, perhaps the "immortal soul," perhaps "the old God," in short, ideas by which one could live better, that is to say, more vigorously and cheerfully, than by "modern ideas"? There is *mistrust* of these modern ideas in this attitude, a disbelief in all that has been constructed yesterday and today; there is perhaps some slight admixture of satiety and scorn, unable to endure any longer the *bric-a-brac* of concepts of the most diverse origin, which is the form in which so-called positivism offers itself on the market today; a disgust of the more fastidious taste at the village-fair motleyness and patchiness of all these reality-philosophasters in whom there is nothing new or genuine, except this motleyness. In this, it seems to me, we should agree with these skeptical anti-realists and knowledge-microscopists of today: their instinct, which repels them from *modern* reality, is unrefuted—what do their retrograde bypaths concern us! The main thing about them is *not* that they wish to go "back," but that they wish to get—*away*. A little *more* strength, flight, courage, and artistic power, and they would want to *rise*—not return! . . .

It is perhaps just dawning on five or six minds that physics, too, is only an interpretation and exegesis of the world (to suit us, if I may say so!) and *not* a world-explanation; but insofar as it is based on belief in the senses, it is regarded as more, and for a long time to come must be regarded as more—namely, as an explanation. Eyes and fingers speak in its favor, visual evidence and palpableness do, too: this strikes an age with fundamentally plebeian tastes as fascinating, persuasive, and *convincing*—after all, it follows instinctively the canon of truth of eternally popular sensualism. What is clear, what is "explained"? Only what can be seen and felt—every problem has to be pursued to that point. Conversely, the charm of the Platonic way of thinking, which was a *noble* way of thinking, consisted precisely in *resistance* to obvious sense-evidence—perhaps among men who en-

joyed even stronger and more demanding senses than our contemporaries, but who knew how to find a higher triumph in remaining masters of their senses—and this by means of pale, cold, gray concept nets
which they threw over the motley whirl of the senses—the mob of the
senses, as Plato said. In this overcoming of the world, and interpreting
of the world in the manner of Plato, there was an *enjoyment* different
from that which the physicists of today offer us—and also the Darwinists and anti-teleologists among the workers in physiology, with their
principle of the "smallest possible force" and the greatest possible stupidity. "Where man cannot find anything to see or to grasp, he has no
further business"—that is certainly an imperative different from the
Platonic one, but it may be the right imperative for a tough, industri-
ous race of machinists and bridge-builders of the future, who have
nothing but *rough* work to do. . . .

There are still harmless self-observers who believe that there are "immediate certainties"; for example, "I think," or as the superstition of
Schopenhauer put it, "I will"; as though knowledge here got hold of
its object purely and nakedly as "the thing in itself," without any falsification on the part of either the subject or the object. But that "immediate certainty," as well as "absolute knowledge" and the "thing in
itself," involve a *contradictio in adjecto,*[3] I shall repeat a hundred times;
we really ought to free ourselves from the seduction of words!

Let the people suppose that knowledge means knowing things entirely; the philosopher must say to himself: When I analyze the process that is expressed in the sentence, "I think," I find a whole series
of daring assertions that would be difficult, perhaps impossible, to
prove; for example, that it is *I* who think, that there must necessarily
be something that thinks, that thinking is an activity and operation on
the part of a being who is thought of as a cause, that there is an "ego,"
and, finally, that it is already determined what is to be designated by
thinking—that I *know* what thinking is. For if I had not already decided within myself what it is, by what standard could I determine
whether that which is just happening is not perhaps "willing" or
"feeling"? In short, the assertion "I think" assumes that I *compare* my
state at the present moment with other states of myself which I know,
in order to determine what it is; on account of this retrospective con-

3. Contradiction between the noun and the adjective.

nection with further "knowledge," it has, at any rate, no immediate certainty for me.

In place of the "immediate certainty" in which the people may believe in the case at hand, the philosopher thus finds a series of metaphysical questions presented to him, truly searching questions of the intellect; to wit: "From where do I get the concept of thinking? Why do I believe in cause and effect? What gives me the right to speak of an ego, and even of an ego as cause, and finally of an ego as the cause of thought?" Whoever ventures to answer these metaphysical questions at once by an appeal to a sort of *intuitive* perception, like the person who says, "I think, and know that this, at least, is true, actual, and certain"—will encounter a smile and two question marks from a philosopher nowadays. "Sir," the philosopher will perhaps give him to understand, "it is improbable that you are not mistaken; but why insist on the truth?"— . . .

O sancta simplicitas![4] In what strange simplification and falsification man lives! One can never cease wondering once one has acquired eyes for this marvel! How we have made everything around us clear and free and easy and simple! how we have been able to give our senses a passport to everything superficial, our thoughts a divine desire for wanton leaps and wrong inferences! how from the beginning we have contrived to retain our ignorance in order to enjoy an almost inconceivable freedom, lack of scruple and caution, heartiness, and gaiety of life—in order to enjoy life! And only on this now solid, granite foundation of ignorance could knowledge rise so far—the will to knowledge on the foundation of a far more powerful will: the will to ignorance, to the uncertain, to the untrue! Not as its opposite, but—as its refinement!

Even if *language,* here as elsewhere, will not get over its awkwardness, and will continue to talk of opposites where there are only degrees and many subtleties of gradation; even if the inveterate Tartuffery of morals, which now belongs to our unconquerable "flesh and blood," infects the words even of those of us who know better—here and there we understand it and laugh at the way in which precisely science at its best seeks most to keep us in this *simplified,* thoroughly artificial, suitably constructed and suitably falsified world—at the way

4. Holy simplicity!

in which, willy-nilly, it loves error, because, being alive, it loves life. . . .

Every choice human being strives instinctively for a citadel and a secrecy where he is saved from the crowd, the many, the great majority—where he may forget "men who are the rule," being their exception—excepting only the one case in which he is pushed straight to such men by a still stronger instinct, as a seeker after knowledge in the great and exceptional sense. Anyone who, in intercourse with men, does not occasionally glisten in all the colors of distress, green and gray with disgust, satiety, sympathy, gloominess, and loneliness, is certainly not a man of elevated tastes; supposing, however, that he does not take all this burden and disgust upon himself voluntarily, that he persistently avoids it, and remains, as I said, quietly and proudly hidden in his citadel, one thing is certain: he was not made, he was not predestined, for knowledge. If he were, he would one day have to say to himself: "The devil take my good taste! but the rule is more interesting than the exception—than myself, the exception!" And he would go *down,* and above all, he would go "inside."

The long and serious study of the *average* man, and consequently much disguise, self-overcoming, familiarity, and bad contact (all contact is bad contact except with one's equals)—this constitutes a necessary part of the life-history of every philosopher, perhaps the most disagreeable, odious, and disappointing part. If he is fortunate, however, as a favorite child of knowledge should be, he will encounter suitable shortcuts and helps for his task; I mean so-called cynics, those who simply recognize the animal, the commonplace, and "the rule" in themselves, and at the same time still have that degree of spirituality and that itch which makes them talk of themselves and their likes *before witnesses*—sometimes they even wallow in books, as on their own dung.

Cynicism is the only form in which base souls approach honesty; and the higher man must listen closely to every coarse or subtle cynicism, and congratulate himself when a clown without shame or a scientific satyr speaks out precisely in front of him.

There are even cases where enchantment mixes with the disgust— namely, where by a freak of nature genius is tied to some such indiscreet billygoat and ape, as in the case of the Abbé Galiani, the profoundest, most clear-sighted, and perhaps also filthiest man of his century—he was far profounder than Voltaire and consequently also a good deal more taciturn. It happens more frequently, as has been hinted, that a scientific head is placed on an ape's body, a subtle exceptional understanding in a base soul, an occurrence by no means rare, especially among doctors and physiologists of morality. And whenever anyone speaks without bitterness, quite innocently, of man as a belly with two requirements, and a head with one; whenever anyone sees, seeks, and *wants* to see only hunger, sexual lust, and vanity as the real and only motives of human actions; in short, when anyone speaks "badly"—and not even *"wickedly"*—of man, the lover of knowledge should listen subtly and diligently; he should altogether have an open ear wherever people talk without indignation. For the indignant and whoever perpetually tears and lacerates with his own teeth himself (or as a substitute, the world, or God, or society) may indeed, morally speaking, stand higher than the laughing and self-satisfied satyr, but in every other sense they are a more ordinary, more indifferent, and less instructive case. And no one *lies* as much as the indignant do. . . .

Anyone who has looked deeply into the world may guess how much wisdom lies in the superficiality of men. The instinct that preserves them teaches them to be flighty, light, and false. Here and there one encounters an impassioned and exaggerated worship of "pure forms," among both philosophers and artists: let nobody doubt that whoever stands that much in *need* of the cult of surfaces must at some time have reached *beneath* them with disastrous results.

Perhaps there even exists an order of rank among these burnt children, these born artists who can find the enjoyment of life only in the intention of *falsifying* its image (as it were, in a longwinded revenge on life): the degree to which life has been spoiled for them might be inferred from the degree to which they wish to see its image falsified, thinned down, transcendentalized, deified—the *homines religiosi* might be included among artists, as their highest rank.

It is the profound, suspicious fear of an incurable pessimism that forces whole millennia to bury their teeth in and cling to a religious interpretation of existence: the fear of that instinct which senses that one might get a hold of the truth *too soon,* before man has become strong enough, hard enough, artist enough.

Piety, the "life in God," seen in this way, would appear as the subtlest and final offspring of the *fear* of truth, as an artist's worship and intoxication before the most consistent of all falsifications, as the will to the inversion of truth, to untruth at any price. It may be that until now there has been no more potent means for beautifying man himself than piety: it can turn man into so much art, surface, play of colors, graciousness that his sight no longer makes one suffer.— . . .

Every morality is, as opposed to *laisser aller*,[5] a bit of tyranny against "nature"; also against "reason"; but this in itself is no objection, as long as we do not have some other morality which permits us to decree that every kind of tyranny and unreason is impermissible. What is essential and inestimable in every morality is that it constitutes a long compulsion: to understand Stoicism or Port-Royal or Puritanism, one should recall the compulsion under which every language so far has achieved strength and freedom—the metrical compulsion of rhyme and rhythm.

How much trouble the poets and orators of all peoples have taken—not excepting a few prose writers today in whose ear there dwells an inexorable conscience—"for the sake of some foolishness," as utilitarian dolts say, feeling smart—"submitting abjectly to capricious laws," as anarchists say, feeling "free," even "free-spirited." But the curious fact is that all there is or has been on earth of freedom, subtlety, boldness, dance, and masterly sureness, whether in thought itself or in government, or in rhetoric and persuasion, in the arts just as in ethics, has developed only owing to the "tyranny of such capricious laws"; and in all seriousness, the probability is by no means small that precisely this is "nature" and "natural"—and *not* that *laisser aller.*

Every artist knows how far from any feeling of letting himself go his "most natural" state is—the free ordering, placing, disposing, giving form in the moment of "inspiration"—and how strictly and subtly he obeys thousandfold laws precisely then, laws that precisely on account of their hardness and determination defy all formulation through concepts (even the firmest concept is, compared with them, not free of fluctuation, multiplicity, and ambiguity).

What is essential "in heaven and on earth" seems to be, to say it once more, that there should be *obedience* over a long period of time and in a *single* direction: given that, something always develops, and

5. Letting go.

has developed, for whose sake it is worth while to live on earth; for example, virtue, art, music, dance, reason, spirituality—something transfiguring, subtle, mad, and divine. The long unfreedom of the spirit, the mistrustful constraint in the communicability of thoughts, the discipline thinkers imposed on themselves to think within the directions laid down by a church or court, or under Aristotelian presuppositions, the long spiritual will to interpret all events under a Christian schema and to rediscover and justify the Christian god in every accident—all this, however forced, capricious, hard, gruesome, and anti-rational, has shown itself to be the means through which the European spirit has been trained to strength, ruthless curiosity, and subtle mobility, though admittedly in the process an irreplaceable amount of strength and spirit had to be crushed, stifled, and ruined (for here, as everywhere, "nature" manifests herself as she is, in all her prodigal and indifferent magnificence which is outrageous but noble).

That for thousands of years European thinkers thought merely in order to prove something—today, conversely, we suspect every thinker who "wants to prove something"—that the conclusions that *ought* to be the result of their most rigorous reflection were always settled from the start, just as it used to be with Asiatic astrology, and still is today with the innocuous Christian-moral interpretation of our most intimate personal experiences "for the glory of God" and "for the salvation of the soul"—this tyranny, this caprice, this rigorous and grandiose stupidity has *educated* the spirit. Slavery is, as it seems, both in the cruder and in the more subtle sense, the indispensable means of spiritual discipline and cultivation, too. Consider any morality with this in mind: what there is in it of "nature" teaches hatred of the *laisser aller,* of any all-too-great freedom, and implants the need for limited horizons and the nearest tasks—teaching the *narrowing of our perspective,* and thus in a certain sense stupidity, as a condition of life and growth.

"You shall obey—someone and for a long time: *else* you will perish and lose the last respect for yourself"—this appears to me to be the moral imperative of nature which, to be sure, is neither "categorical" as the old Kant would have it (hence the "else") nor addressed to the individual (what do individuals matter to her?), but to peoples, races, ages, classes—but above all to the whole human animal, to *man.*

SØREN KIERKEGAARD

Truth Is Subjectivity

Whether truth is defined more empirically, as the conformity of thought and being, or more idealistically, as the conformity of being with thought, it is, in either case, important carefully to note what is meant by being. And in formulating the answer to this question it is likewise important to take heed lest the knowing spirit be tricked into losing itself in the indeterminate, so that it fantastically becomes a something that no existing human being ever was or can be, a sort of phantom with which the individual occupies himself upon occasion, but without making it clear to himself in terms of dialectical intermediaries how he happens to get into this fantastic realm, what significance being there has for him, and whether the entire activity that goes on out there does not resolve itself into a tautology within a recklessly fantastic venture of thought.

If being, in the two indicated definitions, is understood as empirical being, truth is at once transformed into a *desideratum*, and everything must be understood in terms of becoming; for the empirical object is unfinished and the existing cognitive spirit is itself in process of becoming. Thus the truth becomes an approximation whose beginning cannot be posited absolutely, precisely because the conclusion is lacking, the effect of which is retroactive. Whenever a beginning is *made*, on the other hand, unless through being unaware of this, the procedure stamps itself as arbitrary, such a beginning is not the consequence of an immanent movement of thought, but is effected through

a resolution of the will, essentially in the strength of faith. That the
knowing spirit is an existing individual spirit, and that every human
being is such an entity existing for himself, is a truth I cannot too
often repeat; for the fantastic neglect of this is responsible for much
confusion. . . .

The term "being," as used in the above definitions, must therefore
be understood (from the systematic standpoint) much more abstractly,
presumably as the abstract reflection of, or the abstract prototype for,
what being is as concrete empirical being. When so understood there
is nothing to prevent us from abstractly determining the truth as abstractly finished and complete; for the correspondence between
thought and being is, from the abstract point of view, always finished.
Only with the concrete does becoming enter in, and it is from the
concrete that abstract thought abstracts.

But if being is understood in this manner, the formula becomes a
tautology. Thought and being mean one and the same thing, and the
correspondence spoken of is merely an abstract self-identity. Neither
formula says anything more than that the truth is, so understood as to
accentuate the copula: the truth *is,* i.e. the truth is a reduplication.
Truth is the subject of the assertion, but the assertion that it is, is the
same as the subject; for this being that the truth is said to have is
never its own abstract form. In this manner we give expression to the
fact that truth is not something simple, but is in a wholly abstract
sense a reduplication, a reduplication which is nevertheless instantly
revoked.

Abstract thought may continue as long as it likes to rewrite this
thought in varying phraseology, it will never get any farther. As soon
as the being which corresponds to the truth comes to be empirically
concrete, the truth is put in process of becoming, and is again by way
of anticipation the conformity of thought with being. This conformity
is actually realized for God, but it is not realized for any existing
spirit, who is himself existentially in process of becoming. . . .

In that the question of truth is thus raised by an existing spirit *qua*
existing, the above abstract reduplication that is involved in it again
confronts him. But existence itself, namely, existence as it is in the individual who raises the question and himself exists, keeps the two
moments of thought and being apart, so that reflection presents him
with two alternatives. For an objective reflection the truth becomes an
object, something objective, and thought must be pointed away from

the subject. For a subjective reflection the truth becomes a matter of appropriation, of inwardness, of subjectivity, and thought must probe more and more deeply into the subject and his subjectivity. . . .

The way of objective reflection makes the subject accidental, and thereby transforms existence into something indifferent, something vanishing. Away from the subject the objective way of reflection leads to the objective truth, and while the subject and his subjectivity become indifferent, the truth also becomes indifferent, and this indifference is precisely its objective validity; for all interest, like all decisiveness, is rooted in subjectivity. The way of objective reflection leads to abstract thought, to mathematics, to historical knowledge of different kinds; and always it leads away from the subject, whose existence or non-existence, and from the objective point of view quite rightly, becomes infinitely indifferent. Quite rightly, since as Hamlet says, existence and non-existence have only subjective significance. At its maximum this way will arrive at a contradiction, and in so far as the subject does not become wholly indifferent to himself, this merely constitutes a sign that his objective striving is not objective enough. At its maximum this way will lead to the contradiction that only the objective has come into being, while the subjective has gone out; that is to say, the existing subjectivity has vanished, in that it has made an attempt to become what in the abstract sense is called subjectivity, the mere abstract form of an abstract objectivity. And yet, the objectivity which has thus come into being is, from the subjective point of view at the most, either an hypothesis or an approximation, because all eternal decisiveness is rooted in subjectivity. . . .

The subjective reflection turns its attention inwardly to the subject, and desires in this intensification of inwardness to realize the truth. And it proceeds in such fashion that, just as in the preceding objective reflection, when the objectivity had come into being, the subjectivity had vanished, so here the subjectivity of the subject becomes the final stage, and objectivity a vanishing factor. Not for a single moment is it forgotten that the subject is an existing individual, and that existence is a process of becoming, and that therefore the notion of the truth as identity of thought and being is a chimera of abstraction, in its truth only an expectation of the creature; not because the truth is not such an identity, but because the knower is an existing individual for whom the truth cannot be such an identity as long as he lives in time.

Unless we hold fast to this, speculative philosophy will immediately transport us into the fantastic realism of the I-am-I, which modern speculative thought has not hesitated to use without explaining how a particular individual is related to it; and God knows, no human being is more than such a particular individual. . . .

All essential knowledge relates to existence, or only such knowledge as has an essential relationship to existence is essential knowledge. All knowledge which does not inwardly relate itself to existence, in the reflection of inwardness, is, essentially viewed, accidental knowledge; its degree and scope is essentially indifferent. That essential knowledge is essentially related to existence does not mean the above-mentioned identity which abstract thought postulates between thought and being; nor does it signify, objectively, that knowledge corresponds to something existent as its object. But it means that knowledge has a relationship to the knower, who is essentially an existing individual, and that for this reason all essential knowledge is essentially related to existence. Only ethical and ethico-religious knowledge has an essential relationship to the existence of the knower. . . .

In an attempt to make clear the difference of way that exists between an objective and a subjective reflection, I shall now proceed to show how a subjective reflection makes its way inwardly in inwardness. Inwardness in an existing subject culminates in passion; corresponding to passion in the subject the truth becomes a paradox; and the fact that the truth becomes a pardox is rooted precisely in its having a relationship to an existing subject. Thus the one corresponds to the other. By forgetting that one is an existing subject, passion goes by the board and the truth is no longer a paradox; the knowing subject becomes a fantastic entity rather than a human being, and the truth becomes a fantastic object for the knowledge of this fantastic entity.

When the question of truth is raised in an objective manner, reflection is directed objectively to the truth, as an object to which the knower is related. Reflection is not focussed upon the relationship, however, but upon the question of whether it is the truth to which the knower is related. If only the object to which he is related is the truth, the subject is accounted to be in the truth. When the question of the truth is raised subjectively, reflection is directed subjectively to the nature of the individual's relationship; if only the mode of this relationship is in the truth, the individual is in the truth even if he should happen to be thus related to what is not true. . . .

The objective accent falls on WHAT is said, the subjective accent on HOW it is said. This distinction holds even in the aesthetic realm, and receives definite expression in the principle that what is in itself true may in the mouth of such and such a person become untrue. In these times this distinction is particularly worthy of notice, for if we wish to express in a single sentence the difference between ancient times and our own, we should doubtless have to say: "In ancient times only an individual here and there knew the truth; now all know it, except that the inwardness of its appropriation stands in an inverse relationship to the extent of its dissemination. Aesthetically the contradiction that truth becomes untruth in this or that person's mouth, is best construed comically: In the ethico-religious sphere, accent is again on the "how." But this is not to be understood as referring to demeanor, expression, or the like; rather it refers to the relationship sustained by the existing individual, in his own existence, to the content of his utterance. Objectively the interest is focussed merely on the thought-content, subjectively on the inwardness. At its maximum this inward "how" is the passion of the infinite, and the passion of the infinite is the truth. But the passion of the infinite is precisely subjectivity, and thus subjectivity becomes the truth. Objectively there is no infinite decisiveness, and hence it is objectively in order to annul the difference between good and evil, together with the principle of contradiction, and therewith also the infinite difference between the true and the false. Only in subjectivity is there decisiveness, to seek objectivity is to be in error. It is the passion of the infinite that is the decisive factor and not its content, for its content is precisely itself. In this manner subjectivity and the subjective "how" constitute the truth.

But the "how" which is thus subjectively accentuated precisely because the subject is an existing individual, is also subject to a dialectic with respect to time. In the passionate moment of decision, where the road swings away from objective knowledge, it seems as if the infinite decision were thereby realized. But in the same moment the existing individual finds himself in the temporal order, and the subjective "how" is transformed into a striving, striving which receives indeed its impulse and a repeated renewal from the decisive passion of the infinite, but is nevertheless a striving.

When subjectivity is the truth, the conceptual determination of the truth must include an expression for the antithesis to objectivity, a memento of the fork in the road where the way swings off; this expression will at the same time serve as an indication of the tension of the subjective inwardness. Here is such a definition of truth: *An objective uncertainty held fast in an appropriation-process of the most passionate inwardness is the truth*, the highest truth attainable for an *existing* individual. At the point where the way swings off (and where this is cannot be specified objectively, since it is a matter of subjectivity), there objective knowledge is placed in abeyance. Thus the subject merely has, objectively, the uncertainty; but it is this which precisely increases the tension of that infinite passion which constitutes his inwardness. The truth is precisely the venture which chooses an objective uncertainty with the passion of the infinite. I contemplate the order of nature in the hope of finding God, and I see omnipotence and wisdom; but I also see much else that disturbs my mind and excites anxiety. The sum of all this is an objective uncertainty. But it is for this very reason that the inwardness becomes as intense as it is, for it embraces this objective uncertainty with the entire passion of the infinite. In the case of a mathematical proposition the objectivity is given, but for this reason the truth of such a proposition is also an indifferent truth.

But the above definition of truth is an equivalent expression for faith. Without risk there is no faith. Faith is precisely the contradiction between the infinite passion of the individual's inwardness and the objective uncertainty. If I am capable of grasping God objectively, I do not believe, but precisely because I cannot do this I must believe. If I wish to preserve myself in faith I must constantly be intent upon holding fast the objective uncertainty, so as to remain out upon the deep, over seventy thousand fathoms of water, still preserving my faith. . . .

When subjectivity, inwardness, is the truth, the truth becomes objectively a paradox; and the fact that the truth is objectively a paradox shows in its turn that subjectivity is the truth. For the objective situation is repellent; and the expression for the objective repulsion constitutes the tension and the measure of the corresponding inwardness. The paradoxical character of the truth is its objective uncertainty; this uncertainty is an expression for the passionate inwardness, and this passion is precisely the truth. So far the Socratic principle. The eternal and essential truth, the truth which has an essential relationship to an existing individual because it pertains essentially to existence (all other knowledge being from the Socratic point of view accidental, its scope and degree a matter of indifference), is a paradox. But the eternal essential truth is by no means in itself a paradox; but it becomes paradoxical by virtue of its relationship to an existing individual. The Socratic ignorance gives expression to the objective uncertainty attaching to the truth, while his inwardness in existing is the truth. To anticipate here what will be developed later, let me make the following remark. The Socratic ignorance is an analogue to the category of the absurd, only that there is still less of objective certainty in the absurd, and to the repellent effect that the absurd exercises. It is certain only that it is absurd, and precisely on that account it incites to an infinitely greater tension in the corresponding inwardness. The Socratic inwardness in existing is an analogue to faith; only that the inwardness of faith, corresponding as it does, not to the repulsion of the Socratic ignorance, but to the repulsion exerted by the absurd, is infinitely more profound. . . .

When I understood this, it also became clear to me that if I desired to communicate anything on this point, it would first of all be necessary to give my exposition an *indirect* form. For if inwardness is the truth, results are only rubbish with which we should not trouble each other. The communication of results is an unnatural form of intercourse between man and man, in so far as every man is a spiritual being, for whom the truth consists in nothing else than the self-activity of personal appropriation, which the communication of a result tends to prevent. Let a teacher in relation to the essential truth (for otherwise a direct relationship between teacher and pupil is quite in order) have, as we say, much inwardness of feeling, and be willing to publish his doctrines day in and day out; if he assumes the existence of a direct relationship between the learner and himself, his inwardness is not inwardness, but a direct outpouring of feeling; the respect for the learner which recognizes that he is in himself the inwardness of truth, is precisely the teacher's inwardness. Let a learner be enthusiastic, and publish his teacher's praises abroad in the strongest expressions, thus, as we say, giving evidence of his inwardness; this inwardness is not inwardness, but an immediate devotedness; the devout and silent accord, in which the learner by himself assimilates what he has learned, keeping the teacher at a distance because he turns his attention within himself, this is precisely inwardness. Pathos is indeed inwardness, but it is an immediate inwardness, when it is expressed; but pathos in a contrary form is an inwardness which remains with the maker of the communication in spite of being expressed, and cannot be directly appropriated by another except through that other's self-activity: the contrast of the form is the measure of the inwardness. The more complete the contrast of the form, the greater the inwardness, and the less contrast, up to the point of direct communication, the less the inwardness. It may be difficult enough for an enthusiastic genius, who would so gladly make all men happy and bring them to a knowledge of the truth, to learn in this manner to restrain himself, and to give heed to the *nota bene* of reduplication, the truth not being a circular with signatures affixed, but the *valore intrinseco* of inwardness; for an idler and frivolous person this understanding comes more easily. As soon as the truth, the essential truth, may be assumed to be known by everyone, the objective becomes appropriation and inwardness, and here only an indirect form is applicable. The position of an apostle is different, for he has to preach an unknown truth, whence a direct form of communication may in his case have provisional validity.

5
Living Always, Always Dying

That we will all die is as close to certainty as the human frame allows. We all know this, yet we rarely think it; and even when we think about it, the fact seems distant and we lack conviction. We live as though life were endless, and the mere knowledge that it is not rarely suffices to change our acts or values.

By contrast, experiences related to death and dying are vivid and immediate. Even when they involve others, they cause us anxiety, uncertainty, and grief. For when we see others dying, we come face-to-face with the reality of our own death. The fear we then experience is not only of the inescapable nothingness into which we may sink at the end of life, but also of the possibility that life itself has no meaning. Why strive when in the end all achievements follow us to the grave? Why live if everything that lives soon withers and dies?

It is tempting to seek consolation in the view that death is illusory, that through reincarnation or resurrection or in some heavenly place we shall never cease to be. But many persons cannot believe anything like this. They search for some significance *this* life might hold, irrespective of what may follow it. When some of these people, however, find themselves surrounded only by inevitable death and the pervasive presence of dying, they experience despair, see life as meaningless, and commit suicide. Still others lead lives of quiet desperation, continuing the search but finding neither meaning nor rest.

Some people, on the other hand, endow their lives with meaning in the face of imminent extinction. They accept their finitude and experience death and dying as integral parts of their lives. For such people life is, as Socrates said, a preparation for death. For this very reason, their days are filled with joy, vitality, and the special value of things sweet and passing.

What meaning can we find in fleeting life? Is the truth of life found in meaninglessness? How can we convert the prospect of death from a threat to a life-enhancing spur? Such questions become immediate and urgent on occasions of great stress. Open thinking about death and dying at times of relative calm may help us at those other times when the mind is clouded by shock, grief, or pain. It may also render us more sensitive to the variety of meanings in our lives.

JOHN J. COMPTON

Death and
the Philosophical Tradition

The recent interest in death and dying, even risking faddishness as it does, represents an important opening up of our collective consciousness to feelings about death. It is a continuing task to think *toward* those feelings, which we so typically cover up, rather than *away* from them. The great contribution of Dr. Kubler-Ross has been to initiate concrete thinking about the fears of dying persons as well as about the grieving of those who love them and the frequent sense of failure of those who work with them. As a result, it may seem almost too soon to turn attention from those experiences to ideas about death and dying. And yet, we do not have feelings, nor do we live through experiences, without their being informed in some way with meaning. We think of death in ways which inevitably shape our feelings as much as express them. We inherit some of these ways of thinking almost without awareness in our language about death. We speak of a life's being snuffed out, of dying as passing away or departing or as a form of rest, or we speak of someone's being released or taken or lost, and so on. These metaphors surely express depth experiences. But they also contain conceptualities. The ways we commonly speak of death reveal postures toward it and also ways of articulating those postures in ideas.

Conceptualities expressing diverse postures toward death are also found in philosophical attempts to think the meaning of death. I want to explore the hypothesis that the history of Western philosophy

presents us with revealing ways of speaking about death.[1] Through
the development of philosophical thought we can see, both in what is
said and in what is left unsaid, several fundamentally distinct stances
toward death and interpretations of the meaning of death. This history, I believe, forms a record in the consciousness of philosophers of
shifts in the general consciousness of death and dying. When seen in
this way, this history may illuminate our present as well, for through
it we may be able to discern where we are and where we might move
in thinking out implications of our current sense for the human reality
of death.

For philosophy, the crucial linkage is between the concept of death
and the concept of nature, particularly the status of man in nature. The
centrality of this linkage is not difficult to understand, for in a fairly
obvious way death turns us over to natural powers. As the concept of
man's place in nature has shifted in philosophic thought, so has the
concept of death. On this basis it is possible to distinguish three
"families" of concepts of death, each rooted in a distinct way of understanding man's place in nature. The first treats death as a *natural
process*. Man is viewed as an integral part of nature, and the appropriate attitude toward death is one of acceptance, perhaps tinged with
resignation, in keeping with a life which is to be lived in harmony
with nature. The second views death as a *destructive event*. Man is
thought to be over against nature, radically separated from natural
powers. He may defy these powers, struggle with them or hope to
overcome them; he may find them essentially meaningless; but he
cannot identify with them. The third understands death as a *form of
life* or as a *structure of human existence*. Here man is found to be distinctive in nature precisely in the way in which he exists toward his
death; and yet, through this existence he encounters himself as rooted
essentially in nature and as open to responsive, resolute, even affirmative possibilities within it. These three families form strands, or sub-
traditions, with some continuity throughout the history of philosophic
thought, and yet each has its primary home in a particular epoch of
Western history. In what follows I will look at each of them, meditating upon the understandings of certain philosophers within each.

1. Jacques Choron's *Death and Western Thought* (New York: Macmillan, 1963), is the
classic attempt to do this, but whereas he offers an entire history, I am seeking an interpretive analysis.

Death as Natural Process

This conception is the over-arching perspective of classical antiquity. The classical philosopher saw his task to be one of construing all the things that are, or happen, as manifestations of underlying first-principles—principles which, not needing any further explanation, would constitute the way things are "by nature" or "naturally." Death is then simply what can be expected to happen to the kind of being we are in the kind of natural order we inhabit. It is a process of change governed by intelligible laws; it is not restricted to the human sphere, but characteristic of the whole of things. It is, therefore, a process having meaning within the economy and structure of nature, not threatening it or transcending it. Schopenhauer's thesis that "all religious and philosophical systems are . . . antidotes to the certainty of death"[2] gets its measure of justification here. It is not that death is simply understood in terms of a view of nature antecedently adopted, but rather that the entire concept of "the natural" expresses a profound need to find, beyond death and other transiency, permanent elements or principles. This concept is thus a response to death itself. The concept of the natural grows out of the stories of the gods. At first with Anaximander and later with Plato, the order of nature is a kind of "just" or "moral" order. But even where this understanding is explicitly absent, as with the atomists, there is still the rule of necessity, laws which define what may or must take place. Knowledge of these laws brings satisfaction, repose and serenity even in the face of death.

Running through all the very different classical pictures of the cosmos there is, I am suggesting, a common thread. In various ways these pictures make it possible to see a unity of man and nature, a fundamental unity of elements or of structure. In terms of this unity whatever characterizes man, and particularly his dying, may be construed as "natural" for him. Thus, when I group together views which treat death as a "natural process" I want to understand "natural" as a normative term. What is natural in the world is going to fit or be somehow appropriate to what man is; and what man is, including the meaning given to death, will be somehow right or fitting or appropriate to the kind of natural world he inhabits. Different systems pick out differing aspects of nature for emphasis, and human life and death are

2. Schopenhauer, A., *The World as Will and Idea*, trans. Kemp and Haldane (London: 1883), vol. 1, p. 249.

understood quite differently in each; but in each, I think, there is, as a part of the consolation of philosophy, this sense of the fittingness and rightness of human death *sub specie naturae.*

Now for some examples:

As we remember, Socrates, or at least Plato's Socrates, viewed death as "simply the departure of soul from body,"[3] a normal process of separation of the complex into its parts. However, this separation is not just a bare fact; it conforms to the deepest aspirations of the soul—not only within men, but, as the myth of the *Timaeus* tells it, within the cosmos at large. World soul has immediate vision of the true forms of things; it is internally ordered by this vision in its providence for the world of becoming. Human souls cannot find this vision easily within the worldly admixture of bodily and sensuous distraction; but they aspire to it, and if properly prepared, should for its sake welcome dying. Philosophy, says Socrates, is a "training . . . for dying and being dead,"[4] a disciplined attempt to gather the soul together, to struggle through sensory appearances to rational insight. In this sense it separates the soul from the impediment of the body.

Shall then he who truly loves not any human object, but intelligence, and has conceived this same lively hope that in that other world, and there alone, he will attain it in full measure, shall he, I say, complain when death comes? . . . Would it not be utterly unreasonable for such a man to fear death?[5]

Of course it would. Here we have an almost perfect paradigm of the naturalness of death. Death as a separation of soul and body is fitting to the kind of aspiring being man is; and, moreover, man is a part of a fitting larger cosmic order. Therefore, consent to death . . . indeed, welcome it . . . provided you are well prepared!

Turn next to the Stoics, followers of Socrates in so many ways. With a very different concept of nature they also see human death as natural and they derive from this understanding a part of their philosophical therapy. This is the way Epictetus puts it:

Of all existing things some are in our power, and others are not in our power. In our power are thought, impulse the will to get and the will to avoid. . . . Things in our power are by nature free; things not in our power are servile, dependent on others. . . . When anything is attractive or serviceable or an object of affection, remember always to say to yourself "What is its na-

3. Plato, *Phaedo,* trans. Hackforth, S. 64.
4. *Phaedo,* S. 64.
5. *Phaedo,* S. 68.

ture?" If you are fond of a jug, say you are fond of a jug; then you will not be disturbed if it is broken. If you kiss your child or your wife, say to yourself that you are kissing a human being, for then if death strikes it you will not be disturbed. . . . Remember that you are an actor in a play, and the Playwright chooses the manner of it: if he wants it short, it is short; if long, it is long. If he wants you to act a poor man you must act the part with all your powers; and so if your part be a cripple or a magistrate or a plain man. For your business is to act the character that is given to you and act it well; the choice of the cast is Another's.[6]

Many things are going on here. But one major theme is the profound accommodation between man and nature which allows man, if he correctly understands what he is doing, to live with satisfaction and to die with acceptance. Epictetus takes the cosmos to be a material order of events, determined by providential design and lawfully governed like a great city. Human beings are firmly parts of this cosmic order, cast in roles by divine purpose, equipped with reason enabling them to sort out what is fated from what is free. They are called upon to model their free internal lives after the marvelous harmony of the heavens, to achieve self-control, to find their stations, and to perform their duties. One's role and one's mortality are given; for things like jugs and human beings are what they are "by nature." Things like desire, will, and judgment, on the other hand, are within our power "by nature." And we are to live "in accord with nature," to judge the natures of things correctly and to keep desire within the natural limits of our power to satisfy it.

Nature is performing a lot of work in this system! But this is just the point. "Nature" is a justifying word. Nature is a purposive order; what is natural is, therefore, real and right. Mortality is natural to man. Seen this way, and quite apart from any belief in personal survival or immortality, death may rightly be accepted.

As a final example, consider the Epicureans. Here too the power of a vision of man as part of nature is at work. To be sure, we are on very different ground from Plato and the Stoics: Epicurus and Lucretius were rarities in the ancient world in rejecting a purposive view of nature, in rejecting religion, and in rejecting immortality, hell, and judgment, together with the competitive political life which they saw supporting and supported by popular beliefs in these things. They

6. Epictetus, *The Manual of Epictetus*, trans. Matheson, in Whitney Oates, *The Stoic and Epicurean Philosophers* (New York: Random House, 1940), secs. 1, 3, and 17.

apparently held a view of nature which makes no concession to human aspiration or superstition, a rigorous materialism according to which all things visible are composed of combinations of invisible atoms and will, in time, return to them again. And yet it is precisely their thesis that we can with this view of nature achieve what others with alternative systems have failed to achieve, namely, removal of the fear of death. Death is simply a natural process of dispersion of atoms; it is, as Epicurus said, "nothing to us," for *we* no longer exist; sentiency no longer exists, only the atoms do.

The only point I wish to make about the Epicureans is this: the concept of nature which they employ is still, when all is said and done, a normative one. This normative quality is what gives their view of death the aura of fittingness and the power to console, which it undoubtedly possesses. Nature is not just what happens to occur; it is an immanent order, a system of chance and necessity according to law which, albeit not purposed, gives every process in nature meaning as a part of a whole. In their own way the ultimate causes of things both mirror and are mirrored by (ideal) human life and death: in nature there are no aspirations, no designs, no conflicts, and no failures, only serene, sometimes chancy, but largely lawful and necessary coming together and coming apart. Viewing nature in this way permits us to see it as congruent with the simplicity, serenity, and isolation from society which make for true happiness and which eliminate fear. Like the Stoics or Plato, the Epicureans considered nature a fitting place for man when each is properly understood; and man can at death, be seen to rejoin in a fitting way his ultimate origins in the everlasting onrush of the atoms.

Lucretius puts it this way:

What joy it is, when out at sea the stormwinds are lashing the waters, to gaze from the shore at the heavy stress some other man is enduring! Not that anyone's afflictions are in themselves a source of delight; but to realize from what troubles you yourself are free is joy indeed . . . this is the greatest joy of all: to stand aloof in a quiet citadel, stoutly fortified by the teaching of the wise, and to gaze down from that elevation on others wandering aimlessly in a vain search for the way of life, pitting their wits against one another, disputing for precedence, struggling night and day with unstinted effort to scale the pinnacles of wealth and power. O Joyless hearts of men! O minds without vision! How dark and dangerous the life in which this tiny span is lived away! Do you not see that nature is clamouring for two things only, a body free from pain, a mind released from worry and fear for the enjoyment of pleasurable sensations? . . .[7]

And, just because it is so marvelous, I want to add a defense of Lucretius by George Santayana which captures the grandeur of his vision in the face of death:

If we follow Lucretius . . . in narrowing the sum of our personal fortunes to one brief and partial glimpse of earth, we must not suppose that we need narrow at all the sphere of our moral interests. On the contrary, just in proportion as we despise superstitious terrors and sentimental hopes, and as our imagination becomes self-forgetful, we shall strengthen the direct and primitive concern which we feel in the world and in what may go on there before us, after us, or beyond our ken. . . . The soul of nature, in the elements of it, is then, according to Lucretius, actually immortal; only the human individuality, the chance composition of those elements, is transitory; so that if, a man could care for what happens to other men, for what befell him when young and what may overtake him when old, he might perfectly well care, on the same imaginative principle, for what may go on in the world for ever. The finitude and injustice of his personal life would be broken down; the illusion of selfishness would be dissipated; and he might say to himself "I have imagination and nothing that is real is alien to me."[8]

Thus endeth the readings from the sacred texts—at least in so far as my first family of concepts of death as natural process is concerned! I have been concerned only to show the meaning and power of this approach in several of its forms. One could go on to discuss Spinoza or Hegel, for example, or more recent philosophers of nature, such as Alfred North Whitehead, who continue the tradition, but I'll forbear.

Death as Destructive Event

The second family of concepts I have in mind considers death a *destructive event*. Its root experience is the "mere factuality" of death, its merely objective occurrence, its emptiness of any meaning of fittingness such as the philosophies of nature gave it. Because of the human demand for meaning, however, this emptiness appears destructive.

For a complex variety of reasons, philosophy of nature in the clas-

7. Lucretius, *The Nature of the Universe*, trans. Latham (Harmondsworth: Penguin Books, 1951), Bk. II.
8. Santayana, G., *Three Philosophical Poets* (Cambridge, Mass.: Harvard University Press, 1910) pp. 55–56.

sical sense has ceased to be practiced by most modern philosophers. Preeminent among the reasons is the rise of natural science as an analytical and technical intellectual style. As everyone so well knows, this style radically separates questions of value from questions of fact, questions having to do with human interests from questions having to do with the observable, measurable and formalizable aspects of nature—radical separations the ancients never made. What we have, in a sense, is the demise of *physis* and the appearance of *the physical* in the modern sense. Nature as *physis* might be a whole within which man finds himself as an intelligible part; but not so the physical world, to which man relates if at all only as an "object" of his "subjective" perceptions and valuations. Human life and death do not set norms for the physical as they do for the natural; the physical world suggests no model for man as does the natural order. In the new dispensation, nature is not man's home, but his object and his resource; nature has no power, but its rather "matter" for human intervention and transformation. Indeed, as time goes on nature becomes man's construct, his picture—in an intellectual sense, the product of human interpretive intelligence. Nature is then what scientific activity says it is. In such a context, the human reality of life and death is read out of nature entirely.

What I have just described is, in a very rough and overly dramatic way, the development of modern thinking about nature from Galileo to Kant. It is also, I think, a faithful record of changing human experience both of nature and of human death. I want to illustrate this development from several points of view.

First, consider *the* modern philosopher, Immanuel Kant—than whom a less likely candidate for significant remarks about death could, it seems, hardly be found. To my knowledge, Kant never discusses the subject for its own sake, but only refers to it in passing. It is just this nothingness which is fascinating. For objective thought, death is just another event in a space-time region, subject to discoverable causes, and having no particular theoretical significance. And from the moral or practical point of view, death, as a phenomenal event, is equally trivial—not, I think, because it poses no threat, but on the contrary because Kant is so clear that, for the moral man, it *ought* not to be assigned any final significance whatever. Hence, there is a kind of conspiracy of silence about it.

Let me explain this point a little further in order to show Kant's significance even more strikingly: precisely in what he does *not* say about death Kant gives, I think, the most powerful statement in modern times of an affirmative and hopeful approach *to* death! This statement appears in his defense of the belief in immortality. The way in which he argues for immortality shows incisively how vastly our world differs from that of ancient wisdom. He will have none of theoretical arguments for survival. Empirical arguments are totally inconclusive and arguments from pure reason—e.g., that the soul is simple and, thus, indestructible—are fallacious. Who says we are or have a soul in the requisite sense? Human nature is nature, or rather it is the physical, perhaps even the psycho-physical, but never the absolutely simple which is beyond space and time. On the other hand, man is not simply *in* nature *thus* understood; he stands over against it as he knows it and, more importantly, as he acts on it. And in his actions he finds himself bound, unavoidably, by an absolute moral imperative rooted in the principle of human reason itself. This imperative prescribes that he make no exceptions of persons or situations, especially none for himself, and that he choose only in such a manner as can be clearly and openly willed as a law for all human actors.

Thus, the moral man must intend to do what is morally lawful. That is what duty requires. But, as he does so, he has as his object, his end, a world in which all events are as they ought to be. He must strive to realize this world, this highest good, if he truly wills at all. From the absoluteness of the moral imperative, then, Kant proceeds to derive a warrant for the belief in immortality. His argument is this:

> The achievement of the highest good in the world is the necessary object of a will determinable by the moral law. In such a will, however, the complete fitness of intentions to the moral law is the supreme condition of the highest good. This fitness, therefore, must be just as possible as its object, because it is contained in the command that requires us to promote the latter. But complete fitness of the will to the moral law is holiness, which is a perfection of which no rational being in the world of sense is at any time capable. But since it is required as practically necessary, it can be found only in an endless progress to that complete fitness. . . . This infinite progress is possible, however, only under the supposition of the immortality of the soul, and the latter, as inseparably bound to the moral law, is a postulate of pure practical reason.[9]

Now I am certain you will think me audacious to credit *that* piece of argumentation with plausibility, much less the kind of power I earlier

9. Kant, I., *Critique of Practical Reason and Other Writings in Moral Philosophy*, trans. Beck (Chicago: University of Chicago Press, 1949), pp. 225–26.

said it had. And I fear it would take a very long time for me to make out my case. However, let me try to paraphrase:

1. The moral man aims at (strives for) the highest good.
2. This highest good is a world in which all persons, including himself, really are rational agents—they take the law as the motive of their actions, they respect one another as ends in themselves, and, incidentally, they are all happy.
3. But intending to conform to the law, while morally required of us, can only be approached: we can never simply *be* holy wills. As creatures in time, having constantly to choose, we can at best approximate ever more closely to the required state.
4. Thus, what is morally required of us as persons is that we make ever more progress morally.
5. But, here is the unstated brute, empirical fact: *death prevents this progress.* It destroys the possibility of ever more moral improvement.
6. Thus, we must, if we *will* the highest good, also *believe* that human personality continues beyond death. We cannot truly will a goal without believing that it is possible of attainment. Thus, immortality is a necessary postulate—a posit, a demand, of the moral life.

What I think is powerful about this argument is that it incisively reveals the basis for belief in immortality, or for rational hope for immortality (for Kant they come to the same thing). That basis lies in moral will itself and not in nature at all. Nor does it lie in religion. It is a *source* of religion and it is a demand we place *upon* nature in the name of morality. If human personality—human choosing and human striving—is as absolutely important as moral consciousness tells us it is, then it is irrational to suppose that the world is such as to snuff it out utterly and make impossible in principle the fulfillment of its obligations, the attainment of its striving. So we must act *as if* we were immortal. We can ascribe no content to this notion; we have no empirical basis for it; but, as rational agents, Kant argues, we are committed to believing in it.

Perhaps it is now apparent why I find Kant's argument so important and so fascinating. The reason is that, in a negative way, we find there a concept of death which is characteristic of the greater part of modern philosophy, namely, the view that it is essentially a destructive event. It is a threat to the dignity and meaning of human life. Kant himself never puts it this way; indeed, as I said, he never discusses death at all. But the unstated premise necessary for the point of his argument on behalf of the postulate of continued personality is precisely an acknowledgement of this threatening fact. And in acknowledging the threat Kant shows us how far we are from the consolations of classical thought. Human life is precisely *not* meaningful in natural terms, nor is human death. Nature has no human meaning whatsoever. If human meaning is to be given to life or to death it will be given by virtue of the will, the demand of man himself considered over against nature. This will is for Kant the source both of the belief in immortality and in the existence of God. The power not of nature but of human will leads Kant to treat the world of science as a mere phenomenon of grander things.[10]

If I spend so much time on Kant it is because I believe that Kant's predicament is our own. We have come to recognize that the ancient philosophy of nature was mythical and that nature, now scientifically purified and objectified, holds no model for man and provides no sense of fittingness for death. Death *is* brutally disruptive. Kant saw this fact and opted for hope in the face of death. Certain other philosophers have not. For example, Bertrand Russell. His is still the agony. He cannot believe what the moral will demands, but he is outraged by what science reveals. Contrast *his* materialist concept of nature with that of Lucretius and Santayana, for example:

That Man is the product of causes which had no prevision of the end they were achieving; that his origin, his growth, his hopes and fears, his loves and his beliefs, are but the outcome of accidental collocations of atoms; that no fire, no heroism, no intensity of thought and feeling, can preserve an individual life beyond the grave; that all the labors of the ages, all the devotion, all the inspiration, all the noonday brightness of human genius, are destined to extinction in the vast death of the solar system, and that the whole temple of

10. This is not to say that Kant simply rejected the classical concept of nature as an intelligible system. He constantly speaks of nature in Stoic terms, as a purposive whole in which each part or aspect, including man, has a distinctive function. But he transforms the *role* of this concept from a descriptive one to one he calls "regulative" only. The "idea" of nature does not describe the world in its intrinsic reality. On the other hand, it is theoretically useful in order to stimulate detailed scientific study of natural causes. And, above all, it is practically (i.e., morally) useful in directing human life. For if one cannot *discover* in nature an intrinsic, purposive order, one can create in human society and in human history a semblance of such an order. Thus, it is a theme of Kant's essays "Perpetual Peace" and "Idea for a Universal History" that what can only be *believed* about nature may be *achieved* in history by the cumulative efforts of the human species—namely, a significance of individual life beyond the grave.

Man's achievement must inevitably be buried beneath the debris of a universe in ruins—all these things, if not quite beyond dispute, are yet so nearly certain, that no philosophy which rejects them can hope to stand. Only within the scaffolding of these truths, only on the firm foundation of unyielding despair, can the soul's habitation henceforth be safely built. . . . Brief and powerless is Man's life; on him and all his race the slow, sure doom falls pitiless and dark . . . for him, condemned today to lose his dearest, tomorrow himself to pass through the gate of darkness, it remains only to cherish ere yet the blow falls, the lofty thoughts that ennoble his little day . . . proudly *defiant* of the irresistible forces that tolerate, for a moment, his knowledge and his condemnation, to sustain alone, a weary but unyielding Atlas, the world that his own ideals have fashioned despite the trampling march of unconscious power.[11]

A final example will have to suffice for our sample of views of this modern sort. It is the most subtle of all. It is that of Jean-Paul Sartre. I can imagine him retorting to Russell, "Mais Bertrand . . . , don't you see that, by your rage against death you have given it a meaning, and you, Immanuel, you have done the same in your hope that it is overcome? Death, in fact, has neither of these meanings; it is not an outrage unless we rage against it; it is not an obstacle to the moral will unless we will it to vanish." Rather, in the manner of a Stoic sage, Sartre will say that death has no meaning in itself; we give it meanings by our feelings and our desires; but these are within our free control and we are responsible for them. Thus he tries to define our relations to nature in the purest possible form of the modern, basically Kantian, insight that it contains *no* meanings for us, but only those we make. And yet there is a twist. Although death, like our past, our circumstances, and our fellow human beings, is an element in our situatedness—and is in this sense forced upon us to be rendered meaningful as we choose—death is different from them in having a particular power they lack and, in some sense, in having a meaning they do not have. My past, my society, my circumstances all *limit* me, Sartre says, but death *ends* me. Other elements may be transcended by me—as I give them a meaning—but death radically negates my freedom to make anything meaningful at all. So there is something dishonest—almost akin to the dishonesty of covering up one's freedom—about trying to give death a meaning; its meaning, he says, is to be "an always possible annihilation of my possibilities which is *outside* my possibili-

11. Russell, B., "A Free Man's Worship," in *Mysticism and Logic* (London: George Allen and Unwin, 1917), pp. 47–57.

ties."[12] Its meaning is to be the kind of thing to which no meaning can be given. We may take up attitudes to death in general, as Kant and Russell have done; but these leave *their own deaths* untouched; their deaths for them, our deaths for us, are simply given, absurd, externally imposed contingencies. My own death is a limit which I never encounter as a limit, because I never encounter it at all.[13]

I don't think this is gibberish. I think it is a careful, if difficult, attempt to describe the meaning of one's own death as brute fact, the hallmark of this second family of concepts of death. And with Sartre we come to the profoundest sense of the alienation between human freedom and the radically transcendent, simply given character of external nature. This alienation is exemplified in the meaninglessness which is the meaning of death. And even worse, death turns us over to the living! As Sartre says, "The dead life does not thereby cease to change and yet it is all done!"[14] For it is then up to others to determine what we were. Death is seen as *the* destructive or disruptive event par excellence, for with it we become pure objects.

Death as a Form of Life

Is it possible to go beyond this whole approach to death? Is it possible, without returning to some mythical appeal to nature, to overcome the concept of death as disruptive event? I am of deeply divided mind about this matter. My understanding stops with Kant, Russell, and Sartre; but my reason and spirit seek more coherence—just as theirs did. Is there any way of giving philosophical expression to this deeper coherence? Here I am groping. There are hints of another view, I think, of the type of view I called at the beginning *death as form of life* or as *structure of existence.* Karl Jaspers and Max Scheler made contributions to it, but Martin Heidegger is probably the only major thinker to develop it.

Let me try to explain what I understand of his ideas. It is best to begin concretely. We all know, I think, of persons who have, as it were, taken charge of their own deaths. These are persons who have

12. Sartre, J.-P., *Being and Nothingness,* trans. Barnes (New York: Philosophical Library, 1956), p. 537.
13. *Being and Nothingness,* p. 547.
14. *Being and Nothingness,* p. 543.

not avoided or covered up or defied their own death, but who have fit their dying—their entry into death—not to *nature*, nor to some general notion of man-*against*-nature, but precisely to *themselves* as human beings. Such persons, we could say, make their own deaths, or better, they *make their deaths their own*. Socrates seems to have done this; certain Stoics apparently literally made their own deaths as an expression of their freedom. The most powerful example I know, however, was that of a close friend and colleague of mine, a distinguished professor of medicine, who had been undergoing treatment for cancer for years. He was in the hospital, rapidly weakening, and was clearly within weeks or days of death. What he did was to take charge. He instructed that the life-support systems and the treatments be stopped, ordered an ambulance to take him home, and there, with his family and a few close friends, passed his last three days of life. He died, I think, as he lived, with his physician's and teacher's sense of "responsive control"—sensitive to the ultimate limits, but taking up the possibilities that were open. He was fortunate, to be sure, but he was also free and, in a very special way, courageous.

Now Sartre would have it that he was *only* fortunate—he might have died in the ambulance on the way home. For Sartre we can never make our deaths our own. Sartre ridicules Heidegger by holding up the prospect of a man condemned to death who, while waiting in prison, prepares thoughtfully and assiduously for the guillotine, only to be carried off, before the execution date, by the flu! Perhaps it is risky to prepare; but is it not possible to prepare or rather to *be*, such that the contingencies don't defeat you? Would my friend have been less courageous had he failed? I don't think so. Indeed the point of his example is not even that he accepted the fact that he would *die* in three days. I think of another friend, consigned to death by the doctors, who resolved *not* to die and, although not a physician, he used his own educated guess to order his own treatment which, in effect, brought about an (unbelievable) recovery. The point would be the same: There *is* a special sort of courage, or *resolve*, in the face of death. Sartre is simply wrong if he denies this.

The philosophical question is what to make of this phenomenon. Heidegger thinks that examples of this sort require us to understand man's relation to death in a certain way. His argument, in effect, is this:

1. Resolve in the face of death is a readiness to take up the possibilities open to me even in the presence of imminent death; it is, in this way, to make one's death one's own.
2. But of course one is not *in fact* dead (as Sartre would point out); one is alive.
3. Thus, resolve in face of death requires that while *alive*, while not even in immediate danger, I already *can* be in the *presence* of my death in some sense; we are able, while yet alive, to know—to project—with certainty that we will die. (Note: this is true even if we don't happen to die at the time and in the way projected.)
4. But how are we aware of this certainty? How do we know it? Not empirically; not from outside; we cannot know that *we* must die by induction from cases—from *what* cases? Those are the *others;* maybe they will die and we won't!
5. No, rather, we are capable of resolve and know we must die *through the very fact of our being the kind of beings we are;* through the fact that *our very way of existing is a "tending toward death,"* a "being-to-death." Death is, in short, or rather the *being towards death* is, an *essential structure of our existence* as humans.[15]

What this understanding means concretely is that, as human beings, we stand forth from nature in our awareness of mortality and, thus, in the way we live toward death. This awareness gives our entire temporality the sense that it has. At every moment we confront deathliness in the certain uncertainty of the future and the radical perishing of the past. Every transition in time is a grieving for what is lost, and certain periods, such as adolescence and late middle-age, are especially so. We experience our dying in the otherness of our children, of our bodies, and of our guilt. Anxiety in face of death gives form to our lives because it is the foundational fact of human being.

If something like this understanding is true, a number of interesting things fall into place (and Heidegger makes an entire book of them). We are, for example, able to understand the incredible persistence and ingenuity of our attempts to evade our own deaths—indeed, every aspect of our lives is, on this view tinctured with the dishonesty of death-avoidance. Not only do we hide from death in impersonal, idle

15. Heidegger, M., *Being and Time,* trans. Macquarrie and Robinson (New York: Harper and Row, 1962), sections 46–53.

talk about it and put down children and even dying persons who want seriously to talk about it; but as Heidegger sees it, we create our entire "everyday" lives of busy-ness with detailed inessentials and common beliefs and practices, in order to avoid coming to terms with it. We create science and, above all, metaphysical systems, so as systematically to change the subject. We even re-understand history, for example, as a determined sequence of events, in order to evade coming to terms with our own deaths.

On the positive side, however, if we see that resolve in face of death is a possibility for us because our way of being is a vulnerability and openness to death, we are able to understand the new sense of freedom which comes from *letting ourselves be the kind of beings we are*. We are made "free for anxiety in the face of death." [16] And we can understand what is happening in the very structure of the lives of those special persons who make their deaths their own. Time takes on a different meaning, priorities get ordered, energy is suprisingly available, a sense of the "present" is generated, both an assurance and carelessness of self appear, a new openness to others is found. But now these possibilities are understood as possibilities for *any* of us, available, in principle, at *any* time because of the fundamental and defining possibility which we are—"the possibility of the impossibility of any existence at all." [17] Resolve, in short, becomes a model for authentic human existence in general. With a bit of rhetorical flourish, we could sum up Heidegger's view by saying that living resolutely in the presence of death can permit us to avoid a living death.

Enduring Questions

These, then, are my three families of concepts of death. How are we to assess them? This is an ultimate question upon which I can only record my personal and incomplete judgment.

Surely, death is in any full sense precisely *beyond* comprehension. However, the enduring power of these philosophical conceptualities undoubtedly arises because death and dying are indeed experienced by us as natural, as destructive, and as structuring our existence. We should expect to have to try to encompass all three insights in some way. But due to the immense systematic and existential issues at

16. *Being and Time*, p. 254.
17. *Being and Time*, p. 262.

stake, we still seem to be informed by distinct emphases. We inhabit a pluralistic philosophical world. Some persons today find their conceptualities in philosophies of nature, naturalistic visions of the ancient sort. Biological thought, for example, following out the Aristotelian insight of natural cycles, comings to be and passings away both of individuals and of whole populations, provides a concrete comprehension of death: it is functional. In fact, it is essential. Without it, either populations would increase without limit or a stable state would be achieved in which no new individuals would come to be. In either case, selection would be impossible, the drama of evolutionary change would cease, and the significance of individual life would be reduced. Thus, death is seen to be a necessary part of the objective system of life itself. Natural law philosophies and theologies also continue the classical vision. For them, the natural law of living things, including human beings, indeed of *all* created existence, is contingency or mortality. To see this law is to incorporate an existential insight within a naturalistic context that is ultimately ordered and ordained. There is some solace still in the knowledge that, in the order of things, there is a time to live and a time to die. Acceptance—even of an invitation one cannot refuse—can offer serenity if one believes that he is a part, even a tiny part, of an intelligibile whole.

However, others of us find it difficult to accept such naturalistic views for the simple and decisive reason that nature itself, for us, is changed. It has been de-mythologized. It is arguable that Biblical thought, with its radical disjunction between the transcendent Creator and His creation, later tinged with the neo-Platonic doctrine of the complete passivity of matter, prepared the way for the scentific revolution of the seventeenth century. In any case, as I see it, that revolution not only revolutionized physics, it revolutionized human consciousness of nature, essentially depriving it of immanent, intrinsic meaning. As *mere* matter, bits of extension externally related, the blindly running atoms of modern thought differ fundamentally from even the atoms of Democritus and Lucretius. As R. G. Collingwood observed, all the ancient systems of nature—Stoic, Platonic, Aristotelian, even atomistic—saw nature as *alive*.[18] In this lay its intrinsic meaning. Nature was thought to be essentially in motion, a self-moving whole, a system intelligible in itself, according to its own immanent order-

18. Collingwood, R. G., *The Idea of Nature* (Oxford: Clarendon Press, 1945), especially the Introduction and Part I.

—whether explicitly "ensouled" or not. Not so for the "new physics" or for the philosophies which accompany it in the modern period and down to the present. For them nature is intrinsically—leaving its possible relation to God out of account—inert, *dead*, meaningless. And, I would argue, recent systems of a naturalistic sort, such as that of Whitehead, only overcome this result by reinfusing a sense of life, of living process, into nature once again.

As I have tried to suggest, this shift in the concept of nature has been expressed in a massive, historical shift in the concept of death—at least as reflected in philosophic thought—a shift that has put the ancient philosophies of nature and their consolations of death as natural behind many of us, admirable as they are. This shift is experienced in the modern period as a separation of man and nature, an alienation of man from nature, and is expressed in our sense of the meaninglessness of the physical world and the corresponding dependence of all meaning upon human activity—on science and technology, of course, but on all aspects of culture. And in this context death *has* to be experienced as *failure*. And thus it has to be overcome, as Kant thought, or defied, as Russell demanded, or, in the end, with Sartre, acknowledged as absurd. In a certain sense, the entire meaning of modern, technological medicine is founded upon this concept of death as failure. And in the noble ambivalence of this medical way of dealing with death we can see, writ large, the instability and inadequacy of our modern consciousness of man-against-nature.

As soon as we see this point, however, as soon as we see that our dominant modern stance toward death is a function of our philosophy of nature even now—that is, well after the period of antiquity—we can begin to ask ourselves what this means for the third family of approaches to death that has come into view. Is there perhaps some fresh, viable understanding of man in nature presupposed or aborning here? Obviously, I am at the very edge of what I can see or say. But I *do* think there may be a significance beyond itself of the view that being-toward-death is a structure of human existence. I think that death, and how we handle it practically and interpret it intellectually, is a test case for how we handle our relations to nature and to our bodies, practically and intellectually. If this third family of views of death says something to us, and it has almost become banal in recent literature, it may be because in it we are bringing to expression a new sense of our relatedness to nature and to our bodies which is, in a sense, a breakthrough for modern thinking, a way of passing beyond the frustration of earlier modern thought and a way of rejoining traditional philosophies of nature. What we would approach here would be philosophy of nature in a new sense—not one which delivers a system of things in terms of which man is to be understood, but one which discloses the place of nature in and for an authentic human existence.

The key expression in this third view is that of "making one's death one's own." This is an unusual notion. It is quite the opposite of suicide, which is usually a desperate act to which we feel driven; it is rather a resolution of freedom in which we take up our possibilities in face of death, whatever they may be. But it is a "taking up" of those possibilities which precisely realizes that death is essential and unavoidable for us, and finds in that very fact about human being something which determines the urgency of all living moments and relationships. We do not make death at all, but we do try to make our deaths our own. We "make our own death" by *realization*—by running ahead to death as a part of life; by *responsiveness*—by acknowledgement of this as the foundation of our possibilities; and by *resolution*—by a stand which opens the possibilities of relationships in the present.

Now it might seem that becoming, thus, open to one's being-toward-death is finally recognizing what *separates* human existence from the rest of nature, namely, that we, unlike other beings, consciously live our mortality. On the other hand, I believe it may be that precisely in the *way* this separateness is lived, we can see our essential being *with* nature—not as a part within a whole, but as that through which, *in* our distinctive openness, nature can be disclosed in *its* distinctive way as well. What I find in this third way of conceiving death is a clue to a much needed correction of the modern consciousness of alienation from nature generally. Death is, after all, a mark of our link with processes which transcend us. If the event of death can be anticipated with a sense of its meaning for us, perhaps these processes can also.

What might this mean? In the first place, death marks our embodiment. If we could assume our possibilities in the face of death, we would enact a stance of fundamental significance in all our bodily life. We would authentically express our situated freedom.[19] Our bodies

19. See Paul Ricoeur, *Freedom and Nature,* trans. Erajim Kohak (Evanston: Northwestern University Press, 1966).

are *sources* of our experiential and desirous lives—we are moved by our perceptions and our bodily needs and hungers. Our bodies are also *means* through which we live—we act by taking up those motivations, modifying and expressing them through developed, bodily capacities of movement, manipulation, and speech. Our bodies are, finally, the *destinies* we live—they form the limits of our powers, they expose us to pain, fatigue, aging, illness, and, ultimately, to death. We can resign to the body in these respects, or we can (try to) deny it, or, we can, in a spirit of "responsive control," *assume* it. If a measure of our lives is *how* we live our bodies, it would not be surprising that our stance towards our own deathliness should, in some far reaching ways, express and be expressed in our desires, feelings, and actions, and in how we confront bodily limits of all kinds. My sense is that a resolve which is truly open to my mortality should open me also, in a liberating, vital, and responsive way, to all aspects of my embodied life. I could let myself feel, move, be high or tired or sick. I could *let myself be a body*, without fear of submersion in it and without a struggle to overcome it.

But more, my body is my link to the natural world. If I can let myself be a body, I can let myself be with the world of nature as well. If I can live my body authentically, I can dwell on earth authentically too. This became a theme for some of Heidegger's later essays. In "The Thing," for example, he says,

> When and in what way do things appear as things? They do not appear *by means of* human making. But neither do they appear without the vigilance of mortals. The first step toward such vigilance is the step back from the thinking that merely represents—that is, explains—to the thinking that responds and recalls.[20]

Responsive thinking of this sort will not find things simply as material for making, but beings to be acknowledged and allowed to *do* their thinging under human care. It does not seem far-fetched to see in this thinking a possible existential philosophy of environment. Environmental philosophy has typically taken the route of ancient philosophy: "O man, see thyself as a part of nature and then thou wilst see that thou canst not destroy it without destroying thyself." The appeal is essentially to a vision of the whole and to a calculation of consequences. We need that vision. But the calculation of consequences may be

20. Heidegger, M., "The Thing," from *Poetry, Language, Thought,* trans. Albert Hofstadter (New York: Harper and Row, 1971), p. 181.

wholly ineffectual unless self-destruction means something—that is, unless our mortality is genuinely *present* to us. Thus, an existential philosophy of earth suggests another approach to the same result: "O man, become free for thine own mortality and then thou wilst be free to use nature without having to destroy it." The appeal here is to an authentic existence which brings with it responsiveness to the earthly conditions of life. This does not entail renunciation in the face of nature, a return to some pre-technological mode of life, but rather an assumption of our distinctive human possibilities, which are technological, within an openness to the natural possibilities which limit us.

We will probably continue to despoil the environment until we "realize" our own deaths in the death of the environment; until, that is, we are able to see our own temporality, our own priorities, our own care for self, in profound continuity with the temporality, the priorities, and the care-ful provisions of nature. If death can be "made our own," perhaps nature can be made our own too. But "our own" in a very different sense from that of the tradition of modern thinking, or thoughtlessness, about nature. "Our own" not as a utensil, not as life-less matter for use, but as an extension of our bodies. We do not "own" our bodies; we do not even "use" them as we do tools; we *are* our bodies, as Gabriel Marcel put it. We exist with and through them toward our death. If we were able, practically and intellectually, to incorporate this notion into our consciousness, we might be able to open up possibilities for human accommodation to nature which would mean new directions for technology and science. And we might be able to make nature our own without the vain supposition that it can or should be overcome.

ELIE WIESEL

Death with Evil Meaning: A Hanging in a Concentration Camp

I witnessed other hangings. I never saw a single one of the victims weep. For a long time those dried-up bodies had forgotten the bitter taste of tears.

Except once. The Oberkapo of the fifty-second cable unit was a Dutchman, a giant, well over six feet. Seven hundred prisoners worked under his orders, and they all loved him like a brother. No one had ever received a blow at his hands, nor an insult from his lips.

He had a young boy under him, a *pipel*, as they were called—a child with a refined and beautiful face, unheard of in this camp.

(At Buna, the *pipel* were loathed; they were often crueller than adults. I once saw one of thirteen beating his father because the latter had not made his bed properly. The old man was crying softly while the boy shouted: "If you don't stop crying at once I shan't bring you any more bread. Do you understand?" But the Dutchman's little servant was loved by all. He had the face of a sad angel.)

One day, the electric power station at Buna was blown up. The Gestapo, summoned to the spot, suspected sabotage. They found a trail. It eventually led to the Dutch Oberkapo. And there, after a search, they found an important stock of arms.

The Oberkapo was arrested immediately. He was tortured for a period of weeks, but in vain. He would not give a single name. He was transferred to Auschwitz. We never heard of him again.

But his little servant had been left behind in the camp in prison.

Also put to torture, he too would not speak. Then the SS sentenced him to death, with two other prisoners who had been discovered with arms.

One day when we came back from work, we saw three gallows rearing up in the assembly place, three black crows. Roll call. SS all round us, machine guns trained: the traditional ceremony. Three victims in chains—and one of them, the little servant, the sad-eyed angel.

The SS seemed more preoccupied, more disturbed than usual. To hang a young boy in front of thousands of spectators was no light matter. The head of the camp read the verdict. All eyes were on the child. He was lividly pale, almost calm, biting his lips. The gallows threw its shadow over him.

This time the Lagerkapo refused to act as executioner. Three SS replaced him.

The three victims mounted together onto the chairs.

The three necks were placed at the same moment within the nooses.

"Long live liberty!" cried the two adults.

But the child was silent.

"Where is God? Where is He?" someone behind me asked.

At a sign from the head of the camp, the three chairs tipped over.

Total silence throughout the camp. On the horizon, the sun was setting.

"Bare your heads!" yelled the head of the camp. His voice was raucous. We were weeping.

"Cover your heads!"

Then the march past began. The two adults were no longer alive. Their tongues hung swollen, blue-tinged. But the third rope was still moving; being so light, the child was still alive. . . .

For more than half an hour he stayed there, struggling between life and death, dying in slow agony under our eyes. And we had to look him full in the face. He was still alive when I passed in front of him. His tongue was still red, his eyes not yet glazed.

Behind me, I heard the same man asking:

"Where is God now?"

And I heard a voice within me answer him:

"Where is He? Here He is—He is hanging here on this gallows. . . ."

That night the soup tasted of corpses.

VIKTOR FRANKL

Meaning in Life

I doubt whether a doctor can answer this question in general terms. For the meaning of life differs from man to man, from day to day and from hour to hour. What matters, therefore, is not the meaning of life in general but rather the specific meaning of a person's life at a given moment. To put the question in general terms would be comparable to the question posed to a chess champion, "Tell me, Master, what is the best move in the world?" There simply is no such thing as the best or even a good move apart from a particular situation in a game and the particular personality of one's opponent. The same holds for human existence. One should not search for an abstract meaning of life. Everyone has his own specific vocation or mission in life; everyone must carry out a concrete assignment that demands fulfillment. Therein he cannot be replaced, nor can his life be repeated. Thus, everyone's task is as unique as is his specific opportunity to implement it.

As each situation in life represents a challenge to man and presents a problem for him to solve, the question of the meaning of life may actually be reversed. Ultimately, man should not ask what the meaning of his life is, but rather must recognize that it is *he* who is asked. In a world, each man is questioned by life; and he can only answer to life by *answering for* his own life; to life he can only respond by being responsible. . . .

This emphasis on responsibleness is reflected in the categorical imperative of logotherapy, which is: "So live as if you were living already for the second time and as if you had acted the first time as wrongly as you are about to act now!" It seems to me that there is nothing that would stimulate a man's sense of responsibleness more than this maxim, which invites him to imagine first that the present is past and, second, that the past may yet be changed and amended. Such a precept confronts him with life's *finiteness* as well as the *finality* of what he makes out of both his life and himself. . . .

By declaring that man is a responsible creature and must actualize the potential meaning of his life, I wish to stress that the true meaning of life is to be found in the world rather than within man or his own *psyche*, as though it were a closed system. By the same token, the real aim of human existence cannot be found in what is called self-actualization. Human existence is essentially self-transcendence rather than self-actualization. Self-actualization is not a possible aim at all, for the simple reason that the more a man would strive for it, the more he would miss it. For only to the extent to which man commits himself to the fulfillment of his life's meaning, to this extent he also actualizes himself. In other words, self-actualization cannot be attained if it is made an end in itself, but only as a side effect of self-transcendence.

The world must not be regarded as a mere expression of one's self. Nor must the world be considered as a mere instrument, or as a means to the end of one's self-actualization. In both cases, the world view, or the *Weltanschauung*, turns into a *Weltentwertung*, i.e., a depreciation of the world.

Thus far we have shown that the meaning of life always changes, but that it never ceases to be. According to logotherapy, we can discover this meaning in life in three different ways: (1) by doing a deed; (2) by experiencing a value; and (3) by suffering. The first, the way of achievement or accomplishment, is quite obvious. The second and third need further elaboration.

The second way of finding a meaning in life is by experiencing something, such as a work of nature or culture; and also by experiencing someone, i.e., by love.

Love is the only way to grasp another human being in the innermost core of his personality. No one can become fully aware of the very essence of another human being unless he loves him. By the spiritual act of love he is enabled to see the essential traits and features in the beloved person; and even more, he sees that which is potential in him, that which is not yet actualized but yet ought to be actualized. Furthermore, by his love, the loving person enables the beloved person to actualize these potentialities. By making him aware of what he can be and of what he should become, he makes these potentialities come true.

In logotherapy, love is not interpreted as a mere epiphenomenon of sexual drives and instincts in the sense of a so-called sublimation. Love is as primary a phenomenon as sex. Normally, sex is a mode of expression for love. Sex is justified, even sanctified, as soon as, but only as long as, it is a vehicle of love. Thus love is not understood as a mere side effect of sex but sex as a way of expressing the experience of that ultimate togetherness that is called love.

A third way to find a meaning in life is by suffering.

Whenever one is confronted with an inescapable, unavoidable situation, whenever one has to face a fate that cannot be changed, e.g., an incurable disease, such as an inoperable cancer, just then is one given a last chance to actualize the highest value, to fulfill the deepest meaning, the meaning of suffering. For what matters above all is the attitude we take toward suffering, the attitude in which we take our suffering upon ourselves.

Let me cite a clear-cut example: Once, an elderly general practitioner consulted me because of his severe depression. He could not overcome the loss of his wife who had died two years before and whom he had loved above all else. Now how could I help him? What should I tell him? Well, I refrained from telling him anything, but instead confronted him with the question, "What would have happened, Doctor, if you had died first, and your wife would have had to survive you?"

"Oh," he said, "for her this would have been terrible; how she would have suffered!" Whereupon I replied, "You see, Doctor, such a suffering has been spared her, and it is you who have spared her this suffering; but now, you have to pay for it by surviving and mourning her." He said no word but shook my hand and calmly left my office. Suffering ceases to be suffering in some way at the moment it finds a meaning, such as the meaning of a sacrifice.

Of course, this was no therapy in the proper sense since, first, his despair was no disease; and second, I could not change his fate, I could not revive his wife. But in the moment I did succeed in changing his *attitude* toward his unalterable fate inasmuch as from that time on he could at least see a meaning in his suffering. It is one of the basic tenets of logotherapy that man's main concern is not to gain pleasure or to avoid pain, but rather to see a meaning in his life. That is why man is even ready to suffer, on the condition, to be sure, that his suffering has a meaning. . . .

Let me recall that which was perhaps the deepest experience I had in the concentration camp. The odds of surviving the camp were no more than one to twenty, as can easily be verified by exact statistics. It did not even seem possible, let alone probable, that the manuscript of my first book, which I had hidden in my coat when I arrived at Auschwitz, would ever be rescued. Thus, I had to undergo and to overcome the loss of my spiritual child. And now it seemed as if nothing and no one would survive me; neither a physical nor a spiritual child of my own! So I found myself confronted with the question of whether under such circumstances my life was ultimately void of any meaning.

Not yet did I notice that an answer to this question with which I was wrestling so passionately was already in store for me, and that soon thereafter this answer would be given to me. This was the case when I had to surrender my clothes and in turn inherited the worn-out rags of an inmate who had been sent to the gas chamber immediately after his arrival at the Auschwitz railway station. Instead of the many pages of my manuscript, I found in a pocket of the newly acquired coat a single page torn out of a Hebrew prayer book, which contained the main Jewish prayer, *Shema Yisrael.* How should I have interpreted such a "coincidence" other than as a challenge to *live* my thoughts instead of merely putting them on paper?

A bit later, I remember, it seemed to me that I would die in the near future. In this critical situation, however, my concern was different from that of most of my comrades. Their question was, "Will we survive the camp? For, if not, all this suffering has no meaning." The question which beset me was, "Has all this suffering, this dying around us, a meaning? For, if not, then ultimately there is no meaning to survival; for a life whose meaning depends upon such a happenstance—whether one escapes or not—ultimately would not be worth living at all." . . .

I should like to cite the following instance: Once, the mother of a boy who had died at the age of eleven years was admitted to my clinic after a suicide attempt. My associate, Dr. Kocourek, invited her to join a therapeutic group, and it happened that I stepped into the room of the clinic where he was conducting a psychodrama. She was telling her story. At the death of her boy she was left alone with another, older son, who was crippled, suffering from infantile paralysis. The poor boy had to be moved around in a chair. His mother, however, rebelled against her fate. But when she tried to commit suicide together with him, it was the crippled son who prevented her from doing so; he liked living! For him, life had remained meaningful. Why was it not so for his mother? How could her life still have a meaning? And how could we help her to become aware of it?

Improvising, I participated in the discussion, and questioned another woman in the group. I asked her how old she was and she answered, "Thirty." I replied, "No, you are not thirty but instead eighty and lying on your death bed. And now you are looking back on your life, a life that was childless but full of financial success and social prestige." And then I invited her to imagine what she would feel in this situation. "What will you think of it? What will you say to yourself?" Let me quote what she actually said from a tape that was recorded during that session. "Oh, I married a millionaire; I had an easy life full of wealth; and I lived it up! I flirted with men, I teased them! But now, I am eighty; I have no children of my own. Looking back as an old woman, I cannot see what all that was for; actually, I must say, my life was a failure!"

I then invited the mother of the handicapped son to imagine herself similarly looking back over *her* life. Let us listen to what she had to say as recorded on the tape: "I wished to have children and this wish has been granted to me; one boy died, the other, however, the crippled one, would have been sent to an institution if I had not taken over his care. Though he is crippled and helpless, he is after all my boy. And so I have made a fuller life possible for him; I have made a better human being out of my son." At this moment, there was an outburst of tears, and crying, she continued: "As for myself, I can look back peacefully on my life; for I can say my life was full of meaning, and I have tried hard to fulfill it; I have done my best—I have done the best for my son. My life was no failure!" Viewing her life as if from her death bed, she had suddenly been able to see a meaning in it, a meaning that included even all of her sufferings. By the same token, however, it had become clear as well that a life of short duration, like that, for example, of her dead boy, could be so rich in joy and love that it could contain more meaning than a life lasting eighty years.

TED ROSENTHAL

Rosenthal's Account
of His Approach to His Death

The doctor was a lady doctor and she looked a little bit like a hawk. She was a little bit fiendish looking. She said, "I think we have a problem here." And my head flashed. I knew something was disastrously wrong, but I ignored my own warning. Just the look in her eyes. She was blinking, you know, the way people blink when they have something disastrous to tell you. She said, "We have a bit of a problem here" and I asked quite naively, "Well what do you mean?" My heart was racing when she said that. And she said, "Well, you have acute leukemia."

There's something about dying that separates you from all other people. Nobody can come to terms with death. Nobody can walk into death and walk back out the same person. Everybody else, no matter who they are, whether they are a poet, a man of power, a frightened little child, whoever it is, they are afraid of the limitless possibilities of their own nature. Once you have nothing, you can be anything, and that's a feeling of freedom.

Dying is a matter of feeling. I think dying is no different than being born. When I was told that I was going to die in five months I felt that was the same as telling me that I was going to die that afternoon. And the whole idea of going through an awful lot of pain or frustration or embarrassment from one day to the next to prolong my life a few days

or a few weeks or a few months or even a year or so was frightening in
itself.

But it turns out that you can live a lifetime in a day; you can live a lifetime in a moment; you can live a lifetime in a year—so that to the extent they can prolong your life dying is not a lie. It's something that's
beautiful.
    I don't think people are afraid of death. What they are afraid of is
the incompleteness of their life. I think what society does is strip you
of your self-confidence from the moment you are born; strip you of the
sense that what you are is all you're ever going to be.

And so you tell yourself lie after lie after lie, and as you grow older
you begin to feel that whatever life is going to mean to you, it's going
to mean it in the future, depending on what you are grabbing for,
what your ambition is—to get to the other shore, to be enlightened, or
whatever it is. And it isn't until you discover that you're going to die
that you realize that whatever it is you have, you've already got. Right
there. And it makes that moment an eternity. And it doesn't matter if
you die then or a million years from now.

It's that sense of already being dead that makes you feel that you don't
have to be just you, or an extension of what's in your hip pocket, but
the infinite potential of the whole race. Man; first man; last man; all
man. It's like a good trip. Because I had nothing, because I had no
needs of my own, I wasn't self-preoccupied, so I had a feeling of love
for everybody, unilaterally, unequivocally. I loved everybody, which
didn't mean that I had a loss of sensitivity of the pain for other people
who were in the hospital.

I was acutely sensitive to everyone else's pain and I took a great interest, far greater interest, into everyone else's problems, as much as I
could poke my nose into, than I had for my own problems. And it cut
very deeply into me, but in cutting into me it opened me up at the
same time. I didn't feel the resistance to the pain around me or to my
own situation at all. It all went through me almost like a melody. It
was something that I didn't enjoy in a sense that it was fun; it was a
full feeling. I felt full and rich inside and I had no sense of anxiety, no
sense of boredom, no sense of impatience, no sense of time.

I didn't need books. I didn't need crossword puzzles. I didn't need company. I could just sit there and enjoy my environment. Look out the window. I could see the birds for the first time in my life. Instead of just looking at the birds and just saying, "Ah yes, birds," I could see them, without calling them birds; without seeing them as being something. I could see the sky. I could see the clouds and I could lay back and people could talk around me and I could be so receptive to what anybody was saying and yet at the same time just be watching the birds fly across the sky. That's all I could feel, that's all I could care about, without even caring. Just feeling that they were flying through the empty cage of my mind. It was just an open, full, rich feeling.

And as soon as I was told that I had a chance of surviving, this just went crashing to the ground. I just got scared from that point on.

Right now all I want is a little time, a little freedom, a little peace. I want to stretch my bones. I want to stretch my bones where there is room to stretch in this country, where there's a little fresh air. I just want to feel life run through me again. That's all I really want. I am sick of dying. I tell you it's a drag. It's a waste of time. It makes me depressed.

Most people live only for their ambitions and they spend their time boasting about where they have been and where they're going. I was a person whose only ambition was to be without any. So I realized, unconsciously, that I was a happier person once I became sick. That doesn't make sense to most people. It's a state of mind. I remember feeling if only I could live to benefit from my present state of mind. If only I could take this with me and go back, I'd be free. But in so doing and being given the time, I lost the state of mind. You can't have it both ways.

People misunderstand the whole notion of living for the moment versus living in the moment. I think living for the moment is a difficult thing to do and it just sort of makes you goofy anyway. People who are desolate live for the moment; people who have no economic future, say black people in the ghettos, who have no hope of advancing themselves. You see them living for the moment, but they are not happy. But that's very different from living in the moment.

To live in the moment you literally have to have the sense of having nothing to live for. Not in the sense of future economic opportunities and that sort of thing, but just realizing that there is no real purpose to life and being able to live life fully from moment to moment. And that's something I can't even tell myself how to do and I can't tell anybody else how to do it.

I'm changed; I'll always be changed. I'll always be happier for what I have gone through, only because it has enabled me to have the courage to open myself up to anything that happens and I am no longer afraid of death. At least I am not afraid of death the way I might have been had I not become sick. But I do forget that it is me. The days are ticking off and I hate that.

Though you may find me picking flowers
Or washing my body in a river, or kicking rocks,
Don't think my eyes don't hold yours.
And look hard upon them
and drop tears as long as you stay before me
Because I live as a man who knows death
and I speak the only truth
to those who will listen.

Never yield a minute to despair, sloth, fantasy.
I say to you, you will face pain in your life
You may lose your limbs, bleed to death
Shriek for hours on into weeks in unimaginable agony.
It is not aimed at anyone
but it will come your way.
The wind sweeps over everyone.

You will feel so all alone, abandoned,
come to see that life is brief.
And you will cry, "No, it cannot be so,"
but nothing will avail you.
I tell you never to yearn for the past.
Speak certain knowledge.
Your childhood is worthless.
Seek not ritual. There is no escape in Christmas.
Santa Claus will not ease your pain.
No fantasy will soothe you.

You must bare your heart and expect nothing in return.
You must respond totally to nature.
You must return to your simple self.
I do not fool you. There lies no other path.
I have not forsaken you, but I cannot be among you all.
You are not alone
so long as you love your own true simple selves
Your natural hair, your skin, your graceful bodies
your knowing eyes and your tears and tongues.

I stand before you all aching with truth
Trembling with desire to make you know.
Eat, sleep, and be serious about life.
To be serious is to be simple;
to be simple is to love.
Don't wait another minute, make tracks, go home.
Admit you have some place to return to.
The bugs are crawling over the earth, the sun shining over
        everyone
The rains are pounding, the winds driving
The breeze is gentle and the grass burns.
The earth is dusty. Go ankle deep in mud.

Get tickled by the tall cattails.
Kick crazily into the burrs and prickles.
Rub your back against the bark, and go ahead, peel it.
Adore the sun.
O people, you are dying! Live while you can.
What can I say?
The blackbirds blow the bush.
Get glass in your feet if you must, but take off the shoes.
O heed me. There is pain all over!
There is continual suffering, puking and coughing.
Don't wait on it. It is stalking you.
Tear ass up the mountainside, duck into the mist . . .

. . . Roll among the wet daisies. Blow out your lungs
among the dead dandelion fields.
But don't delay, time is not on your side.
Soon you will be crying for the hurt, make speed.

Splash in the Ocean,
leap in the snow.
Come on everybody! Love your neighbor
Love your mother, love your lover,
love the man who just stands there staring.
But first, that's alright, go ahead and cry.
Cry, cry, cry your heart out.
It's love. It's your only path.

O people, I am so sorry.
Nothing can be hid.
It's a circle in the round.
It's group theater,
no wings, no backstage, no leading act.
O, I am weeping, but it's stage center for all of us.
Hide in the weeds but come out naked.
Dance in the sand while lightning bands all around us.

Step lightly, we're walking home now.
The clouds take every shape.
We climb up the boulders; there is no plateau.
We cross the stream and walk up the slope.
See, the hawk is diving.
The plain stretches out ahead, then the hills, the valleys,
          the meadows.
Keep moving people. How could I not be among you?

NANCY CAROLINE

When Dying Is Right

> I prefer to die by the hand of God.
> *Ambrose Paré*

A patient can commit no more grievous offense in a university hospital than to die. Virtually any other lapse in propriety is tolerated—vomiting, incontinence, hemorrhage, seizures, and even behavioral aberrations (the latter forgiven under the heading of "he's not himself"). But to die is an unforgiveable breach of faith with the entire hospital staff, an outrage against doctors, nurses, technicians, orderlies, dieticians, housekeeping maids and all the other major and minor functionaries of that peculiar institution called a hospital.

To die is to cause an enormous inconvenience. Conferences must be held, reports submitted, forms filled out. Endless meetings, discussions and postmortems must be enacted, through which the defeated physician seeks absolution.

Once, in an age not yet blessed with the technology for sustaining life, death was regarded as a natural process, an inevitable consequence of living. And because it was regarded as natural and inevitable, it was accorded a certain dignity and respect. Man, according to one tradition, was like a ship, launched at birth onto a tumultuous sea, returning at journey's end to anchor in a tranquil harbor. The tranquility was a man's due. A human being had a right to die, no less inalienable than his right to live.

Granted, he had no alternative. But neither did. any of the other creatures with whom he shared the earth and sky. So it seemed like a fairly equitable arrangement. And in that dark era, which might in

365

retrospect be termed the Age of Death, man managed somehow—in spite of his mortality, or perhaps even because of it—to write poems and symphonies, to paint frescos, to build colosseums—in short to repudidate the concept of mortality even while submitting to its technicalities. Man in the Age of Death died a hero.

The 20th century—hereafter referred to as the Age of Arrogance—has changed all that. Suddenly man does not have to die, or not, at any rate, at the conventional time. If his kidneys betray him, he can be sustained by dialysis. If his lungs tire of their task, a ventilator can coerce them to breathe. Even his heart can be bypassed or maintained mechanically. Man's appointment with death, albeit still inevitable, is nonetheless now subject to rescheduling according to the arbitrary wish of his physician. And we call this progress. If man no longer dies a hero, it is hardly worth worrying about; there is too much to do.

Death has undergone enormous change. No longer a natural process, no longer a tranquil harbor, death has become The Enemy. To die is to join forces with the enemy. To die is spitefully and ungratefully to proclaim the inadequacy of doctors and their technology. In short, to die in a hospital, most especially in a university hospital, is nothing short of heresy.

Accordingly, every measure is taken in a university hospital to insure that a patient will not commit this impropriety. The most sophisticated techniques are employed to keep vigil over heart beat, blood pressure, oxygenation, renal function. And should the patient show a moment's lapse—a treasonous retreat from life—alarms instantaneously summon the doctors to rescue him from his indiscretion, to forestall his appointment.

Nonetheless, despite the most fervent and conscientious efforts, every so often a patient will elude our sentinels and slip past the barriers beyond which even our extraordinary resuscitative measures cannot penetrate. I cared for one such patient during my internship. He was absolutely bent on dying, and no amount of arguing and cajoling could persuade him otherwise.

His name was Eli Kahn. He was 78 years old. He was admitted to the hospital because of abdominal pain and vomiting. X-rays taken on admission suggested a small bowel obstruction. Having reviewed his films, I walked over to the division to work Mr. Kahn up.

He was a thin, frail old man with a weathered face and marvelously bright eyes. When I entered the room, his attention was fixed on Mr. Kovanich in the next bed, an old man recently operated on for colonic cancer. Mr. Kovanich had not done well, and now he lay entwined in a tangle of drains and tubes, breathing laboriously.

I introduced myself.

Mr. Kahn wrenched his gaze from his neighbor and looked up at me. "I'm dying," he said.

"Don't be silly."

"What's silly about dying?"

"Nothing. But it's not allowed. You are in a hospital, a university hospital, equipped with all the latest technology. Here you must get well."

"My time has come."

"Time is measured differently here."

"What do you understand about time? Wait until you have lived 78 years. Wait until you are 78 years old and tired and alone and have a pain in your belly."

There was no arguing with him.

Physical examination revealed an erratic heart beat, a few crackles in the lungs, a tender, distended abdomen, an enlarged prostate, and arthritic changes in the joints.

"You see," said Mr. Kahn, "the engine is broken down; it is time for the engineer to abandon it."

We discussed the case with our attending and elected to decompress the bowel for a few days before attempting surgery. When I went into Mr. Kahn's room to pass a Miller-Abbott tube, I found him again staring at the patient in the next bed. Mr. Kovanich was comatose.

"We have to pass a tube down into your stomach, Mr. Kahn."

"Like that?" He gestured toward the tube protruding from Mr. Kovanich's nose.

"Something like that."

"Listen, doctor. I don't want to die with tubes sticking out all over me. I don't want that my children should remember their father that way. All my life I tried to be a *mensch*, you understand? All my life, I tried to live so I could hold my head up. Rich I wasn't, but I managed. I put my sons through college. I wanted to be able to hold my head up, to have dignity, even though I didn't have much money and didn't speak good English.

"Now I'm dying. O.K. I'm not complaining. I'm old and tired and have seen enough of life, believe me. But still I want to be a man, not a vegetable that someone comes and waters every day—not like him." He looked over at Kovanich. "Not like him."

"The tube will only be down for a few days, Mr. Kahn. Then we'll take you to surgery and fix you up."

"What, are you going to make me 25 years old again with your surgery?"

"No, we can't accomplish that."

"So what are you trying to do?"

"We're trying to make you feel well again."

He seemed suddenly tired of the conversation. "You don't understand," he said more to himself than to me. "You don't understand."

That evening, I stopped by to start an I.V.

"Another tube?" Mr. Kahn asked.

"You've become dehydrated. We have to get some fluids into you."

He nodded, but said nothing. He watched silently as I started the I.V. and secured the line with tape. Every so often he glanced across at Kovanich. Still he said nothing.

Early the next morning, I heard the hospital page issuing the code for a cardiac arrest. I raced up to the division to find nurses dashing in and out of Mr. Kahn's room. Inside, I saw Mr. Kovanich lying naked on his bed in a pool of excretions with the house officers laboring over him—pounding on his chest, squeezing air into his lungs, injecting one medication after another, trying to thread a pacemaker down his jugular vein. The whole thing lasted about an hour. Mr. Kovanich would not come back, and finally all labors ceased.

The nurses began clearing the resuscitation equipment out of the room, while we filed out to begin the round of postmortem debates.

"Doctor, wait a minute." Mr. Kahn was signalling me. I went over to his bed.

"What is it, Mr. Kahn?"

His eyes were frantic. "Don't ever do that to me. I want you should promise you'll never do that to me."

"Mr. Kahn, I know this has been very upsetting . . ."

"Promise!" He was leaning forward in bed and his eyes were boring through me. There was an interminable silence.

"All right, Mr. Kahn, I promise."

Satisfied, he leaned back against the pillow and closed his eyes. I was dismissed. I wandered out into the hall, where my colleagues were discussing Kovanich's defection.

"It looked like a pulmonary embolism. I knew we should have anticoagulated him."

"Did you get permission for an autopsy?"

"Don't lose his last EKG; we'll need it for the conference."

I walked away. I had other things to think about.

On the fourth hospital day, Mr. Kahn went into congestive heart failure. I found him cyanotic and wheezing on morning rounds. Swiftly the house staff swung into the practised and coordinated action of acute care: morphine, oxygen, IPPB, tourniquets, digitalis, diuretics. But despite our skilled efforts, Mr. Kahn responded poorly. His blood gases continued to show a dangerous degree of hypoxia, and our attending wondered whether he might not have sustained a pulmonary embolism. "He's exhausting himself trying to breathe, and he's still hypoxic," our attending said. "I think he ought to be intubated; it will give him a rest and will help us oxygenate him and get at his secretions."

When the anesthesiologist arrived to intubate him, Mr. Kahn was gasping. I explained to him about the endotracheal tube. His breathing became more labored as he struggled for words. "You promised . . ." was all he could say.

"But this is different, Mr. Kahn. This tube is just for a short while— maybe just a day. It's to help you breathe."

He stared off in another direction. The anesthesiologist intubated him without difficulty, and we hooked him up to the ventilator.

"I think he ought to be monitored also," our attending said. "We don't know what sent him into heart failure, but it may have been an arrhythmia, and if so it could recur."

So we brought in the cardiac monitor and pasted the leads onto Mr. Kahn's chest while he looked on, not stirring, his face expressionless, his eyes dull.

Mr. Kahn was asleep that night when I stopped in for an evening check. The room was still save for the beep-beep of the monitor, the rhythmic whoosh of the ventilator and the hum of the nasogastric suction apparatus. And Mr. Kahn looked suddenly so very old and frail, lost among tubes and wires and enormous, imposing machines. I could not help thinking of the physiology laboratories in medical school where we used to put dogs to sleep and hook them up to all kinds of intricate recording devices. I checked the settings on the ventilator and slipped out of the room. There were a lot of other patients to see.

Sometime late that night, Mr. Kahn woke up, reached over and switched off his ventilator. The nurses didn't find him for several hours. They called me to pronounce him dead. The room was silent when I entered. The ventilator issued no rush of air, the monitor tracked a straight line, the suction machine was shut off. Mr. Kahn lay absolutely still.

I mechanically reached for the pulseless wrist, then flashed my light into the widened, unmoving pupils, and nodded to the nurses to begin their ritual over the body.

On the bedside table, I found a note, scrawled in Mr. Kahn's uneven hand: "Death is not the enemy, doctor. Inhumanity is."

CHARLES E. SCOTT

Healing and Dying

Thinking About Dying

Most people most of the time fear death in a natural way without thinking about it. Or so it seems. Walking happily off a curb, one is seized with a moment of terror as a car bears down on him and only narrowly misses him. He does not want to die. Or we plan our canoeing trip with care because we want adventure but not death. Or a person with a temperature of 105°, emaciated from weeks of pain, sets her jaw and eyes and "holds on" because she does not want to die. We are often threatened by a cool and well planned suicide because our own desire to live is relativized by this event of planned death. We want to want to live.

Our desire to live, our will to be, is so natural and so strong that protection from death and from the power of our fear of death can be a major barrier when our professions have to do with people who are especially or obviously close to death. And death as a possibility is so pervasive of our lives that our fear relating to death can be a major barrier to accepting the finite openness of our own existence.

E. E. Cummings sees, however, that the experiences of growth and joy and freeing immediacy all involve also at once dying and death.

you and I are not snobs. We can never be born enough. We are human beings; for whom birth is a supremely welcome mystery,the mystery of growing:the mystery which happens only and whenever we are faithful to ourselves. You and

I wear the dangerous looseness of doom and find it becoming. Life,for eternal us,is now;and now is much too busy being a little more than everything to seem anything,catastrophic included.

The "now" says, as it were, "impermanence." And our impermanence is our never being tied down finally to how we were or to how we are now. But possible catastrophy is also part of the meaning of impermanence. Dying and death are an essential part of the "mystery of growing, the mystery that happens only and whenever we are faithful to ourselves." We turn with impermanence to ourselves and discover, in being true to ourselves, the meaning of being impermanent and aware. Rilke said in a letter, "even in the most-coming wind we breathe parting." Coming and going, growing and dying, all seem involved with each other. Being here now already bespeaks dying in the very impermanence of the moment—and in the impermanence of ourselves as the moment.

Because dying and death are so central a part of our being as well as of our communal, personal, and professional lives, and because we fear and turn away from it, thinking about it is important. One kind of thinking can be part of our escape: we think away from death by dealing with it in rigid, conceptual categories, or we merely "examine" what important people have said on the topic. That is bad thinking as well as bad psychology because it deals with the reality of death largely by denying and distancing us from the reality of death.

Another way of dealing with death is to think toward it. "Thinking towards death" does not mean that one's thinking culminates with his death. It means that one reflects his experiences of death and dying and interprets those experiences. That process involves a descriptive recognition of the experiences, a search for the words that give most vividness to the way the experiences occur, and the development of judgments or interpretations that relate these experiences to other experiences, i.e., the reflection of experiences of death and dying with other experiential reflections.

By this process we *uncover* pre-reflective experiences—that is the opposite of hiding from them—and we integrate them in relation to other parts of our lives. Our aim in this case is to bring together the experiences related to death and dying with all the basic experiences of our life so that we do not need to protect ourselves from death and fear of death. Nietzsche, in *Twilight of the Idols*, phrased this aim in his own way:

Out of love for life we should want a different death: free, conscious, without hazard, without ambush.

The Experience of Dying and Death

For convenience here I want to use the words *dying* and *death* to name different kinds of events. E. E. Cummings made the distinction in one way:

> dying is fine)but Death
>
> ?o
> baby
> i
>
> wouldn't like
>
> Death if Death
> were
> good:for
>
> when(instead of stopping to think)you
>
> begin to feel of it,dying
> 's miraculous
> why?be
>
> cause dying is
>
> perfectly natural;perfectly
> putting
> it mildly lively(but
>
> Death
>
> is strictly
> scientific
> &artificial&
>
> evil&legal)
>
> we thank thee
> god
> almighty for dying
>
> (forgive us,o life!the sin of Death

Cummings is right in seeing that *dying* names an experience of one dimension of our living, whereas *death* names an objective "thing" that is not immediate in our lives. We often think of dying and death as something we can only go through once, unless we are brought back to life after our hearts have stopped beating. One result of this way of thinking is that we actually separate dying from living, and the idea of the experience of dying seems strange to us. I want to show that the experience of dying, as distinct to death, is very much an aspect of our living and that consequently the meaning of living and the meaning of dying need not be antithetical to each other.

The experience of death, as I think of it, is seeing someone stop breathing or imagining myself as not here. To imagine myself as totally absent is possible only as a leap into a non-imaged state of feeling, an experience that is quite different from imagining my funeral, although the latter may be a step toward the profound sense of my own non-being. These experiences can be highly significant, particularly before we have thoroughly realized and experienced the meaning of our finiteness. But we shall concentrate now on the immediate experience of dying. I stress this latter experience because it is, I believe, the one most difficult to interpret and the one most important for understanding ourselves in relation to our mortality.

I want to emphasize two of the dominant ways of experiencing dying which I shall call the experience of transition and the experience of lapse of meaningful direction.

The Experience of Transition

The experience of transition happens as the loss of some aspect of my existence and as the emergence of some aspect of my existence that is new for me. I experience dying, for example, when my child, or spouse, mother or father dies. I do not experience his or her death. I experience the loss of a living relationship. *I* am changed. I am *bereaved*—that word, *bereaved*, comes from the Anglo-Saxon word which means *to be deprived* or *to be dispossessed*. The loss is not under my control. I *am* deprived. I am changed. I undergo a deep change of relationship. In that sense a part of my reality dies and a new way of being replaces that other aspect of my existence—in this case my relation to someone permanently absent replaces my relation to that person as alive.

Another kind of dying occurs when a person himself changes significantly, when, for example, I become free of an illusion that has dominated my relation to people. Part of me dies in losing that illusion, and I may grieve a loss over which I am also happy. Or I experience dying when I discover, against all my expectations, that some people are not trustworthy, or as I move from childishness to responsibility and independence.

The experience of dying happens as we lose some aspect of the way we are—a relationship, a factor of our identity, a fundamental direction of choice, an ideal. A part of us ceases to be. Such experiences seem to mean that nothing that I am is final and free from radical change. They seem to mean that I am myself a process of changing, that *I* occur as dying and as being reborn. These experiences of dying are themselves the experience of the pre-reflective awareness that my own being is always in question and fundamentally uncertain. I am aware of myself pre-reflectively as a state of transition.

That awareness, although it is one way we are immediately aware of ourselves, can be frightening. It is our non-reflective sense that our best and strongest *control* of ourselves and of our environment does not define our existence. Our own existence is deeply outside of our control. Our experience of dying is our living out that insight. It means that when our professional work and our personal lives are strongest and most integrated, we are a living process that is not defined finally by our work or our personality. It is defined also as a process of changing—growing, declining, transisting—which is lived as an experience of dying that is not within one's control.

The fear or anxiety that can accompany our sense of being outside of our own control may be expressed in attempts to maximize the importance and meaning of what we feel we can control. I may resist knowing deeply and thoroughly that my living is also a process of dying. I may not want to understand what I clearly sense: that all that I love and want and count on is subject to transition, to the process of dying. I may well want more stability and firmness than the dying process of my living allows. The consequence is that I turn away from this central part of my own existence and focus chiefly on what I can keep at my disposal, as though these situations, things, and people were not mortal.

In turning away from my own experiences of dying in the form of transitions, I may avoid, as well as I can, all depth reminders of my own transitoriness. I may avoid people who are experiencing the pain of radical transitions. I may even deny that such transitions are going on. Or I may develop an attitude of distance, perhaps an air of superiority regarding those who suffer radical changes in their lives—a rigid moralism, a secure professionalism, a set of beliefs absolutized into rigidity.

In such cases of denial I reject a significant dimension of my own existence—the experience of transition—and I am consequently inclined to reject people who remind me of that aspect of myself. In refusing this experience of dying I refuse an important part of human living.

Hermann Hesse said it nicely: "As every blossom fades and all youth sinks in to old age, so every life's design, each flower of wisdom, every good, attains its prime and cannot last forever. At each life's call the heart must be prepared to take its leave and to commence afresh, courageously . . . submit itself to other, newer ties. A magic dwells in each beginning and protecting us tells us how to live" (*Magister Ludi*). If one learns how ". . . to take leave and commence afresh . . ." he will have accepted one central way in which we experience dying. As we hold on to what is over as though it were not over, and as we refuse the emerging parts of our lives as though they were not genuinely new and emerging, we deny our own experience of dying. And we very likely will turn away from those who remind us of our own denial.

Experiencing a Lapse of Meaningful Direction

We begin with a situation: You find yourself with nothing to do. You feel strange or ignored and deeply lonely. You don't want to do anything in particular. The options are:

1. Start doing something—anything—go out and find someone. Think about your work. Wash your hair. Pick up something to read. Find an activity.
2. Feel blue, depressed. Sit and stare. Sleep. Think hateful thoughts about the people outside who are laughing.
3. Draw conclusions about reality from your feelings at this moment. Some conclusions that can be drawn: **a.** The universe is a crock of shit. **b.** Mother and Daddy hate me. **c.** My wife is unfaithful to me. **d.** No one really appreciates me. **e.** I'm the only one who understands the way things really are. **f.** I'm a bad person, etc.
4. Feel sympathy for the loneliness which other people experience. Want to help in some way. Want to serve somehow.
5. Ask yourself what is missing, wait for an answer, affirm the direc-

tions of meaning that appear in this sense of emptiness, affirm the sense of emptiness to be valuable.

What has happened in this passing moment? A direction of meaning was not apparent. Without such direction we may experience ourselves, if only for a fleeting moment, disconnected from reality in general. Feeling disconnected is a dying experience. We experience a closure of meaning, separation from the world, an absence of meaningful dialogue. Though alive, we experience a loss of aliveness and vitality.

In the first situation in which I find just anything to do, I distract myself from my situation by some activity or by something that takes my attention. My fear of dissociation, or my unease with it, happens as my scurrying around to find something to do. I am immediately aware of the emptiness of living without a direction of meanings and of the absence of the direction which I need in order to feel deeply and thoroughly alive. I run around anxiously.

In the second situation of sitting and sleeping, I fall prey, at least momentarily to my sense of emptiness. I am deactivated. I am overcome by a sense of detachment and indifference. I feel like I am dying for a while.

In the third situation, as I draw conclusions about things in general, I pull away from the immediacy of my feelings enough to think, instead of sitting and staring, but not enough to grasp the relative place of my feelings. So I absolutize them for a while with mementos of thought writ on marble, little tombstones of reflection.

When I feel close to the loneliness of other people, I discover the relation, the commonness of us all, in the experience of dissociation. I find a basis for hope for relation in my sense of deathliness, my experience of too little meaning for life. In this case, caring for others in our common pain is a dominant way of finding release from the sense of meaninglessness.

In the final instance, when I wait with my sense of emptiness, I attempt to discover who and how I want to be, allowing my loneliness and meaninglessness to be, grieving if need be, hoping for an option, a direction, that I can make mine, being prepared to choose a way for living, but being open now in the absence of something to choose.

In these observations, I have made the experience of meaningful direction a counter pole to the experience of meaninglessness. I have said in effect that the experience of deep loneliness and dissociation is natural, a common kind of happening, and that it is one of our contacts with our contingency and deathliness. I have also said that human living is experienced, as we say, as *really* living according to the directions with which we identify ourselves. Those directions have to be appropriated, chosen in some sense of the word. If we choose them with intensity and if we live out our directions of choice with vigor, we live intensely.

Being overcome by a sense of meaninglessness is an experience of dying—a common experience. As our meanings die away, as they lose their directional force, we experience an absence, sometimes for a moment, sometimes for extended periods, and such an experience is an experience of dying. By *dwelling* with that experience—by *letting it be,* by hearing my own being in the passing away of directions of meaning, I live that *openness,* that *region for hearing,* where *birth* of direction can occur. Letting the experience of meaninglessness happen, but not falling prey to it, just letting it occur, is a painful experience of openness for the future. That is an experience of contingency, of deathliness, which is also *freedom* for possibility, for growth, as well as freedom for death, or for absence.

Meaning and Openness in Human Existence

The *experience* of dying points out that human existence is an experiential process. Our existence does not happen like an object of investigation happens. It happens as a conscious occurrence, as an event of meanings that is alert and subject to pain and fulfillment. When we forget our human reality, we may treat ourselves as mere objects and assume that *dying* refers to no more than physical processes.

Three ordinary occurrences on ward rounds follow:

1. A young man eighteen years old, in the final stages of leukemia. It has come on quickly. His body is still strong and developed. His black skin glistens as the light plays off his sweat. Very low white count. His feet twitch. Danger of dehydration. The attending calls for an I.V. His eyes widen. "Am I goin' a die, Doctor? I don't wan' a die! God, I don't wan' a die!"

2. Eighty years old. Fever of unknown origin. Chronic diarrhea. Now unable to keep food on his stomach. So sunken into his bed that he hardly looks present. Skeletal head. Cheeks sink into his toothless

mouth. A wisp of white hair standing straight up on his otherwise bald pate. Small, wizened, staring at the wall. His wife, white headed, healthy, worried, tired, stands by his bed.

Dr. How is he today, Mrs. R.?

Mrs. R. Oh, he's no good doctor. Nothing we do works. He vomits everything up.

Dr. How's his bowels?

Mrs. R. He had two little dabs, but they was bloody lookin'.

Dr. (after a pause, with a sympathetic and worried look) What are we going to do with him, Mrs. R.?

Mrs. R. All we can do is keep on loving him I reckon, doctor.

3. Thirty-five year old mother of three. Final days. Her fair skin splotched from a body-covering rash that drove her wild with itching for days. Fever, 105°. As the nurse applies the cold washrag, she yields to the movement of the rag, a quick, almost defiant, yet fully cooperative movement. Her eyes, like a flogged animal's eyes, show anger, pain, deep hurt, quiet determination. She lies on her back. Her arms are on the pillow by her head, so that her armpits can be swabbed. But she looks like she has been strapped down and is undergoing, without crying out, some torture.

Dr. Well, J., how are you today?

J. (looks at him long and slow, fully alert. Her eyes tell of no comprehension of her disease, of a life of yielding to forces greater than she.) O.K., I guess.

Dr. I don't know what to do with you next, J. Every time we put you on something you break out like this. Every time we take you off, you don't have enough resistance to fight whatever germs come along. I don't know what to do. (after a long pause) Do you ever wonder why this happens, J.?

J. No, I don't. Maybe it's because I'm a very bad person.

Dr. I don't think that's the reason. I don't think that you are a bad person.

J. Well . . . why then?

Dr. Did you ever hear the hymn that begins, "Courage, brother, do not stumble, though thy path be dark as night."

J. No. I never heard that. (She turns away. The doctor is dismissed.)

I note these three occurrences, which are non-fictional and which are quite ordinary, in order to recall in a focused way the fact that human illness and even the physical process of dying are events of meaning which cannot be understood by physical descriptions only. Fear, desire, etc. are all events of meaning, just as suffering is too. We surely die of physical causes. But dying is itself, in its human reality, a process of meaning that is communicated in words, gestures, eyes, attitudes, and silences. Relation with a person who is dying with some physical malady is never merely a clinical matter. It is a *relation*, an occurrence of meaning, and one possible way to relate is to be clinical about the whole thing: to relate to the person as though he/she were primarily a sick body-object. Relation with the sick, like any relation, is an occurrence of meaning in which the health professional's own relation to himself as well as how he relates with the other person are a central part of the medical situation. To ignore the relationship is to dehumanize, to sicken the situation, even when physical healing is going on. To relate as though the healer's task is primarily with a body-object is to live a deep and dangerous ignorance of human being.

I state the point so starkly in order to underscore that our concern must be with *how* one lives his/her sickness and final days or hours. The *how* is where *human* dying occurs. In order to place this emphasis accurately, we must attend to our existence as a finite, self-aware event of meaning. Short of that point of attention, we very likely will think of dying as something that an inarticulate system of organs undergoes. The person can seem almost extra, vaguely in the way, when our intuitions are centered on such a physical system.

If we are persuaded that human existence is a meaningful event, we are prepared to see that *how* we experience dying will be the fundamental structure for how we approach our death. Our death occurs for us as something final, something we cannot live through. Regardless of our beliefs about immortality, death itself, in *its* time, usually means *loss* of life, *loss* of everything familiar, the most radical transition. It means an eradication of our experience of meaning, a radical separation from all that we value, a loss of direction, an emptying out and giving up.

If I have feared the inevitability of loss, i.e., the transitoriness of my existence, I shall find the specific prospect of death particularly fearful. If I have maximized control in order to turn away from my sense of the uncontrollableness of my being, I shall probably try to control every-thing up to my death and maybe my funeral as well. If frenzy has ac-companied my experience of the loss of meaning, how I shall approach my death is reasonably certain. And if I have been free for loss, for un-controlled openness, for the absence of direction, and so forth, I shall most likely be free for my fear of my death or for my desire for my death. And I shall probably be free also for my death. My experience of dying has already let me know that death, the final loss of my earthly life, is not outside my life, but a culmination for my life.

The living relation between living and dying is discovered by atten-tion to how human existence is intrinsically a process of transition and how it involves both meaningful relations and lapses of meaning. That living relation is experienced as a kind of openness: no moment in life is final, each moment opens out into another moment and is left be-hind. Our meanings and values structure our openness and closedness with things. And this very openness of human being, which we find in a radical way when we experience lapses of meaning and losses of aspects of our own existence, is the way we encounter our mortality, our deathliness. When we are open to our experiences of dying, we are open to our own deathliness. We are then prepared for that most important insight of self-awareness: that we are never finally objects of control or even controlling subjects. We, in our deathliness, are not defined finally by how we control ourselves or by how we are con-trolled by others. And when we do not resist our experiences of dying, we are attuned to our uncontrolled openness for the world. That is at once most threatening, if we have made control central for our lives' meaning, and also most freeing if we have felt the misery of believing that our lives depended on our control of most nearly everything.

So we may say that human living is how we relate meaningfully with ourselves and with other people and things. Human existence is a self-aware, meaning-structured process. This process is character-ized by profound self-alteration and by lapses of meaning. Dying is apparent in these experiences. We discover, when we do not resist the experiences of dying, that *control* can never be a *finally* appropriate relation with ourselves and with others. Release to our own non-ob-jectivity is the experience of being free for our dying. In that freedom, the end of our lives may appear as both a threat to our meanings and as the fulfillment of our finiteness. We become free for our existence when we do not have to hide from what we dread.

The Difference between Being and Having

Gabriel Marcel has developed the difference between having some-thing at one's disposal and being undisposable. *Having* is an experi-ence of keeping, holding, legally owning, using, and so forth. My yard, my house, my profession. But my child? My life? We certainly speak of having children, parents, lovers, and lives. Our language leads us astray in such instances to the extent that we come to think of lives and children (and patients, too) as things defined by how we dispose of them.

We know by common sense that everything we own exceeds our ownership. There is a sense, certainly, in which I have a profession. I choose it. I develop it in certain ways. I use it for certain goals. But there is also a sense in which my profession has me. I am molded by it. It fits me into a history and a future that are not under my control. My yard and my instruments also exceed me. Although I own them, they never fall fully under my possession. They have an independence that is fundamentally different from *my* ownership. I see this indepen-dence particularly when my yard will not grow what I want it to grow or when it makes me work for it. And when my instruments break or will not do what I want them to, I know that there is a sense in which I shall never own them.

When we view things in relation to being able to dispose and not being able to dispose, we find ourselves dealing with two dimensions of reality: our dimension is defined by its availability to us (e.g. we can use this hammer on that person for our own purposes); another dimension is outside of our grasp (e.g. the hammer and the person are not totally defined by our use of them). When we deal with caring and with dying, we are concerned by the unpossessable, i.e., the non-disposable dimension of human reality.

That dimension of reality which never is the same as my relation to it, that excessiveness of my intentions, is mysterious, as Marcel de-scribes it. A mystery, by definition, can never fall into a conceptual scheme. It is not the same as my thinking of it or my intuitions regarding it, or my uses of it. Mystery is what is present as never fit-ting my categories and as never the same as the reality of my thinking and willing processes.

Marcel gives the non-possessable, i.e., the mysterious, the name of *being*. Being cannot be had. It never happens as an object. It is what is independent of whatever I might do regarding it. And our own being is, of course, a non-possessable reality. Our being, our living reality, lives and dies.

That means that to *be* ourselves is a matter of living out the immediacy of whatever we might be *in*—desire, pain, ambition, love, awe, hatred, whatever. Being ourselves human, not being only objects to ourselves, not trying to possess our futures, even when we are planning. It means being open with our aims, not trying to keep who we are. Releasing ourselves as we run ahead toward whatever we have chosen to seek or toward whatever lies ahead unchosen. Being released is being free for our unpossessableness, even when we are tied into a work-a-day world that makes us live by a clock.

And the unpossessable other? Not an object. A being. Encounterable, but not possessable. Not kept. But known. He is to be helped, served, perhaps, when we are healers. But he is not to be treated primarily as an object, not as a sick thing, but as someone living and dying. As a mystery.

Ted Rosenthal wrote *How Could I Not Be Among You* during his terminal illness. He discovered that the meaning of death is to be found in openness in living:

I stand before you all aching with truth
Trembling with desire to make you know.
Eat, sleep, and be simple about life.
To be serious is to be simple;
to be simple is to love.
Don't wait another minute, make tracks, go home.
Admit you have some place to return to.
The bugs are crawling over the earth, the sun is shining over everyone.
Get tickled by the tall cattails.
Kick crazily into the burrs and prickles
Rub your back against the bark, and go ahead, peel it.
Adore the sun.
O people, you are dying. Live while you can.

Openness for living, which means a deep willingness to live through transitions, losses, lapses of meanings, not to forget our mortality, but to live it out with full awareness, this living while we can, impresses me as an opposite of the desire to possess. I am certain that I seek to possess parts of my own life and of the lives of people around me. I often want things to be exact and predictable. Such a desire is often appropriate, but not as a controlling attitude toward myself and other people. I suspect that many people in health professions also attempt, unwittingly, to possess and control the lives of "their" patients. I recall one of so many examples: a physician telling a woman that she would either do what he told her to do or she would have to find another doctor. On the one hand, this person was deeply frustrated by "his" patient's resistances. On the other hand, he felt that he needed to be in total control in order to work his healing techniques. (He had not yet learned the art of healing.) The total control factor is witness to a kind of possessive rigidity, a closure to the frustrating, often maddening non-objectivity of other people and of ourselves. It is also closure to whatever does not fit the grasp of our demands.

When we teach or heal or administer without giving dominance to possessing—when we live at ease with the non-objective mystery of being, to use Marcel's language, we find ourselves free for dying. That freedom creates attitudes toward death which are revolutionary in possession-dominated situations, but which never confuse human life and death with facts or objects. We find in this quiet freedom for dying the feelings and values which will not allow us to oppress life in the name of healing or to deny dying in the name of living.

Ending

I have pointed out that dying is a part of living, as distinct to death, which is the end of living. Some of our experiences of dying occur when relations and aspects of our lives change and when we undergo loss of meaning. How we relate to such transitions and losses reflects to us how we are related to our death. When denial is dominant in our self-relation, for example, denial of the other person in his mortality is highly likely. I have stated further that openness to the inevitability of transition and loss is at the same time openness to birth and regeneration, that we are closed to our mortality at the expense of closure to significant dimensions of possibility of creation. And finally I have suggested that the delivery of health care will reflect the dominance of openness or of possessiveness in our attitudes, that good health care (the art of the healing use of certain techniques) is dependent on our own release to our own mortality. That release will suggest to us that how we die is as important as whether we die. In medical practice the lives of the professional and the patient are always equally in question.

If our thinking about death and dying is "right," we shall be more open to our own dying, and that of other people, and we shall be attuned to our uncertainty, which we recognize as inevitable, concerning the meaning of death and dying. We allow that uncertainty because the "place" of meaning, the context of meaning, itself changes, and thereby all meanings shift as constantly and as inevitably as the sea, without rest and without a final justification. In thinking this inevitability, in accepting uncertainty in our self-image and in our view of our work and our relations with others, we come to a strange peace with death: we may fear it, but we do not need to reject it; we turn toward it as we accept our lives in their mortality; we find freedom for living as we accept the inevitability of dying. And accepting that strange inevitability, we find an attunement with dying and living people which allows us to be free, non-protective, life-affirming, and conversant with our own anxieties in their presence and in their service as healers.

A. ALVAREZ

Can Suicide Tell Us
Something About Living?

That numbness—beyond hope, despair, terror and, certainly, beyond heroics—is, I think, the final quantum to which all the modish forms of twentieth-century alienation are reduced. Under the energy, appetite, and constant diversity of the modern arts is this obdurate core of blankness and insentience which no amount of creative optimism and effort can wholly break down or remove. It is like, for a believer, the final unbudgeable illumination that God is not good. A psychiatrist, Robert Jay Lifton, has defined it, in more contemporary terms, as that "psychic numbing" which occurs in an overwhelming encounter with death. That is, when death is everywhere and on such a vast scale that it becomes indifferent, impersonal, inevitable and, finally, without meaning, the only way to survive, however briefly, is by shutting oneself off utterly from every feeling, so that one becomes invulnerable, not like an armored animal but like a stone. . . .

In other words, that sense of chaos which, I suggested, is the driving force behind the restless experimentalism of the twentieth-century arts has two sources: one developing directly from the period before 1914, the other emerging for the first time during World War I and growing increasingly stronger and more unavoidable as the century has gone on. Both, perhaps, are consequences of industrialism: the first is connected with the destruction of the old social relationships and the related structures of belief during the industrial revolution; the second is produced by the technology itself, which, in the process of creating the wherewithal to make life easier than ever before, has perfected, as a kind of lunatic spin-off, instruments to destroy life completely. More simply, just as the decay of religious authority in the nineteenth century made life seem absurd by depriving it of any ultimate coherence, so the growth of modern technology has made death itself absurd by reducing it to a random happening totally unconnected with the inner rhythms and logic of the lives destroyed.

This, then, is the Savage God whom Yeats foresaw and whose intolerable, demanding presence Wilfred Owen sensed at the front. . . .

There are, of course, other, more obvious pressures, some of which I have already touched on: the collapse of traditional values, impatience with worn-out conventions, the minor pleasures of iconoclasm and experiment for their own sakes. There is also the impact of what Marshall McLuhan calls the "electronic culture," which has so effortlessly usurped both the audience and many of the functions of the "formal" highbrow arts. But beyond all these, and becoming continually more insistent as the atrocities have grown in size and frequency, has been the absolute need to find an artistic language with which to grasp in the imagination the historical facts of this century; a language, that is, for "the destructive element," the dimension of unnatural, premature death.

Inevitably, it is the language of mourning. Or rather, the arts take on the function of mourning, breaking down that "psychic numbness" which follows any massive immersion in death. "The books we need," wrote Kafka in a letter to his friend Oscar Pollack, "are the kind that act upon us like a misfortune, that make us suffer like the death of someone we love more than ourselves, that make us feel as though we were on the verge of suicide, or lost in a forest remote from all human habitation—a book should serve as the axe for the frozen sea within us."

Clearly, books of this order will not be written simply by invoking the atrocities—a gesture which usually guarantees nothing but rhetoric and the cheapening of all those millions of deaths. What is required is something a good deal more difficult and individual: the creative act itself, which gives shape, coherence and some kind of gratuitous beauty to all those vague depressions and paranoias which art is heir to. Freud responded to World War I by positing a death instinct beyond the pleasure principle; for the artist, the problem is to create a language which is both beyond the pleasure principle and at the same time pleasurable.

This ultimately is the pressure forcing the artist into the role of scapegoat. In order to evolve a language of mourning which will release all those backed-up guilts and obscure hostilities he shares with his audience, he puts himself at risk and explores his own vulnerability. It is as though he were testing out his own death in his imagination—symbolically, tentatively and with every escape hatch open. "Suicide," said Camus, "is prepared within the silence of the heart, as is a great work of art." Increasingly, the corollary also seems to be true: under certain conditions of stress, a great work of art *is* a kind of suicide. . . .

After all this, I have to admit that I am a failed suicide. It is a dismal confession to make, since nothing, really, would seem to be easier than to take your own life. Seneca, the final authority on the subject, pointed out disdainfully that the exits are everywhere: each precipice and river, each branch of each tree, every vein in your body will set you free. But in the event, this isn't so. No one is promiscuous in his way of dying. A man who has decided to hang himself will never jump in front of a train. And the more sophisticated and painless the method, the greater the chance of failure. I can vouch, at least, for that. I built up to the act carefully and for a long time, with a kind of blank pertinacity. It was the one constant focus of my life, making everything else irrelevant, a diversion. Each sporadic burst of work, each minor success and disappointment, each moment of calm and relaxation, seemed merely a temporary halt on my steady descent through layer after layer of depression, like an elevator stopping for a moment on the way down to the basement. At no point was there any question of getting off or of changing the direction of the journey. Yet, despite all that, I never quite made it.

I see now that I had been incubating this death far longer than I recognized at the time. When I was a child, both my parents had half-heartedly put their heads in the gas oven. Or so they claimed. It seemed to me then a rather splendid gesture, though shrouded in mystery, a little area of veiled intensity, revealed only by hints and unexplained, swiftly suppressed outbursts. It was something hidden, attractive and not for the children, like sex. But it was also something that undoubtedly did happen to grownups. However hysterical or comic the behavior involved—and to a child it seemed more ludicrous than tragic to place your head in the greasy gas oven, like the Sunday roast joint—suicide was a fact, a subject that couldn't be denied; it was something, however awful, that people did. When my own time came, I did not have to discover it for myself.

Maybe that is why, when I grew up and things went particularly badly, I used to say to myself, over and over, like some latter-day Mariana in the moated grange, "I wish I were dead." It was an echo from the past, joining me to my tempestuous childhood. I muttered it unthinkingly, as automatically as a Catholic priest tells his rosary. It was my special magic ritual for warding off devils, a verbal nervous tic. Dwight Macdonald once said that when you don't know what to do with your hands you light a cigarette, and when you don't know what to do with your mind you read *Time* magazine. My equivalent was this one sentence repeated until it seemingly lost all meaning: "Iwishiweredead . . . Iwishiweredead . . . Iwishiweredead. . . ." Then one day I understood what I was saying. I was walking along the edge of Hampstead Heath, after some standard domestic squabble, and suddenly I heard the phrase as though for the first time. I stood still to attend to the words. I repeated them slowly, listening. And realized that I meant it. It seemed so obvious, an answer I had known for years and never allowed myself to acknowledge. I couldn't understand how I could have been so obtuse for so long.

After that, there was only one way out, although it took a long time—many months, in fact—to get there. We moved to America—wife, child, *au pair* girl, myself and trunk-upon-trunk-load of luggage. I had a term's appointment at a New England university and had rented a great professional mansion in a respectably dead suburb, ten miles from the campus, two from the nearest shop. The house was Germanic, gloomy and far too expensive. For my wife, who didn't drive, it was also as lonely as Siberia. The neighbors were mostly twice her age, the university mostly ignored us, the action was nil. There wasn't even a television set in the house. So I rented one and she sat disconsolately in front of it for two months. Then she gave up, packed her bags, and took the child back to England. I didn't even blame her. But I stayed on in a daze of misery. The last slide down the ice slope had begun and there was no way of stopping it.

My wife was not to blame. The hostility and despair that poor girl provoked in me—and I in her—came from some pure, infantile source, as any disinterested outsider could have told me. I even recognized this for myself in my clear moments. I was using her as an excuse for

troubles that had their roots deep in the past. But mere intellectual recognition did no good, and anyway, my clear moments were few. My
life felt so cluttered and obstructed that I could hardly breathe. I inhabited a closed, concentrated world, airless and without exits. I doubt if
any of this was noticeable socially: I was simply more tense, more nervous than usual, and I drank more. But underneath I was going a bit
mad. I had entered the closed world of suicide, and my life was being
lived for me by forces I couldn't control.

When the Christmas break came at the university, I decided to
spend the fortnight in London. Maybe, I told myself, things would be
easier, at least I would see the child. So I loaded myself up with
presents and climbed on a jet, dead drunk. I passed out as soon as I
reached my seat and woke to a brilliant sunrise. There were dark
islands below—the Hebrides, I suppose—and the eastern sea was on
fire. From that altitude, the world looked calm and vivid and possible.
But by the time we landed at Prestwick the clouds were down like the
black cap on a hanging judge. We waited and waited hopelessly on
the runway, the rain drumming on the fuselage, until the soaking fog
lifted at London Airport.

When I finally got home, hours late, no one was there. The fires
were blazing, the clocks were ticking, the telephone was still. I wandered around the empty house touching things, frightened, expectant.
Fifteen minutes later, there was a noise at the front door and my child
plunged shouting up the stairs into my arms. Over his shoulder I
could see my wife standing tentatively in the hall. She, too, looked
scared.

"We thought you were lost," she said. "We went down to the terminal and you didn't come."

"I got a lift straight from the airport. I phoned but you must have
left. I'm sorry."

Chilly and uncertain, she presented her cheek to be kissed. I obliged, holding my son in my arms. There was still a week until Christmas.

We didn't stand a chance. Within hours we were at each other
again, and that night I started drinking. Mostly, I'm a social drinker.
Like everyone else, I've been drunk in my time but it's not really my
style; I value my control too highly. This time, however, I went at the
bottle with a pure need, as though parched. I drank before I got out of
bed, almost before my eyes were open. I continued steadily through-

out the morning until, by lunchtime, I had half a bottle of whiskey inside me and was beginning to feel human. Not drunk: that first half-bottle simply brought me to that point of calm where I usually begin. Which is not particularly calm. Around lunchtime a friend—also depressed, also drinking—joined me at the pub and we boozed until closing time. Back home, with our wives, we kept at it steadily through the afternoon and evening, late into the night. The important thing was not to stop. In this way, I got through a bottle of whiskey a day, and a good deal of wine and beer. Yet it had little effect. Toward evening when the child was in bed, I suppose I was a little tipsy, but the drinking was merely part of a more jagged frenzy which possessed us all. We kept the hi-fi booming pop, we danced, we had trials of strength: one-arm push-ups, handstands, somersaults; we balanced pint pots of beer on our foreheads, and tried to lie down and stand up again without spilling them. Anything not to stop, think, feel. The tension was so great that without the booze, we would have splintered into sharp fragments.

On Christmas Eve, the other couple went off on a skiing holiday. My wife and I were left staring at each other. Silently and meticulously, we decorated the Christmas tree and piled the presents, waiting. There was nothing left to say.

Late that afternoon I had sneaked off and phoned the psychotherapist whom I had been seeing, on and off, before I left for the States.

"I'm feeling pretty bad," I said. "Could I possibly see you?"

There was a pause. "It's rather difficult," he said at last. "Are you really desperate, or could you wait till Boxing Day?"

Poor bastard, I thought, he's got his Christmas too. Let it go. "I can wait."

"Are you sure?" He sounded relieved. "You could come round at six-thirty, if it's urgent."

That was the child's bedtime; I wanted to be there. "It's all right," I said, "I'll phone later. Happy Christmas." What did it matter? I went back downstairs.

All my life I have hated Christmas: the unnecessary presents and obligatory cheerfulness, the grinding expense, the anticlimax. It is a day to be negotiated with infinite care, like a minefield. So I fortified myself with a stiff shot of whiskey before I got up. It combined with my child's excitement to put a glow of hope on the day. The boy sat among the gaudy wrapping paper, ribbons and bows, positively crowing with delight. At three years old, Christmas can still be a pleasure. Maybe, I began to feel, this thing could be survived. After all, hadn't I flown all the way from the States to pull my marriage from the fire? Or had I? Perhaps I knew it was unsavable and didn't want it to be otherwise. Perhaps I was merely seeking a plausible excuse for doing myself in. Perhaps that was why, even before all the presents were unwrapped, I had started it all up again: silent rages (not in front of the child), muted recriminations, withdrawals. The marriage was just one aspect of a whole life I had decided, months before, to have done with.

I remember little of what happened later. There was the usual family turkey for the child and my parents-in-law. In the evening we went out to a smart, subdued dinner party, and on from there, I think, to something wilder. But I'm not sure. I recall only two trivial but vivid scenes. The first is very late at night. We are back home with another couple whom I know only slightly. He is small, dapper, cheerful, an unsuccessful poet turned successful journalist. His wife is faceless now, but him I still see sometimes on television, reporting expertly from the more elegant foreign capitals. I remember him sitting at our old piano, playing 1930s dance tunes; his wife stands behind him, singing the words; I lean on the piano, humming tunelessly; my wife is stretched, glowering, on the sofa. We are all very drunk.

Later still, I remember standing at the front door, joking with them as they negotiate the icy steps. As they go through the gate, they turn and wave. "Happy Christmas," we call to each other. I close the door and turn back to my wife.

After that, I remember nothing at all until I woke up in the hospital and saw my wife's face swimming vaguely toward me through a yellowish fog. She was crying. But that was three days later, three days of oblivion, a hole in my head.

It happened ten years ago now, and only gradually have I been able to piece together the facts from hints and snippets, recalled reluctantly and with apologies. Nobody wants to remind an attempted suicide of his folly, or to be reminded of it. Tact and taste forbid. Or is it the failure itself which is embarrassing? Certainly, a successful suicide inspires no delicacy at all; everybody is in on the act at once with his own exclusive inside story. In my own case, my knowledge of what happened is partial and second-hand; the only accurate details are in the gloomy shorthand of the medical reports. Not that it matters, since none of it now means much to me personally. It is as though it had all happened to another person in another world.

It seems that when the poet-journalist left with his wife, we had one final, terrible quarrel, more bitter than anything we had managed before, and savage enough to be heard through his sleep by whoever it was who was staying the night in the guest room above. At the end of it, my wife marched out. When she had returned prematurely from the States, our own house was still leased to temporary tenants. So she had rented a dingy flat in a florid and battered Victorian mansion nearby. Since she still had the key to the place, she went to spend the night there. In my sodden despair, I suppose her departure seemed like the final nail. More likely, it was the unequivocal excuse I had been waiting for. I went upstairs to the bathroom and swallowed forty-five sleeping pills.

I had been collecting the things for months obsessionally, like Green Stamps, from doctors on both sides of the Atlantic. This was an almost legitimate activity, since in all that time I rarely got more than two consecutive hours of sleep a night. But I had always made sure of having more than I needed. Weeks before I left America, I had stopped taking the things and begun hoarding them in preparation for the time I knew was coming. When it finally arrived, a box was waiting stuffed with pills of all colors, like jellybeans. I gobbled the lot.

The following morning the guest brought me a cup of tea. The bedroom curtains were drawn, so he could not see me properly in the gloom. He heard me breathing in an odd way but thought it was probably a hangover. So he left me alone. My wife got back at noon, took one look and called the ambulance. When they got me to hospital I was, the report says, "deeply unconscious, slightly cyanosed, vomit in mouth, pulse rapid, poor volume." I looked up "cyanosis" in the dictionary: "A morbid condition in which the surface of the body becomes blue because of insufficient aeration of the blood." Apparently I had vomited in my coma and swallowed the stuff; it was now blocking my right lung, turning my face blue. As they say, a morbid condition. When they pumped the barbiturates out of my stomach, I vomited again, much more heavily, and again the muck went down to my lungs, blocking them badly. At that point I became—that word again—"deeply cyanosed"; I turned Tory-blue. They tried to suck the stuff out, and gave me oxygen and an injection, but neither had much effect. I suppose it was about this time that they told my wife there wasn't much hope. This was all she ever told me of the whole incident; it was a source of great bitterness to her. Since my lungs were still blocked, they performed a bronchoscopy. This time they sucked out a "large amount of mucus." They stuck an air pipe down my throat and I began to breathe more normally. The crisis, for the moment, was over.

This was on Boxing Day, December 26. I was still unconscious the next day and most of the day after that, though all the time less and less deeply. Since my lungs remained obstructed, they continued to give me air through a pipe; they fed me intravenously through a drip tube. The shallower my coma, the more restless I became. On the evening of the second day the airway was removed. During the afternoon of the third day, December 28, I came to. I felt them pull a tube from my arm. In a fog I saw my wife smiling hesitantly, and in tears. It was all very vague. I slept.

I spent most of the next day weeping quietly and seeing everything double. Two women doctors gently cross-questioned me. Two chunky physiotherapists, with beautiful, blooming, double complexions, put me through exercises—it seems my lungs were still in a bad state. I got two trays of uneatable food at a time and tried, on and off and unsuccessfully, to do two crossword puzzles. The ward was thronged with elderly twins.

At some point the police came, since in those days suicide was still a criminal offense. They sat heavily but rather sympathetically by my bed and asked me questions they clearly didn't want me to answer. When I tried to explain, they shushed me politely. "It was an accident, wasn't it, sir?" Dimly, I agreed. They went away.

I woke during the night and heard someone cry out weakly. A nurse bustled down the aisle in the obscure light. From the other side of the ward came more weak moaning. It was taken up faintly from somewhere else in the dimness. None of it was desperate with the pain and sharpness you hear after operations or accidents. Instead, the note was enervated, wan, beyond feeling. And then I understood why, even to my double vision, the patients had all seemed so old: I was in a terminal ward. All around me, old men were trying feebly not to die; I was thirty-one years old, and despite everything, still alive. When I stirred in bed I felt, for the first time, a rubber sheet beneath me. I must have peed myself, like a small child, while I was unconscious. My whole world was shamed.

The following morning my double vision had gone. The ward was filthy yellow and seemed foggy in the corners. I tottered to the lavatory; it, too, was filthy and evil-smelling. I tottered back to bed, rested a little and then phoned my wife. Since the pills and the booze hadn't killed me, nothing would. I told her I was coming home. I wasn't dead, so I wasn't going to die. There was no point in staying.

The doctors didn't see it that way. I was scarcely off the danger list; my lungs were in a bad state; I had a temperature; I could relapse at any time; it was dangerous; it was stupid; they would not be responsible. I lay there dumbly, as weak as a newborn infant, and let the arguments flow over me. Finally I signed a sheaf of forms acknowledging that I left against advice and absolving them from responsibility. A friend drove me home.

It took all my strength and concentration to climb the one flight of stairs to the bedroom. I felt fragile and almost transparent, as though I were made of tissue paper. But when I got into pajamas and settled into bed, I found I smelled bad to myself: of illness, urine and a thin, sour death-sweat. So I rested for a while and then took a bath. Meanwhile my wife, on orders from the hospital, phoned our National Health doctor. He listened to her explanation without a word and then refused, point-blank, to come. Clearly, he thought I was going to die and didn't want me added to his no doubt already prodigious score. She banged down the receiver on him in a rage, but my green face and utter debility frightened her. Someone had to be sent for. Finally the friend who had driven me home from the hospital called in his private family doctor. Authoritative, distinguished, unflappable, he came immediately and soothed everyone down.

This was on the evening of Thursday, the twenty-ninth. All Friday and Saturday I lay vaguely in bed. Occasionally I raised myself to perform the exercises which were supposed to help my lungs. I talked a little to my child, tried to read, dozed. But mostly I did nothing. My mind was blank. At times I listened to my breath coming and going; at times I was dimly aware of my heart beating. It filled me with distaste. I did not want to be alive.

On Friday night I had a terrible dream. I was dancing a savage, stamping dance with my wife, full of anger and mutual threat. Gradually the movements became more and more frenzied, until every nerve and muscle in my body was stretched taut and vibrating, as though on some fierce, ungoverned electrical machine which, fraction by fraction, was pulling me apart. When I woke I was wet with sweat, but my teeth were chattering as if I were freezing. I dozed off almost at once and again went through a similar dream: this time I was being hunted down; when the creature, whatever it was, caught me, it shook me as a dog shakes a rat, and once again every joint and nerve and muscle seemed to be rattling apart. At last I came awake completely and lay staring at the curtains. I was wide-eyed and shuddering with fear. I felt I had tasted in my dreams the death which had been denied me in my coma. My wife was sleeping in the same bed with me, yet she was utterly beyond my reach. I lay there for a long time, sweating and trembling. I have never felt so lonely.

Saturday night was New Year's Eve. Before I even arrived back from the States, we had arranged a party; there seemed no point now, despite everything, in calling it off. I had promised the doctor to spend it in bed, so for a while I held court regally in pajamas and dressing gown. But this was an irritating, self-important posture. Friends came upstairs to see me out of a sense of duty—they had been told I had had pneumonia. Obviously they were bored. The music and voices below were enticing, and anyway, I had nothing now to lose. At ten-thirty I got up, just to see in the New Year, I said. I got back to bed at six the following morning. At ten o'clock I was up again and went down to help clean the house while my wife slept on. The debris of that New Year's binge seemed to me like the debris of the monstrous life I had been leading. I set to work cheerfully and with a will, mopping up, polishing, throwing things away. At lunchtime, when my wife staggered down hung over, the house was sparkling.

A week later I returned to the States to finish the university term. While I was packing I found in the ticket pocket of my favorite jacket, a large, bright-yellow, torpedo-shaped pill, which I had conned off a heavily insomniac American the day I left. I stared at the thing, turning it over and over on my palm, wondering how I'd missed it on the night. It looked lethal. I had survived forty-five pills. Would forty-six have done it? I flushed the thing down the lavatory.

And that was that. Of course, my marriage was finished. We hung on a few months more for decency's sake, but neither of us could continue in the shadow of such blackmail. By the time we parted, there was nothing left. Inevitably, I went through the expected motions of distress. But in my heart, I no longer cared.

The truth is, in some way I *had* died. The over-intensity, the tiresome excess of sensitivity and self-consciousness, of arrogance and idealism, which came in adolescence and stayed on and on beyond their due time, like some visiting bore, had not survived the coma. It was as though I had finally, and sadly late in the day, lost my innocence. Like all young people, I had been high-minded and apologetic, full of enthusiasms I didn't quite mean and guilts I didn't understand. Because of them, I had forced my poor wife, who was far too young to know what was happening, into a spoiling, destructive role she had never sought. We had spent five years thrashing around in confusion, as drowning men pull each other under. Then I had lain for three days in abeyance, and awakened to feel nothing but a faint revulsion at everything and everyone. My weakened body, my thin breath, the slightest flicker of emotion filled me with distaste. I wanted only to be left to myself. Then, as the months passed, I began gradually to stir into another style of life, less theoretical, less optimistic, less vulnerable. I was ready for an insentient middle age.

Above all, I was disappointed. Somehow, I felt, death had let me down; I had expected more of it. I had looked for something overwhelming, an experience which would clarify all my confusions. But it turned out to be simply a denial of experience. All I knew of death were the terrifying dreams which came later. Blame it, perhaps, on my delayed adolescence: adolescents always expect too much; they want solutions to be immediate and neat, instead of gradual and incomplete. Or blame it on the cinema: secretly, I had thought death would be like the last reel of one of those old Hitchcock thrillers, when the hero relives as an adult that traumatic moment in childhood when the horror and splitting off took place; and thereby becomes free and at peace with himself. It is a well-established, much-imitated and persuasive formula. Hitchcock does it best, but he himself did not invent it; he was simply popularizing a new tradition of half-digested psychoanalytic talk about "abreaction," that crucial moment of cathartic truth when the complex is removed. Behind that is the old belief in last-moment revelations, deathbed conversions, and all those old wives' tales of the drowning man reliving his life as he goes down for the last time. Behind that again is an older tradition still: that of the Last Judgment and the afterlife. We all expect something of death, even if it's only damnation.

But all I had got was oblivion. To all intents and purposes, I had died: my face was blue, my pulse erratic, my breathing ineffectual; the doctors gave me up. I had gone to the edge and most of the way over; then gradually, unwillingly and despite everything, I inched my way back. And now I knew nothing at all about it. I felt cheated.

Why had I been so sure of finding some kind of answer? There are always special reasons why a man should choose to die in one way rather than in another, and my own reasons for taking barbiturates were cogent enough, although I did not understand them at the time. As a small baby, I had been given a general anaesthetic when a major operation was performed on my ankle. The surgery had not been a great success and regularly throughout my childhood the thing gave me trouble. Always the attacks were heralded by the same dream: I had to work out a complicated mathematical problem which involved my whole family; their well-being depended on my finding the right answer. The sum changed as I grew, becoming more sophisticated as I learned more mathematics, always keeping one step ahead of me, like the carrot and the donkey. Yet I knew that however complex the problem, the answer would be simple. It merely eluded me. Then, when I was fourteen, my appendix was removed and I was once again put under a general anaesthetic. The dream, by then, had not recurred for a year or two. But as I began to breathe in the ether, the whole thing happened again. When the first sharp draft of gas entered my lungs, I saw the problem, this time in calculus, glowing like a neon sign, with all my family crowding around, dangling, as it were, from the terms. I breathed out and then, as I drew in the next lungful of ether, the figures whirred like the circuits of a computer, the stages of equation raced in front of me, and I had the answer: a simple two-figure number. I had known it all along. For three days after I came around, I still knew that simple solution, and why and how it was so. I didn't have a care in the world. Then gradually it faded. But the dream never returned.

I thought death would be like that: a synoptic vision of life, crisis by crisis, all suddenly explained, justified, redeemed, a Last Judgment in the coils and circuits of the brain. Instead, all I got was a hole in the head, a round zero, nothing. I'd been swindled.

Months later I began to understand that I had had my answer, after all. The despair that had led me to try to kill myself had been pure and unadulterated, like the final, unanswerable despair a child feels, with no before or after. And childishly, I had expected death not merely to end it but also to explain it. Then, when death let me down, I gradually saw that I had been using the wrong language; I had translated the thing into Americanese. Too many movies, too many novels, too many trips to the States had switched my understanding into a hopeful, alien tongue. I no longer thought of myself as unhappy; instead, I had "problems." Which is an optimistic way of putting it, since problems imply solutions, whereas unhappiness is merely a condition of life which you must live with, like the weather. Once I had accepted that there weren't ever going to be any answers, even in death, I found to my surprise that I didn't much care whether I was happy or unhappy; "problems" and "the problem of problems" no longer existed. And that in itself is already the beginning of happiness.

It seems ludicrous now to have learned something so obvious in such a hard way, to have had to go almost the whole way into death in order to grow up. Somewhere, I still feel cheated and aggrieved, and also ashamed of my stupidity. Yet, in the end, even oblivion was an experience of a kind. Certainly, nothing has been quite the same since I discovered for myself, in my own body and on my own nerves, that death is simply an end, a dead end, no more, no less. And I wonder if that piece of knowledge isn't in itself a form of death. After all, the youth who swallowed the sleeping pills and the man who survived are so utterly different that someone or something must have died. Before the pills was another life, another person altogether, whom I scarcely recognized and don't much like—although I suspect that he was, in his priggish way, far more likable than I could ever be. Meanwhile, his fury and despair seem improbable now, sad and oddly diminished.

The hole in my head lasted a long time. For five years after the event I had periods of sheer blankness, as though some vital center had been knocked out of action. For days on end, I went around like a zombie, a walking corpse. And I used to wonder, in a vague, numb way, if maybe I had died, after all. But if so, how could I ever tell?

In time, even that passed. Years later, when the house where it had happened was finally sold, I felt a sharp pang of regret for all the exorbitant pain and waste. After that, the episode lost its power. It became just so much dead history, a gossipy, mildly interesting anecdote about someone half forgotten. As Coriolanus said, "There is a world elsewhere."

As for suicide: the sociologists and psychologists who talk of it as a disease puzzle me now as much as the Catholics and Muslims who call it the most deadly of mortal sins. It seems to me to be somehow as much beyond social or psychic prophylaxis as it is beyond morality, a terrible but utterly natural reaction to the strained, narrow, unnatural necessities we sometimes create for ourselves. And it is not for me. Perhaps I am no longer optimistic enough. I assume now that death, when it finally comes, will probably be nastier than suicide, and certainly a great deal less convenient.

JAMES HILLMAN

Why Might a Person Want To Kill Him/Herself?

In order to get closer to the problem of suicide, we first try to understand the life of the individual whose death is involved. We begin with an individual, not with the concept. The individual's personality is, of course, partly conscious and partly unconscious, so that an enquiry into the unconscious aspects of the individual also becomes necessary. In fact, an enquiry which does not give full share to the inner mythology (as dreams, fantasies, apperceptional modes) of the suicidal individual will give an inadequate picture. All the reasons for suicide mentioned . . .—collective, emotional, intellectual—do not penetrate below the surface, do not get inside the death. Because suicide is a way of entering death and because the problem of entering death releases the most profound fantasies of the human soul, *to understand a suicide we need to know what mythic fantasy is being enacted.* Again, it is an analyst who is in the best position to gain this fuller understanding.

However, this has been contested. The opposition to psychological understanding of individual suicides comes not only from the "outside" position of sociology. (We have already seen the argument: it is useless to delve into the units which happen to make up the suicide quotient.) Opposition comes as well from the "inside." According to Sartre, the one person best able to understand a death is the person who is dead. This means that suicide is incomprehensible because the one person who might give an account no longer can. This is a false dilemma, and we must look more closely at the extreme inside position. We must see whether or not it is true that each individual is the only one who can understand and articulate his own life and death.

The articulate suicide, Socrates or Seneca, is rare. A man who understands his own myth, who is able to follow his pattern so clearly that he can sense the moment of his death and tell of it, is unusual in human history. These are the very few. Their awareness has turned them into legends. The ordinary man has little understanding of his actions, and *because death usually takes him by surprise, it seems to come from without.* Because we are so little connected to the death we carry within us, it seems to strike exogenously as an outer force. Always, what we are unconscious of in ourselves seems to come from without. We do our best to bring fragments of our actions to awareness, but we are more often lived by than live our myth. . . .

Being both "in" and "out" means that an analyst is in a better position to understand and to articulate the psychology of another person. He can follow the pattern because he is at once in it and observing it, while the other person is usually only in it and caught by it. *He is thus able to understand a suicide better than the one who commits it.* The person dead, contrary to Sartre, is not the one having a privileged access to his own death, because part of the meaning of this death was always unconscious to him. It could only have become conscious through the dialectical mirror, a process for which an analyst has been trained.

Where an analyst's understanding may have the effect of prevention, this understanding may not lead to explanation, or give information to others which may be useful in their search for causes and prevention. He understands by appreciating the condition of the soul at the time of death, but owing to the unique relationship his understanding and its articulation cannot be verified by proof. He is alone.

This isolated situation is the crux of viewing the problem from the soul and gives analysis its creatively lonely mission. Like the person whose suicide is not understood by the collective, or interpreted only in terms of conscious motives or alien systems of thought, an analyst's understanding of the suicide is also not understood by the collective. Understanding is not a collective phenomenon. Psychology still awaits the day when this understanding can be explained. Alone of the vocations dealing with human nature and the soul, analysis has no position other than the soul. There is no authority higher than the analysis itself, no medical, legal, or theological point of repair to outside positions which resist death and seek its prevention.

Rules for judging whether a suicide—or any event in analysis—is justified cannot be summarily stated. To do so would be to forsake the inside for the outside. It would mean we are no longer trying to understand the individual event in its uniqueness, but are looking at forms of behaviour, classes of acts. However, this emphasis upon understanding does not mean *tout comprendre, tout pardonner*. Understanding does not mean standing by in sympathetic non-directive acceptance no matter what happens. An analyst has his criteria for justification. These criteria are derived mainly from *an assessment of the conscious mind at the time of death in its relation to objective processes of the unconscious which form the archetypal substructure of behaviour*. Hence, analytical understanding requires knowledge of these objective psychic processes. The knowledge required in meeting the suicide risk is paradoxically about the great unknowable, death. This knowledge is not medical, legal, or theological, which consists anyway of abstractions. It is rather knowledge about the *experience* of death, the archetypal background of death as met in the soul, its meanings, images, and emotions, its import in psychic life, so that one can try to understand the experiences undergone during the suicidal crisis. An analyst makes judgments and tries to operate with an exactitude and an ethic as do other scientists. Nor does he differ from other scientists when he takes his criteria from only his own field. . . .

Death and existence may exclude each other in rational philosophy, but they *are not psychological contraries*. Death can be experienced as a state of being, an existential condition. The very old sometimes inform us of experiences of finding themselves in another world which is not only more real but from which they view this. In dreams and in psychosis one can go through the anguish of dying, or one is dead; one knows it and feels it. In visions, the dead return and report on themselves. Every analysis shows death experiences in all variety, and we shall turn to examples shortly. The experience of death cannot be forced into a logical definition of death. What gives Heidegger—that unpsychological man—his influence in psychotherapy is one crucial insight. He confirms Freud by placing death at the centre of existence. *And analysts cannot get on without a philosophy of death.*

But philosophers provide answers to questions no more than analysts, or rather they provide many sorts of answers by splitting questions open to reveal many seeds of meaning. An analyst turning towards philosophy will not get the same defined viewpoint towards death and suicide as he will from systems of religion, law, and science. The one answer he will get from philosophy is philosophy itself; for when we ask about death we have begun to practise philosophy, the study of dying. This kind of answer is also psychotherapy.

To philosophise is partly to enter death; philosophy is death's rehearsal, as Plato said. It is one of the forms of the death experience. It has been called "dying to the world." The first movement in working through any problem is taking the problem upon oneself as an experience. One enters an issue by joining it. One approaches death by dying. Approaching death requires a dying in soul, daily, as the body dies in tissue. And as the body's tissue is renewed, so is the soul regenerated through death experiences. Therefore, working at the death problem is both a dying from the world with its illusory sustaining hope that there is no death, not really, and a dying into life, as a fresh and vital concern with essentials.

Because living and dying in this sense imply each other, any act which holds off death prevents life. "How" to die means nothing less than "how" to live. Spinoza turned the Platonic maxim around saying (*Ethics* IV, 67) the philosopher thinks of nothing less than death, but this meditation is not of death but of life. Living in terms of life's only certain end means to live aimed towards death. This end is present here and now as the purpose of life, which means the moment of death—at any moment—is every moment. *Death cannot be put off to the future and reserved for old age.* By the time we are old we may no longer be able to experience death; then it may be merely to go through its outer motions. Or, it may have already been experienced, so that organic death has lost all sting. For organic death cannot undo the fundamental accomplishments of the soul. *Organic death has absolute power over life when death has not been allowed in life's midst.* When we refuse the experience of death we also refuse the essential question of life, and leave life unaccomplished. Then organic death prevents our facing the ultimate questions and cuts off our chance for redemption. To avoid this state of soul, traditionally called damnation, we are obliged to go to death before it comes to us.

Philosophy would tell us that we build towards death from day to day. We build each our own "ship of death" within ourselves. From this standpoint, by making our own deaths we are killing ourselves daily, so that each death is a suicide. Whether "from a lion, a precipice, or a fever," each death is of our own making. Then we need not beg with Rilke, "O Lord, give each man his own death," since just that God does give us, though we do not see it because we do not like it. When a man builds the structure of his life upwards like a building, climbing step by step, storey by storey, only to go out the high window or to be brought low by heart attack or stroke, has he not fulfilled his own architectural plan and been given his own death? In his view, suicide is no longer one of the ways of entering death, but *all death is suicide,* and the choice of method is only more or less evident, whether car-crash, heart-attack, or those acts usually called suicide.

By consciously going towards death, philosophy says we build the better vessel. Ideally, as we age, this building becomes more incorruptible, so that the passage to it from the failing flesh may be without fear, felicitous and easy. This death we build within us is that permanent structure, the "subtle body," in which the soul is housed amidst the decay of impermanence. But death is no easy matter; and dying is a rending business, ugly, cruel, and full of suffering. Going towards death consciously as philosophy proposes must therefore be a major human achievement, which is held up to us by the images of our religious and cultural heroes.

An analyst may do well to consider philosophy as a first step in his struggle with the suicide problem. Suicide can be for some an act of unconscious philosophy, an attempt to understand death by joining it. The impulse to death need not be conceived as an anti-life movement; it may be a demand for an encounter with absolute reality, *a demand for a fuller life through the death experience.*

Without dread, without the prejudices of prepared positions, without a pathological bias, suicide becomes "natural." It is natural because it is a possibility of our nature, a choice open to each human psyche. The analyst's concern is less with the suicidal choice as such, than it is with helping the other person to understand the meaning of this choice, *the only one which asks directly for the death experience.*

A main meaning of the choice is the importance of death for individuality. As individuality grows so does the possibility of suicide. Sociology and theology recognise this, as we have seen. Where man is law unto himself, responsible to himself for his own actions (as in the culture of cities, in the unloved child, in protestant areas, in creative people), the choice of death becomes a more frequent alternative. In this choice of death, of course, the opposite lies concealed. Until we can choose death, we cannot choose life. *Until we can say no to life, we have not really said yes to it,* but have only been carried along by its collective stream. The individual standing against this current experiences death as the first of all alternatives, for he who goes against the stream of life is its opponent and has become identified with death. Again, the death experience is needed to separate from the collective flow of life and to discover individuality.

Individuality requires courage. And courage has since classic times been linked with suicide arguments: it takes courage to choose the ordeal of life, and it takes courage to enter the unknown by one's own decision. Some choose life because they are afraid of death and others choose death because they are afraid of life. We cannot justly assess courage or cowardice from the outside. But we can understand why the problem of suicide raises these questions of courage, since the suicide issue forces one to find his individual stand on the basic question—to be or not to be. The courage to be—as it is modishly called—means not just choosing life out there. The real choice is choosing oneself, one's individual truth, including the ugliest man, as Nietzsche called the evil within. To continue life, knowing what a horror one is, takes indeed courage. And not a few suicides may arise from an overwhelming experience of one's own evil, an insight coming more readily to the creatively gifted, the psychologically sensitive, and the schizoid. Then who is the coward and who casts the first stone? The rest of us brutish men who go about dulled to our own shadows.

Each analysis comes upon death in one form or another. The dreamer dies in his dreams and there are deaths of other inner figures; relatives die; positions are lost never to be regained; deaths of attitudes; the death of love; experiences of loss and emptiness which are described as death; the sense of the presence of death and the terrible fear of dying. Some are "half in love with easeful death" for themselves or wish it for others, wanting to be killed or to kill. There is death in soaring sunwards like young Ikaros [Icarus], in climbing for power, in the arrogant ambitions of omnipotence fantasies, where in one stroke of hatred and rage all enemies vanish. Some seem driven to death; others are hounded by it; still others are drawn to it by a call from what can only be empirically described as "the other side," a longing for a dead lover, or parent, or child. Others may have had an acute mystical vision as an encounter with death which has haunted their lives, forming an un-understood experience towards which they yearn. For some, each separation is death, and parting is dying. There are those who feel cursed, certain their life is an ineluctable progress into doom, a chain of destiny, the last link called suicide. Some may have escaped death in a holocaust or war and not yet have inwardly escaped, and the anxiety is enacted again and again. Phobias, compulsions, and insomnia may reveal a core of death. Masturbation, solitary and against the call of love and, like suicide, called the "English disease," evokes fantasies of death. Death can impinge upon the moral "how" of the individual's life: the review of life, one's faith, sins, destiny; how one got to where one is and how to continue. Or, whether to continue.

To understand all these death patterns, analysis cannot turn anywhere but to the soul to see what it says about death. Analysis develops its ideas on death empirically from the soul itself. Again Jung has been the pioneer. He simply listened to the soul tell its experiences and watched the images of the goal of life which the living psyche produces out of itself. Here, he was neither philosopher, nor physician, nor theologian, but psychologist, student of the soul.

He discovered that death has many guises and that it does not usually appear in the psyche as death *per se*, as extinction, negation, and finality. Images of dying and ideas of death have quite other meanings in dreams and fantasies. The soul goes through many death experiences, yet physical life goes on; and as physical life comes to a close, the soul often produces images and experiences that show continuity. The process of consciousness seems to be endless. *For the psyche, neither is immortality a fact, nor is death an end.* We can neither prove nor disprove survival. The psyche leaves the question open.

Searching for proof and demonstration of immortality is muddled thinking, because proof and demonstration are categories of science and logic. The mind uses these categories and the mind is convinced by proof. That is why the mind can be replaced by machines and the soul not. Soul is not mind and has other categories for dealing with its problem of immortality. For the soul, the equivalents of proof and demonstration are belief and meaning. They are as difficult to develop and make clear, as hard to wrestle with, as is proof. The soul struggles with the after-life question in terms of its experiences. Out of these experiences, not out of dogma or logic or empirical evidence, the positions of faith are built. And the fact alone that the psyche has this faculty of belief, unaffected by proof or demonstration, presses us towards the possibility of psychic immortality. Psychic immortality means neither resurrection of the flesh nor personal after-life. The former refers to immortality of the body, the latter to immortality of the mind. Our concern is with immortality of the soul.

What might be the function of these categories of belief and meaning in the soul? Are they not part of the soul's equipment—as proof and demonstration are used by the mind—for dealing with reality? If so, then the objects of belief may indeed be "real." This *psychological argument for immortality* has as its premise the old correspondence idea that the world and the soul of man are intimately linked. The psyche functions in correspondence with objective reality. If the soul has a function of belief it implies a corresponding objective reality for which belief has its function. This psychological position has been stated in the theological arguments that only believers get to Heaven. Without the function of belief, there is no corresponding reality of Heaven.

This psychological approach to immortality can be put another way: following Jung, the concept of energy and its indestructibility was an ancient and widespread notion associated in countless ways with the idea of the soul, long before Robert Mayer formulated the conservation of energy into a scientific law. We cannot get away from this primordial image even in modern scientific psychology, which still speaks of the psyche in dynamic terms. What is immortality and reincarnation of the soul in psychology is conservation and transformation of energy in physics. The mind's certainty that energy is "eternal" is given by law in physics. This corresponds with the soul's conviction that it is immortal, and the sense of immortality is the inner feeling of the eternity of psychic energy. *For if the psyche is an energetic phenomenon, then it is indestructible.* Its existence in "another life" cannot be proved any more than the existence of the soul in this life can be proved. Its existence is given only psychologically in the form of inner certainty, i.e., belief.

When we ask why each analysis comes upon the death experience so often and in such variety, we find, primarily, *death appears in order to make way for transformation.* The flower withers around its swelling pod, the snake sheds its skin, and the adult puts off his childish ways.

The creative force kills as it produces the new. Every turmoil and disorder called neurosis can be seen as a life and death struggle in which the players are masked. What is called death by the neurotic mainly because it is dark and unknown is a new life trying to break through into consciousness; what he calls his life because it is familiar is but a dying pattern he tries to keep alive. The death experience breaks down the old order, and in so far as analysis is a prolonged "nervous breakdown" (synthesising too as it goes along), *analysis means dying*. The dread to begin an analysis touches these deep terrors, and the fundamental problem of resistance cannot be taken superficially. Without a dying to the world of the old order, there is no place for renewal, because, as we shall consider later, it is illusory to hope that growth is but an additive process requiring neither sacrifice nor death. The soul favours the death experience to usher in change. Viewed this way, a suicide impulse is a transformation drive. It says: "Life as it presents itself must change. Something must give way. Tomorrow and tomorrow and tomorrow is a tale told by an idiot. The pattern must come to a complete stop. But, since I can do nothing about life out there, having tried every twist and turn, I shall put an end to it here, in my own body, that part of the objective world over which I still have power. I put an end to myself."

When we examine this reasoning we find it leads from psychology to ontology. The movement toward a complete stop, towards that fulfilment in stasis where all processes cease, is an attempt to enter another level of reality, to move from becoming to being. To put an end to oneself means to come to one's end, to find the end or limit of what one is, in order to arrive at what one is not—yet. "This" is exchanged for "that"; one level is wiped out for another. *Suicide is the attempt to move from one realm to another by force through death.*

This movement to another aspect of reality can be formulated by those basic opposites called body and soul, outer and inner, activity and passivity, matter and spirit, here and beyond, which become symbolised by life and death. The agony over suicide represents the struggle of the soul with the paradox of all these opposites. The suicide decision is a choice between these contradictions which seem impossible to reconcile. Once the choice is made, ambivalence overcome (as the studies of Ringel and of Morgenthaler on suicide notes show), the person is usually deliberate and calm, giving no sign of his intention to kill himself. He has crossed over.

This calm corresponds with the death experience of the physically dying, of whom Sir William Osler said, "A few, very few, suffer severely in the body and fewer still in the mind." The death agony usually takes place before the moment of organic death. Death comes first as an experience of the soul, after which the body expires. "Fear," says Osis, "is not a dominant emotion in the dying," whereas elation and exaltation occur frequently. Other investigations of dying report similar findings. The fear of dying concerns *the experience of death,* which is separable from physical death and not dependent upon it.

If suicide is a transformation impulse we can regard today's concern with mass suicide through the Bomb as an attempt of the collective psyche at renewal by ridding itself of the binds of history and the weight of its material accumulations. In a world where things and the physical life overwhelmingly predominate, where goods have become the "good," that which would destroy them and us with them because of our attachments will, of course, become "evil." Yet, could this evil not somewhere be a good in disguise, by showing how shaky and relative our current values are? Through the Bomb we live in the shadow of death. Where it may bring the death experience nearer, it must not mean that mass suicide is also closer. Where life is clung to, suicide takes on the compulsive attraction of "over-kill." But where collective death is lived with—as in the Nazi concentration camps or during war—suicide is seldom. The point is: *the more immanent the death experience, the more possibility for transformation.* The world is closer to a collective suicide, yes; that this suicide must actually occur, no. What must occur if the actual suicide does not come is a transformation in the collective psyche. The Bomb may thus be God's dark hand which He has shown before to Noah and the peoples of the Cities of the Plain, urging not death, but a radical transformation in our souls.

In individuals where the suicide impulse is not directly associated with the ego, but seems a voice or figure or content of the unconscious that pushes or leads or orders the person to self-murder, again it can be saying: "We cannot meet one another again until a change takes place, a change which ends your identification with your concrete life." *Suicide fantasies provide freedom from the actual and usual view of things,* enabling one to meet the realities of the soul. These realities appear as images and voices, as well as impulses, with which one can communicate. But for these conversations with death one must take the realm of the soul—with its night spirits, its uncanny emotions and shapeless voices, where life is disembodied and highly autonomous—as a reality. Then what appear as regressive impulses can reveal their positive values.

For instance, a young man who would hang himself after an examination failure is drawn to choke off his spirit, or blow out his brains, after having tried too hard to fly too high. Death is dark and easeful; passivity and the inertia of matter draw him down again. Melancholy, that black affliction in which so many suicides occur, shows the pull of gravity downwards into the dark, cold bones of reality. Depression narrows and concentrates upon essences, and suicide is the final denial of existence for the sake of essence. Or, a dead father figure (as Hamlet's ghost) continues to fascinate a woman through suicide thoughts. When she turns to face him she finds him saying: "You are lost in the mundane because you have forgotten your father and buried your aspirations. Die and ascend." Even in those suicide notes where a husband kills himself ostensibly to remove the obstacle to his wife's freedom and happiness, there is an attempt to achieve another state of being through suicide. There is an attempt at transformation.

Transformation, to be genuine and thorough, always affects the body. Suicide is always somewhere a body problem. The transformations from infancy to childhood are accompanied by physical changes both in body structure and libidinal zones; so, too, the major transforming moments of life at puberty, menopause, and old age. Crises are emotional, transfusing the body with joy and anguish and altering looks and habit. Initiation rites are ordeals of the flesh. The death experience emphasises transformation in the body and *suicide is an attack on bodily life.* The Platonic idea that the soul was trapped in the body and released by death has relevance here. Some feel themselves alien in their own bodies all their lives. To encounter the realm of the soul as a reality equal to the usual view of reality, a dying to the world is indeed required. This may produce the impulse to destroy the bodily trap. And, because we can never know whether the old idea of immortal soul in mortal body is true or not, the analyst will at least consider suicide in the light of a body-soul opposition.

The attack on bodily life is for some an attempt *to destroy the affective basis of ego-consciousness.* Suicidal mutilations are extreme distortions of this form of the death experience. Such mutilations can be understood in the light of Eastern meditation techniques or in the universal imagery of sacrificing the animal carrier, bodily life. Because images and fantasies impel action, methods are used for killing off the affective impulse from psychological contents. Memory is washed of desire. For action to be purged of impulse and for image to be free for imaginative play and meditative concentration, bodily desire must die. It must not die directly through suicide, which in this case would be a concrete misinterpretation of a psychological necessity. The necessity is simply that, for an awareness beyond egocentric limitations, affect and image must be separated. This separation proceeds through the introversion of the libido, archetypally represented by the incest complex. Then bodily desire unites with the soul, rather than with the world. The affective impulse becomes then wholly psychic through this conjunction and is transformed.

When the psyche persists in presenting its demands for transformation it may use, besides death, other symbols showing birth and growth, transitions of place and time, and the like. Death, however, is the most effective because it brings with it that intense emotion without which no transformation takes place. The death experience challenges most, requiring a vitally whole response. It means all process is stopped. It is the confrontation with tragedy, for there is no way out, except onward, into it. Tragedy is born *in extremis*, where one is cornered into making a *salto mortale* towards another plane of being. Tragedy is the leap out of history into myth; personal life is pierced by the impersonal arrows of fate. *The death experience offers each life the opening into tragedy*, for, as the Romantics saw it, death extinguishes the merely personal and transposes life on to the heroic key where sounds not only adventure, experiment, and absurdity, but more—the tragic sense of life. Tragedy and death are necessarily interwoven, so that the death experience has the bite of tragedy, and the tragic sense is the awareness of death.

The other symbols of transformation (as birth, growth, transitions of place and time) all openly indicate a next stage. They present this next stage before the present one is over. They unfold new possibilities, affording hope; whereas the death experience never feels like a transition. It is the major transition which, paradoxically, says there is no future. The end has come. It is all over, too late.

Under the pressure of "too late," knowing that life went wrong and there is no longer a way out, suicide offers itself. *Then suicide is the urge for hasty transformation*. This is not premature death, as medicine might say, but the late reaction of a delayed life which did not transform as it went along. It would die all at once, and now, because it missed its death crises before. This impatience and intolerance reflects a soul that did not keep pace with its life; or, in older people, a life that no longer nourishes with experiences a still-hungering soul. For the old there is guilt and sin to be expiated, and so I am my own executioner. The spouse is dead. There may be no certainty about an after-life reunion, yet there may at least be a possibility of joining on the "other side," whereas here is but barren grief. Or there is the sense of having already died; an apathetic indifference that says, "I don't care if I live or die." The soul has already left a world through which the body moves like painted cardboard. In each case time is out of joint and suicide would set it right.

WALT WHITMAN

O Living Always, Always Dying

O living always, always dying!
O the burials of me past and present,
O me while I stride ahead, material, visible, imperious as ever;
O me, what I was for years, now dead, (I lament not, I am content;)
O to disengage myself from those corpses of me, which I turn and look
    at where I cast them,
To pass on, (O living! always living!) and leave the corpses behind.

6

Varieties
of Transcendence

Our lives are shot through with questions. We search. We long for vague and undefined things. We have a sense that we are to *be* in some ways and not to be in others. But which ways? We attach ourselves to solutions so that we may live securely. We embrace answers to our most basic questions so that our search may come to rest in certitude. Yet, again and again we find that our attachments fade and our certainties are shaken.

Discovering this, we deny our doubts. We still our deepest and most uncertain desires. We become absorbed in the day-to-day. We learn to forget or to overlook the meaning of our acts. We attach ourselves to ambitions, accomplishments, social identities, adventures, small enjoyments, and passing happiness. But moments of spontaneous reflection recur. And as we shelter and feed this philosophical flame, we work not to overlook the deepest, the quietest, the highest, the least certain, the wonderful. We think about the transcendence of everyday life, about the enormity of the universe, and about the ultimate meaning or lack of ultimate meaning of our existence.

There are times when the world seems to stop and we feel as though transported to a different reality. Our pains, doubts, attachments, and uncertainties all fade and we are absorbed in a timeless moment. Our awareness is heightened, yet we are without care. There is a sense of well-being, a sense of oneness with self, others, nature, God.

Some call this state contemplation, others simply enjoyment. It need not be mystical and it is not rare; it can occur as a dimension of daily life. People seek this transcendence in various ways—by discipline, meditation, or drugs. When it occurs, it transcends even its causes and reveals a world free of efforts and instrumentalities.

The fact that it liberates us from the world of means and ends makes the transcendent experience particularly sweet. What role does such immediacy play in the good life? Is it a special form of power which, without accomplishing anything in the mundane world, nevertheless fulfills our existence and endows it with meaning? Is it a kind of truth? Is it a deeper understanding of life and death? What forms does transcendence take in our own lives today? Although it happens in many different ways, we shall consider only a few of them.

N. KAZANTZAKIS

Transcending Authority

We entered a long narrow chamber decorated everywhere in gold, with Christ's Passion painted on the walls, and statues of the twelve Apostles on either side. At the far end, seated on a high throne, a bulky old man was meditating, his head resting on his palm, his eyes closed. Apparently he had failed to hear us enter because he did not move. I remained near the door while Francis went forward with trembling steps, approached the throne, knelt, and lowered his forehead to the floor.

For a long moment there was silence. We could hear the old man's heavy, fitful breaths—breaths which sounded just like sighs. Was he sleeping, praying, or observing us furtively with eyes that were only half-closed? I felt he was like a dangerous beast simulating sleep and ready to pounce upon us at any minute.

"Holy Father . . ."—Francis' voice was low, controlled, supplicating—"Holy Father . . ."

The pope raised his head slowly, then looked down and saw Francis. His nostrils were quivering.

"What a stench!" he exclaimed, his eyebrows vibrating with anger. "What are those rags, those bare feet! Who do you think you are?"

Francis replied with his face still against the floor: "I am a humble servant of God from Assisi, Holy Father."

"What pigsty did you come from? I suppose you think you're duplicating the aroma of Paradise—is that it? Couldn't you have washed and dressed yourself for your appearance before me? All right, what do you want?"

In the course of so many sleepless nights, Francis had memorized what he was going to say to the pope. He had pieced together the entire speech with extreme skill, giving it a beginning, a middle, and an end in order to prevent the pope from thinking he did not know what he was about. But now that he found himself before God's shadow, his mind failed him. He opened his mouth two or three times but was unable to utter human speech. Instead, he bleated like a lamb.

The pope frowned. "Can't you talk? Tell me what you want."

"I have come to fall at your feet, Holy Father, and to request a favor of you."

"What favor?"

"A privilege."

"You—a privilege? What privilege?"

"The privilege of absolute Poverty, Holy Father."

"You ask a good deal!"

"We are several friars who wish to marry Poverty. I have come to ask you to bless our marriage, Holy Father, and to grant us permission to preach."

"To preach what?"

"Perfect Poverty, perfect Obedience, perfect Love."

"We have no need of you, seeing that we preach all those things ourselves. Go, if you'll be so kind!"

Francis lifted his eyes from the floor and jumped to his feet "Forgive me, Holy Father," he said, his voice steady now, "but I'm not going. God commanded me to make this journey to speak with you—and I have come. I beg you to hear me out. We are poor and illiterate; when we walk through the streets dressed in our rags we are battered with stones and lemon peels. People fly out of their homes and workshops to jeer at us. That—praise the Lord—is how our journey has begun. On this earth, doesn't every great Hope always start in the same way? All our trust is in our poverty, our ignorance, and in our hearts, which have caught fire. Before I left to come here and find you, Holy Father, I had drawn up clearly in my mind exactly what I intended to lay before you to make you say yes and affix your seal. But now I've forgotten everything. I look at you, and behind you I see Christ Crucified, and behind Christ Crucified, the Resurrection of our Lord, and behind the Resurrection of our Lord, the resurrection as well of the entire forsaken, totally forsaken world. What joy I see before me, Holy Father!

How could it fail to bewilder a man's mind? It has bewildered mine; I am all confused, I don't know where to begin or what is the beginning, what the middle, what the end. Everything is the same now; everything is a sigh, Holy Father, a dance, a great cry that is hopeless and yet full of every hope. Oh, if you could only allow me to sing, Holy Father—then I would be able to convey what I wish to ask of you!"

I watched Francis from my corner and trembled as I heard his words. His feet began to shift impatiently, agitatedly, darting out one step to the right, one step to the left, sometimes slowly, sometimes hastily, like those of skilled dancers who establish their rhythm prior to throwing themselves heart and soul into the sacred intoxication of the dance. Without a doubt, the spirit of God was twirling him around. He would begin clapping his hands at any moment and dancing, whereupon the pope would have us both thrown out.

And in truth, while this thought was passing through my mind, Francis lifted his hands. "You mustn't take this in the wrong spirit, Holy Father," he said. "I simply have a great desire to let out a piercing shout, clap my hands, and begin to dance. God is blowing all around me—above, below, to the right, to the left—and spinning me about like a dry leaf."

I approached on tiptoe. "Francis, my brother," I whispered, "you are in front of the pope. Where is your sense of respect?"

"I am in front of God," he bellowed. "How else do you expect me to approach Him, if not dancing and singing? Make room—I'm going to dance!"

He bent his head to one side, stretched out his arms, advanced one foot, then the other, flexed his knees, leaped into the air, flexed his knees again, squatted down as far as the floor, and the moment he touched it lashed out with his legs and sprang into the air, his arms outstretched on either side—so that it seemed a crucified man was dancing before us.

I fell at the pope's feet. "Forgive him, Holy Father," I implored. "He is drunk with God and doesn't know where he is. He always dances when he prays."

The pope bounded off his throne, restraining his rage with difficulty. "That's enough!" he screamed at Francis, seizing him by the shoulder. "God isn't wine for you to use to make yourself drunk. Go to a tavern if you want to dance."

The Nature
of Mystical Experience

What does the expression "mystical states of consciousness" mean? How do we part off mystical states from other states?

The words "mysticism" and "mystical" are often used as terms of mere reproach, to throw at any opinion which we regard as vague and vast and sentimental, and without a base in either facts or logic. For some writers a "mystic" is any person who believes in thought-transference, or spirit-return. Employed in this way the word has little value: there are too many less ambiguous synonyms. So, to keep it useful by restricting it, I will do what I did in the case of the word "religion," and simply propose to you four marks which, when an experience has them, may justify us in calling it mystical for the purpose of the present lectures. In this way we shall save verbal disputation, and the recriminations that generally go therewith.

1. *Ineffability.*—The handiest of the marks by which I classify a state of mind as mystical is negative. The subject of it immediately says that it defies expression, that no adequate report of its contents can be given in words. It follows from this that its quality must be directly experienced; it cannot be imparted or transferred to others. In this peculiarity mystical states are more like states of feeling than like states of intellect. No one can make clear to another who has never had a certain feeling, in what the quality or worth of it consists. One must have musical ears to know the value of a symphony; one must have been in love one's self to understand a lover's state of mind. Lacking the heart

or ear, we cannot interpret the musician or the lover justly, and are even likely to consider him weak-minded or absurd. The mystic finds that most of us accord to his experiences an equally incompetent treatment.

2. *Noetic quality.*—Although so similar to states of feeling, mystical states seem to those who experience them to be also states of knowledge. They are states of insight into depths of truth unplumbed by the discursive intellect. They are illuminations, revelations, full of significance and importance, all inarticulate though they remain; and as a rule they carry with them a curious sense of authority for after-time.

These two characters will entitle any state to be called mystical, in the sense in which I use the word. Two other qualities are less sharply marked, but are usually found. These are:—

3. *Transiency.*—Mystical states cannot be sustained for long. Except in rare instances, half an hour, or at most an hour or two, seems to be the limit beyond which they fade into the light of common day. Often, when faded, their quality can but imperfectly be reproduced in memory; but when they recur it is recognized; and from one recurrence to another it is susceptible of continuous development in what is felt as inner richness and importance.

4. *Passivity.*—Although the oncoming of mystical states may be facilitated by preliminary voluntary operations, as by fixing attention, or going through certain bodily performances, or in oher ways which manuals of mysticism prescribe; yet when the characteristic sort of consciousness once has set in, the mystic feels as if his own will were in abeyance, and indeed sometimes as if he were grasped and held by a superior power. This latter peculiarity connects mystical states with certain definite phenomena of secondary or alternative personality, such as prophetic speech, automatic writing, or the mediumistic trance. When these latter conditions are well pronounced, however, there may be no recollection whatever of the phenomenon, and it may have no significance for the subject's usual inner life, to which, as it were, it makes a mere interruption. Mystical states, strictly so called, are never merely interruptive. Some memory of their content always remains, and a profound sense of their importance. They modify the inner life of the subject between the times of their recurrence. Sharp divisions in this region are, however, difficult to maké, and we find all sorts of gradations and mixtures.

These four characteristics are sufficient to mark out a group of states of consciousness peculiar enough to deserve a special name and to call for careful study. Let it then be called the mystical group.

Our next step should be to gain acquaintance with some typical examples. Professional mystics at the height of their development have often elaborately organized experiences and a philosophy based thereupon. But you remember what I said in my first lecture: phenomena are best understood when placed within their series, studied in their germ and in their over-ripe decay, and compared with their exaggerated and degenerated kindred. The range of mystical experience is very wide, much too wide for us to cover in the time at our disposal. Yet the method of serial study is so essential for interpretation that if we really wish to reach conclusions we must use it. I will begin, therefore, with phenomena which claim no special religious significance, and end with those of which the religious pretensions are extreme.

The simplest rudiment of mystical experience would seem to be that deepened sense of the significance of a maxim or formula which occasionally sweeps over one. "I've heard that said all my life," we exclaim, "but I never realized its full meaning until now." "When a fellow-monk," said Luther, "one day repeated the words of the Creed: 'I believe in the forgiveness of sins,' I saw the Scripture in an entirely new light; and straightway I felt as if I were born anew. It was as if I had found the door of paradise thrown wide open." This sense of deeper significance is not confined to rational propositions. Single words, and conjunctions of words, effects of light on land and sea, odors and musical sounds, all bring it when the mind is tuned aright. Most of us can remember the strangely moving power of passages in certain poems read when we were young, irrational doorways as they were through which the mystery of fact, the wildness and the pang of life, stole into our hearts and thrilled them. The words have now perhaps become mere polished surfaces for us; but lyric poetry and music are alive and significant only in proportion as they fetch these vague vistas of a life continuous with our own, beckoning and inviting, yet ever eluding our pursuit. We are alive or dead to the eternal inner message of the arts according as we have kept or lost this mystical susceptibility.

A more pronounced step forward on the mystical ladder is found in an extremely frequent phenomenon, that sudden feeling, namely, which sometimes sweeps over us, of having "been here before," as if at some indefinite past time, in just this place, with just these people, we were already saying just these things. As Tennyson writes:

> Moreover, something is or seems,
> That touches me with mystic gleams,
> Like glimpses of forgotten dreams—
>
> Of something felt, like something here;
> Of something done, I know not where;
> Such as no language may declare.

Sir James Crichton-Browne has given the technical name of "dreamy states" to these sudden invasions of vaguely reminiscent consciousness. They bring a sense of mystery and of the metaphysical duality of things, and the feeling of an enlargement of perception which seems imminent but which never completes itself. . . .

Somewhat deeper plunges into mystical consciousness are met with in yet other dreamy states. Such feelings as these which Charles Kingsley describes are surely far from being uncommon, especially in youth:—

When I walk the fields, I am oppressed now and then with an innate feeling that everything I see has a meaning, if I could but understand it. And this feeling of being surrounded with truths which I cannot grasp amounts to indescribable awe sometimes. . . . Have you not felt that your real soul was imperceptible to your mental vision, except in a few hallowed moments?

The next step into mystical states carries us into a realm that public opinion and ethical philosophy have long since branded as pathological, though private practice and certain lyric strains of poetry seem still to bear witness to its ideality. I refer to the consciousness produced by intoxicants and anaesthetics, especially by alcohol. The sway of alcohol over mankind is unquestionably due to its power to stimulate the mystical faculties of human nature, usually crushed to earth by the cold facts and dry criticisms of the sober hour. Sobriety diminishes, discriminates, and says no; drunkenness expands, unites, and says yes. It is in fact the great exciter of the *Yes* function in man. It brings its votary from the chill periphery of things to the radiant core. It makes him for the moment one with truth. Not through mere perversity do men run after it. To the poor and the unlettered it stands in the place of symphony concerts and of literature; and it is part of the deeper mystery and tragedy of life that whiffs and gleams of something that we immediately recognize as excellent should be vouchsafed to so many of us only in the fleeting earlier phases of what in its totality is so degrading a poisoning. The drunken consciousness is one bit of the mystic consciousness, and our total opinion of it must find its place in our opinion of that larger whole.

Nitrous oxide and ether, especially nitrous oxide, when sufficiently diluted with air, stimulate the mystical consciousness in an extraordinary degree. Depth beyond depth of truth seems revealed to the inhaler. This truth fades out, however, or escapes, at the moment of coming to; and if any words remain over in which it seemed to clothe itself, they prove to be the veriest nonsense. Nevertheless, the sense of a profound meaning having been there persists; and I know more than one person who is persuaded that in the nitrous oxide trance we have a genuine metaphysical revelation.

Some years ago I myself made some observations on this aspect of nitrous oxide intoxication, and reported them in print. One conclusion was forced upon my mind at that time, and my impression of its truth has ever since remained unshaken. It is that our normal waking consciousness, rational consciousness as we call it, is but one special type of consciousness, whilst all about it, parted from it by the filmiest of screens, there lie potential forms of consciousness entirely different. We may go through life without suspecting their existence; but apply the requisite stimulus, and at a touch they are there in all their completeness, definite types of mentality which probably somewhere have their field of application and adaptation. No account of the universe in its totality can be final which leaves these other forms of consciousness quite disregarded. How to regard them is the question,—for they are so discontinuous with ordinary consciousness. Yet they may determine attitudes though they cannot furnish formulas, and open a region though they fail to give a map. At any rate, they forbid a premature closing of our accounts with reality. Looking back on my own experiences, they all converge towards a kind of insight to which I cannot help ascribing some metaphysical significance. The keynote of it is invariably a reconciliation. It is as if the opposites of the world, whose contradictoriness and conflict make all our difficulties and troubles, were melted into unity. Not only do they, as contrasted species, belong to one and the same genus, but *one of the species*, the nobler and better one, *is itself the genus, and so soaks up and absorbs its opposite into itself.* This is a dark saying, I know, when thus expressed in terms of common logic, but I cannot wholly escape from its authority. I feel as if it must mean something, something like what the hegelian philosophy means, if one could only lay hold of it more clearly. Those who have ears to hear, let them hear; to me the living sense of its reality only comes in the artificial mystic state of mind. . . .

Certain aspects of nature seem to have a peculiar power of awakening mystical moods. Most of the striking cases which I have collected have occurred out of doors. . . .

I could easily give many instances, but one will suffice. I take it from the Autobiography of J. Trevor.

One brilliant Sunday morning, my wife and boys went to the Unitarian Chapel in Macclesfield. I felt it impossible to accompany them—as though to leave the sunshine on the hills, and go down there to the chapel, would be for the time an act of spiritual suicide. And I felt such need for new inspiration and expansion in my life. So, very reluctantly and sadly, I left my wife and boys to go down into the town, while I went further up into the hills with my stick and my dog. In the loveliness of the morning, and the beauty of the hills and valleys, I soon lost my sense of sadness and regret. For nearly an hour I walked along the road to the 'Cat and Fiddle,' and then returned. On the way back, suddenly, without warning, I felt that I was in Heaven—an inward state of peace and joy and assurance indescribably intense, accompanied with a sense of being bathed in a warm glow of light, as though the external condition had brought about the internal effect—a feeling of having passed beyond the body, though the scene around me stood out more clearly and as if nearer to me than before, by reason of the illumination in the midst of which I seemed to be placed. This deep emotion lasted, though with decreasing strength, until I reached home, and for some time after, only gradually passing away.

Even the least mystical of you must by this time be convinced of the existence of mystical moments as states of consciousness of an entirely specific quality, and of the deep impression which they make on those who have them. A Canadian psychiatrist, Dr. R. M. Bucke, gives to the more distinctly characterized of these phenomena the name of cosmic consciousness. "Cosmic consciousness in its more striking instances is not," Dr. Bucke says, "simply an expansion or extension of the self-conscious mind with which we are all familiar, but the superaddition of a function as distinct from any possessed by the average man as *self*-consciousness is distinct from any function possessed by one of the higher animals."

The prime characteristic of cosmic consciousness is a consciousness of the cosmos, that is, of the life and order of the universe. Along with the consciousness of the cosmos there occurs an intellectual enlightenment which alone would place the individual on a new plane of existence—would make him almost a member of a new species. To this is added a state of moral exaltation, an indescribable feeling of elevation, elation, and joyousness, and a quickening of the moral sense, which is fully as striking, and more important than is the enhanced intellectual power. With these come what may be called a sense of immortality, a consciousness of eternal life, not a conviction that he shall have this, but the consciousness that he has it already.

We have now seen enough of this cosmic or mystic consciousness, as it comes sporadically. We must next pass to its methodical cultivation as an element of the religious life. Hindus, Buddhists, Mohammedans, and Christians all have cultivated it methodically.

In India, training in mystical insight has been known from time immemorial under the name of yoga. Yoga means the experimental union of the individual with the divine. It is based on persevering exercise; and the diet, posture, breathing, intellectual concentration, and moral discipline vary slightly in the different systems which teach it. The yogi, or disciple, who has by these means overcome the obscurations of his lower nature sufficiently, enters into the condition termed *samâdhi*, "comes face to face with facts which no instinct or reason can ever know." He learns—

That the mind itself has a higher state of existence, beyond reason, a superconscious state, and that when the mind gets to that higher state, then this knowledge beyond reasoning comes. . . . All the different steps in yoga are intended to bring us scientifically to the superconscious state or samâdhi. . . . Just as unconscious work is beneath consciousness, so there is another work which is above consciousness, and which, also, is not accompanied with the feeling of egoism. . . . There is no feeling of *I*, and yet the mind works, desireless, free from restlessness, objectless, bodiless. Then the Truth shines in its full effulgence, and we know ourselves—for Samâdhi lies potential in us all—for what we truly are, free, immortal, omnipotent, loosed from the finite, and its contrasts of good and evil altogether, and identical with the Atman or Universal Soul.

The Vedantists say that one may stumble into superconsciousness sporadically, without the previous discipline, but it is then impure. Their test of its purity, like our test of religion's value, is empirical: its fruits must be good for life. When a man comes out of Samâdhi, they assure us that he remains "enlightened, a sage, a prophet, a saint, his whole character changed, his life changed, illumined." . . .

Incommunicableness of the transport is the keynote of all mysticism. Mystical truth exists for the individual who has the transport, but for no one else. In this, as I have said, it resembles the knowledge given to us in sensations more than that given by conceptual thought. Thought, with its remoteness and abstractness, has often enough in the history of philosophy been contrasted unfavorably with sensation. It is a commonplace of metaphysics that God's knowledge cannot be discursive but must be intuitive, that is, must be constructed more after the pattern of what in ourselves is called immediate feeling, than after that of proposition and judgment. But *our* immediate feelings have no content but what the five senses supply; and we have seen and shall see again that mystics may emphatically deny that the senses play any part in the very highest type of knowledge which their transports yield.

In the Christian church there have always been mystics. Although many of them have been viewed with suspicion, some have gained favor in the eyes of the authorities. The experiences of these have been treated as precedents, and a codified system of mystical theology has been based upon them, in which everything legitimate finds its place. The basis of the system is "orison" or meditation, the methodical elevation of the soul towards God. Through the practice of orison the higher levels of mystical experience may be attained. It is odd that Protestantism, especially evangelical Protestantism, should seemingly have abandoned everything methodical in this line. Apart from what prayer may lead to, Protestant mystical experience appears to have been almost exclusively sporadic. It has been left to our mind-curers to reintroduce methodical meditation into our religious life.

The first thing to be aimed at in orison is the mind's detachment from outer sensations, for these interfere with its concentration upon ideal things. Such manuals as Saint Ignatius's Spiritual Exercises recommend the disciple to expel sensation by a graduated series of efforts to imagine holy scenes. The acme of this kind of discipline would be a semi-hallucinatory mono-ideism—an imaginary figure of Christ, for example, coming fully to occupy the mind. Sensorial images of this sort, whether literal or symbolic, play an enormous part in mysticism. But in certain cases imagery may fall away entirely, and in the very highest raptures it tends to do so. The state of consciousness becomes then insusceptible of any verbal description. Mystical teachers are unanimous as to this. Saint John of the Cross, for instance, one of the best of them, thus describes the condition called the "union of love," which, he says, is reached by "dark contemplation." In this the Deity compenetrates the soul, but in such a hidden way that the soul—

finds no terms, no means, no comparison whereby to render the sublimity of the wisdom and the delicacy of the spiritual feeling with which she is filled. . . . We receive this mystical knowledge of God clothed in none of the kinds of images, in none of the sensible representations, which our mind makes use of in other circumstances. Accordingly in this knowledge, since the senses and the imagination are not employed, we get neither form nor impression, nor can we give any account or furnish any likeness, although the mysterious and sweet-tasting wisdom comes home so clearly to the inmost parts of our soul. Fancy a man seeing a certain kind of thing for the first time in his life. He can understand it, use and enjoy it, but he cannot apply a name to it, nor communicate any idea of it, even though all the while it be a mere thing of sense. How much greater will be his powerlessness when it goes beyond the senses! This is the peculiarity of the divine language. The more infused, intimate, spiritual, and supersensible it is, the more does it exceed the senses, both inner and outer, and impose silence upon them. . . . The soul then feels as if placed in a vast and profound solitude, to which no created thing has access, in an immense and boundless desert, desert the more delicious the more solitary it is. There, in this abyss of wisdom, the soul grows by what it drinks in from the well-springs of the comprehension of love, . . . and recognizes, however sublime and learned may be the terms we employ, how utterly vile, insignificant, and improper they are, when we seek to discourse of divine things by their means.

The kinds of truth communicable in mystical ways, whether these be sensible or supersensible, are various. Some of them relate to this world,—visions of the future, the reading of hearts, the sudden understanding of texts, the knowledge of distant events, for example; but the most important revelations are theological or metaphysical.

Saint Ignatius confessed one day to Father Laynez that a single hour of meditation at Manresa had taught him more truths about heavenly things than all the teachings of all the doctors put together could have taught him. . . . One day in orison, on the steps of the choir of the Dominican church, he saw in a distinct manner the plan of divine wisdom in the creation of the world. On another occasion, during a procession, his spirit was ravished in God, and it was given him to contemplate, in a form and images fitted to the weak understanding of a dweller on the earth, the deep mystery of the holy Trinity. This last vision flooded his heart with such sweetness, that the mere memory of it in after times made him shed abundant tears.

Similarly with Saint Teresa. "One day, being in orison," she writes, "it was granted me to perceive in one instant how all things are seen and contained in God. I did not perceive them in their proper form, and nevertheless the view I had of them was of a sovereign clearness, and has remained vividly impressed upon my soul. It is one of the most signal of all the graces which the Lord has granted me. . . . The view was so subtile and delicate that the understanding cannot grasp it."

She goes on to tell how it was as if the Deity were an enormous and sovereignly limpid diamond, in which all our actions were contained in such a way that their full sinfulness appeared evident as never before. On another day, she relates, while she was reciting the Athanasian Creed—

> Our Lord made me comprehend in what way it is that one God can be in three Persons. He made me see it so clearly that I remained as extremely surprised as I was comforted, . . . and now, when I think of the holy Trinity, or hear It spoken of, I understand how the three adorable Persons form only one God and I experience an unspeakable happiness.

On still another occasion, it was given to Saint Teresa to see and understand in what wise the Mother of God had been assumed into her place in Heaven.

The deliciousness of some of these states seems to be beyond anything known in ordinary consciousness. It evidently involves organic sensibilities, for it is spoken of as something too extreme to be borne, and as verging on bodily pain. But it is too subtle and piercing a delight for ordinary words to denote. God's touches, the wounds of his spear, references to ebriety and to nuptial union have to figure in the phraseology by which it is shadowed forth. Intellect and senses both swoon away in these highest states of ecstasy. "If our understanding comprehends," says Saint Teresa, "it is in a mode which remains unknown to it, and it can understand nothing of what it comprehends. For my own part, I do not believe that it does comprehend, because, as I said, it does not understand itself to do so. I confess that it is all a mystery in which I am lost." In the condition called *raptus* or ravishment by theologians, breathing and circulation are so depressed that it is a question among the doctors whether the soul be or be not temporarily dissevered from the body. One must read Saint Teresa's descriptions and the very exact distinctions which she makes, to persuade one's self that one is dealing, not with imaginary experiences, but with phenomena which, however rare, follow perfectly definite psychological types.

To the medical mind these ecstasies signify nothing but suggested and imitated hypnoid states, on an intellectual basis of superstition, and a corporeal one of degeneration and hysteria. Undoubtedly these pathological conditions have existed in many and possibly in all the cases, but that fact tells us nothing about the value for knowledge of the consciousness which they induce. To pass a spiritual judgment upon these states, we must not content ourselves with superficial medical talk, but inquire into their fruits for life.

Their fruits appear to have been various. Stupefaction, for one thing, seems not to have been altogether absent as a result. You may remember the helplessness in the kitchen and schoolroom of poor Margaret Mary Alacoque. Many other ecstatics would have perished but for the care taken of them by admiring followers. The "other-worldliness" encouraged by the mystical consciousness makes this over-abstraction from practical life peculiarly liable to befall mystics in whom the character is naturally passive and the intellect feeble; but in natively strong minds and characters we find quite opposite results. The great Spanish mystics, who carried the habit of ecstasy as far as it has often been carried, appear for the most part to have shown indomitable spirit and energy, and all the more so for the trances in which they indulged. . . .

Mystical conditions may, therefore, render the soul more energetic in the lines which their inspiration favors. But this could be reckoned an advantage only in case the inspiration were a true one. If the inspiration were erroneous, the energy would be all the more mistaken and misbegotten. So we stand once more before that problem of truth which confronted us at the end of the lectures on saintliness. You will remember that we turned to mysticism precisely to get some light on truth. Do mystical states establish the truth of those theological affections in which the saintly life has its root?

In spite of their repudiation of articulate self-description, mystical states in general assert a pretty distinct theoretic drift. It is possible to give the outcome of the majority of them in terms that point in definite philosophical directions. One of these directions is optimism, and the other is monism. We pass into mystical states from out of ordinary consciousness as from a less into a more, as from a smallness into a vastness, and at the same time as from an unrest to a rest. We feel them as reconciling, unifying states. They appeal to the yes-function more than to the no-function in us. In them the unlimited absorbs the limits and peacefully closes the account. Their very denial of every adjective you may propose as applicable to the ultimate truth,—He, the

Self, the Atman, is to be described by "No! no!" only, say the Upanishads,—though it seems on the surface to be a no-function, is a denial
made on behalf of a deeper yes. Whoso calls the Absolute anything in
particular, or says that it is *this*, seems implicitly to shut it off from
being *that*—it is as if he lessened it. So we deny the "this," negating
the negation which it seems to us to imply, in the interests of the
higher affirmative attitude by which we are possessed. The fountain-
head of Christian mysticism is Dionysius the Areopagite. He describes the absolute truth by negatives exclusively.

> The cause of all things is neither soul nor intellect; nor has it imagination,
> opinion, or reason, or intelligence; nor is it reason or intelligence; nor is it
> spoken or thought. It is neither number, nor order, nor magnitude, nor little-
> ness, nor equality, nor inequality, nor similarity, nor dissimilarity. It neither
> stands, nor moves, nor rests. . . . It is neither essence, nor eternity, nor time.
> Even intellectual contact does not belong to it. It is neither science nor truth. It
> is not even royalty or wisdom; not one; not unity; not divinity or goodness;
> nor even spirit as we know it . . .

But these qualifications are denied by Dionysius, not because the
truth falls short of them, but because it so infinitely excels them. It is
above them. It is *super*-lucent, *super*-splendent, *super*-essential, *super-
sublime, super* everything that can be named. Like Hegel in his logic,
mystics journey towards the positive pole of truth only by the "Meth-
ode der Absoluten Negativität."

Thus come the paradoxical expressions that so abound in mystical
writings. As when Eckhart tells of the still desert of the Godhead,
"where never was seen difference, neither Father, Son, nor Holy
Ghost, where there is no one at home, yet where the spark of the soul
is more at peace than in itself." As when Boehme writes of the Primal
Love, that "it may fitly be compared to Nothing, for it is deeper than
any Thing, and is as nothing with respect to all things, forasmuch as it
is not comprehensible by any of them. And because it is nothing re-
spectively, it is therefore free from all things, and is that only good,
which a man cannot express or utter what it is, there being nothing to
which it may be compared, to express it by." . . .

To this dialectical use, by the intellect, of negation as a mode of passage towards a higher kind of affirmation, there is correlated the subtlest of moral counterparts in the sphere of the personal will. Since denial of the finite self and its wants, since asceticism of some sort, is
found in religious experience to be the only doorway to the larger and

more blessed life, this moral mystery intertwines and combines with the intellectual mystery in all mystical writings.

"Love," continues Behmen, is Nothing, for "when thou art gone forth wholly from the Creature and from that which is visible, and art become Nothing to all that is Nature and Creature, then thou art in that eternal One, which is God himself, and then thou shalt feel within thee the highest virtue of Love. . . . The treasure of treasures for the soul is where she goeth out of the Somewhat into that Nothing out of which all things may be made. The soul here saith, *I have nothing*, for I am utterly stripped and naked; *I can do nothing*, for I have no manner of power, but am as water poured out; *I am nothing*, for all that I am is no more than an image of Being, and only God is to me I AM; and so, sitting down in my own Nothingness, I give glory to the eternal Being, and *will nothing* of myself, that so God may will all in me, being unto me my God and all things."

In Paul's language, I live, yet not I, but Christ liveth in me. Only when I become as nothing can God enter in and no difference between his life and mine remain outstanding.

This overcoming of all the usual barriers between the individual and the Absolute is the great mystic achievement. In mystic states we both become one with the Absolute and we become aware of our oneness. This is the everlasting and triumphant mystical tradition, hardly altered by differences of clime or creed. In Hinduism, in Neoplatonism, in Sufism, in Christian mysticism, in Whitmanism, we find the same recurring note, so that there is about mystical utterances an eternal unanimity which ought to make a critic stop and think, and which brings it about that the mystical classics have, as has been said, neither birthday nor native land. Perpetually telling of the unity of man with God, their speech antedates languages, and they do not grow old. . .

I have now sketched with extreme brevity and insufficiency, but as fairly as I am able in the time allowed, the general traits of the mystic range of consciousness. *It is on the whole pantheistic and optimistic, or at least the opposite of pessimistic. It is anti-naturalistic, and harmonizes best with twice-bornness and so-called other-worldly states of mind.*

My next task is to inquire whether we can invoke it as authoritative. Does it furnish any *warrant for the truth* of the twice-bornness and supernaturality and pantheism which it favors? I must give my answer to this question as concisely as I can.

In brief my answer is this,—and I will divide it into three parts:—

1. Mystical states, when well developed, usually are, and have the right to be, absolutely authoritative over the individuals to whom they come.

2. No authority emanates from them which should make it a duty for those who stand outside of them to accept their revelations uncritically.

3. They break down the authority of the non-mystical or rationalistic consciousness, based upon the understanding and the senses alone. They show it to be only one kind of consciousness. They open out the possibility of other orders of truth, in which, so far as anything in us vitally responds to them, we may freely continue to have faith.

I will take up these points one by one.

1.

As a matter of psychological fact, mystical states of a well-pronounced and emphatic sort *are* usually authoritative over those who have them. They have been "there," and know. It is vain for rationalism to grumble about this. If the mystical truth that comes to a man proves to be a force that he can live by, what mandate have we of the majority to order him to live in another way? We can throw him into prison or a madhouse, but we cannot change his mind—we commonly attach it only the more stubbornly to its beliefs. It mocks our utmost efforts, as a matter of fact, and in point of logic it absolutely escapes our jurisdiction. Our own more "rational" beliefs are based on evidence exactly similar in nature to that which mystics quote for theirs. Our senses, namely, have assured us of certain states of fact; but mystical experiences are as direct perceptions of fact for those who have them as any sensations ever were for us. The records show that even though the five senses be in abeyance in them, they are absolutely sensational in their epistemological quality, if I may be pardoned the barbarous expression,—that is, they are face to face presentations of what seems immediately to exist.

The mystic is, in short, *invulnerable,* and must be left, whether we relish it or not, in undisturbed enjoyment of his creed. Faith, says Tolstoy, is that by which men live. And faith-state and mystic state are practically convertible terms.

2.

But I now proceed to add that mystics have no right to claim that we ought to accept the deliverance of their peculiar experiences, if we are ourselves outsiders and feel no private call thereto. The utmost they can ever ask of us in this life is to admit that they establish a presumption. They form a consensus and have an unequivocal outcome; and it would be odd, mystics might say, if such a unanimous type of experience should prove to be altogether wrong. At bottom, however, this would only be an appeal to numbers, like the appeal of rationalism the other way; and the appeal to numbers has no logical force. If we acknowledge it, it is for "suggestive," not for logical reasons: we follow the majority because to do so suits our life.

But even this presumption from the unanimity of mystics is far from being strong. In characterizing mystic states as pantheistic, optimistic, etc., I am afraid I over-simplified the truth. I did so for expository reasons, and to keep the closer to the classic mystical tradition. The classic religious mysticism, it now must be confessed, is only a "privileged case." It is an *extract*, kept true to type by the selection of the fittest specimens and their preservation in "schools." It is carved out from a much larger mass; and if we take the larger mass as seriously as religious mysticism has historically taken itself, we find that the supposed unanimity largely disappears. To begin with, even religious mysticism itself, the kind that accumulates traditions and makes schools, is much less unanimous than I have allowed. It has been both ascetic and antinomianly self-indulgent within the Christian church. It is dualistic in Sankhya, and monistic in Vedanta philosophy. I called it pantheistic; but the great Spanish mystics are anything but pantheists. They are with few exceptions non-metaphysical minds, for whom "the category of personality" is absolute. The "union" of man with God is for them much more like an occasional miracle than like an original identity. How different again, apart from the happiness common to all, is the mysticism of Walt Whitman, Edward Carpenter, Richard Jefferies, and other naturalistic pantheists, from the more distinctively Christian sort. The fact is that the mystical feeling of enlargement, union, and emancipation has no specific intellectual content whatever of its own. It is capable of forming matrimonial alliances with material furnished by the most diverse philosophies and theologies, provided only they can find a place in their framework for its peculiar emotional mood. We have no right, therefore, to invoke its prestige as distinctively in favor of any special belief, such as that in absolute idealism, or in the absolute monistic identity, or in the absolute goodness, of the world. It is only relatively in favor of all these things—it passes out of common human consciousness in the direction in which they lie.

So much for religious mysticism proper. But more remains to be told, for religious mysticism is only one half of mysticism. The other half has no accumulated traditions except those which the text-books on insanity supply. Open any one of these, and you will find abundant cases in which "mystical ideas" are cited as characteristic symptoms of enfeebled or deluded states of mind. In delusional insanity, paranoia, as they sometimes call it, we may have a *diabolical* mysticism, a sort of religious mysticism turned upside down. The same sense of ineffable importance in the smallest events, the same texts and words coming with new meanings, the same voices and visions and leadings and missions, the same controlling by extraneous powers; only this time the emotion is pessimistic: instead of consolations we have desolations; the meanings are dreadful; and the powers are enemies to life. It is evident that from the point of view of their psychological mechanism, the classic mysticism and these lower mysticisms spring from the same mental level, from that great subliminal or transmarginal region of which science is beginning to admit the existence, but of which so little is really known. That region contains every kind of matter: "seraph and snake" abide there side by side. To come from thence is no infallible credential. What comes must be sifted and tested, and run the gauntlet of confrontation with the total context of experience, just like what comes from the outer world of sense. Its value must be ascertained by empirical methods, so long as we are not mystics ourselves.

Once more, then, I repeat that non-mystics are under no obligation to acknowledge in mystical states a superior authority conferred on them by their intrinsic nature.

3.

Yet, I repeat once more, the existence of mystical states absolutely overthrows the pretension of non-mystical states to be the sole and ultimate dictators of what we may believe. As a rule, mystical states merely add a supersensuous meaning to the ordinary outward data of consciousness. They are excitements like the emotions of love or ambi- tion, gifts to our spirit by means of which facts already objectively before us fall into a new expressiveness and make a new connection with our active life. They do not contradict these facts as such, or deny anything that our senses have immediately seized. It is the rationalis- tic critic rather who plays the part of denier in the controversy, and his denials have no strength, for there never can be a state of facts to which new meaning may not truthfully be added, provided the mind ascend to a more enveloping point of view. It must always remain an open question whether mystical states may not possibly be such supe- rior points of view, windows through which the mind looks out upon a more extensive and inclusive world. The difference of the views seen from the different mystical windows need not prevent us from enter- taining this supposition. The wider world would in that case prove to have a mixed constitution like that of this world, that is all. It would have its celestial and its infernal regions, its tempting and its saving moments, its valid experiences and its counterfeit ones, just as our world has them; but it would be a wider world all the same. We should have to use its experiences by selecting and subordinating and substituting just as is our custom in this ordinary naturalistic world; we should be liable to error just as we are now; yet the counting in of that wider world of meanings, and the serious dealing with it, might, in spite of all the perplexity, be indispensable stages in our approach to the final fullness of the truth.

In this shape, I think, we have to leave the subject. Mystical states indeed wield no authority due simply to their being mystical states. But the higher ones among them point in directions to which the religious sentiments even of non-mystical men incline. They tell of the supremacy of the ideal, of vastness, of union, of safety, and of rest. They offer us *hypotheses*, hypotheses which we may voluntarily ig- nore, but which as thinkers we cannot possibly upset. The supernatu- ralism and optimism to which they would persuade us may, in- terpreted in one way or another, be after all the truest of insights into the meaning of this life.

SØREN KIERKEGAARD

Necessary Silence in the Face of the Absolute

The knight of faith is obliged to rely upon himself alone, he feels the pain of not being able to make himself intelligible to others, but he feels no vain desire to guide others. The pain is his assurance that he is in the right way, this vain desire he does not know, he is too serious for that. The false knight of faith readily betrays himself by this proficiency in guiding which he has acquired in an instant. He does not comprehend what it is all about, that if another individual is to take the same path, he must become entirely in the same way the individual and have no need of any man's guidance, least of all the guidance of a man who would obtrude himself. At this point men leap aside, they cannot bear the martyrdom of being uncomprehended, and instead of this they choose conveniently enough the worldly admiration of their proficiency. The true knight of faith is a witness, never a teacher, and therein lies his deep humanity, which is worth a good deal more than this silly participation in others' weal and woe which is honored by the name of sympathy, whereas in fact it is nothing but vanity. He who would only be a witness thereby avows that no man, not even the lowliest, needs another man's sympathy or should be abased that another may be exalted. But since he did not win what he won at a cheap price, neither does he sell it out at a cheap price, he is not petty enough to take men's admiration and give them in return his silent contempt, he knows that what is truly great is equally accessible to all.

Either there is an absolute duty toward God, and if so it is the paradox here described, that the individual as the individual is higher than the universal and as the individual stands in an absolute relation to the absolute/or else faith never existed, because it has always existed, or, to put it differently, Abraham is lost, or one must explain the passage in the fourteenth chapter of Luke as did that tasteful exegete, and explain in the same way the corresponding passages and similar ones.

Was Abraham ethically defensible in keeping silent about his purpose before Sarah, before Eleazar, before Isaac?

The ethical as such is the universal, again, as the universal it is the manifest, the revealed. The individual regarded as he is immediately, that is, as a physical and psychical being, is the hidden, the concealed. So his ethical task is to develop out of this concealment and to reveal himself in the universal. Hence whenever he wills to remain in concealment he sins and lies in temptation (*Anfechtung*), out of which he can come only by revealing himself.

With this we are back again at the same point. If there is not a concealment which has its ground in the fact that the individual as the individual is higher than the universal, then Abraham's conduct is indefensible, for he paid no heed to the intermediate ethical determinants. If on the other hand there is such a concealment, we are in the presence of the paradox which cannot be mediated inasmuch as it rests upon the consideration that the individual as the individual is higher than the universal, but it is the universal precisely which is mediation. The Hegelian philosophy holds that there is no justified concealment, no justified incommensurability. So it is self-consistent when it requires revelation, but it is not warranted in regarding Abraham as the father of faith and in talking about faith. For faith is not the first immediacy but a subsequent immediacy. The first immediacy is the aesthetical, and about this the Hegelian philosophy may be in the right. But faith is not the aesthetical—or else faith has never existed because it has always existed. . . .

But now as for Abraham—how did he act? For I have not forgotten, and the reader will perhaps be kind enough to remember, that it was with the aim of reaching this point I entered into the whole foregoing discussion—not as though Abraham would thereby become more intelligible, but in order that the unintelligibility might become more desultory. For, as I have said, Abraham I cannot understand, I can only admire him. It was also observed that the stages I have described do none of them contain an analogy to Abraham. The examples were simply educed in order that while they were shown in their own proper sphere they might at the moment of variation [from Abraham's case] indicate as it were the boundary of the unknown land. If there might be any analogy, this must be found in the paradox of sin, but this again lies in another sphere and cannot explain Abraham and is itself far easier to explain than Abraham.

So then, Abraham did not speak, he did not speak to Sarah, nor to Eleazar, nor to Isaac, he passed over three ethical authorities; for the ethical had for Abraham no higher expression than the family life.

Aesthetics permitted, yea, required of the individual silence, when he knew that by keeping silent he could save another. This is already sufficient proof that Abraham does not lie within the circumference of aesthetics. His silence has by no means the intention of saving Isaac, and in general his whole task of sacrificing Isaac for his own sake and for God's sake is an offense to aesthetics, for aesthetics can well understand that I sacrifice myself, but not that I sacrifice another for my own sake. The aesthetic hero was silent. Ethics condemned him, however, because he was silent by virtue of his accidental particularity. His human foreknowledge was what determined him to keep silent. This ethics cannot forgive, every such human knowledge is only an illusion, ethics requires an infinite movement, it requires revelation. So the aesthetic hero *can* speak but will not.

The genuine tragic hero sacrifices himself and all that is his for the universal, his deed and every emotion with him belong to the universal, he is revealed, and in this self-revelation he is the beloved son of ethics. This does not fit the case of Abraham: he does nothing for the universal, and he is concealed.

Now we reach the paradox. Either the individual as the individual is able to stand in an absolute relation to the absolute (and then the ethical is not the highest) /or Abraham is lost—he is neither a tragic hero, nor an aesthetic hero.

Here again it may seem as if the paradox were the easiest and most convenient thing of all. However, I must repeat that he who counts himself convinced of this is not a knight of faith, for distress and anguish are the only legitimations that can be thought of, and they cannot be thought in general terms, for with that the paradox is annulled.

Abraham keeps silent—but he *cannot* speak. Therein lies the distress and anguish. For if I when I speak am unable to make myself intelligible, then I am not speaking—even though I were to talk uninterruptedly day and night. Such is the case with Abraham. He is able to utter everything, but one thing he cannot say, i.e. say it in such a way that another understands it, and so he is not speaking. The relief of speech is that it translates me into the universal. Now Abraham is able to say the most beautiful things any language can express about how he loves Isaac. But it is not this he has at heart to say, it is the profounder thought that he would sacrifice him because it is a trial. This latter thought no one can understand, and hence everyone can only misunderstand the former. This distress the tragic hero does not know. He has first of all the comfort that every counter-argument has received due consideration, that he has been able to give to Clytemnestra, to Iphigenia, to Achilles, to the chorus, to every living being, to every voice from the heart of humanity, to every cunning, every alarming, every accusing, every compassionate thought, opportunity to stand up against him. He can be sure that everything that can be said against him has been said, unsparingly, mercilessly—and to strive against the whole world is a comfort, to strive with oneself is dreadful. He has no reason to fear that he has overlooked anything, so that afterwards he must cry out as did King Edward the Fourth at the news of the death of Clarence.

> Who su'd to me for him? who, in my wrath,
> Kneel'd at my feet and bade me be advised?
> Who spoke of brotherhood? who spoke of love?

The tragic hero does not know the terrible responsibility of solitude. In the next place he has the comfort that he can weep and lament with Clytemnestra and Iphigenia—and tears and cries are assuaging, but unutterable sighs are torture. Agamemnon can quickly collect his soul into the certainty that he will act, and then he still has time to comfort and exhort. This Abraham is unable to do. When his heart is moved, when his words would contain a blessed comfort for the whole world, he does not dare to offer comfort, for would not Sarah, would not Eleazar, would not Isaac say, "Why wilt thou do it? Thou canst refrain"? And if in his distress he would give vent to his feelings and would embrace all his dear ones before taking the final step, this might perhaps bring about the dreadful consequence that Sarah, that Eleazar, that Isaac would be offended in him and would believe he was a hypocrite. He is unable to speak, he speaks no human language. Though he himself understood all the tongues of the world, though his loved ones also understood them, he nevertheless cannot speak—he speaks a divine language . . . he "speaks with tongues."

This distress I can well understand, I can admire Abraham, I am not afraid that anyone might be tempted by this narrative light-heartedly to want to be the individual, but I admit also that I have not the courage for it, and that I renounce gladly any prospect of getting further—if only it were possible that in any way, however late, I might get so far. Every instant Abraham is able to break off, he can repent the whole thing as a temptation, then he can speak, then all could understand him—but then he is no longer Abraham.

Abraham cannot *speak,* for he cannot utter the word which explains all (that is, not so that it is intelligible), he cannot say that it is a test, and a test of such a sort, be it noted, that the ethical is the temptation. He who is so situated is an emigrant from the sphere of the universal. But the next word he is still less able to utter. For, as was sufficiently set forth earlier, Abraham makes two movements: he makes the infinite movement of resignation and gives up Isaac (this no one can understand because it is a private venture); but in the next place, he makes the movement of faith every instant. This is his comfort, for he says: "But yet this will not come to pass, or, if it does come to pass, then the Lord will give me a new Isaac, by virtue viz. of the absurd." The tragic hero does at last get to the end of the story. Iphigenia bows to her father's resolution, she herself makes the infinite movement of resignation, and now they are on good terms with one another. She can understand Agamemnon because his undertaking expresses the universal. If on the other hand Agamemnon were to say to her, "In spite of the fact that the deity demands thee as a sacrifice, it might yet be possible that he did not demand it—by virtue viz. of the absurd," he would that very instant become unintelligible to Iphigenia. If he could say this by virtue of human calculation, Iphigenia would surely understand him, but from that it would follow that Agamemnon had not made the infinite movement of resignation, and so he is not a hero, and so the utterance of the seer is a sea-captain's tale and the whole occurrence a vaudeville.

Abraham did not speak. Only one word of his has been preserved, the only reply to Issac, which also is sufficient proof that he had not spoken previously. Isaac asks Abraham where the lamb is for the burnt offering. "And Abraham said, God will provide Himself the lamb for the burnt offering, my son."

This last word of Abraham I shall consider a little more closely. If there were not this word, the whole event would have lacked something; if it were to another effect, everything perhaps would be resolved into confusion.

I have often reflected upon the question whether a tragic hero, be the culmination of his tragedy a suffering or an action, ought to have a last rejoinder. In my opinion it depends upon the life-sphere to which he belongs, whether his life has intellectual significance, whether his suffering or his action stands in relation to spirit.

It goes without saying that the tragic hero, like every other man who is not deprived of the power of speech, can at the instant of his culmination utter a few words, perhaps a few appropriate words, but the question is whether it is appropriate for him to utter them. If the significance of his life consists in an outward act, then he has nothing to say, since all he says is essentially chatter whereby he only weakens the impression he makes, whereas the ceremonial of tragedy requires that he perform his task in silence, whether this consists in action or in suffering. Not to go too far afield, I will take an example which lies nearest to our discussion. If Agamemnon himself and not Calchas had had to draw the knife against Iphigenia, then he would have only demeaned himself by wanting at the last moment to say a few words, for the significance of his act was notorious, the juridical procedure of piety, of compassion, of emotion, of tears was completed, and moreover his life had no relation to spirit, he was not a teacher or a witness to the spirit. On the other hand, if the significance of a hero's life is in the direction of spirit, then the lack of a rejoinder would weaken the impression he makes. What he has to say is not a few appropriate words, a little piece of declamation, but the significance of his rejoinder is that in the decisive moment he carries himself through. Such an intellectual tragic hero ought to have what in other circumstances is too often striven for in ludicrous ways, he ought to have and he ought to keep the last word. One requires of him the same exalted bearing which is seemly in every tragic hero, but in addition to this there is required of him one word. So when such an intellectual tragic hero has his culmination in suffering (in death), then by his last word he becomes immortal before he dies, whereas the ordinary tragic hero on the other hand does not become immortal till after his death.

One may take Socrates as an example. He was an intellectual tragic hero. His death sentence was announced to him. That instant he dies—for one who does not understand that the whole power of the spirit is required for dying, and that the hero always dies before he dies, that man will not get so very far with his conception of life. So as a hero it is required of Socrates that he repose tranquilly in himself, but as an intellectual tragic hero it is required of him that he at the last moment have spiritual strength sufficient to carry himself through. So he cannot like the ordinary tragic hero concentrate upon keeping himself face to face with death, but he must make this movement so quickly that at the same instant he is consciously well over and beyond this strife and asserts himself. If Socrates had been silent in the crisis of death, he would have weakened the effect of his life and aroused the suspicion that in him the elasticity of irony was not an elemental power but a game, the flexibility of which he had to employ at the decisive moment to sustain him emotionally.

What is briefly suggested here has to be sure no application to Abraham in case one might think it possible to find out by analogy an appropriate word for Abraham to end with, but it does apply to this extent, that one thereby perceives how necessary it is that Abraham at the last moment must carry himself through, must not silently draw the knife, but must have a word to say, since as the father of faith he has absolute significance in a spiritual sense. As to what he must say, I can form no conception beforehand; after he has said it I can maybe understand it, maybe in a certain sense can understand Abraham in what he says, though without getting any closer to him than I have been in the foregoing discussion. In case no last rejoinder of Socrates had existed, I should have been able to think myself into him and formulate such a word; if I were unable to do it, a poet could, but no poet can catch up with Abraham.

Before I go on to consider Abraham's last word more closely I would call attention to the difficulty Abraham had in saying anything at all. The distress and anguish in the paradox consisted (as was set forth above) in silence—Abraham cannot speak. So in view of this fact it is a contradiction to require him to speak, unless one would have him out of the paradox again, in such a sense that at the last moment he suspends it, whereby he ceases to be Abraham and annuls all that went before. So then if Abraham at the last moment were to say to Isaac, "To thee it applies," this would only have been a weakness. For if he could speak at all, he ought to have spoken long before, and the weakness in this case would consist in the fact that he did not possess the maturity of spirit and the concentration to think in advance the whole pain but had thrust something away from him, so that the actual pain contained a plus over and above the thought pain. Moreover, by such a speech he would fall out of the rôle of the paradox, and if he really wanted to speak to Isaac, he must transform his situation into a temptation, for otherwise he could say nothing, and if he were to do that, then he is not even so much as a tragic hero.

However, a last word of Abraham has been preserved, and in so far as I can understand the paradox I can also apprehend the total presence of Abraham in this word. First and foremost, he does not say anything, and it is in this form he says what he has to say. His reply to Isaac has the form of irony, for it always is irony when I say something and do not say anything. Isaac interrogates Abraham on the supposition that Abraham knows. So then if Abraham were to have replied, "I know nothing," he would have uttered an untruth. He cannot say anything, for what he knows he cannot say. So he replies, "God will provide Himself the lamb for the burnt offering, my son." Here the double movement in Abraham's soul is evident, as it was described in the foregoing discussion. If Abraham had merely renounced his claim to Isaac and had done no more, he would in his last word be saying an untruth, for he knows that God demands Isaac as a sacrifice, and he knows that he himself at that instant precisely is ready to sacrifice him. We see then that after making this movement he made every instant the next movement, the movement of faith by virtue of the absurd. Because of this he utters no falsehood, for in virtue of the absurd it is of course possible that God could do something entirely different. Hence he is speaking no untruth, but neither is he saying anything, for he speaks a foreign language. This becomes still more evident when we consider that it was Abraham himself who must perform the sacrifice of Isaac. Had the task been a different one, had the Lord commanded Abraham to bring Isaac out to Mount Moriah and then would

Himself have Isaac struck by lightning and in this way receive him as a sacrifice, then, taking his words in a plain sense, Abraham might have been right in speaking enigmatically as he did, for he could not himself know what would occur. But in the way the task was prescribed to Abraham he himself had to act, and at the decisive moment he must know what he himself would do, he must know that Isaac will be sacrificed. In case he did not know this definitely, then he has not made the infinite movement of resignation, then, though his word is not indeed an untruth, he is very far from being Abraham, he has less significance than the tragic hero, yea, he is an irresolute man who is unable to resolve either on one thing or another, and for this reason will always be uttering riddles. But such a hesitator is a sheer parody of a knight of faith.

Here again it appears that one may have an understanding of Abraham, but can understand him only in the same way as one understands the paradox. For my part I can in a way understand Abraham, but at the same time I apprehend that I have not the courage to speak, and still less to act as he did—but by this I do not by any means intend to say that what he did was insignificant, for on the contrary it is the one only marvel.

And what did the contemporary age think of the tragic hero? They thought that he was great, and they admired him. And that honorable assembly of nobles, the jury which every generation impanels to pass judgment upon the foregoing generation, passed the same judgment upon him. But as for Abraham there was no one who could understand him. And yet think what he attained! He remained true to his love. But he who loves God has no need of tears, no need of admiration, in his love he forgets his suffering, yea, so completely has he forgotten it that afterwards there would not even be the least inkling of his pain if God Himself did not recall it, for God sees in secret and knows the distress and counts the tears and forgets nothing.

So either there is a paradox, that the individual as the individual stands in an absolute relation to the absolute/or Abraham is lost.

RUDOLPH OTTO

The Idea of the Holy

The Rational and the Non-rational

It is essential to every theistic conception of God, and most of all to the Christian, that it designates and precisely characterizes deity by the attributes spirit, reason, purpose, good will, supreme power, unity, selfhood. The nature of God is thus thought of by analogy with our human nature of reason and personality; only, whereas in ourselves we are aware of this as qualified by restriction and limitation, as applied to God the attributes we use are "completed," i.e. thought as absolute and unqualified. Now all these attributes constitute clear and definite *concepts:* they can be grasped by the intellect; they can be analysed by thought; they even admit of definition. An object that can thus be thought conceptually may be termed *rational.* The nature of deity described in the attributes above mentioned is, then, a rational nature; and a religion which recognizes and maintains such a view of God is in so far a "rational" religion. Only on such terms is *belief* possible in contrast to mere *feeling.* And of Christianity at least it is false that "feeling is all, the name but sound and smoke";—where "name" stands for conception or thought. Rather we count this the very mark and criterion of a religion's high rank and superior value—that it should have no lack of *conceptions* about God; that it should admit knowledge—the knowledge that comes by faith—of the transcendent in terms of conceptual thought, whether those already mentioned or others which continue and develop them. Christianity not only possesses such conceptions but possesses them in unique clarity and abundance, and this is, though not the sole or even the chief, yet a very real sign of its superiority over religions of other forms and at other levels. This must be asserted at the outset and with the most positive emphasis.

But, when this is granted, we have to be on our guard against an error which would lead to a wrong and one-sided interpretation of religion. This is the view that the essence of deity can be given completely and exhaustively in such "rational" attributions as have been referred to above and in others like them. It is not an unnatural misconception. We are prompted to it by the traditional language of edification, with its characteristic phraseology and ideas; by the learned treatment of religious themes in sermon and theological instruction; and further even by our Holy Scriptures themselves. In all these cases the "rational" element occupies the foreground, and often nothing else seems to be present at all. But this is after all to be expected. All language, in so far as it consists of words, purports to convey ideas or concepts;—that is what language means;—and the more clearly and unequivocally it does so, the better the language. And hence expositions of religious truths in language inevitably tend to stress the "rational" attributes of God.

But though the above mistake is thus a natural one enough, it is none the less seriously misleading. For so far are these "rational" attributes from exhausting the idea of deity, that they in fact imply a non-rational or supra-rational Subject of which they are predicates. They are "essential" (and not merely "accidental") attributes of that subject, but they are also, it is important to notice, *synthetic* essential attributes. That is to say, we have to predicate them of a subject which they qualify, but which in its deeper essence is not, nor indeed can be, comprehended in them; which rather requires comprehension of a quite different kind. Yet, though it eludes the conceptual way of understanding, it must be in some way or other within our grasp, else absolutely nothing can be asserted of it. And even mysticism, in speaking of it as τὸ ἄρρητον, the ineffable, does not really mean to imply that absolutely nothing can be asserted of the object of the religious consciousness; otherwise, mysticism could exist only in unbroken silence, whereas what has generally been a characteristic of the mystics is their copious eloquence.

Here for the first time we come up against the contrast between rationalism and profounder religion, and with this contrast and its signs we shall be repeatedly concerned in what follows. We have here in fact the first and most distinctive mark of rationalism, with which all the rest are bound up. It is not that which is commonly asserted, that rationalism is the denial, and its opposite the affirmation, of the miraculous. That is manifestly a wrong or at least a very superficial distinction. For the traditional theory of the miraculous as the occasional breach in the causal nexus in nature by a being who himself instituted and must therefore be master of it—this theory is itself as massively "rational" as it is possible to be. Rationalists have often enough acquiesced in the possibility of the miraculous in this sense; they have even themselves contributed to frame a theory of it;—whereas anti-rationalists have been often indifferent to the whole controversy about miracles. The difference between rationalism and its opposite is to be found elsewhere. It resolves itself rather into a peculiar difference of *quality* in the mental attitude and emotional content of the religious life itself. All depends upon this: in our idea of God is the non-rational overborne, even perhaps wholly excluded, by the rational? Or conversely, does the non-rational itself preponderate over the rational? Looking at the matter thus, we see that the common dictum, that orthodoxy itself has been the mother of rationalism, is in some measure well founded. It is not simply that orthodoxy was preoccupied with doctrine and the framing of dogma, for these have been no less a concern of the wildest mystics. It is rather that orthodoxy found in the construction of dogma and doctrine no way to do justice to the non-rational aspect of its subject. So far from keeping the non-rational element in religion alive in the heart of the religious experience, orthodox Christianity manifestly failed to recognize its value, and by this failure gave to the idea of God a one-sidedly intellectualistic and rationalistic interpretation.

This bias to rationalization still prevails, not only in theology but in the science of comparative religion in general, and from top to bottom of it. The modern students of mythology, and those who pursue research into the religion of "primitive man" and attempt to reconstruct the "bases" or "sources" of religion, are all victims to it. Men do not, of course, in these cases employ those lofty "rational" concepts which we took as our point of departure; but they tend to take these concepts and their gradual "evolution" as setting the main problem of their inquiry, and fashion ideas and notions of lower value, which they regard as paving the way for them. It is always in terms of concepts and ideas that the subject is pursued, "natural" ones, moreover, such as have a place in the general sphere of man's ideational life, and are not specifically "religious." And then with a resolution and cunning which one can hardly help admiring, men shut their eyes to that which is quite unique in the religious experience, even in its most primitive manifestations. But it is rather a matter for astonishment than for admiration! For if there be any single domain of human experience that presents us with something unmistakably specific and unique, peculiar to itself, assuredly it is that of the religious life. In truth the enemy has often a keener vision in this matter than either the champion of religion or the neutral and professedly impartial theorist. For the adversaries on their side know very well that the entire "pother about mysticism" has nothing to do with "reason" and "rationality."

And so it is salutary that we should be incited to notice that religion is not exclusively contained and exhaustively comprised in any series of "rational" assertions; and it is well worth while to attempt to bring the relation of the different "moments" of religion to one another clearly before the mind, so that its nature may become more manifest.

This attempt we are now to make with respect to the quite distinctive category of the holy or sacred.

"Numen" and the "Numinous"

"Holiness"—"the holy"—is a category of interpretation and valuation peculiar to the sphere of religion. It is, indeed, applied by transference to another sphere—that of ethics—but it is not itself derived from this. While it is complex, it contains a quite specific element or "moment," which sets it apart from "the rational" in the meaning we gave to that word above, and which remains inexpressible—an $\overset{\text{'}}{\alpha}\rho\rho\eta\tau o\nu$ or *ineffabile*—in the sense that it completely eludes apprehension in terms of concepts. The same thing is true (to take a quite different region of experience) of the category of the beautiful.

Now these statements would be untrue from the outset if "the holy" were merely what is meant by the word, not only in common parlance, but in philosophical, and generally even in theological usage. The fact is we have come to use the words "holy," "sacred" (*heilig*) in an entirely derivative sense, quite different from that which they originally bore. We generally take "holy" as meaning "completely good"; it is the absolute moral attribute, denoting the consummation of moral goodness. In this sense Kant calls the will which remains unwaveringly obedient to the moral law from the motive of duty a "holy" will; here clearly we have simply the *perfectly moral* will. In the same way we may speak of the holiness or sanctity of duty or law, meaning merely that they are imperative upon conduct and universally obligatory.

But this common usage of the term is inaccurate. It is true that all this moral significance is contained in the word "holy," but it includes in addition—as even we cannot but feel—a clear overplus of meaning, and this it is now our task to isolate. Nor is this merely a later or acquired meaning; rather, "holy," or at least the equivalent words in Latin and Greek, in Semitic and other ancient languages, denoted first and foremost *only* this overplus: if the ethical element was present at all, at any rate it was not original and never constituted the whole meaning of the word. Any one who uses it today does undoubtedly always feel "the morally good" to be implied in "holy"; and accordingly in our inquiry into that element which is separate and peculiar to the idea of the holy it will be useful, at least for the temporary purpose of the investigation, to invent a special term to stand for "the holy" *minus* its moral factor or "moment," and, as we can now add, minus its "rational" aspect altogether.

It will be our endeavour to suggest this unnamed Something to the reader as far as we may, so that he may himself feel it. There is no religion in which it does not live as the real innermost core, and without it no religion would be worthy of the name. It is preeminently a living force in the Semitic religions, and of these again in none has it such vigour as in that of the Bible. Here, too, it has a name of its own, viz. the Hebrew *qādôsh*, to which the Greek ἅγιος and the Latin *sanctus*, and, more accurately still, *sacer*, are the corresponding terms. It is not, of course, disputed that these terms in all three languages connote, as part of their meaning, *good, absolute goodness*, when, that is, the notion has ripened and reached the highest stage in its development. And we then use the word "holy" to translate them. But this "holy" then represents the gradual shaping and filling in with ethical meaning, or what we shall call the "schematization," of what was a unique original feeling-response, which can be in itself ethically neutral and claims consideration in its own right. And when this moment or element first emerges and begins its long development, all those expressions (*qādôsh*, ἅγιος, *sacer*, &c.) mean beyond all question something quite other than "the good." This is universally agreed by contemporary criticism, which rightly explains the rendering of *qādôsh* by "good" as a mistranslation and unwarranted "rationalization" or "moralization" of the term.

Accordingly, it is worth while, as we have said, to find a word to stand for this element in isolation, this "extra" in the meaning of "holy" above and beyond the meaning of goodness. By means of a special term we shall the better be able, first, to keep the meaning clearly apart and distinct, and second, to apprehend and classify connectedly whatever subordinate forms or stages of development it may show. For this purpose I adopt a word coined from the Latin *numen*. *Omen* has given us "ominous," and there is no reason why from *numen* we should not similarly form a word "numinous." I shall speak, then, of a unique "numinous" category of value and of a definitely "numinous" state of mind, which is always found wherever the category is applied. This mental state is perfectly *sui generis* and irreducible to any other; and therefore, like every absolutely primary and elementary datum, while it admits of being discussed, it cannot be strictly defined. There is only one way to help another to an understanding of it. He must be guided and led on by consideration and discussion of the matter through the ways of his own mind, until he reach the point at which "the numinous" in him perforce begins to stir, to start into life and into consciousness. We can co-operate in this process by bringing before his notice all that can be found in other regions of the mind, already known and familiar, to resemble, or again to afford some special contrast to, the particular experience we wish to elucidate. Then we must add: "This X of ours is not precisely *this* experience, but akin to this one and the opposite of that other. Cannot you now realize for yourself what it is?" In other words our X cannot, strictly speaking, be taught, it can only be evoked, awakened in the mind; as everything that comes "of the spirit" must be awakened.

The Elements in the "Numinous"

Creature-Feeling

The reader is invited to direct his mind to a moment of deeply-felt religious experience, as little as possible qualified by other forms of consciousness. Whoever cannot do this, whoever knows no such moments in his experience, is requested to read no farther; for it is not easy to discuss questions of religious psychology with one who can recollect the emotions of his adolescence, the discomforts of indigestion, or, say, social feelings, but cannot recall any intrinsically religious feelings. We do not blame such an one, when he tries for himself to advance as far as he can with the help of such principles of explanation as he knows, interpreting "aesthetics" in terms of sensuous pleasure, and "religion" as a function of the gregarious instinct and social standards, or as something more primitive still. But the artist, who for his part has an intimate personal knowledge of the distinctive element in the aesthetic experience, will decline his theories with thanks, and the religious man will reject them even more uncompromisingly.

Next, in the probing and analysis of such states of the soul as that of solemn worship, it will be well if regard be paid to what is unique in them rather than to what they have in common with other similar states. To be *rapt* in worship is one thing; to be morally *uplifted* by the contemplation of a good deed is another; and it is not to their common features, · but to those elements of emotional content peculiar to the first that we would have attention directed as precisely as possible. As Christians we undoubtedly here first meet with feelings familiar enough in a weaker form in other departments of experience, such as feelings of gratitude, trust, love, reliance, humble submission, and dedication. But this does not by any means exhaust the content of religious worship. Not in any of these have we got the special features of the quite unique and incomparable experience of solemn worship. In what does this consist?

Schleiermacher has the credit of isolating a very important element in such an experience. This is the "feeling of dependence." But this important discovery of Schleiermacher is open to criticism in more than one respect.

In the first place, the feeling or emotion which he really has in mind in this phrase is in its specific quality not a "feeling of dependence" in the "natural" sense of the word. As such, other domains of life and other regions of experience than the religious occasion the feeling, as a sense of personal insufficiency and impotence, a consciousness of being determined by circumstances and environment. The feeling of which Schleiermacher wrote has an undeniable analogy with these states of mind: they serve as an indication to it, and its nature may be elucidated by them, so that, by following the direction in which they point, the feeling itself may be spontaneously felt. But the feeling is at the same time also qualitatively different from such analogous states of mind. Schleiermacher himself, in a way, recognizes this by distinguishing the feeling of pious or religious dependence from all other feelings of dependence. His mistake is in making the distinction merely that between "absolute" and "relative" dependence, and therefore a difference of degree and not of intrinsic quality. What he overlooks is that, in giving the feeling the name "feeling of dependence" at all, we are really employing what is no more than a very close analogy. Anyone who compares and contrasts the two states of mind introspectively will find out, I think, what I mean. It cannot be expressed by means of anything else, just because it is so primary and elementary a datum in our psychical life, and therefore only definable through itself. It may perhaps help him if I cite a well-known example, in which the precise "moment" or element of religious feeling of which we are speaking is most actively present. When Abraham ventures to plead with God for the men of Sodom, he says (Gen. xviii. 27): "Behold now, I have taken upon me to speak unto the Lord, which am but dust and ashes." There you have a self-confessed "feeling of dependence," which is yet at the same time far more than, and something other than, *merely* a feeling of dependence. Desiring to give it a name of its own, I propose to call it "creature-consciousness" or creature-feeling. It is the emotion of a creature, submerged and overwhelmed by its own nothingness in contrast to that which is supreme above all creatures.

It is easily seen that, once again, this phrase, whatever it is, is not a *conceptual* explanation of the matter. All that this new term, "creature-feeling," can express, is the note of submergence into nothingness before an overpowering, absolute might of some kind; whereas everything turns upon the *character* of this overpowering might, a character which cannot be expressed verbally, and can only be suggested indirectly through the tone and content of a man's feeling-response to it. And this response must be directly experienced in oneself to be understood.

We have now to note a second defect in the formulation of Schleiermacher's principle. The religious category discovered by him, by whose means he professes to determine the real content of the religious emotion, is merely a category of *self*-valuation, in the sense of self-depreciation. According to him the religious emotion would be directly and primarily a sort of *self*-consciousness, a feeling concerning oneself in a special, determined relation, viz. one's dependence. Thus, according to Schleiermacher, I can only come upon the very fact of God as the result of an inference, that is, by reasoning to a cause beyond myself to account for my "feeling of dependence." But this is entirely opposed to the psychological facts of the case. Rather, the "creature-feeling" is itself a first subjective concomitant and effect of another feeling-element, which casts it like a shadow, but which in itself indubitably has immediate and primary reference to an object outside the self.

Now this object is just what we have already spoken of as 'the numinous'. For the "creature-feeling" and the sense of dependence to arise in the mind the "numen" must be experienced as present, a *numen praesens*, as is in the case of Abraham. There must be felt a something "numinous," something bearing the character of a "numen," to which the mind turns spontaneously; or (which is the same thing in other words) these feelings can only arise in the mind as accompanying emotions when the category of "the numinous" is called into play.

The numinous is thus felt as objective and outside the self. We have now to inquire more closely into its nature and the modes of its manifestation.

"Mysterium Tremendum"

The Analysis of "Tremendum"

We said above that the nature of the numinous can only be suggested by means of the special way in which it is reflected in the mind in terms of feeling. "Its nature is such that it grips or stirs the human mind with this and that determinate affective state." We have now to attempt to give a further indication of these determinate states. We must once again endeavour, by adducing feelings akin to them for the purpose of analogy or contrast, and by the use of metaphor and symbolic expressions, to make the states of mind we are investigating ring out, as it were, of themselves.

Let us consider the deepest and most fundamental element in all strong and sincerely felt religious emotion. Faith unto salvation, trust, love—all these are there. But over and above these is an element which may also on occasion, quite apart from them, profoundly affect us and occupy the mind with a wellnigh bewildering strength. Let us follow it up with every effort of sympathy and imaginative intuition wherever it is to be found, in the lives of those around us, in sudden, strong ebullitions of personal piety and the frames of mind such ebullitions evince, in the fixed and ordered solemnities of rites and liturgies, and again in the atmosphere that clings to old religious monuments and buildings, to temples and to churches. If we do so we shall find we are dealing with something for which there is only one appropriate expression, *"mysterium tremendum."* The feeling of it may at times come sweeping like a gentle tide, pervading the mind with a tranquil mood of deepest worship. It may pass over into a more set and lasting attitude of the soul, continuing, as it were, thrillingly vibrant and resonant, until at last it dies away and the soul resumes its "profane," non-religious mood of everyday experience. It may burst in sudden eruption up from the depths of the soul with spasms and convulsions, or lead to the strangest excitements, to intoxicated frenzy, to transport, and to ecstasy. It has its wild and demonic forms and can sink to an almost grisly horror and shuddering. It has its crude, barbaric antecedents and early manifestations, and again it may be developed into something beautiful and pure and glorious. It may become the hushed, trembling, and speechless humility of the creature in the presence of—whom or what? In the presence of that which is a *mystery* inexpressible and above all creatures.

It is again evident at once that here too our attempted formulation by means of a concept is once more a merely negative one. Conceptually *mysterium* denotes merely that which is hidden and esoteric, that which is beyond conception or understanding, extraordinary and unfamiliar. The term does not define the object more positively in its qualitative character. But though what is enunciated in the word is negative, what is meant is something absolutely and intensely positive. This pure positive we can experience in feelings, feelings which our discussion can help to make clear to us, in so far as it arouses them actually in our hearts.

The Element of Awefulness

To get light upon the positive *"quale"* of the object of these feelings, we must analyse more closely our phrase *mysterium tremendum,* and we will begin first with the adjective.

Tremor is in itself merely the perfectly familiar and "natural" emotion of *fear*. But here the term is taken, aptly enough but still only by analogy, to denote a quite specific kind of emotional response, wholly distinct from that of being afraid, though it so far resembles it that the analogy of fear may be used to throw light upon its nature. There are in some languages special expressions which denote, either exclusively or in the first instance, this "fear" that is more than fear proper. The Hebrew *hiqdīsh* (hallow) is an example. To "keep a thing holy in the heart" means to mark it off by a feeling of peculiar dread, not to be mistaken for any ordinary dread, that is, to appraise it by the category of the numinous. But the Old Testament throughout is rich in parallel expressions for this feeling. Specially noticeable is the *'ēmāh* of Yahweh ("fear of God"), which Yahweh can pour forth, dispatching almost like a daemon, and which seizes upon a man with paralysing effect. It is closely related to the δεῖμα πανικόν of the Greeks. Compare Exod. xxiii. 27: "I will send my fear before thee, and will destroy all the people to whom thou shalt come . . ."; also Job ix. 34; xiii. 21 ("let not his fear terrify me"; "let not thy dread make me afraid"). Here we have a terror fraught with an inward shuddering such as not even the most menacing and overpowering created thing can instil. It has something spectral in it.

In the Greek language we have a corresponding term in σεβαστός. The early Christians could clearly feel that the title σεβαστός (*augustus*) was one that could not fittingly be given to any creature, not even to the emperor. They felt that to call a man σεβαστός was to give a human being a name proper only to the *numen*, to rank him by the category proper only to the *numen*, and that it therefore amounted to a kind of idolatry. Of modern languages English has the words "awe," "aweful," which in their deeper and most special sense approximate closely to our meaning. The phrase, "he stood aghast," is also suggestive in this connexion. On the other hand, German has no native-grown expression of its own for the higher and riper form of the emotion we are considering, unless it be in a word like *erschauern*, which does suggest it fairly well. It is far otherwise with its cruder and more debased phases, where such terms as *grausen* and *Schauer*, and the more popular and telling *gruseln* ("grue"), *gräsen*, and *grässlich* ("grisly"), very clearly designate the numinous element. In my examination of Wundt's Animism I suggested the term *Scheu* (dread); but the special "numinous" quality (making it "awe" rather than "dread" in the ordinary sense) would then, of course, have to be denoted by inverted commas. "Religious dread" (or "awe") would perhaps be a better designation. Its antecedent stage is "daemonic dread" (cf. the horror of Pan) with its queer perversion, a sort of abortive offshoot, the "dread of ghosts." It first begins to stir in the feeling of "something uncanny," "eerie," or "weird." It is this feeling which, emerging in the mind of primeval man, forms the starting-point for the entire religious development in history. "Daemons" and "gods" alike spring from this root, and all the products of "mythological apperception" or "fantasy" are nothing but different modes in which it has been objectified. And all ostensible explanations of the origin of religion in terms of animism or magic or folk-psychology are doomed from the outset to wander astray and miss the real goal of their inquiry, unless they recognize this fact of our nature—primary, unique, underivable from anything else—to be the basic factor and the basic impulse underlying the entire process of religious evolution.

Not only is the saying of Luther, that the natural man cannot fear God perfectly, correct from the standpoint of psychology, but we ought to go farther and add that the natural man is quite unable even to "shudder" (*grauen*) or feel horror in the real sense of the word. For "shuddering" is something more than "natural," ordinary fear. It implies that the mysterious is already beginning to loom before the mind, to touch the feelings. It implies the first application of a category of valuation which has no place in the everyday natural world of ordinary experience, and is only possible to a being in whom has been awakened a mental predisposition, unique in kind and different in a definite way from any "natural" faculty. And this newly-revealed capacity, even in the crude and violent manifestations which are all it at first evinces, bears witness to a completely new function of experience and standard of valuation, only belonging to the spirit of man.

Before going on to consider the elements which unfold as the 'tremendum" develops, let us give a little further consideration to the first crude, primitive forms in which this "numinous dread" or *awe* shows itself. It is the mark which really characterizes the so-called "religion of primitive man," and there it appears as "daemonic dread." This crudely naïve and primordial emotional disturbance, and the fantastic images to which it gives rise, are later overborne and ousted by more highly developed forms of the numinous emotion, with all its mysteriously impelling power. But even when this has long attained its

higher and purer mode of expression it is possible for the primitive
types of excitation that were formerly a part of it to break out in the
soul in all their original naïveté and so to be experienced afresh. That
this is so is shown by the potent attraction again and again exercised
by the element of horror and "shudder" in ghost stories, even among
persons of high all-round education. It is a remarkable fact that the
physical reaction to which this unique "dread" of the uncanny gives
rise is also unique, and is not found in the case of any "natural" fear
or terror. We say: "my blood ran icy cold," and "my flesh crept." The
"cold blood" feeling may be a symptom of ordinary, natural fear, but
there is something non-natural or supernatural about the symptom of
"creeping flesh." And any one who is capable of more precise in-
trospection must recognize that the distinction between such a
"dread" and natural fear is not simply one of degree and intensity.
The awe or "dread" *may* indeed be so overwhelmingly great that it
seems to penetrate to the very marrow, making the man's hair bristle
and his limbs quake. But it may also steal upon him almost unob-
served as the gentlest of agitations, a mere fleeting shadow passing
across his mood. It has therefore nothing to do with intensity, and no
natural fear passes over into it merely by being intensified. I may be
beyond all measure afraid and terrified without there being even a
trace of the feeling of uncanniness in my emotion.

We should see the facts more clearly if psychology in general would
make a more decisive endeavour to examine and classify the feelings
and emotions according to their qualitative differences. But the far too
rough division of elementary feelings in general into pleasures and
pains is still an obstacle to this. In point of fact "pleasures" no more
than other feelings are differentiated merely by degrees of intensity:
they show very definite and specific differences. It makes a specific
difference to the condition of mind whether the soul is merely in a
state of pleasure, or joy, or aesthetic rapture, or moral exaltation, or finally in the religious bliss that may come in worship. Such states certainly show resemblances one to another, and on that account can legitimately be brought under a common class-concept ("pleasure"),
which serve to cut them off from other psychical functions, generically
different. But this class-concept, so far from turning the various subordinate species into merely different degrees of the same thing, can do
nothing at all to throw light upon the essence of each several state of
mind which it includes.

Though the numinous emotion in its completest development shows a world of difference from the mere "daemonic dread," yet not even at the highest level does it belie its pedigree or kindred. Even when the worship of "daemons" has long since reached the higher level of worship of "gods," these gods still retain as *numina* something of the "ghost" in the impress they make on the feelings of the worshipper, viz. the peculiar quality of the "uncanny" and "aweful" which survives with the quality of exaltedness and sublimity or is symbolized by means of it. And this element, softened though it is, does not disappear even on the highest level of all, where the worship of God is at its purest. Its disappearance would be indeed an essential loss. The "shudder" reappears in a form ennobled beyond measure where the soul, held speechless, trembles inwardly to the farthest fibre of its being. It invades the mind mightily in Christian worship with the words: "Holy, holy, holy"; it breaks forth from the hymn of Tersteegen:

> God Himself is present:
> Heart, be stilled before Him:
> Prostrate inwardly adore Him.

The "shudder" has here lost its crazy and bewildering note, but not the ineffable something that holds the mind. It has become a mystical awe, and sets free as its accompaniment, reflected in self-consciousness, that "creature-feeling" that has already been described as feeling of personal nothingness and submergence before the awe-inspiring object directly experienced. . . .

The Element of "Overpoweringness" ("Majestas")

We have been attempting to unfold the implications of that aspect of the *mysterium tremendum* indicated by the adjective, and the result so far may be summarized in two words, constituting, as before, what may be called an "ideogram," rather than a concept proper, viz. "absolute unapproachability."

It will be felt at once that there is yet a further element which must be added, that, namely, of "might," "power," "absolute overpoweringness." We will take to represent this the term *majestas*, majesty— the more readily because anyone with a feeling for language must detect a last faint trace of the numinous still clinging to the word. The *tremendum* may then be rendered more adequately *tremenda majestas,* or "aweful majesty." This second element of majesty may continue to be vividly preserved, where the first, that of unapproachability, recedes and dies away, as may be seen, for example, in mysticism. It is especially in relation to this element of majesty or absolute overpoweringness that the creature-consciousness, of which we have already spoken, comes upon the scene, as a sort of shadow or subjective reflection of it. Thus, in contrast to "the overpowering" of which we are conscious as an object over against the self, there is the feeling of one's own submergence, of being but "dust and ashes" and nothingness. And this forms the numinous raw material for the feeling of religious humility. . . .

The Element of "Energy" or Urgency

There is, finally, a third element comprised in those of *tremendum* and *majestas,* awefulness and majesty, and this I venture to call the "urgency" or "energy" of the numinous object. It is particularly vividly perceptible in the ὀργή or "wrath"; and it everywhere clothes itself in symbolical expressions—vitality, passion, emotional temper, will, force, movement, excitement, activity, impetus. These features are typical and recur again and again from the daemonic level up to the idea of the "living" God. We have here the factor that has everywhere more than any other prompted the fiercest opposition to the "philosophic" God of mere rational speculation, who can be put into a definition. And for their part the philosophers have condemned these expressions of the energy of the numen, whenever they are brought on to the scene, as sheer anthropomorphism. In so far as their opponents have for the most part themselves failed to recognize that the terms they have borrowed from the sphere of human conative and affective life have merely value as analogies, the philosophers are right to condemn them. But they are wrong, in so far as, this error notwithstanding, these terms stood for a genuine aspect of the divine nature—its non-rational aspect—a due consciousness of which served to protect religion itself from being "rationalized" away.

For wherever men have been contending for the "living" God or for voluntarism, there, we may be sure, have been non-rationalists fighting rationalists and rationalism. It was so with Luther in his controversy with Erasmus; and Luther's *omnipotentia Dei* in his *De Servo*

Arbitrio is nothing but the union of "majesty"—in the sense of absolute supremacy—with this "energy," in the sense of a force that knows not stint nor stay, which is urgent, active, compelling, and alive. In mysticism, too, this element of "energy" is a very living and vigorous factor, at any rate in the "voluntaristic" mysticism, the mysticism of love, where it is very forcibly seen in that "consuming fire" of love whose burning strength the mystic can hardly bear, but begs that the heat that has scorched him may be mitigated, lest he be himself destroyed by it. And in this urgency and pressure the mystic's "love" claims a perceptible kinship with the ὀργή itself, the scorching and consuming wrath of God; it is the same "energy," only differently directed. "Love," says one of the mystics, "is nothing else than quenched wrath.". . .

The Analysis of "Mysterium"

Ein begriffener Gott ist kein Gott.
"A God comprehended is no God."
                                    Tersteegen

We gave to the object to which the numinous consciousness is directed the name *mysterium tremendum,* and we then set ourselves first to determine the meaning of the adjective *tremendum*—which we found to be itself only justified by analogy—because it is more easily analysed than the substantive idea *mysterium.* We have now to turn to this, and try, as best we may, by hint and suggestion, to get to a clearer apprehension of what it implies.

The "Wholly Other"

It might be thought that the adjective itself gives an explanation of the substantive; but this is not so. It is not merely analytical; it is a synthetic attribute to it; i.e. *tremendum* adds something not necessarily inherent in *mysterium.* It is true that the reactions in consciousness that correpond to the one readily and spontaneously overflow into those that correspond to the other; in fact, anyone sensitive to the use of words would commonly feel that the idea of "mystery" (*mysterium*) is so closely bound up with its synthetic qualifying attribute "aweful" (*tremendum*) that one can hardly say the former without catching an echo of the latter, "mystery" almost of itself becoming "awful mystery" to us. But the passage from the one idea to the other need not by any means be always so easy. The elements of meaning implied in "awefulness" and "mysteriousness" are in themselves definitely different. The latter may so far preponderate in the religious consciousness, may stand out so vividly, that in comparison with it the former almost sinks out of sight; a case which again could be clearly exemplified from some forms of mysticism. Occasionally, on the other hand, the reverse happens, and the *tremendum* may in turn occupy the mind without the *mysterium*.

This latter, then, needs special consideration on its own account. We need an expression for the mental reaction peculiar to it; and here, too, only one word seems appropriate, though, as it is strictly applicable only to a "natural" state of mind, it has here meaning only by analogy: it is the word "stupor." *Stupor* is plainly a different thing from *tremor*; it signifies blank wonder, an astonishment that strikes us dumb, amazement absolute. Taken, indeed, in its purely natural sense, *mysterium* would first mean merely a secret or a mystery in the sense of that which is alien to us, uncomprehended and unexplained; and so far *mysterium* is itself merely an ideogram, an analogical notion taken from the natural sphere, illustrating, but incapable of exhaustively rendering, our real meaning. Taken in the religious sense, that which is "mysterious" is—to give it perhaps the most striking expression—the 'wholly other' (Θάτερον, anyad, alienum), that which is quite beyond the sphere of the usual, the intelligible, and the familiar, which therefore falls quite outside the limits of the "canny," and is contrasted with it, filling the mind with blank wonder and astonishment. . . .

In accordance with laws of which we shall have to speak again later, this feeling or consciousness of the "wholly other" will attach itself to, or sometimes be indirectly aroused by means of, objects which are already puzzling upon the "natural" plane, or are of a surprising or astounding character; such as extraordinary phenomena or astonishing occurrences or things in inanimate nature, in the animal world, or among men. But here once more we are dealing with a case of association between things specifically different—the "numinous" and the "natural" moments of consciousness—and not merely with the gradual enhancement of one of them—the "natural"—till it becomes the other. As in the case of "natural fear" and "daemonic dread" already considered, so here the transition from natural to daemonic amazement is not a mere matter of degree. But it is only with the latter that the complementary expression *mysterium* perfectly harmonizes, as will be felt perhaps more clearly in the case of the adjectival form "mysterious." No one says, strictly and in earnest, of a piece of clockwork that is beyond his grasp, or of a science that he cannot understand: "That is, 'mysterious' to me."

It might be objected that the mysterious is something which is and remains absolutely and invariably beyond our understanding, whereas that which merely eludes our understanding for a time but is perfectly intelligible in principle should be called, not a "mystery," but merely a "problem." But this is by no means an adequate account of the matter. The truly "mysterious" object is beyond our apprehension and comprehension, not only because our knowledge has certain irremovable limits, but because in it we come upon something inherently 'wholly other', whose kind and character are incommensurable with our own, and before which we therefore recoil in a wonder that strikes us chill and numb. . . .

The Element of Fascination

The qualitative *content* of the numinous experience, to which "the mysterious" stands as *form*, is in one of its aspects the element of daunting "awefulness" and "majesty," which has already been dealt with in detail; but it is clear that it has at the same time another aspect, in which it shows itself as something uniquely attractive and *fascinating*.

These two qualities, the daunting and the fascinating, now combine in a strange harmony of contrasts, and the resultant dual character of the numinous consciousness, to which the entire religious development bears witness, at any rate from the level of the "daemonic dread" onwards, is at once the strangest and most noteworthy phenomenon in the whole history of religion. The daemonic-divine object may appear to the mind an object of horror and dread, but at the same time it is no less something that allures with a potent charm, and the creature, who trembles before it, utterly cowed and cast down, has always at the same time the impulse to turn to it, nay even to make it somehow his own. The "mystery" is for him not merely something to be wondered at but something that entrances him; and beside that in it which bewilders and confounds, he feels a something that captivates and transports him with a strange ravishment, rising often enough to the pitch of dizzy intoxication; it is the Dionysiac-element in the numen.

The ideas and concepts which are the parallels or "schemata" on the rational side of this non-rational element of "fascination" are love, mercy, pity, comfort; these are all "natural" elements of the common psychical life, only they are here thought as absolute and in completness. But important as these are for the experience of religious bliss or felicity, they do not by any means exhaust it. It is just the same as with the opposite experience of religious infelicity—the experience of the ὀργή or "wrath" of God:—both alike contain fundamentally non-rational elements. Bliss or beatitude is more, far more, than the mere natural feeling of being comforted, of reliance, of the joy of love, however these may be heightened and enhanced. Just as "wrath," taken in a purely rational or a purely ethical sense, does not exhaust that profound element of *awefulness* which is locked in the mystery of deity, so neither does "graciousness" exhaust the profound element of *wonderfulness* and rapture which lies in the mysterious beatific experience of deity. The term "grace" may indeed be taken as its aptest designation, but then only in the sense in which it is really applied in the language of the mystics, and in which not only the "gracious intent" but "something more" is meant by the word. This "something more" has its antecedent phases very far back in the history of religions.

It may well be possible, it is even probable, that in the first stage of its development the religious consciousness started with only one of its poles—the "daunting" aspect of the numen—and so at first took shape only as "daemonic dread." But if this did not point to something beyond itself, if it were not but one "moment" of a completer experience, pressing up gradually into consciousness, then no transition would be possible to the feelings of positive self-surrender to the numen. The only type of worship that could result from this "dread" alone would be that of ἀπαῖτεισθαι and ἀποτρέπειν, taking the form of expiation and propitiation, the averting or the appeasement of the "wrath" of the numen. It can never explain how it is that "the numinous" is the object of search and desire and yearning, and that too for its own sake and not only for the sake of the aid and backing that men expect from it in the natural sphere. It can never explain how this takes place, not only in the forms of "rational" religious worship, but in those queer "sacramental" observances and rituals and procedures of communion in which the human being seeks to get the numen into his possession.

Religious practice may manifest itself in those normal and easily intelligible forms which occupy so prominent a place in the history of religion, such forms as propitiation, petition, sacrifice, thanksgiving, &c. But besides these there is a series of strange proceedings which are constantly attracting greater and greater attention, and in which it is claimed that we may recognize, besides mere religion in general, the particular roots of mysticism. I refer to those numerous curious modes of behaviour and fantastic forms of mediation, by means of which the primitive religious man attempts to master "the mysterious," and to fill himself and even to identify himself with it. These modes of behaviour fall apart into two classes. On the one hand the "magical" identification of the self with the numen proceeds by means of various transactions, at once magical and devotional in character—by formula, ordination, adjuration, consecration, exorcism, &c.: on the other hand are the "shamanistic" ways of procedure, possession, indwelling, self-fulfilment in exaltation and ecstasy. All these have, indeed, their starting-points simply in magic, and their intention at first was certainly simply to appropriate the prodigious force of the numen for the natural ends of man. But the process does not rest there. Possession of and by the numen becomes an end in itself; it begins to be sought for its own sake; and the wildest and most artificial methods of asceticism are put into practice to attain it. In a word, the *vita religiosa* begins; and to remain in these strange and bizarre states of numinous possession becomes a good in itself, even a way of salvation, wholly different from the profane goods pursued by means of magic. Here, too, commences the process of development by which the experience is matured and purified, till finally it reaches its consummation in the sublimest and purest states of the "life within the Spirit" and in the noblest mysticism. Widely various as these states are in themselves, yet they have this element in common, that in them the *mysterium* is experienced in its essential, positive, and specific character, as something that bestows upon man a beatitude beyond compare, but one whose real nature he can neither proclaim in speech nor conceive in thought, but may know only by a direct and living experience. It is a bliss which embraces all those blessings that are indicated or suggested in positive fashion by any "doctrine of salvation," and it quickens all of them through and through; but these do not exhaust it.

Rather by its all-pervading, penetrating glow it makes of these very blessings more than the intellect can conceive in them or affirm of them. It gives the peace that passes understanding, and of which the tongue can only stammer brokenly. Only from afar, by metaphors and analogies, do we come to apprehend what it is in itself, and even so our notion is but inadequate and confused.

"Eye hath not seen, nor ear heard, neither have entered into the heart of man, the things which God hath prepared for them that love him." Who does not feel the exalted sound of these words and the "Dionysiac" element of transport and fervour in them? It is instructive that in such phrases as these, in which consciousness would fain put its highest consummation into words, "all images fall away" and the mind turns from them to grasp expressions that are purely negative. And it is still more instructive that in reading and hearing such words their merely negative character simply is not noticed; that we can let whole chains of such negations enrapture, even intoxicate us, and that entire hymns—and deeply impressive hymns—have been composed, in which there is really nothing positive at all! All this teaches us the independence of the positive content of this experience from the implications of its overt conceptual expression, and how it can be firmly grasped, thoroughly understood, and profoundly appreciated, purely in, with, and from the feeling itself. . . .

This is where the living "something more" of the *fascinans*, the element of fascination, is to be found. It lives no less in those tense extollings of the blessing of salvation, which recur in all religions of salvation, and stand in such remarkable contrast to the relatively meagre and frequently childish import of that which is revealed in them by concept or by image. Everywhere salvation is something whose meaning is often very little apparent, is even wholly obscure, to the "natural" man; on the contrary, *so far as he understands it,* he tends to find it highly tedious and uninteresting, sometimes downright distasteful and repugnant to his nature, as he would, for instance, find the beatific vision of God in our own doctrine of salvation, or the *henōsis* of "God all in all" among the mystics. "So far as he understands," be it noted; but then he does not understand it in the least. Because he lacks the inward teaching of the Spirit, he must needs confound what is offered him as an expression for the experience of salvation—a mere ideogram of what is felt, whose import it hints at by analogy—with "natural" concepts, as though it were itself just such an one. And so he "wanders even farther from the goal."

It is not only in the religious feeling of longing that the moment of fascination is a living factor. It is already alive and present in the moment of "solemnity," both in the gathered concentration and humble submergence of private devotion, when the mind is exalted to the holy, and in the common worship of the congregation, where this is practised with earnestness and deep sincerity, as, it is to be feared, is with us a thing rather desired than realized. It is this and nothing else that in the solemn moment can fill the soul so full and keep it so inexpressibly tranquil. Schleiermacher's assertion is perhaps true of it, as of the numinous consciousness in general, viz. that it cannot really occur alone on its own account, or except combined and penetrated with rational elements. But, if this be admitted, it is upon other grounds than those adduced by Schleiermacher; while, on the other hand, it may occupy a more or less predominant place and lead to states of calm (ἡσυχία) as well as of transport, in which it *almost* of itself wholly fills the soul. But in all the manifold forms in which it is aroused in us, whether in eschatological promise of the coming kingdom of God and the transcendent bliss of Paradise, or in the guise of an entry into that beatific reality that is "above the world"; whether it come first in expectancy or pre-intimation or in a present experience ("When I but *have* Thee, I ask no question of heaven and earth"); in all these forms, outwardly diverse but inwardly akin, it appears as a strange and mighty propulsion towards an ideal good known only to religion and in its nature fundamentally non-rational, which the mind knows of in yearning and presentiment, recognizing it for what it is behind the obscure and inadequate symbols which are its only expression. And this shows that above and beyond our rational being lies hidden the ultimate and highest part of our nature, which can find no satisfaction in the mere allaying of the needs of our sensuous, psychical, or intellectual impulses and cravings. The mystics called it the basis or ground of the soul.

MIRCEA ELIADE

How Are We To Interpret the Experiences of the Mystic Light?

A Dream

About the middle of last century an American merchant, aged thirty-two, had the following dream: "I was standing behind the counter of my shop in the middle of a bright, sunshiny afternoon, and instantly, in a flash, it became darker than the darkest night, darker than a mine; and the gentleman who was talking with me ran out into the street. Following him, although it was so dark, I could see hundreds and thousands of people pouring into the street, all wondering what had happened. Just then I noticed in the sky, in the far south-west, a bright light like a star, about the size of the palm of my hand, and in an instant it seemed to grow larger and larger and nearer and nearer, until it began to light up the darkness. When it got to the size of a man's hat, it divided itself into twelve smaller lights with a larger one in the centre, and then very rapidly it grew much larger, and instantly I knew that this was the coming of Christ and the twelve apostles. By this time it was lighter than the lightest day that could possibly be imagined, and as the shining host advanced towards the zenith, the friend with whom I was talking exclaimed: 'That is my Saviour!' and I thought he immediately left his body and ascended into the sky, and I thought I was not good enough to accompany him. Then I awoke."

For some days the man was so impressed that he could not tell his dream to anyone. At the end of a fortnight he told it to his family and afterwards to others. Three years later, someone well known for his profound religious life said to this gentleman's wife: "Your husband is born again and don't know it. He is a little spiritual baby with eyes not yet open, but he will know in a very short time." In fact, about three weeks afterwards, when he was walking with his wife in Second Avenue (N.Y.) he suddenly exclaimed: "A—, I have eternal life." He felt at that moment that Christ had just arisen in him and that he would remain in everlasting consciousness.

Three years after this event, whilst on a boat and in a crowd of people, he had a new spiritual and mental experience: it seemed to him that his whole soul, *and his body too,* were suffused with light. But in the autobiographical account that we have just given, he adds that these experiences in the waking state never made him forget the first, the experience he had known in dream.

The principal reasons for my choosing to begin with this example of a spontaneous experience of the light are two:

1. it concerns a business man satisfied with his occupation and seemingly in no way prepared for a semi-mystical illumination;

2. his first experience of the light took place in a dream. He seems to have been deeply impressed by this experience, but he did not grasp its significance. He merely felt that something decisive had happened to him, something that concerned his soul's salvation. The idea that it was a spiritual rebirth only came to him when he heard what another person had said to his wife. Only after this indication from one with authority did he have the conscious experience of Christ's presence and, finally, three years afterwards, the experience of the supernatural light in which both his soul and his body were bathed.

A psychologist would have many interesting things to say about the deep significance of this experience. For his part, the historian of religions will remark that the case of the American businessman admirably illustrates the situation of modern man, who believes himself—or wishes to be—without religion: the religious feeling for existence has in him been pushed back into, or has taken refuge in, the unconscious. Nowadays, as Professor C. G. Jung says, the unconscious is always religious. One could dilate at length on the apparent disappearance of religious feeling in modern man, or more exactly of its banishment to the deep levels of the psyche. But this is a problem outside my purpose.

My intention is to produce a historico-religious commentary on the spontaneous experience of the inner light. The example I have just quoted brings us straight to the heart of the problem; we have just seen how a meeting with the light—even though it took place in a dream—ends by radically changing a human existence by opening it to the world of the Spirit. Now all experiences of the supernatural light present this common denominator: anyone receiving such an experience undergoes a change of being: he acquires another mode of being, which gives him access to the world of the spirit. The actual significance of the change in the individual's being, and of the spirit to which he has now access, constitute quite another problem, which will be discussed later. Let us dwell for the moment on this fact: even in a Far-Westerner of the nineteenth century, a meeting with the light indicates a spiritual rebirth.

This is not an isolated example; there are many similar cases and I shall have occasion to quote some of them. But I approach this subject as a historian of religions. First of all, therefore, it is necessary to know the significances of the interior or supernatural light in the different religious traditions. The subject is enormous; we must therefore observe limits. A satisfactory study of the religious values of the interior light would require not only a careful examination of all varieties of this experience, but also an explanation of the rituals and the different mythologies of the Light. For it is the religious ideologies that justify and, ultimately, give validity to mystical experiences. In so far as I can, I will try briefly to recall the ideological contexts of different experiences of the light in certain great religions. But numerous aspects will be omitted. I shall not speak of mythologies of the Light, nor of solar myths, nor of ritual lamps or fires. Nor shall I speak of the religious significance of the moon's light or of lightning, although all such manifestations of light have great importance for our subject.

Qaumaneq

It is the mythology—or rather the metaphysics—of the lightning-flash that is of especial interest. The rapidity of spiritual illumination has been compared in many religions to lightning. Furthermore, the swift flash of lightning rending the darkness has been given the value of a *mysterium tremendum* which, by transfiguring the world, fills the soul with holy terror. Men killed by lightning are considered to have been snatched up into heaven by the storm gods, and their remains are worshipped as sacred relics. A man who survives being struck by lightning is completely changed; indeed he begins a new existence, he is a new man. A Yakout who was struck but not killed explained that God had come down from heaven, broken his body in pieces and then brought him back to life—but after this initiatory death and resurrection he became a shaman. "Now," he added, "I see everything that happens all around for a distance of thirty versts." It is remarkable that in this example of instantaneous initiation, the familiar theme of death and resurrection is accompanied and completed by the motif of sudden illumination; the blinding flash of lightning causes the spiritual transformation by which man acquires the power of vision. "To see for a distance of thirty versts" is the traditional expression used by the Siberian shaman to indicate clairvoyance.

Now this kind of clairvoyance is, among the Esquimos, the result of a mystical experience called "lightning" or "illumination" (*qaumaneq*), and without it no one can become a shaman. According to the statements of the Iglulik Esquimo shamans, gathered by Rasmussen, the *qaumaneq* consists of "a mysterious light which the shaman suddenly feels in his body, inside his head, within the brain, an inexplicable searchlight, a luminous fire, which enables him to see in the dark, both literally and metaphorically speaking, for he can now, even with closed eyes, see through darkness and perceive things and coming events which are hidden from others; thus they look into the future and into the secrets of others." When the novice first experiences this mystic light "it is as if the house in which he is suddenly rises; he sees far ahead of him, through mountains, exactly as if the earth were one great plain, and his eyes could reach to the end of the earth. Nothing is hidden from him any longer; not only can he see things far, far away but he can also discover souls, stolen souls, which are either kept concealed in far, strange lands or have been taken up or down to the Land of the Dead."

Let us note the essential points of this experience of mystical illumination: (a) it is the consequence of a long preparation, but it always occurs suddenly, like a "lightning-flash"; (b) it is a matter of inner light, felt throughout the body but principally in the head; (c) when a man feels it for the first time it is accompanied by the experience of ascension; (d) it involves vision into the distance and clairvoyance at the same time: the shaman sees everywhere and very far, but he also sees invisible entities (souls of the sick, spirits) and also sees future events.

Let us add that the *qaumaneq* is inseparable from another, specifically shamanistic spiritual exercise; the power to see one's own body reduced to the state of a skeleton. In other words, the shaman is capable of "seeing" what is at the time invisible. By this one can understand either that he sees through the flesh, in the manner of X-rays, or very far in the future, what will happen to his own body after death. In either case, this power too is a sort of clairvoyance, made possible by the illumination. On this point one must insist: although experienced in the form of an inner light and felt as a luminous event, in the almost physical sense of the word, the illumination confers on an Esquimo shaman both paragnomic powers and knowledge of a mystical kind. . . .

India: The Light and the Atman

In Indian religions and philosophies, as might be expected, the mystique of the Light is much more complex. In the first place there is the basic idea that light is creative. "Light is procreation" (*jyotir prajanaman*) says the *Satapatha Brahmana* (VIII, 7, 2, 16–17). It "is the procreative power" (*Taittirya Samhita*, VIII, 1, 1, 1). Already the *Rig Veda* (I, 115, 1) affirmed that the Sun is the Life or the *atman*—the Self—of all things. The Upanishads particularly insist on this theme: that being manifests itself by the pure Light and that man receives knowledge of being by an experience of supernatural Light. Now, says the *Chandogya Upanishad* (III, 13, 7), the light that shines beyond this Sky, beyond all things, in the highest worlds beyond which there are none higher, is in fact the same light that shines within a man (*antah puruse*).

Consciousness of the identity between the interior light and the super-cosmic light is accompanied by two well-known phenomena of subtle physiology: a rise in the temperature of the body and the hearing of mystical sounds (*ibid.*, III, 13, 8). There are signs that the revelation of the *atman-brahman* in the form of Light is not simply an act of metaphysical cognition but a deeper experience to which a man commits his existential governance. The supreme gnosis brings a modification of his way of being. In the words of the *Bradaranyaka Upanishad* (I, 3, 28), "from non-being (*asat*) lead me to being (*sat*), from darkness lead me to the light (*tamaso ma jyotir gamaya*), from death lead me to immortality."

The light then is identical with being and immortality. The *Chandogya Upanishad* (III, 17, 7) cites two verses of the *Rig Veda* which speak of the contemplation of the "Light that shines above the Sky," and adds: "By contemplating (this) Very-high Light, beyond the Darkness, we attain the Sun, the god of gods . . ." According to the famous expression of the *Bradaranyaka Upanishad* (IV, 3, 7) the *atman* is identified with the entity that is to be found at the heart of man, in the form of "a light in the heart" (*hrdy antarjyotih purusah*). "This calm being, rising from his body and reaching the highest light, appears in its own form (*svena rupenabhinispadyate*). It is the *atman*. It is the immortal, the fearless. It is Brahman. In fact the name of Brahman is *The True*" (*Chandogya Upanishad*, VIII, 3, 4). At the moment of death, the *Chandogya Upanishad* (VIII, 6, 5) goes on to tell us, the soul rises upwards on the rays of the Sun. It approaches the Sun, "the Gate of the World." Those who know how can enter, but the Gate is closed for those who do not know.

We are concerned therefore with a science of a transcendental and initiatory character, for he who gains it not only gains knowledge but also, and principally, a new and superior way of being. The revelation is sudden; that is why it is compared to lightning—and we have analysed in another context the Indian symbolism of "instantaneous illumination." The Buddha himself received his illumination in a moment outside time—when at dawn, after another night passed in meditation, he raised his eyes to the sky and suddenly perceived the morning star. In Mahayana philosophy the light of the sky at dawn, when there is no moon, has come to symbolise the "Clear Light named the Universal Void." In other words, the Buddha state, the condition of one who is free of all relativity, is symbolised by the Light that Gautama perceived at the moment of his illumination. This Light is described as "clear," "pure," that is to say not only without spot or shadow, but also colourless, and without qualities. For this reason it is called "the Universal Void," since the term void (*sunya*) exactly signifies that it is free of all attributes, of all differentiation: it is the *Urgrund*, the ultimate reality. Comprehension of the Universal Void, like the act of knowledge of the identity of brahman and atman in the Upanishads, is an instantaneous action, comparable to the lightning-flash. Just as nothing precedes the dazzling flash that suddenly rends the mass of darkness, nothing appears to precede the experience of illumination; it belongs to another contextual plane, there is no conti-

nuity between the time before it and the timeless moment in which it
takes place. . . .

Buddhism

Buddha himself says in the *Dighanikaya* that the precursory sign of the
manifestation of Brahma is "the light that rises and the glory that
shines." A Chinese sutra affirms that in the *Rupaloka*, thanks to the
practice of contemplation and the absence of all unclean desires, the
gods (Devas) reach the state of *samhadi* known as the "flash of fire"
and their bodies become more radiant than the Sun and Moon. This
extreme radiance is a result of their perfect purity of heart. According
to the *Abhidharmakosa*, gods of the Brahma class are white as silver,
while those that belong to the Rupadhatu are yellow and white. According to other Buddhist texts the eighteen classes of gods all have
bodies that shine like silver and live in palaces as yellow as gold.

A fortiori, the Buddha is pictured as radiant also. At Amaravati he is
represented in the form of a column of fire. At the end of a discourse
he relates: "I have become a flame and I have risen into the air to the
height of seven palm trees" (*Dighanikaya*, III, 27). The two images that
express transcendence of the human condition—a fiery brightness and
ascension—are here used together. The Buddha's brightness becomes
almost a cliché in the texts (*Divyavadana*, XLVI–VII, 75; *Dhammapada*
XXVI, 51, etc.). The statues of the Gandhara school show flames coming out of the Buddha's body, particularly from his shoulders. Certain
Buddhas are pictured flying in the air; which has given rise to a confusion between flames and wings.

That this light is yogic in essence, that is to say the result of the experimental realisation of a transcendent unconditioned state, is affirmed by a number of texts. When Buddha is in *samadhi*, says the
Lalitavistara, "a ray named the Ornament of the Light of Knowledge
(*jnanalokalanakram nama rasmih*) rising from the cranial suture (*usnisa*)
shines above the head." This is why iconography represents the Buddha with a flame rising above his head. A. K. Coomaraswamy recalls
this question from the *Saddharmapundarika* (p. 467); "On account of
what knowledge (*jnana*) does the cranial protuberance of the Tathagata
shine?"—and he finds the answer in a verse of the *Bhagavadgita* (XIV,
II): "When there is knowledge the light shines through the orifices of
the body." The shining of the body is, therefore, a symptom of the

transcendence of all conditioned states: gods, men and Buddhas shine when they are in *samadhi*, that is to say when they are one with the ultimate reality, Being. According to traditions elaborated by Chinese Buddhism, five lights shine at the birth of every Buddha—and a flame springs out of his corpse. And every Buddha can light the whole Universe with the tuft of hair which grows between his eyebrows. It is well known that Amita, the Buddha of the Boundless Light, is the central figure of Amidism, the mystical school which attaches capital importance to the experience of the Light.

Another mystical theme important for our researches is the Indra's visit to the Buddha when he was meditating in the cave (*Indrashailaguha*). According to this myth, Indra, accompanied by a crowd of gods, descended from the sky to Magadha, where Tathagata was meditating in a cave in the mountain Vediyaka. Roused from his meditation by a Gandharva's singing, Buddha magically widened the cave so that his guests could enter, and received them courteously. A bright light lit the cavern. According to *Dighanikaya* (Sakka Panha Sutta), the light emanated from the gods, but other sources (*Dirghanana-Sutra*, x, etc.) attribute it to the "fiery ecstasy" of the Buddha. Indra's visit is not mentioned in the classical biographies of the Buddha written in Pali and Sanskrit. But this episode occupies an important place in the art of Gandhara and Central Asia. This mystical theme affords a parallel to the legend of Christ's Nativity in a cave and the visit of the Magi (see below, pp. 51ff.). As Monneret de Villard observed, both legends relate how a King of the Gods (Indra), or "Kings, sons of Kings" enter a cave to pay homage to the Saviour, and in the course of their visit the cave is miraculously lit. This mythical theme is certainly older than Indo-Irano-Hellenistic syncretism; it is one with the myth of the Sun God's victorious emergence from the Primordial Cave.

We must now say something about the relations between the cosmogony and the metaphysics of the light. We have seen that the Mahayana identifies the Tathagatas with the cosmic elements (*skandha*) and considers them luminous entities. This is a bold ontology which only becomes really intelligible if we take into account the whole history of Buddhist thought. But it is possible that similar ideas, or at least presentiments of the grand conception of the cosmogony as a manifestation of the Light, had already been expressed in earlier times. Coomaraswamy associates the Sanskrit word *lila*—meaning "play," especially cosmic play—with the root *lelay*, "to flame," "to sparkle," "to shine." This word *lelay* may convey notions of Fire, Light or Spirit. Indian thought seems then already to have found a certain relationship between, on the one hand, cosmic creation conceived as a divine game, and on the other, the play of flames, the dancing of a well-fed fire. Clearly it was only possible to relate the image of cosmic creation to that of dancing flames because flame was already considered the exemplary manifestation of divinity. In view of the Indian evidence that we have quoted, this conclusion seems to us to be established. Flame and light, then, symbolise in India the cosmic creation and the very essence of the Cosmos, on account of the fact that the Universe is conceived as a free manifestation of the divine or, in the last analysis, its "play."

A parallel series of images and concepts, crystallised round *maya*, reveal a similar vision: cosmic creation is a divine play, a mirage, an illusion magically projected by the deity. One knows how great an importance the notion of *maya* has had in the development of Indian ontology and soteriology. Less stress has been laid on this point: that to tear the veil of *maya* and pierce the secret of cosmic illusion amounts primarily to understanding its character as "play"—that is to say free, spontaneous activity of the divine—and consequently to imitating the divine action and attaining liberty. The paradox of Indian thought is that the idea of liberty is so concealed by the idea of *maya*—that is of illusion and slavery—that it takes a long detour to find it. It is enough, however, to discover the deep meaning of *maya*—divine "play"—to be already on the way to deliverance. . . .

Mysticism of the Light

Any phenomenological study of the mystic light should take into account the light that blinded Saint Paul on the road to Damascus, various experiences of the light by Saint John of the Cross, Pascal's famous and mysterious paper on which the word "Fire" was written in capitals, and Jacob Boehme's ecstasy, which was started by the sun's reflection on a dish and followed by an intellectual illumination so perfect that he seemed to have understood all mysteries; also many other less famous experiences like that of the Venerable Serafina di Dio, a Carmelite of Capri (d. 1699) whose face in prayer or after Communion shone like a flame, and whose eyes threw sparks like a fire; and even those of the unfortunate Father Surin who, after suffering for so many years for the deeds of the devils of Loudun, knew some hours of beatitude: once when he was walking in the garden "the sunlight seemed to grow incomparably brighter than usual, and yet was so soft and bearable" that he seemed "to be walking in Paradise." No less significant are the luminous visions that accompany the Moslem mystics' different phases of the *dhikr;* the seven "coloured lights" seen successively by the inner eye of the ascetic at the stage of the *dhikr* of the heart, and the effulgent light to which one attains during the most inward *dhikr,* which is a divine light that never goes out.

Spontaneous Experiences of the Light

But here we must conclude our examples of religious experiences involving the light. I should like, however, to quote also a few interesting cases of persons indifferent to or almost entirely ignorant of theology and the mystical life. We shall now in fact return to the spiritual horizon of that American merchant whose inward adventures we related at the beginning of this study. One particularly instructive case is that of Dr. R. M. Bucke (1837–1902), one of the best known Canadian psychiatrists of his time. He occupied the chair of Nervous and Mental Diseases at Western University, Ontario, and in 1890 was elected President of the American Medico-Psychological Association. At the age of thirty-five he had a strange experience, which I will relate and which radically changed his ideas of life. A little before his death he published *Cosmic Consciousness,* a book which William James considered "an important contribution to psychology." Dr. Bucke believed that certain persons are capable of attaining a higher level of consciousness, which he named "cosmic consciousness." The reality of this state seemed to him to be proved in the first instance by an experience of subjective light. His book assembles a great number of such experiences, from those of the Buddha and Saint Paul to those of his own contemporaries. His analyses and interpretations have only a slight interest, but the book is valuable for its documentation: he gives many unpublished experiences, gathered principally from his contemporaries.

This is how Dr. Bucke describes in the third person what happened to him in the early spring, at the beginning of his thirty-sixth year: He and two friends had spent the evening reading Wordsworth, Shelley, Keats, Browning, and especially Whitman. They parted at midnight, and he had a long drive in a hansom (it was an English city). "He was in a state of quiet, almost passive enjoyment. All at once, without warning of any kind, he found himself wrapped round as it were by a flame-coloured cloud. For an instant he thought of fire, some sudden conflagration in the great city; the next he knew the light was within himself. Directly afterwards came upon him a sense of exaltation, of immense joyousness accompanied or followed by an intellectual illumination impossible to describe. Into his brain streamed one momentary lightning-flash of Brahmic splendour, leaving thenceforward for always an after-taste of Heaven . . . He saw and he knew that the Cosmos is not dead matter but a living Presence; that the soul of man is immortal . . . that the foundation principle of the world is what we call love and that the happiness of everyone is, in the long run, absolutely certain. He claims that he learnt more within the few seconds during which the illumination lasted than in previous months or even years of study, and that he learnt much that no study could have taught him."

Dr. Bucke adds that for the rest of his life he never had a similar experience. And these are the conclusions he comes to: the realization of cosmic consciousness comes as a sense of being immersed in a flame or in a rose-coloured cloud, or, perhaps rather a sense that the mind is itself filled with such a cloud or haze. This sensation is accompanied by an emotion of joy, assurance, triumph, "salvation," and with this experience comes, simultaneously or instantly afterwards, an intellectual illumination quite impossible to describe. The instantaneousness of the illumination can be compared with nothing so well as with a dazzling flash of lightning in the middle of a dark night, bringing the landscape that had been hidden into clear view.

There is much that could be said about this experience. Let us be content to make a few observations: 1. the inner light is at first perceived as coming from without; 2. not until he understands its subjective nature does Dr. Bucke feel inexplicable happiness and receive the intellectual illumination which he compares to a lightning-flash passing through his brain; 3. this illumination definitely changed his life, bringing a spiritual rebirth. Typologically, one could relate this case of illumination to the illumination of the Esquimo shaman and, to a certain extent, to the self-illumination of the *atman*. A friend and admirer of Whitman, Dr. Bucke speaks of "cosmic consciousness" and of "Brahmic splendour": these are retrospective conceptions, derived from his own ideology. The character of the experience—its transcendence of the personality and its association with love recall rather a Buddhist climate of thought. A Jungian psychologist or a Catholic theologian would say that it was a realisation of selfhood. But the fundamental point, in our opinion, is that, thanks to this experience of the inner light, Dr. Bucke had access to a spiritual world the existence of which he had not even suspected till then, and that the access to this transcendental world constituted for him an *incipit vita nova*. . . .

The morphology of the subjective experience of Light is extremely large. Certain of the more frequent forms can however be noted:

1. The Light may be so dazzling that it somehow blots out the surrounding world; the man to whom it appears is blinded. This was the experience of Saint Paul, for instance, on the road to Damascus, and of many other saints—also, up to a point, of Arjuna in the *Bhagavad-gita*.

2. There is the Light that transfigures the World without blotting it out: the experience of a very intense supernatural light, which shines into the depths of matter, but in which forms remain defined. This is like the Heavenly Light which reveals the World as it was in its primal perfection—or, according to the Judaeo-Christian tradition, as it was before Adam's fall. In this category lie the majority of experiences of the light undergone by mystics, Christian and non-Christian.

3. Rather close to this type is the illumination (*qaumanek*) of the Esquimo shaman, which enables him to see far into the distance, but also to perceive spiritual entities: an extra-retinal vision, as one might say, which permits him to see not only very far, but in all directions at once, and finally reveals to him the presence of spiritual beings, or unveils to him the ultimate structure of matter, and brings him a staggering growth of understanding. Here one must also note the differences between the various Universes mystically perceived during the experience: the Universe whose structure seems to be like that of the natural Universe, with the difference that now it is truly understood—and the Universe that reveals a structure beyond the reach of the intelligence in the waking state.

4. A distinction must also be made between the instantaneous experience and the various types of progressive perception of the light, in which the growing intensity is accompanied by a feeling of deep peace or a certainty that the soul is immortal, or a comprehension of a supernatural kind.

5. Finally we must distinguish between a light which reveals itself

as a divine, personal Presence and a light which reveals an impersonal holiness: that of the World, Life, man, reality—ultimately, the holiness one discovers in the Cosmos contemplated as a divine creation.

It is important to stress that whatever the nature and intensity of an experience of the Light, it always evolves into a religious experience. All types of experience of the light that we have quoted have this factor in common: they bring a man out of his worldly Universe or historical situation, and project him into a Universe different in quality, an entirely different world, transcendent and holy. The structure of this holy and transcendent Universe varies according to a man's culture and religion—a point on which we have insisted enough to dispel all doubt. Nevertheless they share this element in common: the Universe revealed on a meeting with the Light contrasts with the worldly Universe—or transcends it—by the fact that it is spiritual in essence, in other words only accessible to those for whom the Spirit exists. We have several times observed that the experience of the Light radically changes the ontological condition of the subject, by opening him to the world of the Spirit. In the course of human history there have been a thousand different ways of conceiving or evaluating the world of the Spirit. That is evident. How could it have been otherwise? For all conceptualization is irremediably linked with language, and consequently with culture and history. One can say that the meaning of the supernatural light is directly conveyed to the soul of the man who experiences it—and yet this meaning can only come fully to his consciousness clothed in a pre-existent ideology. Here lies the paradox: the meaning of the light is, on the one hand, ultimately a personal discovery and, on the other, each man discovers what he was spiritually and culturally prepared to discover. Yet there remains this fact which seems to us fundamental: whatever his previous ideological conditioning, a meeting with the Light produces a break in the subject's existence, revealing to him—or making clearer than before—the world of the Spirit, of holiness and of freedom; in brief, existence as a divine creation, or the world sanctified by the presence of God.

What the Symbols "Reveal"

The task of the historian of religions remains incomplete if he fails to discover the function of symbolism in general. We know what the theologian, the philosopher and the psychologist have to say about this problem. Let us now examine the conclusions which the historian of religions reaches when he reflects on his own documents.

The first observation that he is forced to make is that the World "speaks" in symbols, "reveals" itself through them. It is not a question of a utilitarian and objective language. A symbol is not a replica of objective reality. It *reveals* something deeper and more fundamental. Let us try to elucidate the different aspects, the different depths of this revelation.

1. Symbols are capable of revealing a *modality of the real or a condition of the World which is not evident on the plane of immediate experience.* To illustrate the sense in which the symbol expresses a modality of the real inacessible to human experience, let us take an example: the symbolism of the Waters, which is capable of revealing the pre-formal, the potential, the chaotic. This is not, of course, a matter of rational cognition, but of apprehension by the active consciousness prior to reflection. It is of such apprehensions that the World is made. Later, by elaborating the significances thus understood, the first reflections on the creation of the World will be set in motion; this is the point of departure of all the cosmologies and ontologies from the Vedas to the Pre-Socratics.

As for the capacity of symbols to reveal an inner pattern of the World, we will refer to what we said earlier about the principal significances of the Cosmic Tree. The Tree reveals the World as a living totality, periodically regenerating itself and, thanks to this regeneration, continually fertile, rich and inexhaustible. Here, too, it is not a question of considered knowledge, but of an immediate comprehension of the "cipher" of the World. The World "speaks" through the medium of the Cosmic Tree, and its "word" is directly understood. The World is apprehended as Life and, for primitive thought. Life is a disguise worn by Being.

A corollary of the preceding observations: religious symbols which touch on the patterns of life reveal a deeper Life, more mysterious than that grasped by everyday experience. They reveal the miraculous, inexplicable side of Life, and at the same time the sacramental dimension of human existence. "Deciphered" in the light of religious symbols, human life itself reveals a hidden side: it comes from "elsewhere," from very far away; it is "divine" in the sense that it is the work of Gods or supernatural Beings.

2. This brings us to a second general observation: for primitives,

symbols are always religious, since they point either to something *real* or to a *World-pattern.* Now, at the archaic levels of culture, the *real*— that is to say the powerful, the significant, the living—is equivalent to the *sacred.* Moreover, the World is a creation of the Gods or of supernatural Beings: to discover a World pattern amounts to revealing a secret or a "ciphered" meaning of the divine work. It is for this reason that archaic religious symbols imply an ontology; a pre-systematic ontology, of course, the expression of a judgement both of the World and of human existence: judgement which is not formulated in concepts and which cannot always be translated into concepts.

3. An essential characteristic of religious symbolism is its *multivalence,* its capacity *to express simultaneously several meanings the unity between which is not evident on the plane of immediate experience.* The symbolism of the Moon, for example, reveals a connatural unity between the lunar rhythms, temporal becoming, the Waters, the growth of plants, women, death and resurrection, the human destiny, the weaver's craft, etc. In the final analysis, the symbolism of the Moon reveals a correspondence of a "mystical" order between the various levels of cosmic reality and certain modalities of human existence. Let us observe that this correspondence is not indicated by immediate and spontaneous experience, nor by critical reflection. It is the result of a certain mode of "viewing" the World.

Even if we admit that certain of the Moon's functions have been discovered by careful observation of the lunar phases (their relation with rainfall, for instance, and menstruation), it is difficult to imagine that the symbolism could have been built up in its entirety by an act of reason. It requires quite another order of cognition to reveal, for example, the "lunar destiny" of human existence, the fact that man is "measured" by temporal rhythms which are one with the phases of the Moon, that he is consigned to death but that, like the Moon which reappears in the sky after three days of darkness, he also can begin his existence again, and that, in any case, he nourishes the hope of a life beyond the tomb, more certain or better as a consequence of initiation.

4. This capacity of religious symbolism to reveal a multitude of structurally united meanings has an important consequence: the symbol is capable of *revealing a perspective in which diverse realities can be fitted together or even integrated into a "system."* In other words, a religious symbol allows man to discover a certain unity of the World and

at the same time to become aware of his own destiny as an integral part of the World. In the case of lunar symbolism, it is clear in what sense the different meanings of the symbols form a "system." On different registers (cosmological, anthropological, and "spiritual") the lunar rhythm reveals homologous patterns: always it is a matter of modalities of existence subject to the law of Time and cyclic becoming, that is to say of existences destined for a "Life" which carries, in its very structure, death and rebirth. Thanks to the Moon symbolism, the World no longer appears an arbitrary assembly of heterogeneous and divergent realities. The various cosmic levels are mutually related, they are, in a sense, "bound together" by the same lunar rhythm, just as human life is "woven" by the Moon and predestined by the Spinning Goddesses.

Another example will illustrate even better this capacity of symbols to open up a perspective in which things can be understood as united in a system. The symbolism of Night and Darkness—which can be discerned in cosmogonic myths, in initiatory rites, in iconographies featuring nocturnal or underground creatures—reveals the structural unity between the pre-cosmogonic and pre-natal Darkness, on the one hand, and death, rebirth and initiation on the other.[1] This renders possible not only the intuition of a certain mode of being, but also the comprehension of the "place" of that mode of being in the constitution of the World and the human condition. The symbolism of cosmic Night enables man to see what existed before him and before the World, to understand how things came into existence, and where things "were" before they were there, before him. Once again, this is no speculation but a direct understanding of the mystery that things had a beginning, and that everything which precedes and concerns this beginning has a supreme value for human existence. Consider the great importance of initiatory rites involving a *regressus ad uterum,* as a result of which man believes himself able to start a new existence. Remember also the innumerable ceremonies intended periodically to restore the primordial "Chaos" in order to regenerate the World and human society.

5. Perhaps the most important function of religious symbolism— especially important because of the role it will play in later philosophical speculations—is its *capacity for expressing paradoxical situa-*

---

1. It must be added that Darkness symbolizes not only the pre-cosmic "chaos" but also "orgy" (social confusion) and "madness" (disintegration of the personality).

tions or certain patterns of ultimate reality that can be expressed in no other way. One example will suffice: the symbolism of the Symplegades as it can be deciphered in numerous myths, legends and images presenting the paradox of a passage from one mode of existence to another—transfer from this world to another, from Earth to Heaven or Hell, or passage from a profane, purely carnal existence to a spiritual existence, etc. The following are the most frequent images: to pass between two clashing rocks or icebergs, or between two mountains in perpetual movement, or between two jaws, or to penetrate the *vagina dentata* and come out unharmed, or enter a mountain that reveals no opening, etc. One understands the significance of all these images: if the possibility of a "passage" exists, it can only be effectuated "in the spirit"—giving the word all the meanings that it is capable of carrying in archaic societies: a discarnate being, the imaginary world and the world of ideas. One can pass through a Symplegades in so far as one behaves "as a spirit," that is to say shows imagination and intelligence and so proves oneself capable of detaching oneself from immediate reality. No other symbol of the "difficult passage"— not even the celebrated motif of the bridge filed to the sharpness of a swordedge, or the razor mentioned in the *Katha Upanishad* (III, 14)— reveals more clearly than the Symplegades that there is a way of being inaccessible to immediate experience, and that this way of being can only be attained by renouncing a crude belief in the impregnability of matter. . . .

6. Finally, we must stress the *existential value of religious symbolism*, that is to say the fact that a symbol *always points to a reality or a situation concerning human existence.* It is above all this existential dimension that distinguishes and divides symbols from concepts. Symbols preserve contact with the deep sources of life; they express, one might say, "the spiritual as life experience." This is why symbols have a kind of "numinous" aura: they reveal that the *modalities of the spirit are at the same time manifestations of Life,* and that consequently, they *directly concern human existence.* A religious symbol not only reveals a pattern of reality or a dimension of existence, it brings at the same time a *meaning to human existence.* This is why even symbols concerning ultimate reality also afford existential revelations to the man who deciphers their message.

A religious symbol translates a human situation into cosmological terms, and vice versa; to be more precise, it reveals the unity between human existence and the structure of the Cosmos. Man does not feel himself "isolated in the Cosmos, he is open to a World which, thanks to the symbol, becomes "familiar." On the other hand the cosmological significances of a symbolism allow him to escape from a subjective situation and recognize the objectivity of his personal experiences.

It follows that the *man who understands a symbol not only "opens himself" to the objective world, but at the same time succeeds in emerging from his personal situation and reaching a comprehension of the universal.* This is to be explained by the fact that symbols "explode" immediate reality as well as particular situations. When some tree or other incarnates the World Tree, or when the spade is assimilated to the phallus and agricultural labour to the act of generation, etc., one may say that the immediate reality of these objects or activities "explodes" beneath the irruptive force of a deeper reality. The same thing takes place in an individual situation, for example that of the neophyte shut in the initiatory hut: the symbolism "explodes" this particular situation by revealing it as exemplary, that is to say endlessly repeatable in many different contexts (for the initiatory hut is approximated to the mother's womb, and also to the belly of a Monster and to Hell, and the darkness symbolizes, as we have seen, cosmic Night, the pre-formal, the foetal state of the World, etc.). *Thanks to the symbol, the individual experience is "awoken" and transmuted into a spiritual act.* To "live" a symbol and correctly decipher its message implies an opening towards the Spirit and finally access to the universal.

Claims About How One May Achieve Religious Elevation

There are different kinds of transcendentalists who are called *yogī*—*haṭha-yogīs, jñāna-yogīs, dhyāna-yogīs* and *bhakti-yogīs*—and all of them are eligible to be transferred to the spiritual world. The word *yoga* means "to link up," and the *yoga* systems are meant to enable us to link with the transcendental world. As mentioned in the previous chapter, originally we are all connected to the Supreme Lord, but now we have been affected by material contamination. The process is that we have to return to the spiritual world, and that process of linking up is called *yoga*. Another meaning of the word *yoga* is "plus." At the present moment we are minus God, or minus the Supreme. When we add Kṛṣṇa—or God—to our lives, this human form of life becomes perfect.

At the time of death we have to finish that process of perfection. During our lifetime we have to practice the method of approaching that perfection so that at the time of death, when we have to give up this material body, that perfection can be realized.

One who, at the time of death, fixes his life air between the eyebrows and in full devotion engages himself in remembering the Supreme Lord, will certainly attain to the Supreme Personality of Godhead. (Bg. 8.10)

Just as a student studies a subject for four or five years and then his examination and receives a degree, similarly, with the subject of life, if we practice during our lives for the examination at the time of death, and if we pass the examination, we are transferred to the spiritual world. Our whole life is examined at the time of death.

Whatever state of being one remembers when he quits his body, that state he will attain without fail. (Bg. 8.6)

There is a Bengali proverb that says that whatever one does for perfection will be tested at the time of his death. In *Bhagavad-gītā*, Kṛṣṇa describes what one should do when giving up the body. For the *dhyāna-yogī* (meditator) Śrī Kṛṣṇa speaks the following verses:

Persons learned in the *Vedas*, who utter *omkāra* and who are great sages in the renounced order, enter into Brahman. Desiring such perfection, one practices celibacy. I shall now explain to you this process by which one may attain salvation. The yogic situation is that of detachment from all sensual engagements. Closing all the doors of the senses and fixing the mind on the heart and the life air at the top of the head, one establishes himself in *yoga*. (Bg. 8.11–12)

In the *yoga* system this process is called *pratyahara*, which means, "just the opposite." Although during life the eyes are engaged in seeing worldly beauty, at death one has to retract the senses from their objects and see the beauty within. Similarly, the ears are accustomed to hearing so many sounds in the world, but at the moment of death one has to hear the transcendental *omkāra* from within.

After being situated in this *yoga* practice and vibrating the sacred syllable *om*, the supreme combination of letters, if one thinks of the Supreme Personality of Godhead and quits his body, he will certainly reach the spiritual planets. (Bg. 8.13)

In this way, all the senses have to be stopped in their external activities and concentrated on the form of *viṣṇumūrti*, the form of God. The mind is very turbulent, but it has to be fixed on the Lord in the heart. When the mind is fixed within the heart and the life air is transferred to the top of the head, one can attain perfection of *yoga*.

At this point the *yogī* determines where he is to go. In the material universe there are innumerable planets, and beyond this universe there is the spiritual universe. The *yogīs* have information of these places from Vedic literatures. Just as one going to America can get some idea what the country is like by reading books, one can also have knowledge of the spiritual planets by reading Vedic literatures. The *yogī* knows all these descriptions, and he can transfer himself to any planet he likes without the help of spaceships. Space travel by mechanical means is not the accepted process for elevation to other planets. Perhaps with a great deal of time, effort and money a few men may be able to reach other planets by material means—spaceships, spacesuits, etc.—but this is a very cumbersome and impractical method. In any case, it is not possible to go beyond the material universe by mechanical means.

The generally accepted method for transferral to higher planets is the practice of the meditational *yoga* system or *jñāna* system. The *bhakti-yoga* system, however, is not to be practiced for transferral to any material planet, for those who are servants of Kṛṣṇa, the Supreme Lord, are not interested in any planets in this material world because they know that on whatever planet one enters in the material sky, the four principles of birth, old age, disease and death are present. On higher planets, the duration of life may be longer than on this earth, but death is there nonetheless. By "material universe" we refer to those planets where birth, old age, disease and death reside, and by "spiritual universe" we refer to those planets where there is no birth, old age, disease and death. Those who are intelligent do not try to elevate themselves to any planet within the material universe.

If one tries to enter higher planets by mechanical means, instant death is assured, for the body cannot stand the radical changes in atmosphere. But if one attempts to go to higher planets by means of the *yoga* system, he will acquire a suitable body for entrance. We can see this demonstrated on this earth, for we know it is not possible for us to live in the sea, in a watery atmosphere, nor is it possible for aquatics to live on the earth. As we understand that even on this planet one has to have a particular type of body to live in a particular place, so a particular type of body is required for other planets. On the higher planets, bodies live much longer than on earth, for six months on earth is equal to one day on the higher planets. Thus the *Vedas* describe that those who live on higher planets live upward to ten thousand earth years. Yet despite such a long life span, death awaits everyone. Even if one lives twenty thousand or fifty thousand or even millions of years, in the material world the years are all counted, and death is there. How can we escape this subjugation to death? That is the lesson of *Bhagavad-gītā*. (Bg. 2.20)

For the soul there is never birth nor death. Nor, once having been, does he ever cease to be. He is unborn, eternal, ever-existing, undying and primeval. He is not slain when the body is slain.

We are spirit soul, and as such we are eternal. Why then should we subject ourselves to birth and death? One who asks this question is to be considered intelligent. Those who are Kṛṣṇa conscious are very intelligent because they are not interested in gaining entrance to any planet where there is death. They will reject a long duration of life in order to attain a body unlike unto God's. *Īśvaraḥ paramaḥ kṛṣṇaḥ saccidānanda-vigrahaḥ. Sat* means eternal, *cit* means full of knowledge, and *ānanda* means full of pleasure. Kṛṣṇa is the reservoir of all pleasure. If we transfer ourselves from this body into the spiritual world— either to Kṛṣṇaloka, Kṛṣṇa's planet, or any other spiritual planet—we will receive a similar *sac-cid-ānanda* body. Thus the aim of those who are in Kṛṣṇa consciousness is different from those who are trying to promote themselves to higher planets within this material world.

The self or soul of the individual is a minute spiritual spark. The perfection of *yoga* lies in the transferral of this spiritual spark to the top of the head. Having attained this, the *yogī* can transfer himself to any planet in the material world according to his desire. If the *yogī* is curious to know what the moon is like, he can transfer himself there, or if he is interested in higher planets, he can transfer himself there, just as travellers go to New York, Canada, or other cities on the earth. Wherever one goes on earth, he finds the same visa and customs systems operating, and on all the material planets one can similarly see the principles of birth, old age, disease and death operating.

At the point of death the *yogī* can pronounce *om, omkāra,* the concise form of transcendental sound vibration. If the *yogī* can vibrate this sound and at the same time (*mām anusmaran*) remember Kṛṣṇa or Viṣṇu, he attains the highest goal. It is the process of *yoga* to concentrate the mind on Viṣṇu. The impersonalists imagine some form of the Supreme Lord, but the personalists do not imagine this; they actually see. Whether one imagines Him or actually sees Him, one has to concentrate his mind on the personal form of Kṛṣṇa.

For one who remembers Me without deviation, I am easy to obtain, O son of Pṛthā, because of his constant engagement in devotional service. (Bg. 8.14)

Those who are satisfied with temporary life, temporary pleasure and temporary facilities are not to be considered intelligent, at least not according to *Bhagavad-gītā.* One whose brain substance is very small is interested in temporary things, according to the *Gītā.* We are eternal, so why should we be interested in temporary things? No one wants a nonpermanent situation. If we are living in an apartment and the landlord asks us to vacate, we are sorry, but we are not sorry if we move into a better apartment. It is our nature, because we are permanent, to want permanent residence. We don't wish to die because in actuality we are permanent. Nor do we want to grow old or be diseased because these are all external or nonpermanent states. Although we are not meant to suffer from fever, sometimes fever comes, and we have to take precautions and remedies to get well again. The fourfold miseries are like a fever, and they are all due to the material body. If somehow we can get out of the material body, we can escape the miseries that are integral with it.

For the impersonalists to get out of this temporary body, Kṛṣṇa here advises that they vibrate the syllable *om*. In this way they can be assured of transmigration into the spiritual world. However, although they may enter the spiritual world, they cannot enter into any of the planets here. They remain outside in the *brahmajyoti*. The *brahmajyoti* may be likened unto the sunshine, and the spiritual planets may be likened unto the sun itself. In the spiritual sky the impersonalists remain in the effulgence of the Supreme Lord, the *brahmajyoti*. The impersonalists are placed in the *brahmajyoti* as spiritual sparks, and in this way the *brahmajyoti* is filled with spiritual sparks. This is what is meant by merging into the spiritual existence. It should not be considered that one merges into the *brahmajyoti* in the sense of becoming one with it; the individuality of the spiritual spark is retained, but because the impersonalist does not want to take a personal form, he is found as a spiritual spark in that effulgence. Just as the sunshine is composed of so many atomic particles, so the *brahmajyoti* is composed of so many spiritual sparks.

However, as living entities, we want enjoyment. Being in itself is not enough. We want bliss (*ānanda*) as well as being (*sat*). In his entirety, the living entity is composed of three qualities—eternality, knowledge and bliss. Those who enter impersonally into the *brahmajyoti* can remain there for some time in full knowledge that they are now merged homogeneously with Brahman, but they cannot have that eternal *ānanda*, bliss, because that part is wanting. One may remain alone in a room for some time and may enjoy himself by reading a book or engaging in some thought, but it is not possible to remain in that room for years and years at a time, and certainly not for all eternity. Therefore for one who merges impersonally into the existence of the Supreme, there is every chance of falling down again into the material world in order to acquire some association. This is the verdict of *Śrīmad-Bhāgavatam*. Astronauts may travel thousands and thousands of miles, but if they do not find rest on some planet, they have to return again to earth. In any case, rest is required. In the impersonal form, rest is uncertain. Therefore *Śrīmad-Bhāgavatam* says that even after so much endeavor, if the imperialist enters into the spiritual world and acquires an impersonal form, he returns again into the material world because of neglecting to serve the Supreme Lord in love and devotion. As long as we are here on earth, we must learn to practice to love and serve Kṛṣṇa, the Supreme Lord. If we learn this, we can enter into those spiritual planets. The impersonalist's position in the spiritual world is nonpermanent, for out of loneliness he will attempt to acquire some association. Because he does not associate personally with the Supreme Lord, he has to return again to the world and associate with conditioned living entities there.

It is of utmost importance, therefore, that we know the nature of our constitutional position: we want eternity, complete knowledge and pleasure also. When we are left alone for a long time, we cannot have pleasure—we accept the pleasure given by the material world. In Kṛṣṇa consciousness, real pleasure is enjoyed. In the material world it is generally accepted that the highest pleasure is sex. This is a perverted reflection of the sex pleasure in the spiritual world, the pleasure of association with Kṛṣṇa. But we should not think that pleasure there is like the sex pleasure in the material world. No, it is different. But unless sex life is there in the spiritual world, it cannot be reflected here. Here it is simply a perverted reflection, but the actual life is there in Kṛṣṇa, who is full of all pleasure. Therefore, the best process is to train ourselves now so that at the time of death we may transfer ourselves to the spiritual universe, to Kṛṣṇaloka, and there associate with Kṛṣṇa. In *Brahma-saṁhitā* Śrī Kṛṣṇa and His abode are described thus:

I worship Govinda, the primeval Lord, the first progenitor, who is tending the cows, fulfilling all desire, in abodes built with spiritual gems, surrounded by millions of wish-fulfilling trees, always served with great reverence and affection by hundreds and thousands of *lakṣmīs*, or *gopīs*. (Bs. 5.29)

This is a description of Kṛṣṇaloka. The houses are made of what is called "touchstone." Whatever touchstone touches immediately turns into gold. The trees are wish-fulfilling trees or "desire trees," for one can receive from them whatever he wishes. In this world we get mangoes from mango trees and apples from apple trees, but there from any tree one can get whatever he desires. Similarly, the cows are called *surabhi*, and they yield an endless supply of milk. These are descriptions of the spiritual planets found in Vedic scriptures.

In this material world we have become acclimatized to birth, death and all sorts of suffering. Material scientists have discovered many facilities for sense enjoyment and destruction, but they have discovered no solution to the problems of old age, disease and death. They cannot make any machine that will check death, old age or disease. We can manufacture something that will accelerate death, but nothing that will stop death. Those who are intelligent, however, are not concerned with the fourfold miseries of material life but with elevation to the spiritual planets. One who is continuously in trance does not divert his attention to anything else. He is always situated in trance. His mind is always filled with the thought of Kṛṣṇa, without deviation. *Satatam* refers to anywhere and anytime.

In India I lived in Vṛndāvana, and now I am in America, but this does not mean that I am out of Vṛndāvana because if I think of Kṛṣṇa always, then I'm always in Vṛndāvana, regardless of the material designation. Kṛṣṇa consciousness means that one always lives with Kṛṣṇa on that spiritual planet, Goloka Vṛndāvana, and that one is simply waiting to give up this material body. *Smarati nityaśaḥ* means continuously remembering, and for one who is continuously remembering Kṛṣṇa, the Lord becomes *tasyāhaṁ sulabhaḥ*—easily purchased. Kṛṣṇa Himself says that He is easily purchased by this *bhakti-yoga* process. Then why should we take to any other process? We can chant Hare Kṛṣṇa, Hare Kṛṣṇa, Kṛṣṇa Kṛṣṇa, Hare Hare / Hare Rāma, Hare Rāma, Rāma Rāma, Hare Hare twenty-four hours daily. There are no rules and regulations. One can chant in the street, in the subway or at his home or office. There is no tax and no expense. So why not take to it?

FRIEDRICH NIETZSCHE

Joyful Wisdom
and the Death of God

That impulse, which rules equally in the noblest and the ignoblest, the impulse to the conservation of the species, breaks forth from time to time as reason and passion of spirit; it has then a brilliant train of motives about it, and tries with all its power to make us forget that fundamentally it is just impulse, instinct, folly and baselessness. Life *should* be loved, *for . . . !* Man *should* benefit himself and his neighbour, *for . . . !* And whatever all these *shoulds* and *fors* imply, and may imply in future! In order that that which necessarily and always happens of itself and without design, may henceforth appear to be done by design, and may appeal to men as reason and ultimate command,—for that purpose the ethiculturist comes forward as the teacher of design in existence; for that purpose he devises a second and different existence, and by means of this new mechanism he lifts the old common existence off its old common hinges. No! he does not at all want us to *laugh* at existence, nor even at ourselves—nor at himself; to him an individual is always an individual, something first and last and immense, to him there are no species, no sums, no noughts. However foolish and fanatical his inventions and valuations may be, however much he may misunderstand the course of nature and deny its conditions—and all systems of ethics hitherto have been foolish and anti-natural to such a degree that mankind would have been ruined by any one of them had it got the upper hand,—at any rate, every time that "the hero" came upon the stage something new was attained: the frightful counterpart of laughter, the profound convulsion of many individuals at the thought, "Yes, it is worth while to live! yes, I am worthy to live!"—life, and thou, and I, and all of us together became for a while *interesting* to ourselves once more.—It is not to be denied that hitherto laughter and reason and nature have *in the long run* got the upper hand of all the great teachers of design: in the end the short tragedy always passed over once more into the eternal comedy of existence; and the "waves of innumerable laughters"— to use the expression of Aeschylus—must also in the end beat over the greatest of these tragedies. But with all this corrective laughter, human nature has on the whole been changed by the ever new appearance of those teachers of the design of existence,—human nature has now an additional requirement, the very requirement of the ever new appearance of such teachers and doctrines of "design." Man has gradually become a visionary animal, who has to fulfil one more condition of existence than the other animals: man *must* from time to time believe that he knows *why* he exists; his species cannot flourish without periodically confiding in life! Without the belief in *reason in life!* And always from time to time will the human race decree anew that "there is something which really may not be laughed at." And the most clairvoyant philanthropist will add that "not only laughing and joyful wisdom, but also the tragic with all its sublime irrationality, counts among the means and necessities for the conservation of the race!"— And consequently! Consequently! Consequently! Do you understand me, oh my brothers? Do you understand this new law of ebb and flow? We also shall have our time! . . .

The Madman

Have you ever heard of the madman who on a bright morning lighted a lantern and ran to the market-place calling out unceasingly: "I seek God! I seek God!"—As there were many people standing about who did not believe in God, he caused a great deal of amusement. Why! is he lost? said one. Has he strayed away like a child? said another. Or does he keep himself hidden? Is he afraid of us? Has he taken a sea-voyage? Has he emigrated?—the people cried out laughingly, all in a hubbub. The insane man jumped into their midst and transfixed them with his glances. "Where is God gone?" he called out. "I mean to tell you! *We have killed him,*—you and I! We are all his murderers! But how have we done it? How were we able to drink up the sea? Who gave us the sponge to wipe away the whole horizon? What did we do when we loosened this earth from its sun? Whither does it now move? Whither do we move? Away from all suns? Do we not dash on unceasingly? Backwards, sideways, forewards, in all directions? Is there still an above and below? Do we not stray, as through infinite nothingness? Does not empty space breathe upon us? Has it not become colder? Does not night come on continually, darker and darker? Shall we not have to light lanterns in the morning? Do we not hear the noise of the grave-diggers who are burying God? Do we not smell the divine putrefaction?—for even Gods putrefy! God is dead! God remains dead! And we have killed him! How shall we console ourselves, the most murderous of all murderers? The holiest and the mightiest that the world has hitherto possessed, has bled to death under our knife,— who will wipe the blood from us? With what water could we cleanse ourselves? What lustrums, what sacred games shall we have to devise? Is not the magnitude of this deed too great for us? Shall we not ourselves have to become Gods, merely to seem worthy of it? There never was a greater event,—and on account of it, all who are born after us belong to a higher history than any history hitherto!"—Here the madman was silent and looked again at his hearers; they also were silent and looked at him in surprise. At last he threw his lantern on the ground, so that it broke in pieces and was extinguished. "I come too early," he then said, "I am not yet at the right time. This prodigious event is still on its way, and is travelling,—it has not yet reached men's ears. Lightning and thunder need time, the light of the stars needs time, deeds need time, even after they are done, to be seen and heard. This deed is as yet further from them than the furthest star,— *and yet they have done it!"*—It is further stated that the madman made his way into different churches on the same day, and there intoned his *Requiem aeternam deo.* When led out and called to account, he always gave the reply: "What are these churches now, if they are not the tombs and monuments of God?"—

WALLACE STEVENS

Of Mere Being

The palm at the end of the mind,
Beyond the last thought, rises
In the bronze distance,

A gold-feathered bird
Sings in the palm, without human meaning,
Without human feeling, a foreign song.

You know then that it is not the reason
That makes us happy or unhappy.
The bird sings. Its feathers shine.

The palm stands on the edge of space.
The wind moves slowly in the branches.
The bird's fire-fangled feathers dangle down.